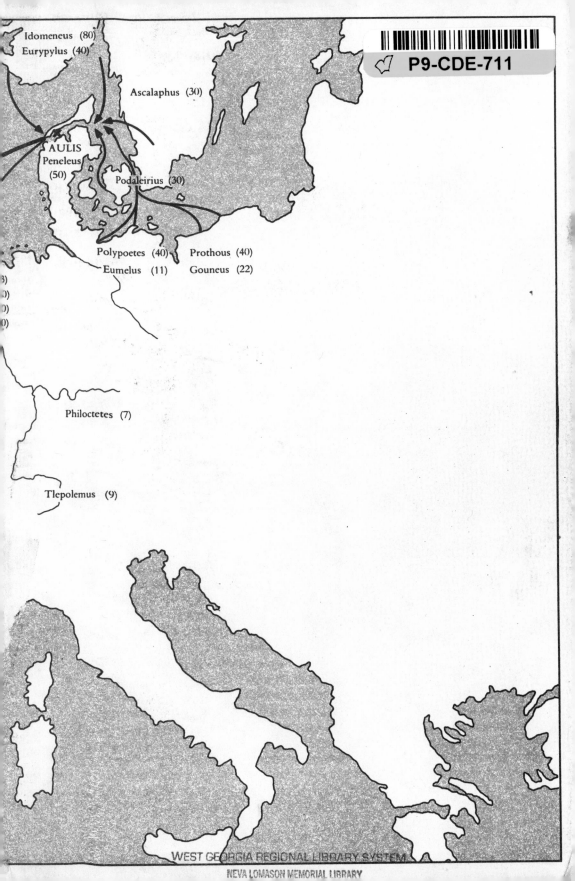

Idomeneus (80)
Eurypylus (40)

Ascalaphus (30)

AULIS
Peneleus
(50)

Podaleirius (30)

Polypoetes (40)   Prothous (40)
Eumelus (11)   Gouneus (22)

)
)
)
)

Philoctetes (7)

Tlepolemus (9)

WHERE TROY ONCE STOOD

Contents

Part III: The World of the *Odyssey*

List of Maps

Acknowledgements

I would like to express my sincere thanks to the many people who have given of their knowledge and helped in various ways, in particular the following: Mr Hugo Haarbosch, who commented on the nautical aspects of the Odyssey; Ms Mary Fransen van de Putte, who provided me with valuable information on Zeeland with the kind assistance of the archivists of the Zeeuwse Bibliotheek (Library of Middelburg); Mr Pete Moss for taking on the daunting task of translating my unfinished French manuscript; Ms Felicity Bryan for her whole-hearted support for my book; Ms Felicity Carter for editing and picture research; Ms Anita Lawrence for all the line drawings; Mr Ron Dixon (Taurus Graphics) for designing the maps; Ms Erica Smith and her staff in Century Hutchinson for their enthusiastic professional support, and, last but not least, the late Mr Oliver Caldecott for his valuable comments and encouragement.

Illustration Credits
The reference used in preparation of Plate 10, Armorial Devices of Zeeland, was K1. Siersma, *De gemeentewapens van Nederland*, Prisma-Boeken, Utrecht, 1960. Thanks are due to the Cambridge Antiquarian Society for Map 4.

The photographs were by:
J. W. den Beer Poortugael   Cover photo of the author
Janet and Colin Bord   Plates 3a, 3b and 7
Cambridge University Collection of Air Photographs   Plate 2
Danish National Museum, Copenhagen   Plate 6
Bram Gideonse   Plates 4a and 5
Metropolitan Museum of Art, New York   Plate 1
A. Van Pagee   Plates 4b and 8

Part
I
The Mystery

Iam seges est ubi Troia fuit
Ovid

(Now there are fields where Troy once stood . . .)

1

Homer's Epics:
Myth and Reality

Since classical antiquity, man has sought to elucidate what is, perhaps, the greatest mystery in European civilization: the origin, background and meaning of the two most ancient European poems, the *Iliad* and the *Odyssey*, which are attributed to Homer, about whom virtually nothing is known. The *Iliad* describes part of the Trojan War which, according to evidence from the text, took place in the Bronze Age, probably about 1200 BC. The detailed nature of the descriptions suggest that the works were composed by one or more eyewitnesses of the conflict and passed on orally for several centuries until they were written down in Ionian Greek around the eighth century BC. Although there is no doubt that the *written* version of the epics originated in Greece, the thesis is here advanced that the *oral* version originated in western Europe at a much earlier date. This, of course, in no way detracts from the prestige of classical Greek culture as it developed after Homer, and which is rightly admired by all.

Someone reading the *Iliad* for the first time with no preconceived ideas would not, on the evidence of the text, locate the theatre of war in the eastern Mediterranean (if it were not for a number of familiar place-names) as there is mention of tides, a salty, dark or misty sea and a climate of rain, fog and snow, while the trees are generally more typical of regions with a temperate climate rather than of subtropical southern Europe. Also the tall, long-haired warriors, travelling overseas in 'symmetrical' ships, 'eager to kill their enemies' are more reminiscent of the dreaded Norsemen of the Dark Ages than the more peaceful Greeks of the classical era. Several commanders even had the honorific but little reassuring title of 'sacker of cities'. As the ancient Greeks themselves could hardly imagine that these people were their ancestors, they relegated them to an imaginary 'heroic age'.

My doubts about the location of the Trojan War go back to the years I spent in a Dutch grammar school where, like many of my readers, I had the dubious privilege of translating Homer's beautiful but difficult verses. Once, on a rainy November day, I looked out of the window, while struggling with the Greek text speaking of 'ceaseless' rains in the Trojan plain. The adjective employed by Homer is, of course, much more elegant and poetic: *athesphatos* which means, approximately: 'what even a god cannot measure', which must therefore describe something that has neither beginning nor end. Such seemingly endless rains are so typical of the north Atlantic climate that I wondered whether the Trojan War had taken place in northern Europe. But this could apparently not be the case because Homer situates Troy close to Lesbos and the Hellespont, while Crete and Egypt are just a few days distant by boat. Had there been a great change in climate, then? This cannot be ruled out since we know that climate does change over the centuries. But, above all, how could the tides be explained? The usual argument that the entire work of Homer was a mere product of fantasy has never satisfied me as the descriptions of geographical places appear too detailed for a work of pure imagination.

But how could I find out more about the Trojan War? Even the earliest Greek historians lived too long after the conflict to be able to confirm its authenticity. Thucydides, who lived in the fifth century BC, carried out research into the ancient history of his country and informs us that before his time, 'nothing in Greece reached great proportions, the wars no more than anything else'. According to him this was due to a number of weaknesses in ancient Greece. For instance, there was little contact between the different peoples as navigation and trade was very poorly developed if not nonexistent. Because of widespread piracy, people travelled in Greece, 'more by land than by sea', and in general 'ancient Greece was not inhabited in a stable fashion'.[1] He was therefore unable to understand how Greece could have waged a great offensive against Troy.

Thucydides also found a number of what seemed to him anomalies in Homer's text. He was surprised at the total absence of the word 'barbarian' (foreigner) with which the Greeks always designated non-Greeks, for as he writes, 'this word ought to have been used by the poet if the Greeks had really united to wage war against non-Greeks'. Thucydides further relates that, as far as he knew, Mycenae had always been a village without great importance (today there are 600 inhabitants), but Homer called it the 'town with broad streets', the 'opulent' capital of the kingdom of Agamemnon, the most powerful king of the Achaeans who started the war.

Finally, Thucydides mentions something that is of the utmost importance for our research: he writes that barbarians were living in various parts of Greece, and names in particular the Taulentians, 'of the

Illyrian race', who were living on the shores of the Ionian Gulf, on the west coast of Greece. We also know from classical mythology that a certain Galatea gave birth to three sons: Galas, Celtus and Illyrius, who founded the three major Celtic peoples: the Gauls, the Celts and the Illyrians, so that Professor Henri Hubert's hypothesis[2] that the ancient Greeks had been in contact with Celtic culture through the intermediation of the Illyrians is thus confirmed by two ancient sources.

Celtic Influences

If the west of Greece was inhabited by Celtic peoples, it is quite possible that Homer's epics, which I take to be of Celtic origin, spread throughout the country from there. Subsequently, the Greeks, fascinated by the epics sung by the bards, gave many names taken from Homer to geographical locations in Greece and on the Turkish coast. They identified the Ionian islands with Odysseus' kingdom, as the port of Thiaki happens to correspond to the poet's description of Ithaca's port. This is one of several coincidences that contributed to a great mystification. The ancient Greeks soon became convinced that the Trojan War had been waged by their own heroic ancestors against an overseas power, which they situated across the Aegaean Sea on the Turkish coast. In the nineteenth century, when Heinrich Schliemann found ruins on the west coast of Turkey which he believed to be those of Troy, the mystification was complete and ever since then all those readers of Homer who, like myself, had the distinct impression that there was something fundamentally wrong, found themselves confronted with an inextricable problem.

Quite apart from the difficulty of fitting most places described in the *Iliad* and the *Odyssey* into the physical reality of the lands surrounding the Aegean Sea, there is also a problem with the spiritual content of Homer's works. Plato (427-348 BC) had doubts as to their Greek origin, and the great philosopher was by no means an admirer of this imaginative poet whose gods, with their jealousies and vengeances, behaved like spoilt children. Plato was particularly worried about the corrupting influence of Homer's poems on the minds of Greek youth, above all because of their 'lack of respect' for the gods. He suggested that certain passages of the *Iliad* and *Odyssey* should be corrected or even expurgated[3] and if he had been the dictator of his 'ideal state', he would probably have had them burned, thus breaking the chain of transmission of these unique and extremely ancient poems.

Once I had passed my final examinations, I did the same as schoolboys the world over: I threw away my textbooks with a great sigh of relief, except for the *Iliad* and the *Odyssey*. I could not part with the world's most beautiful and celebrated poems, even if only out of respect and admiration for their author. (Is it not said that one cannot read Homer without loving him?) But I also kept these books because I had a score to settle with the author – in exchange for all those hours of suffering, I had sworn to myself that one day I would penetrate his secret. He continued to hold the upper hand for thirty years but now I believe I have solved the mystery after being lost in many blind alleys. Just as some people like to spend rainy weekends doing jigsaw puzzles, I had my own: the *Iliad* and the *Odyssey*. Reading the text with an atlas of Greece on one's knee it is hard to understand the descriptions of many places, or the distances between places, or the sailing directions, or how it was possible to travel or drift in a boat with a head wind. In short, the place-names in Greece, the pieces of the puzzle, seem completely jumbled. Once these names are sought in western Europe, however – and about 90 per cent of them can still be found there, far more than in Greece – all the pieces of the puzzle fall perfectly into place and the events described by Homer become entirely logical and comprehensible. But what is the use of such a discovery? Many of Homer's readers perhaps do not feel the need for explanation and are quite happy to read the poems whether the places and events are real or not. I take the contrary view and believe that elucidation of this mystery will contribute much to our knowledge of European prehistory and will benefit archeologists, historians, linguists and, above all, readers of Homer who will discover a whole new dimension to his epics.

I am certainly not the first to have the impression that the Trojan War must have taken place in western Europe. As early as 1790, Wernsdorf[4] thought that the stories about the Cimmerians, one of the peoples mentioned by Homer (*Od.* XI, 14), were of Celtic origin. He had a very precise reason for this: the classical Greek author Aelian mentions them in connection with the 'singing' swan, *Cygnus musicus*, which is found in the British Isles and northern Europe, whereas Greece and the rest of southern Europe knew only the 'silent swan', *Cygnus olor*. In 1804, M. H. Vosz[5] believed that the *Odyssey* most probably described certain landscapes in the British Isles and, in 1806, C. J. de Grave[6] arrived at the general conclusion that the historical and mythical background of Homer's works should be sought not in Greece but in western Europe. Towards the end of the nineteenth century, Th. Cailleux[7] wrote that Odysseus' adventures had taken place in the Atlantic, starting from Troy, which by a process of deduction he concluded to be near Cambridge in England. More recently, E. Gideon[8] further developed the ideas of Cailleux, though without adding much factual evidence and leaving too many essential questions unanswered to be convincing.

Nowadays, it is considered very unlikely that the Trojan War took place on the west coast of Turkey, as was long believed, for it is impossible to reconcile most of the details recorded by Homer with the geographical reality of Greece and western Turkey (see Appendix Note 1, The *Iliad* in Greece), unless the conflict was an event of minor importance blown up into a fully-fledged epic by the genius of Homer as E. V. Rieu believes. Others consider the epics to be purely and simply a myth but, as we shall see, they are not entirely a myth as they contain a large share of reality. Contrary to what was always thought, it turns out to be perfectly possible to separate reality from fiction and to identify the site of Troy and the itinerary of Odysseus, thus confirming what de Grave already suspected nearly two centuries ago: 'If Homer had not been faithful to the facts and to the geographical details, his works would never have achieved the great renown that is theirs today'.[9]

Transposition of Place-names

We shall find that there has been a transfer of western European geographical names to the eastern Mediterranean, but this was not due to large-scale migration of all sorts of western European peoples to Greece, as was the case very much later when European emigrants gave familiar names to places in the New World. It rather appears that geographical names were taken directly from the *Iliad* and the *Odyssey*, Europe's 'sacred books' of the time. This transposition of names was facilitated by the fact that, as archeology tells us, Greece was very sparsely populated after the decline of Mycenaean culture, with the probable exception of the provinces of Attica and Euboea.[10] During this period, the Taulentians, mentioned by Thucydides, and other foreign peoples had settled in Greece, the former mainly on the Ionian islands and the northwest coast of the mainland. The transposition of geographical names probably began about 1000 BC and continued for several centuries, in particular as regards places outside mainland Greece, as we shall see. However, it would appear that a few Homeric place-names were already in use in Greece before the Trojan War but these are likely to have been settlements of the so-called 'Sea Peoples' who, according to Egyptian records, had come from the 'Green Sea' in the fourteenth century BC. The Sea Peoples were probably Illyrians from the Adriatic, or Celts from the Atlantic seaboard if the name 'Green Sea' meant the Atlantic Ocean.

With the exception of the Bible, no works of western literature have been more commented on than the *Iliad* and the *Odyssey*, but the entirely new approach presented here enables us to discover the existence of a great Celtic civilization in Europe long before the Greek and Roman eras. Some may question the validity of applying detective methods to ancient texts, but this turned out to be an effective way of using the scant sources available. Under these circumstances, I had to take the clues given by Homer and other classical authors, test a great many hypotheses, deductions and combinations until I had built up a coherent picture of a period of European prehistory. If my thesis is correct in its essentials, despite any errors of detail I may have made, it may help solve some of the problems at present facing archeology, both in western Europe and in Greece and throw new light on a period about which still very little is known, the transition period between the Bronze Age and the Iron Age (about 1500 to 750 BC).

I now invite the reader to follow me, step by step, towards the discovery of the true site of Troy and many other places mentioned by Homer. This will be a very enlightening journey and almost as exciting as the voyages of Odysseus himself.

When I began my research on Homer, I had no idea where it would lead, so I was just as surprised as the reader will be to find, for example, Troy in England and Mycenae in France, but I would advise the reader not to start this book in the middle or near the end, nor to study the maps without first following their explanation in the text, for with such a complex subject it is easy to lose one's bearings. He or she will soon find that solving a Greek mystery means 'working like a Trojan'.

Notes

1 Thucydides, *The Peloponnesian War*, Book A. I-XIII.
2 Henri Hubert, *Les Celtes et l'expansion celtique*, Vol. I, Albin Michel, Paris 1974, p. 144.
3 Plato, *The Republic*, Chapter 3.
4 Wernsdorf, cited by Prof. R. Hennig: *Wo lag das Paradis?*, 1958.
5 M. H. Vosz, *Alte Weltkunde*, Stuttgart, 1928.
6 C. J. de Grave, *République des Champs-Elysées ou Monde Ancien*, P-F de Goesen-Verhaeghe, Ghent, 1906.
7 Théophile Cailleux, *Pays Atlantiques décrits par Homère*, Paris, 1879.
8 Ernst Gideon, *Homerus, Zanger der Kelten*, Ankh-Hermes, Deventer, 1973.
9 C. J. de Grave, op. cit., Vol. I, p. 181.
10 N. K. Sandars, *The Sea Peoples, 1250-1150 BC*, Thames & Hudson, London, 1978, Chapter 8.

2

The *Iliad* and *Odyssey*: A Message

Before we start to investigate the origin and meaning of Homer's epics, it may be helpful to give a short outline of the story.

If, in our time, the public's interest in Homer seems to be waning, this may be because the geography and historicity of his poems have never been satisfactorily established, despite the efforts of countless scholars over the last few centuries. Until now, it was not even certain whether the Trojan War had ever taken place and whether ruins found in Turkey were the remains of the legendary town of Troy. As to Odysseus' adventures at sea, there is no unanimity on the identification of the hero's ports of call described by the poet, as particular features seldom correspond to designated places in the Mediterranean.

Modern readers also have difficulty in believing that the *Iliad* and the *Odyssey* could ever have had the religious value of a 'Bible of the ancients' because of the highly immoral behaviour of the pagan gods who were not a particularly enlightening example for mankind. But it turns out that the epics, as we read them, hide an entirely different story where, very surprisingly, the gods do give the right example to mankind.

We will see that appearance and reality are in sharp contrast, but this was known in ancient times only to a small number of initiates into the Mysteries, while revelation of the Mysteries to the profane was punishable by death. It seems that the esoteric explanation of Homer's works (and of classical mythology in general) was already gradually lost in antiquity, to be reconstituted early last century, in particular by Professor Creuzer[1] and, more recently, by R. Emmanuel[2] and others. The subject being very complex, their works do not make for easy reading and are therefore little known.

By explaining in this book the essentials of the historic, geographic and esoteric aspects of Homer's epics it is to be hoped that the interest in Europe's oldest and most outstanding poet will be revived.

The *Iliad*

The first epic, the *Iliad*, recounts fifty-one days of the tenth and final year of the Trojan War, which is waged by two groups of people: on the one side the *Trojans* or *Dardanians*, and on the other the *Achaeans*, also often called the *Danaans* or *Argives*, who cross the sea to lay siege to Troy, or *Ilium* (the meaning of these seven names will be explained later).

Among the sons of Priam, the aged king of Troy, there are two who play a particularly important role in the war: Hector, commander-in-chief of the Trojan armies, and Paris, also called Alexander, who caused the war by carrying off Helen, the wife of Menelaus, one of the Achaean kings.

There are also two famous brothers in the Achaean camp: the Atreidae or sons of Atreus, one of whom, King Agamemnon, is commander-in-chief of the Achaean armies, while the other is King Menelaus, husband of Helen.

Homer must assume that his public already knows the causes of this war, since he only devotes two lines to the subject. The legend which describes the cause is as follows: Eris, the goddess of strife, was furious because the Olympian gods had 'forgotten' to invite her to a banquet. She had the perverse idea of throwing a golden apple inscribed with the words 'For the fairest' into the hall where the feast was taking place. Although all the goddesses present wanted the apple, the choice was very quickly whittled down to three of them: Here (consort of Zeus), Athene, and Aphrodite. They asked Zeus to be the judge, but he refused the honour (see Appendix Note 2, Trinities) and sent them to the young Prince Paris, a connoisseur of female beauty, who was herding the cattle of his father, King Priam, outside Troy. Each of the three goddesses tried to buy Paris by offering him a special gift. Here promised power and riches and Athene wisdom, but Aphrodite, goddess of Love, made the winning offer – the most beautiful woman in the world. Paris, who was more interested in love than anything else, declared Aphrodite the winner and gave her the golden apple. This turned out to be a real apple of discord, because from that moment on there was a series of misfortunes. First, Helen, the most beautiful woman in the world, was already married to King Menelaus, which meant that Aphrodite had to help Paris to abduct her and take her to Troy. Menelaus subsequently asked his brother Agamemnon and the other Achaean kings to fit out a fleet to cross the sea and recover Helen by force, thus triggering the Trojan War.

It is difficult to believe that this quarrel over a kidnapped woman, even if she was the wife of King Menelaus, was anything more than a pretext for the war. In fact, Homer does give a clue as to the real reason when he speaks of a warrior who 'was one of those who went to Ilium to fight the Trojans in Agamemnon's cause'. (*Od.* XIV, 70-71). This reason was no doubt a dispute over the hegemony of the seas or the monopoly of trade rather than the conquest of new territory. This seems plausible, because the Achaeans do not occupy Troad after their victory, but return home. It is nonetheless true that women were highly thought of in Homer's time, which was the age of the matriarchy and the Amazons - female warriors who considered marriage to be a dishonour. Women were men's equals while remaining different. In some respects they were very influential because among the immortals it was the goddesses who did all the plotting and scheming, while among the mortals it was also women who were the source of many problems and misfortunes, including the Trojan War (see Appendix Note 3, Women in the Bronze Age).

But let us get back to the story. The Achaean warrior most feared by the Trojans was Achilles, son of Peleus and grandson of Aeacus and hence often called 'the Aeacean'. He was a demi-god because his mother Thetis was a Sea-Nymph. Achilles was an introverted man who came into conflict with his superior, Agamemnon, who was his opposite, concerned with covering himself with wealth and glory. This conflict, which is the central theme of the *Iliad*, was also caused by a woman. While laying waste to a town in Troad, the Achaeans capture some women, the most beautiful of whom, Chryseis, daughter of a priest of Apollo, is reserved for Agamemnon, while another, Briseis 'of the beautiful girdle', is given to Achilles who subsequently becomes deeply attached to her.

In the early years of the war the Achaeans had dominated the battlefield to such an extent that the Trojans scarcely dared to emerge from their city. Achilles had taken advantage of this to sack twelve towns on the coast and eleven others on the Trojan plain, while the Achaean army built long war dykes on the battlefield.

The *Iliad* commences when the plague is raging in the Achaean camp. The warriors, fearing that this sickness is caused by the black magic of Chryseis' father, beg Agamemnon to give her back. He agrees, but as compensation asks for Briseis. Achilles cannot stand this humiliation and having lost his loved one refuses to fight any more. He and his troops remain camped near the boats. This enables the Trojans to gain the upper hand on the field of battle, and when they penetrate the Achaean camp near the sea they almost succeed in destroying the barracks and the fleet. In this situation Agamemnon begs Achilles to take up arms again, promising him all he wants – riches, towns, women and even Briseis, but Achilles is stubborn and refuses to forget the insult he has suffered. In his stead, his best friend Patroclus offers to lead the troops into battle and borrows Achilles' arms and chariot. Despite his experience in combat and great courage, Patroclus is soon killed by Hector, because he does not possess Achilles' superhuman force. Achilles is so affected by Patroclus' death that his sullenness turns into uncontrollable hatred. He rushes to the field of battle and kills many Trojans, including Hector, whom he first chases three times round the walls of Troy in front of everybody. On his return to the Achaean camp, he drags Hector's body three times round Patroclus' bier, then leaves it to the dogs, as the ultimate humiliation for the Trojans. Some days later old King Priam takes the risk of going alone in the evening to visit Achilles in the Achaean camp to beg for the return of his son's body. Achilles hands over Hector's remains, still intact, which are burned and buried eleven days later, the fighting having been suspended for this period. The *Iliad* ends with Hector's burial.

The particular charm of Homer's epic lies in a judicious blend of reality and myth. On the one hand it is a detailed account of war and on the other a mythical tale in which the gods intervene personally in the war, even at the risk of being injured. What strikes the reader who might think that our Bronze Age ancestors were all primitive people with no kind of education is the respect and politeness with which the various parties address one another, for the poems bear witness to great refinement and elegance in language and social relations.

To give the reader unfamiliar with Homer an impression of his epic, I have chosen a few extracts of the *Iliad* in the translation of A. T. Murray, which is not the most modern one, but very close to the Greek text (see Appendix Note 4, Translation of Homer). Let us allow the poet to introduce the major actors in the drama in the following passages:

And Helen, fair among women, answered him [Priam], saying: "Revered art thou in mine eyes, dear father of my husband, and dread. Would that evil death had been my pleasure when I followed thy son hither, and left my bridal chamber and my kinsfolk and my daughter, well-beloved, and the lovely companions of my girlhood. But that was not to be; wherefore I pine away with weeping. Howbeit this will I tell thee, whereof thou dost ask and enquire. Yon man is the son of Atreus, wide-ruling Agamemnon, that is both a noble king and a valiant spearman. And he was husband's brother to shameless me, as sure as ever such a one there was." (Il. III, 171-179)

And next the old man saw Odysseus, and asked: "Come now, tell me also of yonder man, dear child, who he is. Shorter is he by a head than Agamemnon, son of Atreus, but broader of shoulder and of chest to look upon. His battle-gear lieth upon the bounteous earth, but himself he rangeth like the bell-wether of a herd through the ranks of warriors. Like a ram he seemeth to me, a ram of thick fleece, that paceth through a great flock of white ewes."

To him made answer Helen, sprung from Zeus: "This again is Laërtes' son, Odysseus of many wiles, that was reared in the land of Ithaca, rugged though it be, and he knoweth all manner of craft and cunning devices."   (II. III, 191-202)

In the hope of putting an end to the war, Paris, also called Alexander ('The Protected'), proposed a duel with Menelaus. The winner would keep Helen and her possessions, as was agreed in advance, but the duel had an unexpected outcome:

So saying, he [Menelaus] sprang upon him, and seized him by the helmet with thick crest of horse-hair, and whirling him about began to drag him towards the well-greaved Achaeans; and Paris was choked by the richly-broidered strap beneath his soft throat, that was drawn tight beneath his chin to hold his helm. And now would Menelaus have dragged him away, and won glory unspeakable, had not Aphrodite, daughter of Zeus, been quick to see, and to his cost broken in twain the thong, cut from the hide of a slaughtered ox; and the empty helm came away in his strong hand. This he then tossed with a swing into the company of the well-greaved Achaeans, and his trusty comrades gathered it up; but himself he sprang back again eager to slay his foe with spear of bronze. But him Aphrodite snatched up, full easily as a goddess may, and shrouded him in thick mist, and set him down in his fragrant, vaulted chamber, and herself went to summon Helen. (II. III, 369-383)

We shall never know if the duel between Paris and Menelaus really took place. According to some historians it is not even certain that Helen was ever in Troy, for the very down-to-earth reasons put forward by Herodotus as early as the fifth century BC:

If Helen really was in Troy, she would have been returned to her husband with or without the consent of Paris, for I cannot believe that Priam would have been so stupid as to have risked the lives of himself and his children simply to enable Paris to live with Helen. What is more, Paris was not even heir to the throne and would thus not have been able to reign in the place of his aged father, since it was Hector, his elder brother and a far better man, who would have taken the succession on the death of Priam. It was unlikely that Hector would have approved of the illegal behaviour of his brother, particularly because his attitude was the cause of such distress, for himself as much as for the other Trojans.[3]

However, the poet gives such a lively description of the beautiful Helen in the *Iliad* that it seems she must have really existed. Since war and kidnappings were probably part of daily life in the Bronze Age, there is no reason to believe that a queen, Helen, could not have been abducted. But logical as Herodotus' argument appears at first sight, his conclusion is wrong. It reflects the opinion of a historian and not of a diplomat experienced in negotiation. The latter knows very well that it is no good making concessions to a country that has decided to go to war against another, because a pretext for war can always be found. In this instance, the pretext was Helen, but if the Trojans had surrendered her, the Achaeans would certainly have found another. King Priam, seeing the futility of meeting the enemy's demands, therefore allowed his son Paris to keep Helen. She had already been in Troy for nine years before the outbreak of hostilities, for at the end of the *Iliad*, after ten years of war, we learn that she has been there for nineteen years. Preparations for the war must thus have taken no less than nine years, which should not really surprise us when we think of the time necessary to coordinate the actions of the various Achaean peoples at a time when there were no rapid means of communication. Moreover, it certainly required time to mobilize public opinion in favour of such a big enterprise. But the commanders were well aware of the economic reasons for the military expedition, although they make the warriors think they are fighting for the injured honour of a king and a splendid queen, a chivalresque cause of war, which must have appealed to the poet Homer and, of course, his public.

Herodotus and other classical authors had also overlooked the fact that Helen was particularly remarkable: she is described as an immortal who was the daughter of Zeus and Nemesis. This unusual descendance is a sure indication that there must be another story hidden between the lines of Homer's epic which, more precisely, has to do with initiation into the Mysteries. To be an initiate, candidates had to surpass themselves, not only physically but also intellectually, and even mentally by getting rid of prejudices and other imperfections of their character. Their efforts were believed to bring humans closer to the Olympian gods from where they originated and make the heroes 'godlike', as Homer calls some of the warrior chiefs. The imperfect candidate will not pass the final test, as was the case with Achilles who perished before Troy because he had a weakness of character, his excessive stubbornness, symbolized by the famous Achilles heel. For people to make a huge effort however, an incentive is needed, which in the *Iliad* is Helen (and, in the *Odyssey*, Circe, as we will see). She is not only the most beautiful woman in the world, but also an incarnation of wisdom, which is exactly what candidates for initiation try to obtain. Helen is therefore what R. Emmanuel calls 'an allurement of the gods' but certainly not an ordinary unfaithful woman who can be bribed to leave her husband, as the surface of the story makes believe the profane. That Helen was a symbol of initiation has been understood by some people throughout the ages, as evidenced for instance by Goethe's remark that 'he who has seen Helen is never the same again'. For the initiate, Helen was a lower emanation of Here (the second goddess in the divine hierarchy symbolizing Wisdom was Athene) while her counterpart in the drama, her abductor Paris, was an emanation of the god Hermes. This explains why Paris suddenly disappeared in a cloud during the duel with Menelaus, who was thus deprived of his victory, as we just saw, and for good reason: gods do not lose battles with mortals. Moreover, Hermes was not only the messenger of the Olympian gods, as we learn in school, but also the god of redemption whose task it was to accompany the initiates to and from Hades, the Underworld (we will meet him again in this particular function in the Odyssey). It turns out, therefore, that the Trojan War which is a historical event, was used by Homer as the background for another drama where both Helen and Paris are closely associated with the race to initiation in which many of the Trojan and Achaean nobles participate.

As the Trojans do not pay their due after Menelaus' duel with Paris, this is considered by the Achaeans to be a violation of the oath and the war recommences, with all its horrors described in detail by the poet, not because he was an admirer of warfare, but clearly because he wanted to stress its ultimate futility. When Patroclus is killed by Hector, Achilles prepares a magnificent funeral for his friend, as we read in the following passage, which gives an idea of the last honours paid to a high-ranking warrior in the Bronze Age. There is the symbolic gesture of the offering of the hair of the mourning warriors and sacrifices of animals – and humans. Homer does not seem to approve of human sacrifice, but the practice was customary with the Celts until the Roman era, more than a thousand years later.[4] This extract is taken from Book XXIII of the *Iliad*, which describes Patroclus' funeral and the games in his honour:

Then when the king of men Agamemnon heard this word, he forthwith dispersed the folk amid the shapely ships, but they that were nearest and dearest to the dead abode there, and heaped up the wood, and made a pyre of an hundred feet this way and that, and on the topmost part thereof they set the dead man, their hearts sorrow-laden. And many goodly sheep and many sleek kine of shambling gait they flayed and dressed before the pyre: and from them all great-souled Achilles gathered the fat, and enfolded the dead therein from head to foot, and about him heaped the flayed bodies. And thereon he set two-handled jars of honey and oil, leaning them against the bier; and four horses with high-arched necks he cast swiftly upon the pyre, groaning aloud the while. Nine dogs had the prince, that fed beneath his table, and of these did Achilles cut the throats of twain, and cast them upon the pyre. And twelve valiant sons of the great-souled Trojans slew he with the bronze – and grim was the work he purposed in his heart – and thereto he set the iron might of fire, to range at large. Then he uttered a groan, and called on his dear comrade by name: "Hail, I bid thee, O Patroclus, even in the house of Hades, for now am I bringing all to pass, which aforetime I promised thee. Twelve valiant sons of the great-souled Trojans, lo all these together with thee 'the flame devoureth; but Hector, son of Priam, will I nowise give to the fire to feed upon, but to dogs."   (Il. XXIII, 161-183)

In order to avenge the death of Patroclus, Achilles kills many Trojans before attacking Hector, whom he also kills. With Hector, Priam loses his oldest and best-loved son. After some days of mourning, the old king conceives the bold plan of infiltrating the enemy camp at night to beg Achilles to let him have Hector's remains in return for a large ransom. Achilles agrees, but his pride will not let him accept the ransom and he even claims that he had already decided to return Hector's body to his father. Here is the account of that dramatic tête-à-tête between the two men:

So spake he [Priam], and in Achilles he roused desire to weep for his father; and he took the old man by the hand, and gently put him from him. So the twain bethought them of their dead, and wept; the one for man-slaying Hector wept sore, the while he grovelled at Achilles' feet, but Achilles wept for his own father, and now again for Patroclus; and the sound of their moaning went up through the house. But when goodly Achilles had had his fill of lamenting, and the longing therefor had departed from his heart and limbs, forthwith then he sprang from his seat, and raised the old man by his hand, pitying his hoary head and hoary beard; and he spake and addressed him with winged words: "Ah, unhappy man, full many in good sooth are the evils thou hast endured in thy soul. How hadst thou the heart to come alone to the ships of the Achaeans, to meet the eyes of me that have slain thy sons many and valiant? Of iron verily is thy heart. . . ." (Il. XXIV, 507-521)

And the old man, godlike Priam, answered him: "Seat me not anywise upon a chair, O thou fostered of Zeus, so long as Hector lieth uncared-for amid the huts; nay, give him back with speed, that mine eyes may behold him; and do thou accept the ransom, the great ransom, that we bring. So mayest thou have joy thereof, and come to thy native land, seeing that from the first thou hast spared me." (Il. XXIV, 552-557)

The *Odyssey*

Hector's remains are burned and the bones collected in a golden urn. The *Iliad* does not recount the subsequent battles, nor the death of Achilles, nor even the fall of Troy. Homer recalls these facts for us in the second epic, the *Odyssey*, which is otherwise devoted mainly to Odysseus and his many adventures on the seas. Odysseus was also one of the heroes of the Trojan War, but he excelled more by his sound advice and cunning tricks than by his physical prowess. He had the brilliant idea of introducing the great wooden horse, packed with Achaean warriors, into Troy, thus bringing about the downfall of the city. When Odysseus left Ithaca to participate in the war, he had left behind his wife, Penelope, and his infant son, Telemachus. When the conflict ended ten years later, the surviving commanders returned home, among them their chief, Agamemnon, king of Argos (who was promptly murdered by his wife, Clytemnestra) as well as Menelaus, king of Sparta and Nestor, king of Pylos, both territories situated close to Ithaca. But Odysseus' ship was caught in a storm which was the beginning of ten years of adventures at sea. The first part of the *Odyssey* relates the voyage of Telemachus to Pylos and Sparta to inquire about the fate of his father, already absent for nineteen years. The central part of the epic describes Odysseus' wanderings over the ocean, while the latter part recounts his homecoming and the massacre of Penelope's suitors.

The epic starts with the decision by the assembly of the Olympian gods to let Odysseus – who has been retained for many years already by the nymph Calypso, a daughter of Atlas, on the island of Ogygia – return finally to his homeland Ithaca, following Athene's intervention with Zeus:

"But my heart is torn for wise Odysseus, hapless man, who far from his friends has long been suffering woes in a sea-girt isle, where is the navel of the sea. 'Tis a wooded isle, and therein dwells a goddess, daughter of Atlas of baneful mind, who knows the depths of every sea, and himself holds the tall pillars which keep earth and heaven apart. His daughter it is that keeps back that wretched, sorrowing man; and ever with soft and wheedling words she beguiles him that he may forget Ithaca. But Odysseus, in his longing to see were it but the smoke leaping up from his own land, yearns to die. Yet thy heart doth not regard it, Olympian. Did not Odysseus beside the ships of the Argives offer thee sacrifice without stint in the broad land of Troy? Wherefore then didst thou conceive such wrath against him, O Zeus?"

Then Zeus, the cloud-gatherer, answered her and said: "My child, what a word has escaped the barrier of thy teeth? How should I, then, forget godlike Odysseus, who is beyond all mortals in wisdom, and beyond all has paid sacrifice to the immortal gods, who hold broad heaven?" (Od. I, 48-67)

Hermes, the messenger god, flies from Mount Olympus to the island of Ogygia, situated in the middle of the ocean to transmit Zeus' decision to Calypso while Athene goes to Ithaca to set courage in the heart of the young and inexperienced Telemachus. She visits him, in the disguise of the Taphian leader Mentes, to exhort him to get rid of his mother's suitors, who have for many years been feasting in the palace, squandering Odysseus' fortune while insisting that Penelope chooses a new husband. In the evening of the following day, after he has given an unusually strong warning to the suitors, Telemachus, accompanied by Athene, sails in all secrecy to Pylos to question Nestor about the fate of his father, then continues overland to Sparta to inquire with Menelaus, but neither king has any information about Odysseus. When the suitors discover Telemachus' absence, they assume that he is seeking help from his powerful neighbours to get rid of them and they decide to try to kill him in an ambush on his return.

In the meantime, Odysseus floats on a raft from Ogygia to Ithaca, when he is driven off course by a heavy storm that lands him on the island of Scheria, where he is well received by Alkinoos, the king of the Phaeacians. During the farewell dinner given in his honour, Odysseus recounts his terrible adventures – which constitute the central part of the epic – such as his encounter with the Cyclops, the descent into the Underworld, the temptation of the Sirens and the two dangerous passages through Scylla and Charybdis, both on his way to and from the island of the sungod Helios.

'Thence for nine days was I borne, and on the tenth night the gods brought me to Ogygia, where the fair-tressed Calypso dwells, dread goddess of human speech, who gave me welcome and tendance. But why should I tell thee this tale? For it was but yesterday that I told it in thy hall to thyself and to thy noble wife. It is an irksome thing, meseems, to tell again a plain-told tale."

So he spoke, and they were all hushed in silence, and were spellbound throughout the shadowy halls.   (Od. XII/XIII)

When the farewell dinner is over, a Phaeacian ship laden with gifts from his hosts sees Odysseus home during the night.

The third and longest part of the epic starts with Odysseus' awakening on a remote beach of his native Ithaca. On the advice of Athene, who disguises him as a beggar, Odysseus first visits his faithful swineherd Eumaeus, to inquire about Penelope and to find out what has happened in the royal palace during his long absence. Meanwhile, Telemachus is sailing home from Pylos, avoiding – thanks to Athene – the ambush of the suitors by landing near Eumaeus's hut. After Odysseus has revealed his identity to Telemachus the two men devise a plan to massacre the suitors. Still disguised as a beggar, Odysseus enters his palace where he is promptly pelted and taunted by the suitors. He does not yet reveal his identity to Penelope who has been faithful to him for twenty years, putting off the date of her remarriage by a trick become famous: she had promised to choose a new husband as soon as she had finished weaving a shroud for Odysseus' father Laërtes. But each night she undid her work of the previous day, until she was found out by the suitors. She then promised to marry the winner of a contest with Odysseus' bow to shoot an arrow through the holes of twelve aligned axes, a contest which was to take place on the day of Odysseus' return. When none of the suitors is able to even *bend* Odysseus' bow, the 'beggar' is allowed to give it a try. After accomplishing the task at first shot Odysseus reveals his identity to the suitors and kills them all with the help of his son and the discreet interventions of Athene. Only after the massacre Odysseus reveals his identity to Penelope, removing her lingering doubts by describing their nuptial bed. The following day, Odysseus visits his old father in the countryside. A battle with the relatives of the slain suitors is averted thanks to the intervention by Athene – disguised as Mentor – and peace is restored in Ithaca.

We will discover that the *Odyssey* describes real, identifiable places while at the same time telling the allegorical story of the difficult path to illumination and redemption of Odysseus. The underlying message of this epic much resembles the older myth of Heracles and his twelve labours, which is considered the archetypal example of an initiation and, as such, well explained by Alice Bailey.[5] Odysseus, like Heracles, has to fight terrible monsters, which of course, are not real beings but the monsters deep inside ourselves, the dark instincts in our subconscious which we must dominate if we want to become better, more 'godlike' humans. Odysseus, like Heracles, visits Hades, the Underworld, which suggests that he had a ritual contact with death, in order to be symbolically 'reborn' with a new personality. The Gnostic concept of spiritual 'rebirth' is also found in Christianity, as evidenced by Jesus' words: 'Unless a man is born again, he cannot see the Kingdom of God' (John 3:3). For the ancients, the symbolic rebirth was deemed necessary for the novices to become conscious and responsible beings and a prerequisite for access to the teaching of the Mysteries, the understanding of the Universe, in the expectation of a better life in the Other World. These Gnostic beliefs persisted well into our era, as Mystery schools are known to have existed in Europe and the Near East as late as the fifth century AD. As to Odysseus, after a dozen terrible adventures, which were, symbolically speaking, as many tests for an initiate, he had finally become:

> a man the peer of the gods in counsel, one who in time past had suffered many griefs at heart in passing through wars of men and the grievous waves. (Od. XIII, 90)

In Part III of this book, we will accompany Odysseus in both his real and symbolic voyages, citing some relevant passages in Homer. But the beginning of the *Odyssey*, recounting Telemachus' visit to Pylos and Sparta, will be discussed in Part II, the *Iliad*, where this story is needed for the research on the geographical origin of the regiments led by Nestor and Menelaus, who, together with Agamemnon, Achilles and Odysseus himself, were the most important commanders of the Achaean army before Troy.

Notes

1 G.F. Creuzer, *Symbolik und Mythologie der alten Völker, besonders der Griechen*, 4 Vols, Heidelberg, 1819.

2 R. Emmanuel, *Pleins feux sur la Grèce antique, la mythologie vue par ses écoles des Mystères*, Dervy-Livres, Paris, 1982.

3 Herodotus, *The Histories*, II 120, translation by A. de Selincourt, Penguin Classics.

4 Caesar, *The Conquest of Gaul*, VI, 16, translation by S. A. Handford, Penguin Classics.

5 Alice A. Bailey, *The Labours of Hercules*, Lucis Trust, 1981.

3

The Location of Troy

Why Troy cannot have been in Turkey

Before setting off to search for the site of the famous city of Troy, we need to be convinced that it is not possible for the ruins found on the west coast of Turkey to be those of Troy. From ancient times until the last century it was thought that Troy was located near the town of Bunar-Bashi but this site does not correspond to Homer's descriptions in several vital respects. First, because of the mountains, it is impossible to go round the walls of the city, as Achilles did when pursuing Hector. Second, the river Menderès (or Kücük) would have lain between the two armies, and nowhere does Homer mention that the warriors have to cross a river before engaging in battle. His descriptions of the war and the circumstances in which it took place are so detailed, however, that we have the impression he was present in person as a 'war correspondent' with the job of providing the maximum of information for his audience. Towards the end of last century, it was thought that the location of Troy in the Bunar-Bashi valley had been confirmed, when, in 1873, Heinrich Schliemann (1822-1890), a German businessman, linguist and archeologist, discovered some ruins at Hissarlik, a few kilometres from Bunar-Bashi, and assumed them to be those of the city of Ilium.

Schliemann had in fact found the ruins of seven towns, one on top of the other, some of which seemed to have been destroyed by fire, but none of them was destroyed at the time of the Trojan War, somewhere around 1200 BC. The ruins are either very much older or very much more recent. Another serious problem is that the Hissarlik ruins are more the size of a village, not to say a hamlet, as they cover only two hectares. Schliemann himself admitted that this fortress could not have held more than 5,000 people, while according to W. Leaf the figure would be more like 2,000, whereas Homer's Troy held an army of 50,000 men in addition to the civilian population (*Il.* VIII, 562). Homer also describes Ilium as a large town with broad streets, where there was the acropolis of Pergamus, Priam's palace with over sixty rooms and an agora. If Hissarlik is already much too small, so is the neighbouring plain – it is less than five kilometres from the ruins to the sea. In the time of Strabo[1] and Pline[2] it was scarcely more than two kilometres, and must have been even less in Homer's day, because over the past 3,000 years the silt washed down by the river has considerably extended the plain. It would therefore have been virtually impossible to install an attacking army of at least 65,000 men, plus the prisoners, the women (servants, slaves) and the livestock required for food. What is more, the Achaean army commanders had a barracks of several rooms with a courtyard in front of it. Once such an army was installed, there would scarcely have been any room to deploy the troops and certainly none to carry out the long pursuits recounted in the *Iliad*. The Turkish valley is also too small to have contained the fourteen rivers named by Homer and the eleven towns that Achilles laid waste. It is also difficult to understand why the poet should have called Troy the 'steep' city when the Hissarlik hill rises scarcely thirty metres above the surrounding plain. Neither is there any trace of the springs mentioned by Homer. On the coast there is no port and no bay capable of receiving almost 1,200 vessels, yet there were that many according to the 'catalogue of ships' in Book Two of the *Iliad*. The Turkish gulf opposite Lesbos is also ruled out as the possible site because this is surrounded by high mountains, up to 1,700 metres, which is contrary to the description of the poet who says that between the Achaean camp near the sea and the city of Troy there was a 'vast plain'.

The list of inconsistencies is long and it thus seems impossible to support Hissarlik as the site of ancient Troy unless one assumes grostesque exaggeration on the part of Homer. There are no other sites on the west coast of Turkey that fit the descriptions, either. What is more, there is also a geopolitical argument against looking for Troy on this coast. We understand from the Homeric texts that Troy had influence over a very wide area because of its varied activities and that allies came from afar to help defend it. Asia Minor has never been the seat of such an important centre, with the support of allies to defend it. Further to the north, and after Homer's time, Constantinople came to fulfil this role, inherited from the Roman Empire, but the sphere of influence of this city was the Balkans rather than Asia Minor, and its strategic role was, and still is, to watch over the sea passage through the Bosphorus and the land traffic between Europe and Asia.

However, throughout the ages, since classical antiquity, many kings, out to conquer or on official tours, have visited the presumed site of Troy in Turkey. Herodotus tells us that Xerxes, king of the Persians, stopped at Troy on his way to attack Greece, making an offering of 1,000 oxen in honour of the gods and heroes of the Trojan War.[3] Later, Alexander the Great also visited Troy to pay homage to his ancestors

The Location of Troy

Map 1
The Troad in Turkey.

before embarking on the conquest of the Near East. But these ceremonies obviously prove nothing about the existence of Priam's city in this area. They prove only that the mystery of the *Iliad* goes back a very long way indeed.

Not only Homer's topography but also written material from the Bronze Age fail to provide grounds for thinking that Troy was in northwest Turkey. Neither the extensive diplomatic correspondence of the Hittites living in Asia Minor nor the Mycenaean Linear B tablets from Greece ever mention the city of Troy or a Trojan War in the region. What is more, archeological finds are often in direct conflict with Homer's epics so that we are confronted with 'this paradox, that the more we know the worse off we are' in the words of Sir Moses Finley, who arrived at the conclusion that 'Homer's Trojan War...must be evicted from the *history* of the Greek Bronze Age'.[4]

Notes
1 Strabo, *Geography*, XIII, 1, 36.
2 Pline, *Natural History*, V, 33.
3 Herodotus, *The Histories*, VII, 42.
4 M. I. Finley, *The World of Odysseus*, Appendix II: "Schliemann's Troy—One Hundred Years After", Penguin, 2nd ed., 1979.

4

Twelve Keys
to the Mystery

Before we start the search for the many places mentioned in the *Iliad* and the *Odyssey*, let us first examine the more general indications provided by the poet. This approach gives us already a rough idea about their possible location and helps to avoid inconsistencies at a later stage.

(i) The Combatants

In principle it should be easy approximately to locate a theatre of war if the names of the peoples involved are known. We have already seen that the attackers of Troy are called alternatively Achaeans, Argives or Danaans. Hitherto, it has always been thought that they were Greeks, to the extent that some translations simply speak of 'Greeks', even though neither the noun nor the adjective 'Greek' appears anywhere in the original text. This erroneous identification is based on the fact that the Argives were thought to owe their name to a Greek province, but, as we shall see, in the Bronze Age, Argos was the name of a region elsewhere in Europe. The Danaans are so called after Danaus, a king of Argos. As for 'Achaeans', this is a general term that could be translated as 'Allies', as it is cognate with the Celtic (and Hebrew) 'ach', meaning 'brother'.[1]

The name 'Hellenes' does appear in the original text (*Il.* II, 684), but according to the Greek historian Thucydides, writing in the fifth century BC, 'it seems that this name [Hellenes] did not even exist in Greece at the time of the Trojan War, and in any event 'it took a long time before it came to be used for the whole population'.[2] The Hellenes were originally a people living on the shores of, and owe their name to, the Helle Sea ('Hellespont' in Greek) which was not in the Mediterranean area, as we will discover.

Since Homer's work is written in Ionian Greek it might be thought that the Trojan War involved the Ionian people, but this name is nowhere to be found in the texts, though the poet does once mention a people called the 'Iaones' (*Il*, XIII, 685), a name generally rendered in the translations as 'Ionians'. It certainly shows remarkable modesty on the part of this people if their name is mentioned only once in an epic describing their victory over the Trojans. What is more, according to Thucydides, the Ionians or other Greek tribes did not possess a large fleet 'until many generations after the Trojan War'.[3]

As for the Trojans, they obviously owe their name to the city of Troy but, as we have seen, this cannot be in Turkey. The location of Troy will be identified elsewhere in Europe. Their other name, the Dardanians, is derived from Dardanos, an ancestor of Priam and also king of Troad.

(ii) The Ocean and the Tides

Both the *Iliad* and the *Odyssey* are epics of seafarers, or in Homer's words, 'friends of the oar'. The sea, which he often calls the ocean, is omnipresent in his works, but although he uses many adjectives to describe it, there is one which is totally absent from the *Iliad* and rarely found in the *Odyssey* – blue, which is the predominant colour of the Mediterranean. Instead, the sea is variously described as grey, black, wine–dark, salty, misty, whitening (reference to foam and spray), brilliant (in good weather), turbulent, dangerous and immense. The waves are sometimes as 'high as mountains' and Homer's ocean is so vast that 'the birds do not even come back for a year'. What is more, the Greeks in fact never used the word *okeanos* to designate the Mediterranean, but always used other words: *pontos*, *pélagos* and *thalassa* or *thalatta*. For the ancient Greeks 'ocean' meant exclusively 'the river that surrounds the world' outside the Mediterranean basin and the known world. The ocean 'comes back on itself' (*Il.* XVIII, 399 and *Od.* XX, 65), implying that it is subject to tides. There can be no doubt, because the word used is *apsorroos*, which more precisely means 'flowing back', or 'ebbing', the movement of the sea after high tide. Nearly two millenia ago, the Greek geographer Strabo already noted that 'Homer was not ignorant about the ebb and flow of Oceanus'[4] and concluded that several events described by the poet must therefore have taken place in the Atlantic Ocean. Strabo was not able to identify any specific places, however, as he knew of the Atlantic only by hearsay.

Of all the arguments in favour of locating the action of the *Iliad* and the *Odyssey* in the Atlantic area rather than the Mediterranean, the phenomenon of the tides is so important as to make all other arguments virtually redundant. The movement of the tides is often evoked in Homer, in both the literal and figurative senses. The difference in the level of the sea between low and high tides, insignificant in the Mediterranean, is several metres on the Atlantic coasts. In Homer's works the difference is also considerable, because when his sailors want to take to the sea they dig a channel between the boat and the sea at low tide so that it fills with water at high tide. This obviously facilitates the departure of the vessel, which was held upright on the beach by props:

> ... and they with loud shouting rushed towards the ships; and from beneath their feet the dust arose on high. And they called each one to his fellow to lay hold of the ships and draw them into the bright sea, and they set themselves to clear the launching–ways, and their shouting went up to heaven, so fain were they of their return home; and they began to take the props from beneath the ships.　　　　　　　　　　　　　　　　　(*Il.* II, 149-154)

It was indeed necessary to clear out the channels which had been used to drag the ships as far as possible up the beach during high tide because they had subsequently been eroded by the sea. But Homer also speaks of tides in the figurative sense, for example when he invites his audience to imagine the clash between the two great armies, Trojan and Achaean, and the subsequent battle in terms of the rising tide meeting the current of a river:

> Then the Trojans drave forward in close throng, and Hector led them. And as when at the mouth of some heaven-fed river the mighty wave roareth against the stream, and the headlands of the shore echo on either hand, as the salt-sea belloweth without. (*Il.* XVII, 262-265).

The Greek *kuma* is here usually translated by 'wave', although its meaning was more precisely 'swelling', and the swelling of the sea is much more than a wave: it is the rising tide. The image invoked by the poet is in fact much more powerful and appropriate when he opposes the continuing force of the rising tide against the current of the river rather than the temporary force of a single wave. Greek audiences, for whom tides were unknown, must never have been able to appreciate this powerful image. If Homer's sea is the Atlantic Ocean, which is not only darker but also foggier than the Mediterranean, it is also easier to appreciate the following comparison:

> As far as a man seeth with his eyes into the haze of distance as he sitteth on a place of outlook and gazeth over the wine–dark deep, even so far do the loud–neighing horses of the gods spring at a bound.　　　　　　　　　　　　　　　　　(*Il.* V, 770-772).

In the *Odyssey* we shall, significantly, discover many more references to tides.

(iii) The Climate

In the beginning of this book we already saw briefly that the climate of the Troad is more like that of England than of Turkey. I already mentioned the 'ceaseless' rains, which some translators render as 'sudden' rains to fit the Turkish climate. Such seemingly never-ending rains are very typical of the north Atlantic climate during autumn and winter. When the Achaeans are preparing to join battle with the Trojans, Homer recounts:

> Now when they were marshalled, the several companies with their captains, the Trojans came on with clamour and with a cry like birds, even as the clamour of cranes ariseth before the face of heaven, when they flee from wintry storms and measureless rain, and with clamour fly toward the streams of Ocean . . . (*Il.* III, 1-5)

and a few lines later he even mentions thick fog:

> . . . a mist that the shepherd loveth not, but that to the robber is better than night, and a man can see only so far as he casteth a stone.
> (*Il.* III, 10-13)

A Greek or Turkish thief, unlike his English counterpart, would risk starving to death if he had to wait for thick mists to help him. In the same Book, Homer uses another image rather poorly chosen for a Greek public:

> But whenso he uttered his great voice from his chest, and words like snowflakes on a winter's day. . . . (*Il.* III, 221-222)

However, his original public must have been very familiar with snow judging by the following passage, where Homer describes warriors hurling stones at one another:

> And as flakes of snow fall thick on a winter's day, when Zeus, the counsellor, bestirreth him to snow, shewing forth to men these arrows of his, and he lulleth the winds and sheddeth the flakes continually, until he hath covered the peaks of the lofty mountains and the high headlands, and the grassy plains, and the rich tillage of men; aye, and over the harbours and shores of the grey sea is the snow strewn, albeit the wave as it beateth against it keepeth it off, but all things beside are wrapped therein, when the storm of Zeus driveth it on: even so from both sides their stones flew thick . . .
> (*Il.* XII, 278-287)

There is not only rain, mist and snow in Homer but also a great deal of wind and he often calls Troy the city 'whipped by winds'. The reader may think that I have deliberately selected only passages that speak of bad weather, leaving aside those that celebrate the sun, but the fact is that nowhere in the *Iliad* does Homer mention climatic conditions typical of the Mediterranean. Some such passages are to be found in the *Odyssey* but, as we shall see, these refer to more distant places.

(iv) The Vegetation

Most of the trees mentioned by Homer are typical of the temperate areas of Europe with an oceanic climate. The beech, for example, is practically nonexistent in the Mediterranean countries because it requires friable soil. The trees found on the island of Hades are 'tall black poplars and willows' (*Od.* X, 510). The first, green–leaved despite their name, have the shape of cypresses, growing as tall as forty metres. They prefer moist soils and are therefore generally found near rivers, ponds and canals in temperate zones. Willows have a similar preference and there are dozens of indigenous species to be found along the rivers of northwest Europe. The mention of these trees and 'deep forests' is complemented by other indications that suggest that the poet was describing places located in the temperate zone, except for one region, Odysseus' homeland Ithaca, where there are olive trees, which are an exclusively subtropical species. Other trees mentioned, such as oaks and elms are unreliable indicators as they are at home in different climates. In the Trojan plain there is a 'fig tree lashed by the winds' and, surprising as it may seem, fig trees are present in the north of France, Belgium and England. Other trees have northern and southern varieties, such as the cornel (dogwood) and the ash, the common variety being found only in the north where its foliage can provide useful fodder. As for the tamarisk, this shrub also can be found anywhere in Europe, but it is so typical of the temperate Atlantic climate that the Latin botanical name of the main variety is *Tamaris Galliae* or *Tamaris Celtis*. Because of its resistance to winds, drought and soil salinity, and because of its lóng roots, it is now often planted near sea shores to keep the dunes in place.

Homer mentions vineyards in nearly all regions. But vineyards are not a very useful clue either as they were found virtually all over Europe in the Bronze Age, when the summers were warmer than they are today. Traces of vineyards dating from about 1000 BC have been found even in Sweden, while England also always had vineyards. Since the quality of the wine of the Bronze Age was perhaps mediocre, it was mixed with honey in a 'mixing bowl' (*krater* in Greek).

Homer often writes of 'thick turf', again something one does not usually associate with Mediterranean countries, while the Trojan plain is 'beautiful with its orchards and wheatfields' and its 'lush meadows dotted with flowers' where the Achaean invaders install themselves:

> So they took their stand in the flowery mead of Scamander, numberless, as are the leaves and the flowers in their season. (*Il.* II, 467–473)

Judging by the descriptions of the vegetation, most of the regions must lie in the temperate zone which is rich in deciduous trees:

> Even as are the generations of leaves, such are those also of men. As for the leaves, the wind scattereth some upon the earth, but the forest, as it bourgeons, putteth forth others when the season of spring is come; even so of men one generation springeth up and another passeth away. (*Il.* VI, 146–149)

This comparison would not be very meaningful for a Greek public, more familiar with evergreens.

(v) Horses

The horse occupies a very special place in Homer's works and in the hearts of his warriors. They fought using a battle chariot drawn by two horses. There were two men on the chariot, the warrior and his charioteer. The warrior either remained on the chariot and used his lance or descended for close combat. This method of waging war is thus nothing like that of the Greeks, who fought if they had to, but always on foot (the 'hoplites') until the time of Alexander the Great (third century BC). In earlier times, the horse as an instrument of war was even unknown in Greece. The Egyptians, on the other hand, had known the horse-drawn chariot since the occupation of their country by the Hyksos, a people coming from the steppes of Asia in the seventeenth century BC, and they had subsequently used them themselves in their wars in the Middle East, where the plains are more suited to this type of combat than is the rocky soil of Greece.[5]

But the peoples who inhabited the vast plains of Europe, from England and France to Russia, have always considered the horse as the most important domesticated animal, absolutely essential for work on the farm, for transport and for making war. From West to East the Celts, the Germans, the Slavs, the Hittites (who invaded Turkey), the Huns (who threatened central Europe), the Hyksos (who invaded Egypt), and the Aryans (who invaded Persia and northern India) all

41

used horses for warfare. But neither the Greeks nor the Romans used chariots drawn by horses for this purpose, so that the Roman armies were unnerved by the mere sight of the Celtic chariot fighters, as Caesar recounts.[6]

Both the Trojans and the Achaeans raised horses in their respective countries, Troad and Argos, which are often mentioned by the poet as being lands 'nurturing horses' or 'rich in horses'. The Troad is so rich in horses that Homer relates that an ancestor of King Priam had no less than 3,000. It is scarcely likely that this country, where so many aspects of life centred around horses, was the west coast of Turkey, where these animals were the exception rather than the rule. By contrast, it is well known, as W. Rutherford observed, that 'the Celts were particularly renowned as horse-breeders, pioneering many advances. Their reputation in this field is brought out by the fact that almost all the words in Latin connected with horses are Celtic loan-words.[7] Homer's warriors thought so much of their horses that some were even considered to be divine, such as Achilles' horses Xanthus and Balius. These two animals, which his father had received as a gift from a god, weep when Achilles' best friend Patroclus is killed by Hector:

> But the horses of the son of Aeacus being apart from the battle were weeping, since first they learned that their charioteer had fallen in the dust beneath the hands of man-slaying Hector. In sooth Automedon, valiant son of Diores, full often plied them with blows of the swift lash, and full often with gentle words bespake them, and oft with threatenings; yet neither back to the ships to the broad Hellespont were the twain minded to go, not yet into the battle amid the Achaeans. Nay, as a pillar abideth firm that standeth on the tomb of a dead man or woman, even so abode they immovably with the beauteous car, bowing their heads down to the earth. And hot tears ever flowed from their eyes to the ground, as they wept in longing for their charioteer, and their rich manes were befouled, streaming from beneath the yoke-pad beside the yoke on this side and on that. (*Il.* XVII, 426-440)

In one instance, Xanthus is even able to speak, predicting that Achilles is shortly to die on the field of battle:

> Then from beneath the yoke spake to him the horse Xanthus, of the swift-glancing feet; on a sudden he bowed his head, and all his mane streamed from beneath the yoke-pad beside the yoke, and touched the ground; and the goddess, white-armed Hera, gave him speech: "Aye verily, yet for this time will we save thee, mighty Achilles, albeit the day of doom is nigh thee, nor shall we be the

cause thereof, but a mighty god and overpowering Fate. For it was not through sloth or slackness of ours that the Trojans availed to strip the harness from the shoulders of Patroclus, but one, far the best of gods, even he that fair-haired Leto bare, slew him amid the foremost fighters and gave glory to Hector. But for us twain, we could run swift as the blast of the West Wind, which, men say, is of all winds the fleetest; nay, it is thine own self that art fated to be slain in fight by a god and a mortal.' *(Il. XIX, 405-417)*

It is only in reading the *Odyssey* that we learn that Achilles perished before Troy, as he had heard from 'his horse's mouth'.

(vi) Cattle

Homer frequently speaks of cows 'with dragging step' and uses the image of cows and calves in a figurative sense, as when Odysseus recounts his reunion with his companions who believed him dead:

> . . . and there I found my trusty comrades by the swift ship, wailing piteously, shedding big tears. And as when calves in a farmstead sport about the droves of cows returning to the yard, when they have had their fill of grazing – all together they frisk before them, and the pens no longer hold them, but with constant lowing they run about their mothers – so those men, when their eyes beheld me, thronged about me weeping. *(Od. X, 407-415)*

If the calves can knock down their enclosures, then the latter were made not of stone but of wood. The meadows full of cows and enclosed by wooden fences strongly suggest that Homer had the lowlands of western Europe in mind.

(vii) The Food

According to Homer, his contemporaries ate not only bread, beef, mutton and pork, but also oysters, a delicacy found all along the Atlantic coast. Admittedly, there are smaller varieties in the Mediterranean, but it is noteworthy that the poet compares a warrior falling head first from his chariot to a man diving for oysters rather than for sponges which would be more typical for Greece (and which were already in the bathrooms in Homer's time):

> Hah, look you; verily nimble is the man; how lightly he diveth! In sooth if he were on the teeming deep, this man would satisfy many by seeking for oysters, leaping from his ship were the sea never so stormy, seeing that now on the plain he diveth lightly from his car. Verily among the Trojans too there be men that dive.
>
> *(Il. XVI, 745-750)*

Even more striking is the mention of eels, which are born in the Sargasso Sea, east of the Bahamas, from where the elvers cross the Atlantic with the Gulf Stream. Eels are still prized as food in certain regions of western Europe rather than in Greece:

> He spake, and drew forth from the bank his spear of bronze, and left Asteropaeus where he was, when he had robbed him of his life, lying in the sands; and the dark water wetted him. With him then the eels and fishes dealt, plucking and tearing the fat about his kidneys;
> (*Il.* XXI, 200-204)

We will soon find out where these swarms of eels were having their banquet.

(viii) The Dykes

Homer mentions dykes, these 'splendid works of young men', so typical of the low-lying areas of northwest Europe, which risk being burst at any moment by the flooding of a river or the violence of the sea. The Greek word for dyke, *teichos*, even seems to be a borrowing from north European languages (*Deich* in German, for example). As dykes were rare or perhaps nonexistent in Greece, an ancient Greek audience would have difficulty in appreciating the comparison between an impetuous warrior and a river bursting through the dyke:

> For he stormed across the plain like unto a winter torrent at the full, that with its swift flood sweeps away the embankments; this the close-fenced embankments hold not back, neither do the walls of the fruitful vineyards stay its sudden coming when the rain of Zeus driveth it on; and before it in multitudes the fair works of men fall in ruin. Even in such wise before Tydeus' son were the thick battalions of the Trojans driven in rout. . . .
> (*Il.* V, 87-94)

This comparison suggests that Homer's public was familiar with dykes, which they needed to protect their low-lying lands from flooding by rivers or the sea. It was only about a millenium later that classical authors, such as Aristotle and Strabo, became aware of the Celts' struggle against the sea without really understanding the problem. Strabo recounts that floods in northern Europe caused more deaths than wars.[8]

It seems that there have indeed been several cataclysms, the memory of which was kept alive by the Celts in the usual form of myths.[9] A poem attributed to the Celtic bard Taliesin mentions one of these catastrophes:

The storm raged for four nights in the summer
the men fell, the woods themselves were no longer any protection
against the wind from the sea
Math and Hyvedd, masters of the magic wand, had liberated the
elements
Then Gwyddyon and Amaethon held council – they made a shield
so strong that the sea could not engulf the best troops[10]

The 'strong shield' was no doubt a dyke, but Aristotle thought that the
Celts took up their arms against the waves, thus making them
ridiculous in the eyes of Mediterranean people.[11] But in northern
Europe, the struggle against the sea has always been a matter of survival
which even recently called for a truly Pharaonic work: the construction
of the 'Dyke of Piles' in the Eastern Schelde (Netherlands). The huge
movable steel vanes, which stop the sea during heavy storms, are a
curious reminder of the 'strong shields' of the Celtic wizards. It only
took more than a magic wand to put them in place.

(ix) Art

Homer's descriptions of the art of his time, such as the decorations on
arms and vases do not correspond with those found in Greek
excavations of the Mycenaean era. Lasserre expresses surprise at this:

> [The *Iliad*] speaks of the choirs of Knossos, it mentions a vase
> ornamented with flowers, a decoration unknown in classical Greek
> art; it describes a cup with handles decorated with doves, similar to
> one of those found in the excavations, but while it often speaks of
> the opulence of the kings of Mycenae, never on the occasion of the
> death of a hero does it make any allusion to the characteristic
> custom of making a funeral mask of gold leaf, or of sword blades
> incrusted with hunting scenes that have been found in such great
> number in Mycenaean tombs.[12]

It must not be forgotten, however, that Homer's dead were not buried
but cremated, which was a typical Celtic custom. The heroes are
therefore honoured not with a gold mask, but with a golden urn to hold
their bones, as is described explicitly for Achilles, Patroclus and Hector.
In any event, the culture described by Homer cannot be that of
Mycenae, as this civilization disappeared when the Trojan War was
about to begin. How could a declining people wage a great war and
emerge as victors? I therefore agree with Vidal-Naquet who writes that
the theory that Homer was describing Mycenaean culture 'is a corpse
that has to be killed over and over again'.[13] Similarly, the scholar John

Chadwick, who assisted Michael Ventris to decipher the Linear B script of the Mycenaean culture and had hoped that those tablets would throw light on the world of Homer was so disappointed that he came to the conclusion that Homer was 'a liar'.[14] None of these scholars who were disappointed because they had not succeeded in finding traces of the Homeric world in Greece ever realized that Homer was not describing Greek civilization at all, but quite a different one thousands of kilometres to the northwest!

(x) Religion

In the Bronze Age, men worshipped many gods and guardian angels. There were, no doubt, several hundred of them because, for a start, each river had its god. Certain animals were also considered to be sacred, but we have no very precise idea how the rites were performed or how people imagined their gods. One thing that is certain, however, is that nowhere in Europe were the gods represented by beautiful statues such as the ones later sculpted in Greece and which have become so familiar and dear to us through centuries of classical education. The reader therefore needs to try to forget these aesthetic images, for we are going to change the scenery and return to the Bronze Age, when men's ideas and their cultural and religious manifestations were quite different from those of classical Greece.

It seems that in these very ancient times the gods could take any form in men's minds. They very often took human form, for example, Homer speaks of Here 'of the white arms', or Athene 'of the blue–green eyes'. Sometimes they can transform themselves into animals, for example Zeus into a bull, Athene an eagle or Hermes a seagull. Zeus sometimes even takes the form of a tree, as we learn when Odysseus goes to consult, 'the sacred voice of Zeus from the tall and leafy oak' (*Od.* XIV, 327 and XIX, 296). It is therefore not surprising that in Celtic art, human, animal and plant forms are often mixed, because people believed in very close links between all life in the universe. Although Homer does not mention it, the Druids had a name for the invisible force that governed both life and the material universe: *Nwywre*, symbolized by the serpent, which is a universal symbol already familiar to us from the statues of the Pharaohs, who were believed to represent the divinity on earth. According to Moreau, *Nwywre* 'was the creative power of the physical world. Nothing happened without it. It was the cosmic fluid, the ether, the light and the great creative and divine Principle that linked Heaven and Earth. Its union with the other elements created life, movement and the spirit. A Gallic bard sang that it is smaller than the smallest and bigger than worlds because it is subtleness and power itself. For the Druids, *Nwywre* was the thread mysteriously linking the human world to the divine world'.[15]

The gods, of course, could not only see what happened on earth from distances of hundreds of miles, but could also travel with the speed of thought. This may seem a very modern concept to us, but was already very familiar to our Bronze Age ancestors:

> So spake he (Zeus), and the goddess, white-armed Hera, failed not to hearken, but went her way from the mountains of Ida unto high Olympus. And even as swiftly darteth the mind of a man who hath travelled over far lands and thinketh in the wisdom of his heart, 'Would I were here, or there,' and many are the wishes he conceiveth: even so swiftly sped on in her eagerness the queenly Hera. . . . (*Il.* XV, 78-82)

Writing of the supreme god, known to the Romans as Jupiter, Maximus Tyrius relates that, 'The Celts worshipped Zeus, whose effigy was the oak'.[16] The effigy of this god had thus remained unchanged from the Bronze Age – Homer's time – to the beginning of our own era. Homer never mentions statues of divinities, only altars; while his temples were sanctuaries in the open air.

'But Odysseus had gone to Dodona to hear the will of Zeus from the high-crested oak of the god.' (Od. XIV, 327 and XIX, 296).

The destruction of Celtic culture was so complete that we know very little about their religion as compared, for example, with that of the Scandinavians and Germans of Nordic religion, as is pointed out by Jan de Vries in a recent book on the subject[17], but we do know that both the Celts and the Germans celebrated their rites in forests and by lakes, without erecting any covered temples or statues of divinities. According to Tacitus, the reason for this was that:

> They do not think it in keeping with the divine majesty to confine gods within walls, or to portray them in the likeness of any human countenance. Their holy places are woods and groves and they apply the names of deities to that hidden presence which is seen only by the eyes of reverence.[18]

Offerings to the gods were thrown into the water, and it is thanks to this religious practice that many gold, silver and bronze objects have been recovered from the bottom of lakes and rivers in western Europe. Numerous statuettes in human or animal form have also been found, for example in Anglesey and near the sources of the Seine and the Marne. These were probably personal votive offerings. It was only much later, a few centuries BC, that the Celts, under the influence of the Mediterranean cultures, started to make statues of their divinities, but they were nothing like the Greco–Roman style. Celtic art may seem primitive compared to classical Greek art, as it stands at the opposite end of the aesthetic spectrum. The former is schematic and abstract, while the latter is naturalistic and mimetic. One can therefore not apply the same criteria to both types of art, just as today we do not directly compare abstract painting with, say, works of the seventeenth century. Considering that the metalworking technology of the Celts was very advanced for the time, we may assume, with Miranda Green, that the emphasis on abstraction was deliberate, as it had the specific purpose of relating the image directly to the supernatural.[19] Celtic statues of the Gallo–Roman period often bear inscriptions that have made it possible to identify them. In more ancient times, however, the gods were apparently considered more as invisible forces of nature, supernatural beings with magic powers enabling them to take any desired form.

It is thus at present difficult to give any precise description of the shadowy universe of religion and culture in the Bronze Age. This, and in particular the absence of any written sources, makes the study of European prehistory extremely frustrating. Neither the megalithic monuments, nor the very numerous objects that have been found, notably arms, utensils and pottery, suffice to reconstruct the history of our remote ancestors. If, later in the book it is attempted to demonstrate that such and such a god was worshipped in a precise part of Europe during the Bronze Age, it is impossible to point to concrete proof in the shape of temples or statues found in that location, because they simply did not exist. For this reason research has to be based essentially on linguistic evidence, and in particular the etymology of place-names. As we shall see, this type of evidence can be extremely useful, especially when there are several indicators pointing in the same direction.

Homer gives us to understand that the two opposing camps, the Achaeans and the Trojans, are in some way related peoples, with identical culture and religion. This obviously poses a problem for the gods, who are themselves divided into two camps; Here, consort of Zeus, Athene, Poseidon and Hephaistos support the Achaeans, while Zeus, Aphrodite, Apollo, Ares and Hermes support the Trojans. However, the support of the gods is not constant and they can sometimes change sides and even enter the combat directly when it suits them. Both groups of peoples venerate the same pantheon, however, and we will find therefore places of worship dedicated to the same gods on both sides of the sea separating the opposing forces.

Although Zeus was the supreme god, he was not the creator of the universe, a particularity which, however stunning to modern man, is not devoid of a certain logic (see Appendix Note 18, Creation). Zeus was chief of a myriad of gods and demi-gods, who seem to have been aspects or functions of himself and ranked in a hierarchy according to their importance, much like human society itself. The subordinate gods each represented a concrete or abstract phenomenon, such as fire, water, earth, fertility, wisdom, jealousy, revenge and so on. One can easily imagine that the people of the time would in first instance pray to the lower god responsible for a particular aspect of life. Just as Homer invokes the Muse to help him compose his epics, a peasant, fearing inundation of his land by a swollen river, would address the local river god. Similarly, a blacksmith would invoke the god of fire, a barren woman a fertility goddess, and a victim of injustice the goddess of revenge. If we consider the subordinate gods as mere intermediaries between man and Zeus, Bronze Age religion would in fact be much closer to monotheism than generally assumed. It appears that, for important matters, Zeus could be invoked directly, as Menelaus did before his duel with Paris, which was intended to put an end to the Trojan War.

Man has always wondered whether there is a god who controls our destiny and, if so, whether he is 'good' or 'bad' or perhaps both at once. In the Bronze Age there was no doubt on this subject and it was firmly believed that there was a supreme god who provided human beings sometimes with good things and sometimes with bad, as Homer explains:

> For on this wise have the gods spun the thread for wretched mortals, that they should live in pain; and themselves are sorrowless. For two urns are set upon the floor of Zeus of gifts that he giveth, the one of ills, the other of blessings. To whomsoever Zeus, that hurleth the thunderbolt, giveth a mingled lot, that man meeteth now with evil, now with good; but to whomsoever he giveth but of the baneful, him he maketh to be reviled of man, and direful madness driveth him over the face of the sacred earth, and he wandereth honoured neither of gods nor mortals.
>
> (*Il.* XXIV. 525-533)

Although it may appear to the reader that the Homerian gods have 'typically Greek' names, the fact is that various classical authors tell us that the Celts worshipped Zeus and the other gods under their Greek names, which must therefore have originally been Celtic or proto-Celtic names. The conclusion must be that the Greeks inherited the whole pantheon from Homer's works, as we shall discover.

(xi) Philosophy

Plato had very good reasons for his doubts about the Greek origin of Homer's works because not only do the physical descriptions in his poems not correspond to the Greek world, but also the Homeric philosophy is very different from the mainstream Greek. The latter is based on the dualism of two opposing elements (thesis/antithesis, good/bad, body/soul, life/death, form/content) while Homer's philosophy contains a third element that links the two extremes while incorporating certain of their characteristics. Between the body and the soul there is the spirit ('Three times he considered it in his soul and in his heart' [*Il.* VIII, 169]), between life and death there is the transformation (see Part III, Chapters 10 and 11), between father and mother there is the child, who takes the characteristics of both father and mother (for this reason Homer usually mentions only one child per couple, for example, the son of Hector and Andromache or of Odysseus and Penelope), and between good and bad there is the specific situation that determines what is to be done at a given moment.

Homer's philosophy is thus based on three simultaneous determinants, which makes it typically Celtic. (The symbol of this philosophy is the triskele, representing three waves joined together.)

The simultaneous existence of the third element by no means implies that the notion of good and evil did not exist or was not reflected in the law, because Homer tells us that the society of the time was well organized – there was an assembly, a council, a tribunal and judges. But a judge may well have decided, for example, not to pursue Odysseus for the multiple murders of his wife's suitors, who had run down his possessions during his absence, because the circumstances perhaps justified his act, just as today under French law a murderer may be freed after a crime of passion.

Celtic philosophy had such an influence on the early Greek philosophers that Aristotle considered Gaul to be Greece's teacher and the Druids to be the inventors of philosophy, for they were the first to formulate theories on the origins and end of humanity (by fire and water).[20] The Greeks also considered the Druids to be the world's greatest scholars, whose mathematical knowledge rivalled that of Pythagoras[21] and, according to certain writers of the early centuries of the Christian era, it was through contact with the Druids that Pythagoras learned his mathematics.[22, 23] However, this assertion cannot be confirmed as Pythagoras himself left no writings and his very existence is even in doubt. It also appears that the Romans had considerable respect and admiration for the Druids, and Cicero even had a Druid friend who lived in Rome under a Latinized name, Diviciacus.[24]

Among the earliest Greek philosophers of Celtic inspiration was Heraclites (540–480 BC), who believed that everything that exists is in constant evolution caused by the simultaneous action of decay and reconstitution that annihilates opposing elements. A century later, Plato summed up this philosophy (which he did not embrace) in the famous phrase *panta rhei* ('everything evolves' or 'all is flux, nothing stays still').

Whereas the world of Plato is the static universe of the mind, which attempts to analyse everything, the Celtic world was profoundly attached to nature, which is in constant movement. These differences between the two approaches to life were evident to the ancient Greeks themselves. Since we have all been educated on the basis of Greek and Judao-Christian philosophy, we are so accustomed to thinking in terms of extreme categories, such as black/white, that we have the greatest difficulty in understanding Homer on a number of points, for example, the spontaneous admiration often expressed for the enemy. The reader is surprised to see the enemy warriors variously described as 'valiant', 'goodly', god-like, etc. For 2,500 years we have ceased to admire the enemy, for we are invariably 'the good' and the enemy invariably 'the

51

bad'. Anyone who dares to say otherwise would be branded as suspect, or even worse, a traitor. This inability to think in more relative terms unfortunately leads to polarization and may lead to extremism. Our Bronze Age Celtic ancestors often fought with one another, but once the dispute was settled by force it seems that the two sides bore no grudge and could become friends again. Here is an example from the *Iliad*:

> . . . and amazement came upon all that beheld, on horse-taming Trojans and well-greaved Achaeans: and thus would a man say with a glance at his neighbour: "Verily shall we again have evil war and the dread din of battle, or else friendship is set amid the hosts by Zeus, who is for men the dispenser of battle." *(Il. IV, 79-84)*

Without wishing to advocate one philosophy rather than another, I should simply like to point out, in the framework of our research into the origin of Homer's works, that there is a fundamental difference between the Homeric stance and classical Greek philosophy as it developed after the fourth century BC, despite Homer's great influence on Greek culture and that of Europe as a whole right down to the present day.

(xii) A Mismatch in Time

As work on Homer's puzzle progressed, it turned out that many towns, islands and countries were not yet known in the eastern Mediterranean at the time of the Trojan War by the names mentioned by the poet. Places like Thebes, Crete, Lesbos, Cyprus and Egypt had entirely different names in the Bronze Age, as we now know from archeological research. The theatre of action of Homer's epics can therefore never have been in the Mediterranean, just as, say, an epic found in the United States about a Medieval war, mentioning European place-names (which can be found in that country) could not have taken place there, as the American continent had not yet been discovered! As to Homer's place-names, we are confronted with a similar problem but it is not really surprising that such a fundamental error in chronology could persist for some 2,700 years as traditional beliefs handed down over a long period are seldom challenged: each generation simply repeats the teachings of the previous one without asking itself the proper questions. But now that this problem of timing has come to light, we are obliged to look for Homer's places elsewhere than the eastern Mediterranean, and situated near the ocean and its tides, in particular where dykes prevented low-lying areas from flooding. In other words:

we have to look for Homer's places along the Atlantic coast (the coast of the Indian Ocean does not fit the descriptions of climate and vegetation). The outcome of this research will be unsettling to many and I also realize from my own experience that it takes some time to get accustomed to the Bronze Age geography of Europe. The best way of adjusting is by reading Homer together with the explanations and maps of this book. Those who remain sceptical should realize that the problem of place-name *chronology* in general and the phenomenon of *oceanic tides* in particular *exclude any alternative solution.*

Notes

1 Ernst Gideon, *Homerus, Zanger der Kelten*, Ankh-Hermes, Deventer 1973, p. 15.
2 Thucydides, *The Peleponnesian War*, Book A. III, 2.
3 Thucydides, op. cit., Book A. XIII, 6 and XIV, 1.
4 Strabo, *Geography*, I, 1, 7.
5 N.K. Sandars, *The Sea Peoples, 1250-1150 BC*, Thames & Hudson, London, 1978, Chapter 8.
6 Caesar, *The Conquest of Gaul*, IV, 33-34.
7 W. Rutherford, *The Druids*, Aquarian Press, 1978, p.33.
8 Strabo, op. cit., VII, 2.
9 Markale, Jean, *Les Celtes*, Payot, Paris, 1973, p. 30.
10 *Book of Taliesin*, poem XV.
11 Aristotle, *Moral for Eudemus*, III. 1, 26.
12 E. Lasserre, *L'Iliade*, Introduction, Garnier, Paris, 1960, p. 18.
13 P. Vidal-Naquet, *Introduction to the Iliad*, French translation by P. Mazou, Gallimard, Paris, 1975.
14 John Chadwick 'Homère le menteur', in Diogène 77, (1972)
15 M. Moreau, *La tradition celtique dans l'art roman*, Le Courrier du Livre, Paris 1975, p. 55.
16 Maximus Tyrius, VIII, 8.
17 Jan de Vries, *La religion des Celtes*, Payot, Paris, 1984.
18 Tacitus, *Germania*, 9, English translation by H. Mattingly, Penguin Classics.
19 Miranda Green, *The Gods of the Celts*, Allan Sutton, Gloucester, 1986.
20 Diogenes Laertius, *De clarorum philosphorum vatis*.
21 Valerius Maximus, *Memorabilia*, II, 6, 10.
22 Ammianus Marcellinus, XV, 9.
23 Clement of Alexandria, *Stromates*, p. 359.
24 Cicero, *De divinatione*, I, 41, 90.

5

The Celts

In the introduction to his French translation of Homer, Lasserre remarks that Homer's Achaeans were originally an Indo-European people who had invaded Greece from the north, bringing with them their religion in which the main gods were Zeus and an earth-mother goddess.[1] Since we also know from various classical sources that Zeus and other 'Greek' gods were worshipped by the Celts, it follows that the invading Achaeans were of Celtic origin. It is precisely this rather unexpected 'Celtic connection' that put me on the right track.

But who were the Celts? We learn virtually nothing at school about these distant ancestors of ours, despite the fact that there is a very rich Celtic vernacular literature including myths, stories and poems, much of which has been translated into modern languages.

It was during my research into the origins of Homer's poems that I began to realize, and regret, my own ignorance about this mysterious people, forgotten by the majority of modern Europeans, and started reading some of the many books about them. Celtic literature itself, in its written form, dates mainly from the Middle Ages, but it is based on oral transmission frequently going back to the pre-Christian era. Of all the old Celtic territories, Ireland and, to a lesser extent, Wales are the main sources of this literature, that of Gaul having practically disappeared. Celtic culture was better preserved in Ireland than elsewhere because that country was never occupied by the Roman army.

It is very difficult to obtain a clear picture of the pre-Christian Celts from the transmitted texts, not only because of the typical mixture of myth and reality, but above all because of the very great lapse of time between events and their eventual recording in writing. This greatly hampers any rigorous and systematic analysis of the type that I have tried to apply to Homer's work, which itself certainly combines myth and reality, but has the very great advantage of being an eye-witness account transmitted orally for a relatively short period and written down as early as the eighth century BC, the original text being preserved practically intact until our own time, as I shall demonstrate below.

The impression one gets of the Celts is that of a dynamic, but somewhat undisciplined people, proud, full of imagination, loving freedom, adventure, feats of arms, tournaments and fêtes. The Celts were renowned for their eloquence and their poetry, to such an extent that a poet was held in much greater esteem than a common priest. The bards accompanied their ballads on a type of lyre. Despite their individualism, the Celts often acted together, while remaining suspicious of any centralized authority. Their lack of discipline finally brought about their downfall, but for a long period they dominated Europe militarily and even sacked Rome in 387 BC.

The Druids

One of the principal historians of the Roman era, Julius Caesar, tells us that the Celtic peoples were ruled by a privileged caste, the Druids, who were exempt from taxes and military service.[2] This caste held all knowledge. The word 'Druids' in fact means 'the very wise ones', and according to Pline is connected with the Greek *drus*, meaning oak, a tree symbolizing strength, for by holding the knowledge the Druids also held the power. This also explains why their sanctuaries were surrounded by oaks, their sacred trees. The Druids dominated all intellectual activities and were by no means confined to a religious role. They were involved in medicine and even in the command of the army and they were also poets and satirists. Their influence was such that the Druid spoke before the king, at least in Gaul and Ireland. According to Caesar, students of Druidism devoted as much as twenty years of their lives to their studies, learning geography, astronomy, physics and theology. There were Druids who spoke fluent Latin, Greek and Hebrew, according to various classical authors. They believed in reincarnation, at least for those who had not reached the stage of perfection. This belief probably helped them overcome the fear of death. They were very superstitious and made human sacrifice, believing that the only way to save a man's life was to placate the gods by offering another life in its stead. Their religion prohibited the transmission of teaching in writing, even though they used the Ogam or, according to Caesar, the Greek alphabet, at least in Gaul, for purely administrative purposes. It is obviously this lack of written texts that causes the greatest problem for historians. But why the taboo?

The most important reason was that in this way the élite class could maintain itself in power by guarding the secret of certain types of knowledge and could hide anything it considered incomprehensible to the people or dangerous for public opinion. This reason seems even more important than the one advanced by Lévy-Bruhl: 'If the sacred myths were revealed, they would become profaned and thus lose their mystic virtues'.[3]

Although the Druids kept their knowledge secret from all but the initiates, it seems that certain memorized texts, and in particular the epic poems, could be chanted before the general public. It is even probable that some non-initiates also knew them by heart, because the ancients often hid messages in their texts through using symbol, metaphor and parable that only the initiated could understand. In this way it was possible to pass on messages, through time, to those intended to understand them. But in the pre-Christian era, revelation of the mysteries to non-initiates carried the death penalty, something which is hard to understand in our time with its compulsory schooling and free access to knowledge for anyone eager to learn.

Some readers may think I am going too far in trying to demonstrate that the *Odyssey* can be interpreted at various levels: as a precise historical account, as a navigator's chart and as an initiation story. But let us remember the dispute between Aristotle (384–322 BC) and his pupil Alexander, the future Alexander the Great (356–323 BC), on the subject of revealing texts considered secret. Aristotle gave secret lessons (known as 'esoteric' or 'acroamatic' lessons) in his school in the mornings, before a privileged audience. In the afternoons he gave lessons open to all ('exoteric' lessons). The 'secret' books were written in an obscure manner and couched in such terms as to be intelligible only to initiates. But when Aristotle had published his esoteric books, a correspondence (preserved by Aulus-Gellius, an erudite Roman of the second century AD) ensued between him and Alexander. The royal pupil wrote to his master: 'Now that you have made available to everyone the teachings you gave me, in what way shall I be superior to others?' The philosopher replied, 'Know that my published acroamatic lessons can be considered as *not* being published, because only those who have heard me explain them will understand them'.[4]

If this was true of Aristotle's acroamatic books, it was also true of many other ancient texts as diverse as the Bible, the Cabala, the Celtic myths or the works of Homer – only the initiate who has heard the explanations will be able to understand them. Unfortunately, the oral explanation of Homer's works was no longer given in the age of the ancient Greeks, who, for this reason, do not seem to have understood its full significance, or at any rate there is no trace of any written explanation.

There were also other reasons for the ban on writing, however. First, the desire of the initiates to preserve their privileges and, again according to Caesar, the Druids' concern that their pupils should not neglect the training of their memories by relying on written texts. It is worth noting here that in the nineteenth century it was observed that the illiterate Yugoslav bards, who used to recite interminable poems relating their wars against the Turks, sadly had lost their incredible ability to memorize once they had learned to read and write.

Although the Druids prohibited writing, they do not appear to have been completely illiterate. For one thing, it is impossible to mobilize an army of 100,000 men without a certain minimum of administration, which implies at least the ability to keep records. Celtic writings in Ogamic script have indeed been found on ancient stones (see Note 5, The Ogamic alphabet). The name comes from the divinity associated with the magic power of the word, Ogme (in Irish) or Ogmios (in continental Celtic). According to Greek dictionaries, Ogmios was also the alternative Celtic name for Heracles. It is likely that the Celts wrote administrative records and messages on wood, bark or hides rather than on stone tablets. Already in the Bronze Age there was a form of writing for sending messages, judging by the following lines in which Homer tells the story of a perfidious woman:

> Now the wife of Proetus, fair Anteia, lusted madly for Bellerophon, to lie with him in secret love, but could in no wise prevail upon wise-hearted Bellerophon, for that his heart was upright. So she made a tale of lies, and spake to king Proetus: 'Either die thyself, Proetus, or slay Bellerophon, seeing he was minded to lie with me in love against my will.' So she spake, and wrath gat hold upon the king to hear that word. To slay him he forbare, for his soul had awe of that; but he sent him to Lycia, and gave him baneful tokens, graving in a folded tablet many signs and deadly, and bade him show these to his own wife's father, that he might be slain. So he went his way to Lycia under the blameless escort of the gods. And when he was come to Lycia and the stream of Xanthus, then with a ready heart did the king of wide Lycia do him honour: for nine days' space he shewed him entertainment, and slew nine oxen. Howbeit when the tenth rosy-fingered Dawn appeared, then at length he questioned him and asked to see whatever token he bare from his daughter's husband, Proetus. But when he had received from him the evil token of his daughter's husband, first he bade him slay the raging Chimaera. She was of divine stock, not of men, in the fore part a lion, in the hinder a serpent, and in the midst a goat, breathing forth in terrible wise the might of blazing fire. And Bellerophon slew her, trusting in the signs of the gods. (*Il.* VI, 160-183)

Caesar recounts that the Celts were using the Greek alphabet when the Romans arrived in Gaul, in the first century BC:

> In the camp of the Helvetii were found, and brought to Caesar, records written out in Greek letters . . .[5]

However, the knowledge possessed by the initiates was transmitted entirely orally, often in the form of verse or a kind of limerick. In the case of Homer's works, this technique has helped considerably to preserve the original text without too many modifications. One has the impression that the powerful rhythm of Homeric verse also reflects the movement of the ocean waves, but this effect is unfortunately lost in prose translations.

Celtic Origins

There is uncertainty about the origin of the Celts. According to the more generally accepted theory, they spread outwards from Central Europe, where many Celtic objects have been found, notably in excavations at Hallstatt (Austria) and La Tène (French-speaking Switzerland), to establish themselves on the Atlantic Coast, in the British Isles, the north of Italy and Yugoslavia. However, according to another theory, the movement was in the other direction, from the Atlantic coast and islands to the interior of Europe. The second theory would appear to be confirmed by the analysis in this book of the origin of the peoples engaged in the Trojan War, for they were already well-established on the Atlantic coast before the dates generally put forward (see Map 9, Part II, Chapter 14).

Excavations have confirmed that the Celts were also well-established in Denmark during the Bronze Age (from about 1500 to 500 BC) and it was there that the famous Gundestrup silver cauldron was found (see Plate 6). The Celtic tribe that has moved the least is that of the Helvetii, who have been in Switzerland for a very long time (see Part IV, Regiment 18). The Italo-Celts lived in the north of Italy and the Illyrians on the Adriatic coast. In Germany, the frontier between Celts and Germans was ill-defined and in some cases we do not know whether a certain tribe were Celts, Germans, Celticized Germans (i.e. converted to Celtic rites) or Germanized Celts. It should not be forgotten that at that period peoples of sometimes very different origins and cultures could be scattered throughout the same region. Examples are the Germans and the Celts in Central Europe (as shown by archeological evidence), and the non-Greeks and autochthons in Greece, (as mentioned by Thucydides).

Thanks to the Roman historians we have a good picture of where the various Celtic peoples, from Scotland to the Balkans and from Spain to the Baltic, were living at the beginning of our own era. That Celts were living for a long time in the region of Cadiz in the extreme southwest of

The Celts

Spain (Celtiberia) and in the north of Morocco is clear not only from archeological evidence, but also from the writings of historians such as Ephorus, who demonstrated Celtic greatness in his *Universal History*.

There was a certain unity of language, religion and culture among the Celts throughout Europe. Although they never formed a great national or political entity they were prepared to help one another against a common enemy, even though they also fought among themselves. There was also another very important link between them, at any rate for those who lived in coastal regions – the sea routes. The Celts of the Atlantic regions were sea-faring peoples, 'friends of the oar', as Homer calls them, who often undertook long voyages, as we shall discover below.

During their voyages or migrations, communication between the different Celtic tribes must have been linguistically easier than it would be today, because the different languages of the Indo-European family were more homogeneous 3,000 years ago. Many words had the same root from one end of Europe to the other; for example, 'horse' was *epo* in Celtic and *hippos* in Greek. We shall see many other examples in this book. From the grammatical standpoint, too, the languages of Europe more closely resembled one another, for example, the conjugation of Gothic verbs contained elements close to Latin (see Appendix Note 6, Indo-European Languages). What is more, according to Louis Kervan:

> When Rome conquered Gaul, the latter had been in contact with Greek civilization whose bridgehead, since 600 BC, had been Marseille, at the mouth of the Rhône . . . After the arrival of the Romans, as a sign of resistance against the occupiers, Greek continued to be the language of the intellectual élite.[6]

Under these circumstances it must not have been very difficult to translate Homer's works from a Celtic language into Ionian Greek, at the same time committing them to writing, since the Greeks had no taboo on writing. Translation was certainly necessary, for despite a certain number of words in common, Greek is far from being a Celtic language. But was it possible to make a translation in hexameters (lines of six feet: see Appendix Note 7, Metrics) without losing too many details of the original text? The answer is affirmative, since there are examples of translations into Dutch, one in hexameters and one in pentameters, the former, in particular, being very close to the original. It is thus perfectly possible that the epic history of the Trojan War was transmitted by Celts living in central Europe to find its way to Greece, where it was translated and preserved entirely intact, especially, as

Henri Hubert assures us, when talking about the period before 800 BC, that:

> If it can be taken as proven that the Greeks came from the north, i.e. from central Europe, it is not unreasonable to assume that they had contacts not only with the Illyrians (thus confirming Thucydides), but also with the Italo–Celts and even the Celts.[7]

On the other hand, it is unlikely that a Greek author would have composed the work himself on the basis of echoes he had heard of a war that had taken place in some distant part of Europe several centuries before his time, as the hundreds of coherent details in the text are so many indications that the original poem was composed by an eye-witness. However, these details correspond so little to the Greece of the period, or of today, that certain commentators have concluded that the poet did not have a precise idea of the places he was describing. We shall see below that the truth is quite the reverse – the poet knew exactly what he was describing, but it had nothing to do with Greece.

I write in this book of 'Celts', although it would perhaps have been more correct to call them 'proto–Celts' for their culture had not yet come to match entirely what the traditional archeologists call 'Celtic', which dates only from 800 BC. However, Homer mentions the legendary mother of the Celts – 'glorious Galatea' – and describes the Celtic custom of cremation. I therefore adopted the general rule of the archeologist Bosch–Guimpéra, who always speaks of Celts where funeral urns are found, and Homer mentions such urns several times. Furthermore, when I am writing about Celts and their migrations in Europe, I am not always referring to the time of Homer, but possibly to any time in the thousand years before Christ, because as yet we have no precise chronology of the development of their culture. Let us hope that further research will enable us to establish such a chronology. In the meantime, I have sometimes had to work back from elements known about the Celts in the Roman era. In Part III we will come back to Galatea, who will turn out to be a major key for our research as she will be proof that the Celts were already around in the Bronze Age – much earlier than assumed hitherto.

Celtic Culture

The dynamic and inventive Celtic culture brought a certain civilization to Europe before the Greeks and the Romans. They were the first to construct harvesting implements and war chariots. They invented tools still used today, such as pincers; they had keys; they forged iron rims for their chariot wheels; they produced coats of mail. They shod their horses. These shoes, at first in bronze, were not nailed, but had rings round the edge through which a thong was passed to tie them in place. This explains the use of such expressions as horses 'with flashing feet' or 'single-hooved horses' in Homer. The Celts taught the Greeks and Romans the use of soap – *sapo* in Celtic. They have left us some very beautiful ornaments, in gold, such as fibulae (decorated clasps) and torques (collars), and in bronze, such as phalerae (decorative bosses for horses' harness), oenochoe (wine pitchers – it should not be forgotten that the Celts had vineyards even in the north of Europe), situlae (square-shouldered vessels in bronze or glass) and pans for evaporating seawater for salt. Other finds include numerous decorated bronze swords and axes and chiefs' helmets covered with gold or decorated with a bird of prey and, of course, a great deal of pottery. But the Celts excelled above all in the non-plastic arts, such as eloquence, poetry and music.

Certain Celtic practices have persisted down to our own day, such as that of starting the new day as from midnight, and certain feast days have been adopted and adapted by the Christian religion. An example of the latter is the 1 November, which was the feast of Samrain, which marked the beginning of the new year for the Celts. They lit fires in the night, not only to celebrate the new year, but also to communicate with their dead, for if the barriers between the natural and supernatural were already narrow, they believed them to be absent during Samrain night. All Saints, the day the dead are specially remembered, is now celebrated on the 1 November, and on Halloween fires are still lit. The beginning of spring was 1 May, the day of Beltene (or Apollo) when fires were lit and fertility rites were celebrated, with dancing clockwise in circles. The flocks were let out and the sailors went to sea after sacrificing the first vessel they had built during the winter to the gods of the sea. Other major feast days were that of Imbolc on 1 February and Lug (or Zeus) on 1 August.

Notes

1 E. Lasserre, *L'Iliade*, Introduction, Garnier, Paris, 1960, p. 2.
2 Caesar, *The Conquest of Gaul*, VI. 14.
3 Levy-Bruhl, *La Mythologie primitive*, 1935.
4 Aulus-Gellius, *Attic Nights*, XX. 5. English translation by J. C. Rolfe, Loeb Classical Library.
5 Caesar, op cit., I. 29.
6 Louis Kervran, *Brandan, le grand navigateur celte du VIème siècle*, Robert Laffont, Paris, 1977, p. 30.
7 Henri Hubert, *Les Celtes et l'expansion celtique*, Albin Michel, Paris, 1974, Vol. I, p. 144.

6

The Missing Links: Dares and Dictys

If the Trojan War was fought between Celts in western Europe, as I am convinced it was, the crucial question arises of how such a major event could be completely forgotten there. This is so incomprehensible in fact that we have to find a satisfactory answer. As for Homer's epic, there must have been an early break in the chain of oral transmission in western Europe, due to wars, epidemics and the systematic persecution of the Druids by the Romans. This chain was already weak by its very nature, as the number of people capable of reciting some 28,000 lines by heart was obviously very limited. But what is less well known is that there was a second ancient poem describing the war and the fall of Troy, this time from the Trojan side. This work, dating in its written form from about the fifth century AD and ascribed to a certain Dares Phrygius, was the source of inspiration for many early medieval authors in western Europe who wrote about the Trojan War, such as Joseph of Exeter, Joffroi of Waterford, Albert of Stade, Jean de Fixencourt, Servan Copale and, probably the best known, Benoît de Saint-Maure, whose *Roman de Troie* (154-60) is a long epic relating not only the earlier destruction of Troy by Jason the Argonaut and Hercules, the reconstruction of the city by Priam and its subsequent famous siege, but also Helen's abduction by Paris and the wanderings of Odysseus.

The latter epic was retold in abridged form by a Sicilian judge, Guido delle Colonne, who in turn inspired Raoul le Fèvre to write his *Recueil des histoires de Troye* (1464), which was translated into English by William Caxton (1474), while other translations were made into Dutch, Danish, Icelandic, Czech and Spanish.

Since the works of all the medieval authors known to us were directly or indirectly based on the work of Dares, they took the side of the Trojans, contrary to Homer, whose work was apparently unknown to them.

The Missing Links: Dares and Dictys

Dares

But who was this mysterious author by the name of Dares? Most surprisingly, he turns out to have been a priest living in Troy during the war, and he is even mentioned in passing by Homer in the *Iliad:*

> Now there was amid the Trojans one Dares, a rich man and blameless, a priest of Hephaestus, and he had two sons, Phegeus and Idaeus, both well skilled in all manner of fighting. (*Il.* V, 9-11)

Homer seems surprised to see the sons of Dares make their appearance on the battlefield. Since he knew their father's name, function, wealth, reputation, the number of his sons and their names, without having access to the besieged city, he must have met Dares before the war, most probably at the place where they had both received their education, a place we shall identify in Part III. Homer does not tell us much more about Dares, as he did not know that this priest was to survive the war, and even less that he would compose an epic of his own about it. This work, too, must have been transmitted orally for a long time. The versions we have now are in Latin, probably from the fifth century AD, but the Latin author claims to have translated the story from a Greek manuscript, and since we have already seen that the Druids were using Greek at the time the Romans came, this seems not unlikely. The work, generally referred to as *Daretis Phrygii de excidio Troiae historia* (The history of the destruction of Troy by Dares Phrygius), has been translated into various modern languages at different times, but not into English until very recently. The *Encyclopedia Britannica* has little doubt that Dares Phrygius and Homer's Dares were one and the same man, considering the descriptions of the war to be so detailed that they seem to be an eyewitness account. Hitherto, of course, it has always been believed that he was from Asia Minor, because he was known as Dares Phrygius, or 'Dares the Phrygian'. However, as we shall see in Part II, there were already two regions in western Europe called 'Phrygia' in the Bronze Age, long before this name migrated to Turkey. Besides, Dares could well be a name from England, Celtic or otherwise, preserved in the villages of Daresbury in Cheshire and Darsham in East Anglia.

Dictys

In addition to Homer and Dares, there was yet a third author on the Trojan War, Dictys Cretensis, whose work was translated from Greek into Latin in the fourth century AD under the title *Ephemeris belli Trojani* (Diary of the Trojan War). Dictys accompanied the Cretan leader

Idomeneus to Troy, but neither of these men were from the Crete we know, but from a west-European country, again as we shall see in Part II. This would make it much easier to understand how it came about that medieval authors in western Europe were so deeply influenced by the works of Dares and Dictys, and why they took it for granted that the war had taken place in the west of Europe.

Although the works of Dares and Dictys are much shorter than the *Iliad*, they cover the full ten years of the war, which makes them a very interesting complementary source of information about the conflict. For instance, it appears that there have been very long intervals in the war. We also learn that there were about one million casualties, of which 250,000 were Trojans and 750,000 Achaeans. From the latter figure we may conclude that the Achaean army was reinforced on many occasions, as the initial number of warriors can hardly have exceeded 120,000, judging by the 'Catalogue of Ships' in Book II of the *Iliad*. Apparently, the greater part of these reinforcements had to make up for the numerous victims of epidemics, such as the pest that raged in the Achaean camp according to Homer. If the staggering overall number of casualties is correct, the Trojan War is indeed the largest battle ever fought for a single city, in particular if one takes into account the sparse population of Europe in the Bronze Age.

Before the Renaissance, there was even a widespread belief that dispersed Trojans had founded several western European nations, including England and France. For example, the 'Trojan origin' of the Franks is related by Fredegarius, who lived in the seventh century AD, and the 'Trojan origin' of western Europe was still vivid as late as the sixteenth century, as evidenced by Jean Lemaire de Belge's *Illustrations de Gaule et Singularités de Troie* (1510-13) and by Ronsard's epic *La Franciade* (1572).

The siege of Troy is known in Breton tradition as the war between the Asches and the Ecks, a clear reference to Achilles and Hector respectively. From the Renaissance onwards, however, when Homer's works returned to western Europe, it was taken into its culture, and not surprisingly since it was far longer and of far greater literary merit, Homer's work completely overshadowed that of Dares, his Trojan counterpart.

What is more serious, however, is that because Homer was written in Greek, it was considered to be a purely 'Greek' story, although he does not once mention the Greeks, as we have seen. This series of unfortunate coincidences of history has greatly contributed to the confusion leading to a 'Trojan mystery' which can be solved only by going right back to square one, the Bronze Age of the twelfth century BC.

The Missing Links: Dares and Dictys

Back to Square One

At first sight it seems impossible to penetrate such a very distant past, but it turns out to be still feasible to discover what happened over 3,000 years ago, and precisely where, thanks to the branch of linguistics dealing with the history of word forms – etymology. While the Greek spelling of Homer's geographical names was fixed once and for all when the poems were written down 2,700 years ago, place-names in western Europe went on changing in accordance with more or less well-established etymological rules, to be fixed by spelling only relatively recently. Taking this fact into account, we shall see how virtually 400 odd Homeric place-names can be matched in a coherent and logical fashion with western European place-names as we know them today. Many of them are still easily recognizable, others very much less so, often because they have changed by invaders speaking a different language. Even over the last few centuries, some place-names around the world have changed beyond recognition, due to pronunciation by peoples of different languages. (see Appendix Note 8, Etymology). Who, for example, would believe that Brooklyn in New York comes from the Dutch place-name Breukelen, if it were not a documented fact? While it is not possible to 'prove' anything that occurred more than 3,000 years ago, I hope that my detective work has at least produced sufficient circumstantial evidence to convince the judges – my readers – that the famous city of Troy was situated in western Europe.

In my quest for clues that the Trojan War really did take place in the West, I was struck by another idea, this time from Jean Markale, who, discussing geographic names, thinks that those of rivers in particular are among the most ancient, sometimes dating from the Bronze Age or even earlier. Through following this clue I have been able to identify in western Europe not only dozens of rivers mentioned by Homer, but also hills and towns (though the latter are not always in the same location as 3,000 years ago). The reason for the longevity of place-names in general and river names in particular is that conquerors generally adopt the already-existing name, although often modified or adapted to their own tongue.

A major exception to this rule is Greece, where invaders arriving in a country almost emptied of its population gave new names to many places – names familiar to them and appearing in Homer's works. But people arriving in a new and sparsely populated country of course give familiar names to places in a haphazard kind of way. In Australia, for example, Cardiff, Gateshead, Hamilton, Jesmond, Stockton, Swansea and Walsend, widely scattered in Britain, are all suburbs of Newcastle,

New South Wales. It is precisely this haphazard transposition of names that explains, for example, why Rhodes is an island in Greece, but a region in Homer; Euboea is another Greek island, but part of the continent in Homer; Chios yet another island, but not in Homer. Similarly, Homer speaks of an island called Syria which clearly cannot be Syros in the Cyclades. The reader may object that these are simply imprecisions due to the extreme antiquity of the text. But we have evidence that the present Egypt, Cyprus, Lesbos and Crete, all names appearing in Homer, were not known by those names in the Bronze Age. And why does Homer talk about Dorians in Crete when we know that this people did not invade Greece until very much later, if at all? The list of such anomalies is long, as we shall see (*see also* Appendix Note 1, The *Iliad* in Greece). Even the identification of such Homeric places as Ithaca and Pylos has led to endless and inconclusive discussion among scholars, and the difficulty of making sense of Homer in Greece or Turkey is brought out in recent studies by Malcolm Wilcock[1] and G.S. Kirk[2].

It is therefore clear that the poet, though he uses names we recognize, was not talking about the places that now bear those names. What places was he talking about, then? That is the subject I now intend to tackle.

Notes

1 Malcolm M. Wilcock, *A Companion to the Iliad*, University of Chicago Press, Illinois, 1976.
2 G.S. Kirk, *The Iliad: A Commentary*, Vol. I, Books I-IV, Cambridge University Press, 1985.

Part II
The World of the *Iliad*

Be fire with fire;
threaten the threatener,
and outface the brow of bragging horror.

SHAKESPEARE

1

The Troad, Troy and Priam, King of England

In Part I, we saw a great deal of evidence that excluded even the possibility of Troy being located in Turkey, and at the same time found many reasons for seeking the site of this city in a country with a temperate climate and, because of the mention of tides, open to the Atlantic. We also saw that Homer's *Iliad* contains many Celtic elements. It is therefore only logical to look for the Troad on the map of Europe, in a country formerly inhabited by the Celts, with an Atlantic climate, separated from the Continent by the sea and having on its east coast a broad plain with a large bay capable of sheltering a big fleet of ships. There are, in fact, only two big islands off the Atlantic coast of Europe, Ireland and Great Britain. The choice is soon made in favour of the latter, because there is in England an area corresponding perfectly to all the descriptions in Homer – the East Anglian plain between the city of Cambridge and the Wash, a large bay in the North Sea. The Wash not only has the capacity to hold a fleet of almost 1,200 ships, but also affords good shelter against storms from the west. What is more, on its southern shore, it is possible in summer to see the sun not only rise over the sea (in the northeast), but also set in the sea (in the northwest).

The East Anglian plain is not only wide enough easily to contain a big encampment covering several square kilometers, but also to have contained the eleven towns sacked by Achilles. In addition, there still exist two long war dykes, almost intact, between the river Cam and the hills to the east of the plain. However, the mere fact of finding a plain that fits all the requirements of the Homeric text still proves nothing, even if the two war dykes are still there, for these are just as anonymous as the ruins found by Schliemann in Turkey last century. It would be more convincing if we could find Homer's place-names.

Homer's Rivers

Knowing that many rivers have kept their names more or less intact since very ancient times, I hoped to find some resemblance between the names of the East Anglian rivers and those mentioned in the *Iliad*. Homer names no less than fourteen rivers in the region of Troy, eight of them being listed together in the passage where he describes how, after the Trojan War, the violence of these rivers in flood sweeps away the wood and stone rampart built round the Achaean encampment and the ships. It appears that generations of readers must have skipped over these lines, thinking they contained fictitious names of no interest, for otherwise it is difficult to understand how nobody, not even people from the Cambridge area, was ever struck by the resemblance between the names of Homer's rivers and those of this area because, as we shall see, it is still possible to recognize most of them. Here is the passage from the *Iliad* listing the eight rivers in the Trojan plain that the gods unleash against the Achaean rampart because when it was built the proper sacrifices had not been made:

> But when . . . the city of Priam was sacked in the tenth year, and the Argives had gone back in their ships to their dear native land, then verily did Poseidon and Apollo take counsel to sweep away the wall, bringing against it the might of all the rivers that flow forth from the mountains of Ida to the sea – Rhesus and Heptaporus and Caresus and Rhodius, and Granicus and Aesepus, and goodly Scamander, and Simoïs, by the banks whereof many shields of bull's-hide and many helms fell in the dust, and the race of men half-divine – of all these did Phoebus Apollo turn the mouths together, and for nine days' space he drave their flood against the wall; and Zeus rained ever continually, that the sooner he might whelm the wall in the salt sea. And the Shaker of Earth, bearing his trident in his hands, was himself the leader, and swept forth upon the waves all the foundations of beams and stones, that the Achaeans had laid with toil, and made all smooth along the strong stream of the Hellespont, and again covered the great beach with sand, when he had swept away the wall; and the rivers he turned back to flow in the channel, where aforetime they had been wont to pour their fair streams of water.
> Thus were Poseidon and Apollo to do in the aftertime. . . .
>
> (*Il.* XII, 17-35)

Elsewhere in the *Iliad*, Homer mentions six other rivers in the Troy area; Satniois (*Il.* VI, 34; XIV, 445; XXI, 87), Thymbre, also the name of a town, (*Il.* X, 430), Larisa, also the name of a fertile region (*Il.* II, 841; XVII, 301), Caystrius (*Il.* II, 461), Cilla, also the name of a town, (*Il.* I, 38 and 452) and Callicolone, name of a hill and two rivers (*Il.* XX, 53 and 151). Unfamiliar as the names of Homer's rivers might appear to us at first sight, we shall soon see that these names were not only the actual names of real rivers, but have in most cases been preserved sufficiently intact to be recognizable thirty centuries later. It is therefore

69

possible to identify not only the fourteen rivers mentioned above, but also many other rivers mentioned by Homer, elsewhere in England and on the Continent. My approach was simply to assume that the East Anglian plain was the Trojan plain and compare the names of the rivers on a modern map with those found in Homer. I now invite the reader to compare Homer's names, as they generally appear in the translations, with the modern English names (see Map 2 for their location). The river Temese, mentioned in the *Odyssey* (*Od*. I, 184) has been added to the list. The reader who is unfamiliar with the rules of phonetic change is referred to Appendix Note 8, Etymology.

	Greek		Usual rendering	Modern name
1	*Aisépos*	Ἀίσηπος	Aesepus	*Ise*
2	*Rhésos*	Ῥῆσος	Rhesus	*Rhee*
3	*Rhodios*	Ῥόδιος	Rhodius	*Roding*
4	*Grénikos*	Γρήνῑκος	Granicus	*Granta*
5	*Skamandros*	Σκαμανδρος	Scamander	*Cam*
6	*Simoeis*	Σιμόεις	Simoïs	Great *Ouse*
7	*Satnioeis*	Σατνιόεις	Satniois	Little *Ouse*
8	*Larisa*	Λάρῑσα	Larisa	*Lark*
9	*Kaüstrios*	Καΰστριος	Caystrius or Cayster	*Yare* (*Caister*-on-sea and *Caistor* castle at the mouth)
10	*Thumbré*	Θύμβρη	Thymbre	*Thet*
11	Karésos	Κάρησος	Caresus	*Hiz*
12	Heptaporos	Ἑπτάπορος	Heptaporus	*Tove*
13	Kallikolone (Beautiful *Kolone*) (Beautiful Hill)	Καλλικολώνη	Callicolone	*Colne*
14	*Killa*	Κίλλα	Cilla	*Chillesford*
15	*Temesé*	Τεμέση	Temese	*Thames*

Comparing the names of the rivers around Cambridge with those mentioned by Homer in the region of Troy shows such a high degree of correlation that there is every reason to think that it must be one and the same group of rivers, and hence the same region. Half of these rivers have kept their name virtually intact for 3,000 years. Only the Caystrius has radically changed its name to become the Yare, but the original name is preserved by two small towns, Caister-on-Sea at the estuary and Caistor St Edmund in the suburbs of Norwich, a town situated on the Yare. Four other names have changed so much as to be difficult to recognize, but the original elements are still there. Such phonetic change is scarcely surprising in a region that since the Bronze Age has been invaded more than once by continental peoples of different tongues. Homer also calls the main river, the Scamander, by another name, Xanthus, and he explains why: '. . . the great, deep-eddying river, that gods call Xanthus and men Scamander' (*Il.* XX, 74). The name Scamander designates both the river and the god of the river; *andros* being the Greek genitive for 'man'. The famous university city of Cambridge ('bridge over the Cam') has since been built on this river. Homer tells us that the other major river in the Trojan plain, the Simois, flows into the Scamander not far from the sea, thus making it possible to identify the Simois with the present-day Great Ouse (and consequently the Satniois with the Little Ouse), which flows into the Cam north of Cambridge on the way to the Wash, the great North Sea bay.

> When they came to the land of Troy and the two rivers, where the Simois and Scamander join their streams, the goddess, white-armed Here, stopped her horses and loosed them from the chariot and spread thick mist about them. And Simois made ambrosia spring up for their pasture. (*Il.* V, 773-777)

It is impossible to identify all these rivers in a similar way in Turkey (see Map 1, Part I, Chapter 3). All that can be found are four rivers that were given Homeric names without regard to the descriptions in the *Iliad*. It is equally impossible to find all these rivers elsewhere in Europe, so that it would appear in order formally to identify 'the broad plain of Troy' with that of Cambridge. This evidence is backed up by the poet's descriptions, such as the fertile soil, rich land, water meadows, flowering meadows, fine orchards, fields of corn and a host of other details.

The Whereabouts of Troy
If it is possible to identify the Trojan plain, we should also be able to find the exact location of Holy Ilium, as Homer often calls the city of Troy. The poet tells us that it was situated on a hill ('steep Troy'), but which hill? The plain of Cambridge is bounded by hills to the west, the south and the east. However, still using the evidence of the text, we can pinpoint the hill that interests us by two different methods.

First, as already mentioned, there still exist the very substantial remains of two enormous earth ramparts, running parallel with one another, to the northeast of Cambridge, one twelve kilometres long and the other fifteen. The ditches dug in front of these dykes are on the

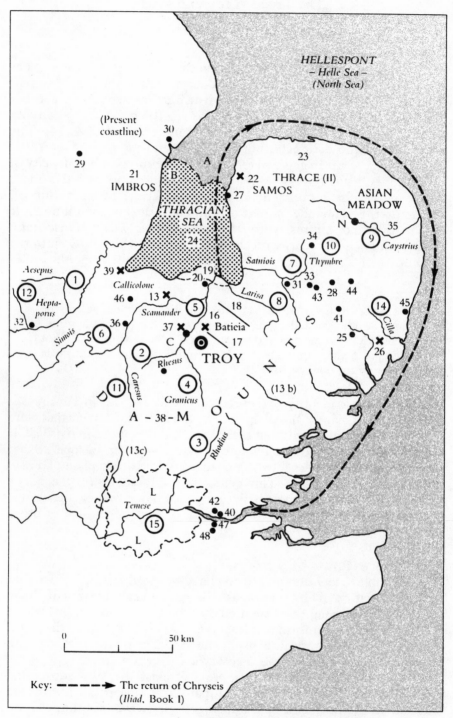

HELLESPONT
– Helle Sea –
(North Sea)

(Present
coastline)
30

29

21
IMBROS

B

A

THRACIAN
SEA
24

23

×22
27

THRACE (II)
SAMOS

ASIAN
MEADOW

N
9
35
Caystrius

34
10
Satniois
7
Thymbre

Aesepus
1

12
Hepta-
porus

39 ×
Callicolone
46 ●   13 ×
Scamander

32 ●

36
6

5
37 ×

C
2

11

Caresis

Rhesus
4
Granicus

A – 38 – M

Simois

19
20

Larisa

31
33
43 28 44

8
16
18
Baticia ×
17
⦿
TROY

(13 b)

41

45
14
Cilla

25
×
26

L

(13c)

3
Rhodius

Temese
42
40
15
48 47

L

O   U   N   T   S

0   50 km

Key: ━ ━ ━► The return of Chryseis
                 (Iliad, Book I)

Map 2
The Trojan Plain in East Anglia. (Bronze Age).
72

Key to Map 2

Reference points
A   The Wash
B   The Fens: this land was under water 3,000 years ago
C   Cambridge
L   London
N   Norwich

Rivers (these names are discussed in detail in the text)

1	Aesepus	Ise
2	Rhesus	Rhee
3	Rhodius	Roding
4	Granicus	Granta
5	Scamander	Cam
6	Simois	Great Ouse
7	Satniois	Little Ouse
8	Larisa	Lark
9	Caystrius	Yare (Cayster)
10	Thymbre	Thet
11	Caresus	Hiz
12	Heptaporus	Tove
13	Callicolone	Colne (hill)

(13b and 13c are rivers with similar names but do not figure in Homer)

14	Cilla	Chillesford
15	Temese	Thames

Other geographical features
N.B. When comparing place-names, it is necessary to forget all the suffixes that are much later than Homer. Examples are: -ham, -ton ('house' in Old English); -by ('village' in Scandinavian); -ford; -field. Further research is required to improve this list. The towns marked with an asterisk are among those sacked by Achilles (only six of them are mentioned by Homer).

16	Batieia, hill (*II*, 811-15)	Bottisham, village
17	Fleam Dyke (Archer's dyke)	} War dykes
18	Devil's Dyke	
19	Achaean camp and rampart	(Destroyed by floods in Homer's time)
20	Tomb of Ilos (*Il*. XI, 166)	Site of Ely Cathedral
21	Imbros (*Il*. XIII, 33)	Region and town west of the Wash (Humber)
22	Samos, hill (*Il*. XXIV, 78)	East of the Wash (Sandringham)
23	Thrace II, region	Norfolk. (There were other Thraces, see Chapter 18, ii.)
24	Sea of Thrace (*Il*. XXIII, 230)	The Wash, 'deep coastline' (*Il*. II, 92)
25	Thebes★ of the Trojans (*Il*. I, 366)	Debenham or another town further downstream the river Deben. (Trojan Thebes not to be confused with Egyptian Thebes, now Dieppe, France)

26	Placus (Wooded hill near Trojan Thebes, VI, 396)	Forest region near Blaxhall
27	Lyrnessus*, town of King Mynes (*Il.* II, 691 and XIX, 296)	King's Lynn (hometown of Briseis, Achilles' girlfriend) was situated on the sea.
28	Tenedos I* (*Il.* I, 452)	Denton
29	Aesyme (*Il.* VIII, 304)	Aisby
30	Scuros* (*Il.* IX, 668)	Skirbeck, a Boston suburb
31	Thymbre (*Il.* X, 430)	Thetford
32	Zeleia (near Aesepus river, *Il.* IV, 103, 121)	Shelton, hamlet near the Ise river (*see also* Part IV, Regiment C)
33	Roiteion (not in Homer)	Roydon (near Diss)
34	Pedasos* (on Satniois river, *Il.* VI, 35)	Besthorpe; name also preserved by the ancient Peddars Way crossing the Little Ouse
35	Asian Meadow (near Cayster river, *Il.* II, 461)	Region of the Yare river and Cayster on Sea. (Asia was a daughter of Oceanus)
36	Eetion* (*Il.* IX, 189)	Eton Socon
37	Gargarus (hill, *Il.* VIII, 48)	Girton
38	Ida (mounts) (*Il.* VIII, 47)	Ditton Woods ('Ida' = woods)
39	Lecton (hill, *Il.* XIV, 284)	Leighton Bromswold
40	Chryse, 'deep harbour', *Il.* I, 430)	Grays on the Thames
41	Pedaeum (*Il.* XIII, 173)	Bedingfield
–	Pergamus (*Il.* IV, 508)	Acropolis of Troy

Other place names (not found in Homer):

42	Ockendon	Former place of worship of Pallas Okke (= Pallas Athene)
43	Diss (Pt III, 11)	Former place of worship of Dis or Hades
44	Homersfield (Pt III, 21)	Named after Homer
45	Darsham (Pt I, 6)	Named after Dares
46	Alconbury	Possibly named after Alalcomenus, responsible for the upbringing of Athene (whence her title Alalcomene meaning 'Patron')
47	Erith	Possibly ancient Erythie (no similar name is found on all of the European continent) where Heracles stole the cattle of the monster Geryon. On his way home, he separated the continents, the original Pillars of Hercules (the Strait of Dover, in line with Tacitus' observations, see Pt II, Chapter 13) and founded Alesia (see Map 15, no. 117)
48	Crayford	Geryon's father was Chrysaion, whose name seems to be preserved by the towns of Crayford and Grays, (no. 40), Homer's Chryse

* Towns sacked by Achilles

74

side facing inland, not towards the sea, which means that they were built by those invading the territory, not defending it (Homer mentions one of them in *Il.* XX, 48ff). These earthworks are known today as Fleam Dyke and Devil's Dyke and appear on most maps of East Anglia (see Map 2). It is obvious that the invader who built these enormous defences was preparing for a long war (the Trojan war lasted ten years) and must have had a very large army to be able to shift the huge volume of earth needed for the dykes, which are 20 m high and 30 m wide at the base (see Plate 2). The estimate usually put forward that the Achaean army numbered between 65,000 and 100,000 men would therefore seem to be no exaggeration, and perfectly corresponds with the number of ships in the fleet multiplied by the average number of warriors in each, as related by Homer. The two dykes are about 10 km apart, giving enough room for two large armies to deploy if the defenders of the town should succeed in passing the first rampart. A line drawn perpendicularly through the centres of the two dykes and extended inland cuts a hill, the highest in the Cambridge area and only a few kilometres from the city, now known as Wandlebury Ring, which is part of a plateau called the Gog Magog Hills. It has become a place for outings where visitors get a good view over the plain. There has been a certain amount of archeological digging here, but it is clear that nobody has had any idea of the illustrious past that finds there may have.

A second indication that Wandlebury was the site of Troy is provided by a further detail of Homer's text, where he tells how the Trojan army (apparently before the construction of the ramparts) gathered on a small isolated hill before Troy:

> Now there is before the city a steep mound afar out in the plain, with a clear space about it on this side and on that; this do men verily call Batieia, but the immortals call it the barrow of Myrine, [an Amazon] light of step. There on this day did the Trojans and their allies separate their companies. *(Il.* II, 811-815)

Some kilometres to the north of Wandlebury, there is indeed an isolated hill where the village of Bottisham now stands. It seems permissible to associate the Homeric name of Batieia (often translated as Briar Hill) with that of Bottis(ham), the 'ham' being a common enough suffix added much later.

During the Trojan War, the god Poseidon, who sides with the Achaeans, installs himself on another hill close to the sea, from where he can see the Achaean ships, the field of battle and, at a distance of some 40 km, the heights of Troy. The sea god's vantage point is usually rendered as Samothrace:

> But the lord, the Shaker of Earth, kept no blind watch, for he sat marvelling at the war and the battle, high on the topmost peak of wooded Samothrace, for from thence all Ida was plain to see; and plain to see were the city of Priam, and the ships of the Achaeans. There he sat, being come forth from the sea, and he had pity on the Achaeans that they were overcome by the Trojans, and against Zeus was he mightily wroth. (*Il.* XIII, 10-16)

The best place to the north of the plain from which to overlook the field of combat is a wooded height on the east side of the Wash from where the Gog Magog Hills, east of Cambridge, are clearly visible, even in fairly overcast weather. Could the wooded hill of Samos in Thrace be the site of one of the residences of the British Royal Family, Sandringham House, which is surrounded by magnificent parkland? The name Sandring(ham) is indeed cognate with Samo-thrace, for in the Ionian in which Homer was first written down the full name is 'Samos-thréîkié', which contracted to Samthrik or Sandrig. Close to the Samos Hill was the Achaean camp, where Achilles invokes the north and west winds blowing over the sea to fan the flames of the funeral pyre of his dead comrade Patroclus. Homer calls the sea in question the Thracian Sea (*Il.* XXIII, 230), which corresponds perfectly with the Wash, where the Acheaean camp was situated on the southeastern shores, right under the northwest wind (see Map 2, p.72). The sea was named after the adjacent region of Thrace, where Samos Hill stood. This tends to confirm that Samo-thrace is none other than the heights of Sandringham. In Bronze Age Europe there were several more regions called Thrace, as we shall see in Chapter 18. ii.

Other features of the Cambridge plain also correspond with the *Iliad*. First, as can be seen on Map 2, p.72, no rivers cross the battlefield and Homer indeed nowhere says that either army has to cross a river to engage in combat. The Scamander bounds the area to the west, as is evident in several passages in Homer, for example, when he describes the position of the Trojan commander-in-chief, Hector:

> Nor did Hector as yet know aught thereof, for he was fighting on the left of all the battle by the banks of the river Scamander, where chiefly the heads of warriors were falling, and a cry unquenchable arose, round about great Nestor and warlike Idomeneus.
> (*Il.* XI, 497-501)

When Priam, with a herald, is on his way from Troy to the Achaean camp by the sea to ask Achilles to return the body of his son, Hector, they apparently follow the course of the Scamander and stop to water their horses at another place that is of great interest to us:

> When the others had driven past the great barrow of Ilus, they halted the mules and the horses in the river to drink, for darkness was by now come down over the earth. (*Il.* XXIV, 349-351)

A modern map shows us that half way between where Troy was and the Achaean camp, on the river Cam, lies the small town of Ely, which very likely owes its name to Ilus, an ancestor of Priam and the founder of Troy. It may well be, therefore, that the great gothic cathedral of Ely was built on the site where Homer saw the tomb of the first Trojan king. As regards the river Granicus (present Granta), it is sufficiently far south of the hill of Troy to allow Achilles to chase Hector round the ramparts, 'These two circled three times with swift feet about the city of Priam' (*Il.* XXII, 165). It remains to explain how it was that Homer's warriors were able to get so easily from Troy to the Achaean camp and the sea, if Wandlebury lies some 40 km from the Wash. The proximity of the Achaean camp to the sea is mentioned frequently, for example:

> But when those others [Nestor and Machaon] were come to the hut of the son of Neleus, they stepped forth upon the bounteous earth, and Eurymedon the squire loosed old Nestor's horses from the car, and the twain dried the sweat from their tunics standing in the breeze by the shore of the sea; and thereafter they went into the hut and sate them down on chairs. (*Il.* XI, 618-623)

and on another occasion, Odysseus and Diomedes first bathe in the sea, then take a bath in the camp, apparently close by:

> So spake he, and drave the single-hooved horses through the trench, exultingly, and with him went joyously the rest of the Achaeans. But when they were come to the well-builded hut of the son of Tydeus, the horses they bound with shapely thongs at the manger where stood the swift-footed horses of Diomedes, eating honey-sweet corn. And on the stern of his ship did Odysseus place the bloody spoils of Dolon until they should make ready a sacred offering to Athene. But for themselves they entered the sea and washed away the abundant sweat from shins and necks and thighs. And when the wave of the sea had washed the abundant sweat from their skin, and their hearts were refreshed, they went into polished baths and bathed. But when the twain had bathed and anointed them richly with oil, they sate them down at supper, and from the

full mixing-bowl they drew off honey-sweet wine and made
libation to Athene. *(Il.* X, 564-579)

A glance at a relief map showing land below sea level in a distinctive
colour shows immediately that the North Sea once covered the whole
of the plain north of Ely, which is itself situated on a rise known as the
Isle of Ely. Certain areas of this reclaimed land are now as much as three
metres below sea level. Part of the Wash had already dried out before
the Roman era, enabling the Romans to build an east-west road, the
Roman Fen Causeway, about 20 km north of Ely. In the fifth century
AD, the sea again took possession of this land, which was finally
reclaimed by means of dykes in the seventeenth century.

The big Achaean fleet needed a very large beach on which to land,
and despite the fact that the southshore of the Wash is about 25 km long,
the ships had to be drawn up in rows:

> For albeit the beach was wide, yet might it in no wise hold all the
> ships, and the host was straitened; wherefore they had drawn up
> the ships row behind row, and had filled up the wide mouth of all
> the shore that the headlands shut in between them. *(Il.* XIV, 33)

Homer tells us that the beached ships were vulnerable to northerly
storms. Map 2, p.72 shows that this is indeed the case for a camp on the
southern shore of the Wash:

> And the sea surged up to the huts and ships of the Argives, and the
> two armies clashed with a mighty din. Not so loudly bellows the
> wave of the sea upon the shore, driven up from the deep by the
> dread blast of the North Wind. . . . *(Il.* XIV, 393-395)

Fortunately the weather is not always bad, and the waters of the Wash
can be calm, as for example, when Iris, the messenger of the gods, goes
to see Achilles' mother, Thetis, a sea goddess:

> . . . and storm-footed Iris hasted to bear his message, and midway
> between Samos and rugged Imbros she leapt into the dark sea, and
> the waters sounded loud above her. Down sped she to the depths
> like a plummet of lead, the which, set upon the horn of an ox of the
> field, goeth down bearing death to the ravenous fishes. And she
> found Thetis in the hollow cave, and round about her other
> goddesses of the sea sat in a throng, and she in their midst was
> wailing for the fate of her peerless son, who to her sorrow was to
> perish in deep-soiled Troy, far from his native land. *(Il.* XXIV, 77-86)

The Troad, Troy and Priam

Since Samos is clearly the region (not to be confused with the island of Samos near Ithaca) of Samothrace or wooded Samos, which, as we have seen, is a hill on the eastern shore of the Wash, Imbros must be the region on the western shore, where, a little further north, the name of the river Humber reminds us of this name.

Homer gives us a very good idea of the scale of the military operation, which for its time must have been at least the equivalent of the allied landing in Normandy in June 1944. The mass invasion by the Achaeans is most impressive, because even today, despite all the sophisticated equipment now available, nothing is more difficult and hazardous for an army than to invade a country across the sea, because of the risks inherent in the landing and the problems of supply. The Achaean fleet, like the Allied fleets, needed a very large bay to effect their landing successfully. It is obvious that such a big fleet could not have landed in Turkey near the presumed site of Troy because there is neither port nor bay. As for supplies, Homer recounts that boats arrived every day bringing wine (and, by extension, other victuals) for the Achaean army from another region called Thrace (which we shall identify later):

> [Nestor to Agamemnon]: "Full are thy huts of wine that the ships of the Achaeans bring thee each day from Thrace, over the wide sea. All manner of entertainment hast thou at hand seeing thou art king over many."
> (*Il.* IX, 71)

After landing in Troad and setting up camp, the great Achaean army advances in the plain of the Scamander (Cam) the warriors being as numerous as the birds in the nearby plain of Asia on the banks of the Caystrius (Yare) in the area where Norwich now stands. Their advance is a terrifying sight:

> Even as a consuming fire maketh a boundless forest to blaze on the peaks of a mountain, and from afar is the glare thereof to be seen, even so from their innumerable bronze, as they marched forth, went the dazzling gleam up through the sky unto the heavens.
> And as the many tribes of winged fowl, wild geese or cranes or long-necked swans on the Asian mead by the streams of Caÿstrius, fly this way and that, glorying in their strength of wing, and with loud cries settle ever onwards, and the mead resoundeth; even so their many tribes poured forth from ships and huts into the plain of Scamander, and the earth echoed wondrously beneath the tread of men and horses. So they took their stand in the flowery mead of Scamander, numberless, as are the leaves and the flowers in their season.
> (*Il.* II, 455-468)

79

The name Asia, a daughter of Oceanus, seems to have disappeared in England, but, as we have seen, the nearby river Caystrius is the present-day Yare. Zeus watched the battles from the Heights of Ida (Greek *ida* = woods) which were to the south of Troy, from where the rivers flowed. On modern maps they are called Ditton Woods. The site of Troy itself was on the Gog Magog Hills. This curious name is mentioned in the Bible. The prophet Ezekiel, who lived about five centuries after the Trojan War, announced as a warning to the people of Israel the words of God, evoking an attack from outside by an alliance of peoples wearing armour and accompanied by horses, under the command of Gog, king of Magog, which provokes such carnage that the birds and animals come to feed on the flesh and blood of kings and heroes:

> And thou, son of man, thus saith the Lord God; Speak unto every feathered fowl, and to every beast of the field, assemble yourselves and come; gather yourselves on every side to my sacrifice that I do sacrifice for you, even a great sacrifice upon the mountains of Israel, that ye may eat flesh and drink blood. Ye shall eat the flesh of the mighty, and drink the blood of the princes of the earth . . . And ye shall eat fat till ye be full, and drink blood till ye be drunken, of my sacrifice which I have sacrificed for you. Thus ye shall be filled at my table with horses and chariots, with mighty men, and with all men of war, saith the Lord God. *(Ezekiel, 39, 17-20)*

It seems that the prophet has taken the terrible example of the Trojan War as a warning to his people, the memory of this conflict having spread throughout the world from distant England. Why was this particular model chosen, in a world that has always and everywhere known bloody war? The reason was that in this case the stakes were very high: Troy, or Holy Ilium, was not just a great city, but was also and above all the centre and symbol of a great nation, which was probably trying to gain control of sea routes and trade in Europe.

Troy did not exercise political power over the whole of Great Britain, however, judging by the fact that the neighbouring peoples who came to defend it were called the 'allies'. They came from as far away as Cornwall, Wales and Scotland, as we shall see. These warriors spoke different languages and therefore had to fight under the command of their own army leaders, but all came to rally to the defence of the Trojans and their city, which obviously meant something very important to these people.

Troy was the illustrious symbol of a country and people whose name, fame and tragedy have remained alive throughout the centuries to our own time.

The Legacy of Troy

But why did the Trojans lose the war and why did the 'gods decide to abandon them'? The reason was no doubt internal weakness, symbolized by Homer in the undying image of the Trojan horse. Quite near the beginning of the *Iliad*, Homer draws attention to this weakness, always a threat to peoples living in peace and comfort and thus underestimating possible dangers. In this extract, Iris, messenger of the gods, is talking to Priam, king of Troy:

> "Old sir, ever are endless words dear to thee, now even as of yore in time of peace; but war unabating is afoot. Verily full often have I entered ere now into battles of warriors, but never yet have I seen a host so goodly and so great; for most like to the leaves or the sands are they, as they march over the plain to fight against the city. Hector, to thee beyond all others do I give command, and do thou even according to my word. Inasmuch as there are allies full many throughout the great city of Priam, and tongue differs from tongue among men that are scattered abroad; let each one therefore give the word to those whose captain he is, and these let him lead forth, when he has marshalled the men of his own city."
>
> (*Il.* II, 796–806)

As everybody knows, Troy was wiped off the map for ever after ten years of war and innumerable deaths. But some town must have taken over from Troy to fulfil the functions of the former metropolis after its total destruction by the Achaeans. The city was clearly not rebuilt on the same spot, and no doubt already at that time the silting up of the Wash made the inhabitants establish their new capital in a place giving better access to the sea. The place they chose was on the Thames, at Ilford ('ford of Ilium') east of the present City of London. The Romans called the new city Londinium Troia Nova ('New Troy') or Trinobantum, while the Celts called it Caer Troia ('town of Troy'). There are still reminders that London took over from Troy: huge wooden effigies of Gog and Magog can be seen in the Guildhall (see Appendix Note 9), while London gold merchants fix their prices per Troy ounce, a unit slightly heavier than the avoirdupoids ounce and used for precious metals only. Tradition dies hard in England!

In subsequent chapters, we shall identify other rivers and towns in the Troad. Sometimes a town had the same name as the river on which it stood (see Appendix Note 10, Homeric Geography). In the *Odyssey*, Homer mentions one such place the reader can easily identify himself, without recourse to an atlas. Here is the passage:

> Then the goddess, flashing-eyed Athene, answered him:
> "Therefore of a truth will I frankly tell thee all. I declare that I am
> Mentes, the son of wise Anchialus, and I am lord over the oar-
> loving Taphians. And now have I put in here, as thou seest, with
> ship and crew, while sailing over the wine-dark sea to men of
> strange speech, on my way to *Temese* for copper; and I bear with
> me shining iron. . . . "   (*Od.* I, 179-184)

The reference is clearly to the Thames, Latin *Tamesa*, Old English
Temes (see Appendix Note 11, Temese: the Thames). It is on this river
that London continues to exercise the power and influence of the
famous city of Troy. But were there already cities of as many as 100,000
inhabitants at the time of Homer? It seems quite possible, and this
number does not even seem excessive in the light of recent estimates by
archeologists, who consider that the population of England was
probably about three million at the end of the Bronze Age, as many as in
the Middle Ages. The population certainly fluctuated widely over time,
due to wars and epidemics, but, according to P. Muir, England at the
transition from the Bronze Age to the Iron Age was already a populous
country with a well-developed agriculture.[1] Naturally, the inhabitants
of a large town have to be fed by surplus agricultural produce from the
farming population, and we do in fact read in the *Iliad* about orchards,
vines and fields of corn. Evidently farming was organized on a settled
and long-term basis, so that there must have been surplus production
for sale. This implies that there was a type of 'capitalistic' market
economy existing in western Europe in the Bronze Age with private
ownership of land. The inheritance went to the sons, or if there were
none, to cousins, according to Homer.

The existence of a well-structured society in England during the
Bronze Age is confirmed by Dillon and Chadwick,[2] cited by Colin
Renfrew, who actually compared it with Homeric society:

> About 2000 BC came Bell-beaker people, whose burials are in single
> graves, with individual grave-goods. The remarkable Wessex
> Culture of the Bronze Age which appears about 1500 BC is thought
> to be based on this tradition. The grave-goods there suggest the
> existence of a warrior aristocracy 'with a graded series of
> obligations of service . . . through a military nobility down to the
> craftsmen and peasants', as in the Homeric society. This is the sort
> of society which is described in the Irish sagas, and there is no
> reason why so early a date for the coming of the Celts should be
> impossible. As we shall see, there are considerations of language
> and culture that rather tend to support it.[3]

In this chapter, we have found a great deal of evidence that Troy was a large city situated in East Anglia. It must have been the capital of the surrounding territory, which bore a very similar name, the Troad. As we shall discover in the following chapters, the Troad was very large indeed, as it corresponded to the greater part of present England. We may therefore consider the Troad and Troy as the cradle of modern England, and Priam the first king of England in documented history, living in the twelfth century BC.

Around 1100 BC, Troia Nova (London) was founded by Brutus, who heads the long list of Trojan kings of England mentioned by Geoffrey of Monmouth in the 12th Century AD.[4] This explains why Queen Elizabeth I was greeted as 'that sweet remain of Priam's state, that hope of springing Troy'.[5]

Notes

1 P. Muir, *Reading the Celtic Landscapes*, Michael Joseph, London, 1985.
2 M. Dillon and N. Chadwick *The Celtic Realms*, Weidenfeld and Nicolson, London, 1972.
3 Colin Renfrew, *Archaeology and Language: The Puzzle of European Origins*, Jonathan Cape, London, 1987, p. 243.
4 Geoffrey of Monmouth, *The History of the Kings of Britain*, translated by Lewis Thorpe, Penguin, 1966 and 1986.
5 M. Wood, *In Search of the Trojan War*, BBC Books, 1985, page 34.

2

The Gog
Magog Hills

What remains today of the ancient city of Troy and the field of battle? The rampart surrounding the Achaean camp had already been washed away in Homer's time (*Il*. XII, 17-35), but two long war dykes, Fleam Dyke and Devil's Dyke (Plate 2), still remain, though documentation available locally is more than vague about their origin. The feeling seems to be that they were built during the Saxon invasions, but nothing is known for certain, which is very strange. If these enormous earthworks had been used for war during the Roman era, this would have been recorded by Caesar, Tacitus or one of the other historians, and if they dated from the Christian era their history would also be known. Their construction and the reasons for it must therefore lie in prehistory, with the chain of oral transmission of their story by the inhabitants of the area having been broken somewhere along the line. It is logical to think of the great Trojan War as taking place here for several reasons. First, the sheer size of the dykes makes it most unlikely that they were built for local wars between tribes of the region. Second, the volume of earth shifted indicates the presence of a large army preparing for a war of attrition, and it is clear that they were built by the invaders and not the defenders because the anti-chariot ditches are on the inland, not the seaward, side. As for the city of Troy itself, the traces of three round fortifications and of war ditches have been found on the Gog Magog Hills southeast of Cambridge (see Map 3, p.85).

Archeological Finds

Unfortunately, archeological excavation work carried out on this site over the past century has been very intermittent and far too fragmentary, due partly to lack of funds and more especially to the fact that nobody has had the slightest suspicion that this is one of the most famous sites in the whole of history.

The first round hillfort, that of Cherry Hinton, was rapidly investigated at the turn of the century and has since been almost entirely

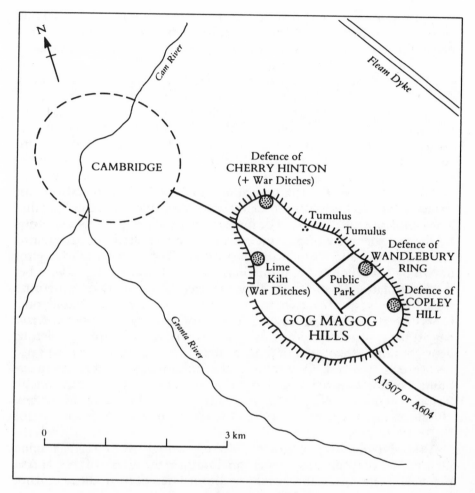

Map 3
Troy on the Gog Magog Hills.

destroyed by the construction of a cement works on the site.[1] The fort had a diameter of 165 m and was surrounded by a ditch 4.50 m deep. Skeletons, pottery and Iron Age objects were found, but in his final report of 1904, Professor McKenny Hughes, who led the work, remarked that it was very difficult to date the finds because all of them were in some way 'exceptional'. The Copley Hill fort, 3 km southeast of Cherry Hinton, suffered a similar fate and is no longer visible today, but between the two there is the better-preserved Wandlebury Ring, located in a public park of 150 hectares. The curious name seems to date from Roman times and owe its origins to the Vandals (Wandle) and Burgundians (Bury), warriors forming part of the Roman army occupying this area. This site has been investigated more thoroughly (see Map 4, p.88). This hillfort consisted of a circular rampart with a diameter of 310 m enclosing an area of 6 hectares. Surrounding it was a ditch 5.50 m wide and 4.50 m deep. The earth excavated was used for the rampart where it was held in place by two wooden palisades. In the course of history the ramparts were destroyed and rebuilt several times, with the result that the most ancient seems to date back only to the third century BC. Numerous urns and skeletons have been found, together with fired pottery and objects in bronze and iron. We know from Homer's text (see, for example, the quotation at the end of the last chapter) that iron was already being used alongside bronze in his time. The simultaneous discovery of funeral urns and skeletons is explained by the fact that only important people were cremated. The mutilated remains of men and women and the upper half of a child, obviously cut in two by a weapon, were found in three pits. It is not known whether these mutilations were caused by massacres, accidents or gruesome rites. Recently, in 1975, two skeletons of warriors were found under the roots of a tree torn up during a gale. One of them had the nose and jaw cut off by a sword, but it is impossible to say whether these skeletons date from the Trojan War or from a later period, because they have not been precisely dated. One thing that is certain is that there are many human remains in the area, for they are constantly being found by farmers, builders and pipe-layers, although, as Professor McKenny Hughes says, the region was not known to have been the site of a major battle.

Although the Gog Magog Hills are not high, they form a small plateau 71-117 m above sea level and dominate the whole of the plain to the Wash. They are easily visible, as Homer stated, from the heights of Samothrace, Sandringham on the east coast of the Wash, some 40 km away. As for Homer's other clues – oysters, eels, vineyards and springs – all are present in the region. The excavations have revealed oyster shells, and even today visitors are offered oysters, especially in Colchester, near the North Sea oyster beds. As for eels, there are so many in the river Cam that the inhabitants of Ely, a small town on this river, think that the name probably comes from eel. They cannot know that their town is more likely to owe its name to Ilos, the ancestor of Priam, whose barrow, according to Homer, was precisely there, half way between Troy and the sea. The magnificent Ely Cathedral is thus built on what must have been an important pagan cult site before the Christian era. There is still an old street called Vineyards in Ely,

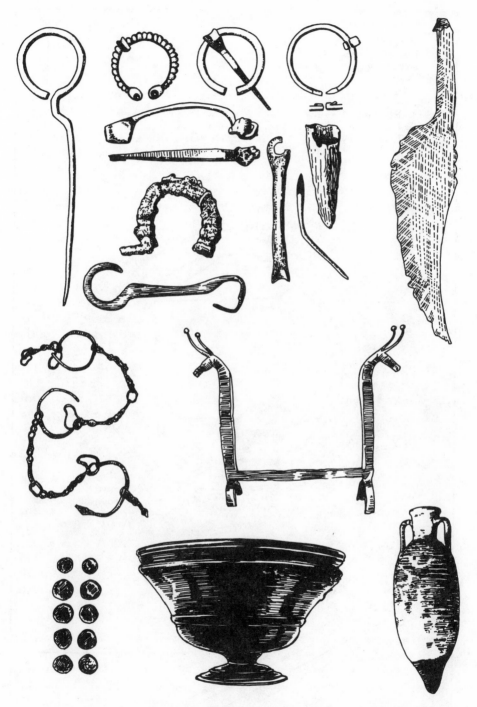

Archaeological finds from the area of the Gog Magog hills in Cambridgeshire, site of the legenday city of Troy.

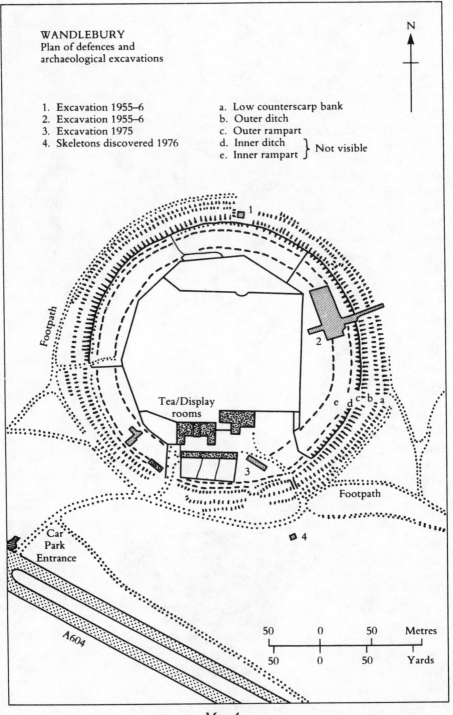

WANDLEBURY
Plan of defences and
archaeological excavations

N

1. Excavation 1955–6
2. Excavation 1955–6
3. Excavation 1975
4. Skeletons discovered 1976

a. Low counterscarp bank
b. Outer ditch
c. Outer rampart
d. Inner ditch
e. Inner rampart } Not visible

Footpath

1

2

e d c b a

Tea/Display
rooms

3

Footpath

Car
Park
Entrance

4

A604

| 50 | 0 | 50 | Metres |
| 50 | 0 | 50 | Yards |

Map 4
Wandlebury, one of the circular fortifications on the Gog Magog Hills,
former site of Troy.

indication of a tradition of viticulture and even today there are some local wines available. There are many springs in the region, some near the Cherry Hinton hillfort and others at Nine Wells.

There have been two other archeological finds of the greatest interest in this area. First, in 1923, C. Fox discovered brooches and other objects dating from the Hallstatt period (approximately 700–400 BC) that had been imported from northern Italy,[2] while an even more ancient find was made by the Hon. R. C. Neville near Mutlow Hill, 5 km east of Wandlebury Ring (Plate 3b). These were glass objects from the eastern Mediterranean which were dated as being from the fifteenth century BC.[3] Objects of a similar date and origin have also been found in other parts of England, thus proving that there were contacts between the Atlantic and Mediterranean peoples long before our own era, though the extent of trade and contact is not yet known.

The earliest reference to the biblical name of Gog Magog for the hills near Cambridge is found in a decree of 1574 forbidding students to visit such places as the Gog Magog Hills, on pain of a fine of 6/8d, and Michael Dayton's *Poly-olbion*, dating from the end of the sixteenth century, contains a map on which the 'Gogmagog Hills' appear and a poem in which Old Gogmagog tries to woo the Nymph of the river Granta. Historians consider it likely that these hills got their present name because of the innumerable human bones that have been found there, silent witnesses to a battle so deadly that it reminded the local inhabitants of the prophet Ezekiel's evocation of the terrible battle started by Gog, king of Magog. However, as suggested in the last chapter, the truth may be the other way round. Although Homer does not mention the name Gog Magog anywhere, it is not impossible that the Trojans used this name themselves for the hills, for the poet, living in the Achaean camp, was not necessarily aware of all that happened or was said in the enemy city. If this were the case, it is possible that Ezekiel, who lived in the seventh century BC (the prophecies date mainly from 695–690 BC), had heard of the terrible war of Troy, which had taken place a few centuries earlier, under the name Gog Magog, and even if he did not know exactly where, he was sufficiently impressed to refer to this war to warn his own people against such a disaster.

Be this as it may, the names of both Troy and Gog Magog have been associated for thousands of years with an archetypal battle, as archetypal as that between good and evil, and the historic event has remained graven on the collective memory of peoples, even though its cause and place may have been forgotten. If it should turn out to be simply a coincidence that the site of Troy is situated on hills today called Gog Magog, then it is one of the happier accidents of history.

The name of Wandlebury, in the form 'Wandlebiria', is found in Gervase of Tilbury's *Otia Imperialia*, of 1211, where he recounts an old legend according to which any warrior setting foot on the site and crying 'Knight to Knight, come forth' would be confronted by a knight on horseback ready to fight. According to Gervase, a visitor to Cambridge, Osbert, son of Hugh, fought and defeated the mysterious knight and took his horse as proof. But the knight managed to wound Osbert in the thigh with his lance. Osbert showed the magnificent horse to his friends, but at cockcrow it disappeared, and each year on the anniversary of the encounter Osbert's wound reopened.[4] England would not be England without its legends and ghosts, but there can be no doubt that the Gog Magog Hills saw violent battles in the far distant past, and probably the worst in prehistory, the Trojan War, recalled as a warning by the prophet Ezekiel.

For the future, the Bible again evokes the name of Gog and Magog, in the book of Revelation, usually ascribed to St John, and better known as the Apocalypse, where the last battle of humanity in which there will be few survivors is announced:

> And when the thousand years are expired, Satan shall be loosed out of his prison, and shall go out to deceive the nations which are in the four quarters of the earth, Gog and Magog, to gather them together to battle: the number of whom is as the sand of the sea. And they went up on the breadth of the earth, and compassed the camp of the Saints about, and the beloved city: and fire came down from God out of heaven, and devoured them.   (Revelation 20, 7-9)

In referring to the first great war of humanity, the Trojan War, the Bible thus also announces the last, which is to be the most devastating conflict in history. We can only hope that it never happens.

Notes

1 H.C. Coppock, *Over the Hills to Cherry Hinton*, Plumridge, Linton, Cambridge, 1984.

2 C. Fox, *Archaeology of the Cambridge Region*, Cambridge University Press, 1923, p. 115.

3 T.C. Lethbridge, *Gogmagog: The Buried Gods*, Routledge & Kegan Paul, p. 9.

4 Wendy Clark, *Once Around Wandlebury*, Cambridge Preservation Society, 1985.

3

The Game of Troy

The Spiral Labyrinth

If Troy was in England, it also becomes clear why prehistoric spiral labyrinths engraved on rocks or laid out on the ground with stones are still called 'Troy towns' or 'walls of Troy' in England, 'Caer*droia*' in Wales and '*Troja*borgs' in Scandinavia. In Greece, the legendary labyrinth of Minos was never found, although labyrinths do appear on Cretan coins dating from about 300 BC. In northern Europe, the treading of a maze is called the 'Game of Troy',[1] which suggests a common characteristic between the circular Troy town labyrinths – or 'unicursal' labyrinths in the terminology of Matthews[2] – and the circular hillforts of the ancient city of Troy: both protect something valuable at the centre.

The labyrinths were clearly related to the Mysteries, as the spirals and blind alleys symbolized the difficulties of life, while the exit route from the centre represented resurrection to a new life, or, in the words of Dr Jaffé, 'the Troy town labyrinth symbolized a rite of passage from life to death and rebirth'.[3] The word 'rebirth' should be taken in the spiritual sense, as Berteaux explains that 'the ritual path through the labyrinth leads the initiate into the depths of the subconscious while following a complex but guided path'.[4]

The Gnostic schools indeed considered knowledge of the self and the universe as the path to illumination and delivery of the soul. But the way to redemption required great courage of the initiate and domination of his animal instincts. This is why Theseus on his way into the labyrinth had to overcome his fear and slay the Minotaur, the bull which guarded the centre, before he was able to return, thanks to the thread of Ariadne which represented the knowledge required to emerge into a new life. As soon as he was saved, he abandoned Ariadne, who merely represented his 'anima', in the terminology of C.G. Jung. Since the personalities of the initiates and life's experiences vary between individuals, the itinerary through the labyrinth is different for each person. This is an important aspect of Gnostic philosophy to which we will return when discussing the *Odyssey*.

The symbolism of the labyrinth was perpetuated in our era by maze decorations in churches in particular, (see Plate 3a) the most famous example being found in the cathedral of Chartres. But the Christians had, of course, replaced knowledge by faith as the means to redemption, which may be why in the Middle Ages the faithful trod the maze on their knees as a sort of penitence. The labyrinth also remained a recurrent theme in literature, the best known example being Dante's description of Hell in his *Divine Comedy*, which, according to Jaffé, 'remains faithful to the mystical prototype of the labyrinth which is the profoundly human myth of a transition – henceforth in the Christian sense of the word – of the life of mortals through death to a new life acquired by the grace of God'. In India, the labyrinth was perpetuated under the name *mandala*, which is Sanskrit for 'circle' although mandalas can take a great variety of forms just like labyrinths.[5]

There is not only a symbolic relationship between the spiral labyrinths called Troy towns and the city of Troy, but also a linguistic one. The origin of the name Troy is found, according to K. Kerényi, in the root of the word *truare* which means 'a circular movement around a stable centre'.[6] In the figurative sense, turning round a problem, while finding more answers to our questions leads to solving the mystery. While the word Troy means a circular hillfort in the concrete sense, it designates a spiral labyrinth in the figurative sense. It appears that the symbolism of the circular labyrinth is much older than Homer's time as it goes back as early as the Stone Age. Western Europe is rich in rock engravings of that era which show a close resemblance between the circular labyrinth and the womb, symbol of return to the origin and (re-)birth,[7] whence the presence of umbilical cords equated by Rank[8] with Ariadne's threads (see illustration opposite).

The linguistic explanation through the word *truare* explains still another, entirely abstract, form of labyrinth: the movement of people dancing in circles, a ritual that may well be as old as the rock engravings themselves. Until recently, such ritual dances were occasionally performed in England around a pole to which each dancer was linked by a long string. The first movement was in anticlockwise direction, symbolizing the return to the origin, i.e. death. Once the strings were entirely wrapped up around the pole, the dance resumed clockwise, symbolizing the release to a new life. In Scandinavia, a very similar dance was performed around a virgin, whence the local name *Jungfrudans*. Homer mentions such a circular dance when describing the decorations on the shield of Achilles (*Il.* XVIII, 590 ff), while the

Bronze Age rock engravings of mazes: (a) Province of Vigo, northwest Spain; (b) and (c) Knowth, Scotland; (d) San Jorge de Mogor, Spain; (e) Auchnabreach, Scotland. Note the 'umbilical cords' or 'Ariadne's threads!'.

meaning of the directions is explained by the poet in another context: a bird flying in front of a subject from right to left augured trouble, while the opposite direction was a good omen.

In the *Odyssey*, we will find a Troy town of the figurative sort, a labyrinth containing knowledge. We will make acquaintance with the goddess Circe, the Great Initiatrice into the Mysteries and, as such, the central figure of the epic. Her name, Circe, is not accidental, for in its dialect form, Kirke, it is related, amongst others, to the word *kirkos*, which designated any bird of prey that *circles* above its prey, such as sparrowhawks, harriers and serpent eagles do, whose generic name is, very appropriately, Circeatinae. Although these birds disappeared from western Europe as they fell victim to hunters and agrochemicals, it is well known that they glide first in large circles above their prey, then spiral inwards, finally to drop like a stone on their victim. In a very similar way, a person eager to learn turns around the mystery, gradually approaching the centre in the learning process. Since the epics of Homer are deeply rooted in the teachings of the Mystery schools, it is not surprising to find that the Troy town or spiral labyrinth is the key symbol of both the *Iliad* and the *Odyssey*.

Notes

1 E. Krause, *Die Trojaburgen Nord-Europas*, Glogau, 1893.
2 W.H. Matthews, *Mazes and Labyrinths*, Longman, Green & Co., London, 1922.
3 Dr H.L.C. Jaffé in *The Situationist* 4, Times, Copenhagen, 1963.
4 R. Berteaux, *La voie symbolique*, Edimaf, Paris, 1975, p. 110.
5 R. Dahlke, *Mandalas der Welt*, Hugendubel, Munich, 1985.
6 K. Kerényi in *The Situationist* 4, Times, Copenhagen, 1963.
7 C.G. Jung, *Psychologie et alchimie*, Buchet/Chastel Paris, 1988, p. 235.
8 R.L. Rousseau, *L'Envers des contes*, Dangles, St-Jean-de-Braye, 1988, p. 83.

4

The Frontiers of
the Troad

(The Channel, the North Sea, Scotland, the Isle of Wight)

If fourteen rivers in the same region of England correspond linguistically and geographically with those of the Trojan plain as described by Homer, the coincidence is so great that it cannot be accidental, and we must indeed be talking about the same plain. However, I can already hear critics saying that this still proves nothing, because at the end of the *Iliad*, Homer states explicitly where Troy was located, speaking through the voice of Achilles talking to the old King Priam, come to claim the body of his son, Hector:

> And of thee, old sire, we hear that of old thou wast blest; how of all that toward the sea Lesbos, the seat of Macar encloseth, and Phrygia in the upland, and the boundless Hellespont, over all these folk, men say, thou, old sire, wast pre-eminent by reason of thy wealth and thy sons. (*Il.* XXIV, 543-546)

This does seem to delimit Priam's kingdom fairly precisely, and these places are indeed now to be found in the Mediterranean. Lesbos is a Greek island off the Turkish coast, Phrygia is the high plateau of western Turkey and the Hellespont is the classical name for the Strait of the Dardanelles. It is precisely this description that inspired Schliemann to seek the ruins of Troy in a plain in northwest Turkey. However, as we have seen, the indications that the true Troy was in England are so strong that we have to assume that there was a general shift of Homeric place-names from western Europe to Greece and the neighbouring countries about twenty-five centuries ago. If this is really what happened, we still have a great many places to identify, so a considerable part of this book will be a study of place-names. This may sound rather daunting, but the reader should not be too discouraged, for he will find that there are some exciting discoveries to be made, and he will be as surprised as I was myself as my research progressed. The

95

Map 5
The identification of the Hellespont or Helle Sea with the North Sea,
Channel and Bay of Biscay. (Bronze Age.)

most logical way to approach this work of identification is to start with the frontiers of the Troad, and first of all the sea.

The Hellespont

Homer calls the sea on whose shores the Troad lies the Hellespont, which means 'Sea of Helle', but who or what was Helle? According to legend she was a girl who fell from the back of a winged ram and drowned in the sea which subsequently took her name. She was the daughter of Athamas, king of Orchomenus and the sister of Phrixus. This additional information will prove to be extremely valuable. The name Hel or Helle (also written as El or Elle by those who do not pronounce the 'h') is of very ancient Indo-European origin. Not only was El the name of the principal god of the pantheon of Ugarith, the ancient Syrian town on the Mediterranean (16th-12th century BC) but 'el' also means 'god' in the Semitic languages.[1] In another legend, found in Nordic mythology, Hel or Hella was the personification of the Kingdom of the Dead, as we learn from the Edda poems:

> Of his goods each man decides only until a certain day, for at a given time every man has to go from here to the house of Hel.
>
> (Fáfnismál, Poem X)

In the course of this book we shall see that there is a close connection between Hel and Helle, and it so happens that they have left many traces to this day. The atlas of Europe contains so many place-names beginning with Hel-, Helle-, El- and Elle- that it is well worthwhile marking them on a blank map of this old continent (see Map 5, p.96). This procedure gives us a frequency distribution of such names that shows a very marked concentration on the shores of the North Sea, the Channel and the Baltic. Elsewhere in western Europe, we find only Hellin, a small town in the south of Spain, and Helvetia, the old name for Switzerland, which may well date from the Bronze Age as we saw when discussing the Celts (see Part I, Chapter 5 and Part IV, Regiment 18). On the other hand, the name Hellas for Greece does not come from Helle, but from Hellen, the son of Deucalion.

Apart from the waters off the western tip of France, still called Chenal de la Helle, the name Hellespont or Helle Sea has disappeared from western Europe, but there are very good reasons for thinking that it must have been the sea on the shores of which so many traces of the name Helle remain, for 'Hell' and 'hel' in English and the Nordic languages means the Kingdom of the Dead, and for the ancients, the Other World was symbolized by the sea, as we shall find (Part III,

Chapter 10 and 11). This explains why Homer sometimes speaks of the 'sterile sea' or the 'watery home of Hades', the god of the Other World (although he also sometimes calls the sea 'rich in fish' and 'source of all things'; the apparent contradiction will be elucidated when we discuss Odysseus' descent into the Kingdom of the Dead).

If the name of the Sea of Helle has virtually disappeared, those of two entrances to it still exist, for in the Rhine delta there remains an estuary called Hellegat, or 'Gate to Helle', while the origin of the name of the small French resort of Houlgate on the Channel coast is no doubt the same, Hellegat.

Confirmation of the connection between Hellespont or Sea of Helle and the English word 'hell' is provided by two well-established etymologies. First, the name of the port of Hull on the northeast coast of England comes from the word 'hell', according to the *Oxford Dictionary of English Etymology*. Second, the name of Brocéliande, the vast forest of Paimpont in Brittany, known from the cycle of the Knights of the Round Table and the Wizard Merlin, is 'Bro–Hellean' in Armorican Breton meaning 'Land near Hell'.[2]

It therefore seems logical to conclude that Homer's 'vast' Hellespont was not the narrow strait of the Dardanelles in northwestern Turkey, but the sea separating England from the continent of Europe, in other words the Channel, the North Sea and the Baltic, all the more so because the Greek adjective used to describe the Hellespont, *apeiros*, is much stronger than 'vast': it means 'boundless' which can only apply to the seas off the western shores of Europe, or, in other words, the Atlantic.

Phrygia

The second frontier of the Troad mentioned by Homer is Phrygia, which he describes as an upland. There are a number of reasons for thinking that this must be Scotland, as the name Phrygia is phonetically very close to that of the Nordic goddess Frigg (or Freya). But we should also look for the etymology of Phrygia in the name of Phrixos, the brother of Helle. This has the advantage of explaining the names of other places in Scotland through the name of the kingdom of their father Athamas, which was called Orchomenus. There is, in fact, still a place in the west of Scotland called Orchy, while off the north of Scotland are the Orkney Islands, the spelling on old maps being Orcheny. On the Orkneys there is a small town with a typically Celtic name, Aith, the same name as Agamemnon's horse. Many other Homeric names will be found in Scotland when we come to study the list of allied armies (see Part IV) which came to help the Trojans defend their city of 'Holy Ilion'. The name of King Athamos himself is possibly preserved in the name of Edinburgh: Atham > Ethem > Eden > Edin (on etymology in general, see Appendix Note 8).

It might be thought that in Homer's time Scotland must have been a very sparsely populated and backward country, but many recent archeological discoveries prove the contrary. Remains of big farms have been found dating from as far back as the Neolithic Age (4000 to 2000 BC), for example at Balbridge near Aberdeen, witness of a very advanced culture for its time, that subsequently spread to the south of Great Britain.[3]

Lesbos
Since we have now provisionally identified two of the frontiers of the Troad named by Homer, the Hellespont to the east, and Phrygia to the north, it should not be too difficult to find the third. Lesbos would then be the Isle of Wight, situated in the Channel, just off the south coast of England. Homer does not say anywhere that Lesbos is an island, only that the site is beautiful, the country well-established and that the Lesbian women (with none of the present homosexual connotation) are very beautiful. The name Lesbos has disappeared, but the name of the main river on the Isle of Wight, the Medina, is cognate with the Greek Methymna, as we shall see shortly. The narrow strait separating the Isle of Wight from the mainland is called the Solent, a name related to the Greek noun *solén* meaning channel or strait). The mainland port of Portsmouth facing the Isle of Wight no doubt later gave its name to the Strait of Porthmos in Greece. What is more, the noun *porthmos* itself originally meant both 'strait' and 'ferry'. Maps of the island also show a promontory known as Egypt Point, a detail that will have its importance when I bring further evidence that Lesbos was indeed the Isle of Wight (see Chapter 10 below). Some readers may still have doubts, because the Greek original of the lines of the *Iliad* quoted at the beginning of this chapter speak of 'Lesbos above', while the Isle of Wight is off the south coast of England and thus not 'above' on the map. The Greek *ano* means indeed 'above, on top', but this does not imply north. Quite to the contrary, in Homer's time *ano* meant 'south', the point where the sun reaches the highest point, the zenith. Our explanation is thus in perfect concordance with Homer's text. There were no maps at the time, and even our habit of projecting north at the top of maps is fairly recent, for example on the maps produced for Roger II of Sicily by the celebrated Arab geographer al-Idrisi in the twelfth century, south is at the top.

However, the few pieces of the puzzle found so far are still totally useless if they do not fit in with numerous others to form a complete picture of Homeric geography. Let us therefore now try to find the original locations of four other key names in his poems: Egypt, Crete, Ithaca and Argos.

Notes

1 M. Eliade, *Histoire des croyances et des idées religieuses*, Payot, Paris, 1989, Vol. I, p. 164.
2 Jean Markale, *Les Celtes*, Payot, Paris, 1973, p. 30.
3 Ann Tweedy, 'A startling new look at Ancient Scotland', in *International Herald Tribune*, 28 September, 1978.

5

Egypt

(Seine–Maritime, northern France)

According to Homer, Egypt is only a few days' voyage from Troy, so if we are convinced that Troy was in England, Egypt must be sought not far from the British Isles. Somewhere in western Europe there should be a region that subsequently gave its Bronze Age name to the land of the Pharaohs. At first sight the very idea seems ridiculous, because Egypt possessed a very ancient civilization and could boast one of the most highly developed cultures the world has ever known, even long before the Trojan War. However, there is a very strong initial argument: at the time of Homer the land of the Pharaohs was not yet called Egypt, but Misr, Al-Khem or Kemi and sometimes Meroë, which means, depending on the authority, 'those blackened by the sun' or 'black earth'. This latter name applied above all to Upper Egypt and what is now Ethiopia (which is yet another Homeric name). The biblical name was Mitsrayim, also modern Hebrew for Egypt. Since independence the official Arabic name of the country has returned to Masr. It was Herodotus, the first Greek to visit the pyramids, which he described in his *Histories*, who first called the Land of the Pharaohs by a name taken from Homer, Egypt. Alexander the Great made this the official name of the country when it became a Greek colony in 332 BC. The Greeks did exactly what the colonial powers of western Europe were to do so many centuries later: they gave familiar names to places in their colonies and imposed their language as the official language of the administration. It was in fact due to this bilingualism in Egypt that the French orientalist Jean-François Champollion (1790–1832) was able to decipher the hieroglyphics, thanks to the famous Rosetta stone, found near Alexandria, on which the same text appears in hieroglyphics, demotic and Greek.

What is more, Homer's descriptions of Egypt do not at all correspond with the Land of the Pharaohs, as was already noted by the Greek Philosopher Eratosthenes (284–192 BC), who himself lived in Alexandria, for Homer uses the name Egypt to designate sometimes a river 'fed by the water of the sky' and sometimes the surrounding country with its 'fine fields'. But he never mentions the celebrated pyramids, several of which were already a thousand years old at the time. It is not inconceivable that the pyramids are not mentioned in Homer because part of the text has been lost, but neither are they mentioned in the Egypt described by Aeschylus (fourth century BC) in his drama *The Suppliants*, the subject of which is clearly based on the Druidic tradition come from the north. He first tells how the suppliants, a group of fifty young women who wish to escape forced marriages, flee Egypt 'across the salty waves to reach the land of Argos'. Later on in the play (and in his *Prometheus Enchained*) we learn how the young Io, pursued by a gadfly, returns from Argos to Egypt, and 'arrives in the holy land of Zeus, rich in fruits of all sorts, in the meadows fed by the melting snow and assailed by the fury of Typhon, on the banks of the Nile whose waters are always pure'.

These lines are bewildering for a number of reasons. First, Argos has never been part of, or near to, the Land of the Pharaohs. Second, the supreme god in Egypt was Râ or Rê the Sun God, while Zeus was completely unknown. Third, meadows watered by melting snow clearly do not describe the Egypt we know today. The only thing mentioned in the translations of Aeschylus that sounds typical of the Land of the Pharaohs is papyrus, but the word in the Greek text is *bublos*, a word of semitic origin meaning 'roll' (of parchment or other writing material).

Since the descriptions by both Homer and Aeschylus do not fit the country we know as Egypt, and as it is also highly unlikely that two authors would have forgotten to mention the pyramids, we can be sure that they were not talking about the Land of the Pharaohs. So, where was the Egypt of the Bronze Age? Once more, using the knowledge that the names of rivers tend to be preserved through the ages, I looked for a river in western Europe whose name resembled 'Egypt' as closely as possible, i.e. at least kept the consonants -gpt-. There is no such river, but there is just one that contains the letters -pt-, the Epte. This river flows from the north to join the Seine near Vernon, half-way between Paris and Rouen. Could the Epte be the E(gy)pt of 3,000 years ago?

The region corresponds to the descriptions by both Homer and Aeschylus. Zeus was certainly known in France, to the extent that one day of the week, *jeudi* (Thursday), comes from his name (Zeus' day), and it is the right distance from Troy. However, the name Epte alone is slim evidence on which to claim that we have found Homer's Egypt, so we must look for further confirmation. In present-day Egypt there is a town and a branch of the Nile, both close to the Mediterranean, that the Greeks called Bolbitiron and Bolbitinon respectively. Is it possible that they borrowed these names, too, from western Europe (they do not appear in Homer, but could have been transmitted by other means). There is only one place-name in the whole of Europe that begins with the letters Bolb-, the small town of Bolbec, which lies exactly where I had hoped to find it, near the mouth of the Seine, 15 km east of Le Havre. There may also be a connection between the village of Vatteville on the other side of the Seine and another branch of the Nile, the Phatnitic Mouth.

If Egypt was originally the name of a region of northwest France, where the river Epte still recalls this ancient past, what has happened to the Nile? It turns out that there are still many reminders of this name in northern France, where many villages contain -nil- (French for Nile) in their name, such as Mesnil, near Le Havre, which in twelfth-century church Latin was called 'Mas-nilii', or 'house in the Nile country'. Other examples are Miromesnil, Ormesnil, Frichemesnil, Longmesnil, Vilmesnil, etc. In Paris there are reminders of this ancient past in the district of Ménilmontant ('house on the upper Nile') and the suburb of Blanc-Mesnil to the north. What is more, the god of the Nile had a daughter called Europe, whose name is preserved by the present river Eure, a southern confluent of the Seine (see Appendix Note 12, Europe). It thus appears that the Greeks have given a Homeric name, Nile, to the longest river in Africa, just as later the colonizers of Brazil gave another Homeric name, Amazon, to the longest river in the world. In the time of the Pharaohs, the Nile was called Ar or Aur, and during the periods when it flooded, Hape the Great, which was also the name of the river god. It would thus appear that in the Bronze Age the lower reaches of the Seine were called the Nile by the inhabitants of the right bank, and we shall see below that the inhabitants of the left bank also called it the Asopus, a name perpetuated by a village called Aizier. The upper Seine was called Séné or Séna, after a Celtic tribe living in this area, the Sénones. The fact that the same river was called by different names should not worry us unduly, for this is still the case with the Rhine, for example, which changes its name several times in Holland before reaching the sea.

Homer mentions a town in Egypt, Thebes, which cannot be the town we know in the land of the Pharaohs, because in their time it was called Wase or Wo-se. It was only eight centuries after Homer that the Greek occupiers of Egypt gave it the new name of Thebes, inspired by the *Iliad* and perhaps also by the Pharaonic name of the nearby site now known as Luxor, Tao-pe. Homer's Thebes is now called Dieppe.

According to etymological dictionaries the 'd' was formerly pronounced 't' and the name is connected with the Germanic *tief* (English 'deep') for the harbour lies deep in the country. Let us recall that Homer, who always chose sound and concise descriptions, speaks of a country of 'fair fields' and a 'heaven fed' river. Dieppe's hinterland is a beautiful farming region and the rain is never far away in this part of France. What is more, recent archeological research has revealed that large farms existed in many parts of France in the Celtic period, so well-kept fields were a feature of the countryside even in that remote era.

Let us now return to Lesbos or the Isle of Wight for further confirmation that Egypt was in Normandy. We have seen that there is a promontory called Egypt Point, situated in the northwest of the island, which was the point where ships turned to head for Egypt (Seine Maritime). Vessels leaving the port in the north went west rather than by a more direct route because the eastern part of the Solent is known for its dangerous sandbanks and currents.

The initial evidence found so far is thus in favour of identifying the Bronze Age Egypt as corresponding approximately to the present department of Seine-Maritime. We shall find further confirmation of this in Chapter 13.

6

Crete

(Scandinavia)

Like so many other places, the Mediterranean island of Crete owes its present name to Homer, this name having been given to it by the people who settled there after the Bronze Age. Before that time, it was known as Kabturi, Keftiu or Kaftor.[1] It is clear for a number of reasons that Homer was talking about quite a different country. First, how could the poet have described Crete as a prosperous country when we know that the Minoan civilization was destroyed about 1380 BC by a combination of structural weakness and invaders from the Peloponnese? It is true that Minoan civilization was replaced by the Mycenaean, which had its centre of gravity in the Peloponnese, but this too was in decline at the time of the Trojan War, to such an extent that the peoples who invaded Greece later seem to have found a country almost devoid of population. Whether this was due to epidemics, genocide by invaders or natural disaster is not known.

Also, the fact that Homer mentions the Dorians among the peoples living in Crete has long been a source of embarrassment to historians, because in the Mediterranean this would be a definite anachronism, as it is well known that the Dorians (or the people who subsequently came to be called the Dorians) established themselves in the Peloponnese and Crete long after the Trojan War. It seems likely that the Dorians were in fact a people who originated in central Europe, whence certain tribes emigrated first to western Europe (where many place-names seem to evoke their presence – Doorn in Holland, Doornik in Belgium, Dorchester in England, and perhaps even the 'doric accent' in English, usually associated with a broad northern dialect), while other tribes later migrated to Greece.

The ancient civilization of Crete was called Minoan after the 'race of Minos', who were its inhabitants according to Homer, and the famous ruins of a palace is known by the Homeric name of Knossos or Cnossus. But, as we have seen (Part I, Chapter 4), the culture described by Homer so little resembles Minoan or Mycenaean culture that the expert

105

John Chadwick called him a liar. The poet scarcely deserved the insult, for he was in fact describing a region that had nothing to do with the Mediterranean island of Crete but was virtually at the other end of Europe – Scandinavia.

I admit it took me a long time to identify Crete in western Europe, thinking first of all that I had to look for an island in the Atlantic. However, re-reading Homer, I realized that it was not necessarily an island, since he talks of a 'vast land surrounded by water', a description he uses only for Crete. The Greek adjective used, *perirrutos* means 'sea-girt' or 'with water flowing round', and can apply equally well to peninsulas such as Jutland or the mainland of Scandinavia:

> There is a land called Crete, in the midst of the wine–dark sea, a fair, rich land, begirt with water and therein are men, past counting, and ninety cities. They have not all the same speech, but their tongues are mixed. (*Od.* XIX, 172-174)

Elsewhere, the poet tells us that from 'vast Crete, far over the sea', where the 'race of Minos' lives, to Egypt is five days voyage, with the vessel taking advantage of the north wind. Not only the direction, but also the distance covered by a sailing boat in five days (roughly 1,200 km) correspond with the voyage from southern Norway to the mouth of the Seine (whereas in the Mediterranean the distance between Crete and Egypt is only 600 km). Through the mouth of Odysseus, Homer tells us that there are snowy mountains in Crete and that its climate is very cold, at least in winter: it can be assumed that he means the winter, because Odysseus is speaking at the moment of his departure after a long stay in that country, and he must have left in the spring, as the sailors of antiquity did not put to sea in winter:

> ". . . verily cloaks and bright coverlets became hateful in my eyes on the day when first I left behind me the snowy mountains of Crete, as I fared on my long-oared ship . . ." (*Od.* XIX, 338)

The only part of Europe that combines all the characteristics mentioned by Homer is Scandinavia. The area is rich, largely thanks to the 'fair, rich' soil, found mainly in Denmark and southern Sweden, where the countryside resembles that of northern France and the fertile north European plains in general. The area is vast enough to have counted ninety towns. The 'snowy mountains' are found in Norway, where certain peaks remain covered in snow even in summer. Since it is surrounded by water there are many ports where 'tongues are mixed'.

In order formally to identify Scandinavia as Homer's Crete, however, we need the names of rivers, but Homer only mentions two in the first instance, the more important of which is the Iardanus. At first, I could find no Scandinavian river with the consonants -yrdn- and had almost abandoned the search, when one morning I woke up with the answer, Hardanger. I had the impression of being 'inspired by a Muse,' as Homer would put it, for Iardan(os) must be Hardan(ger), Norway's biggest fjord which opens to the North Sea just south of Bergen. Homer also mentions another river, the Celadon, close to the mouth of the Iardanos. The map shows the Sildefjord not far from the Hardangerfjord, and phonetically Celadon could well have become Silde. Elsewhere, in the list of armies, we find three other Scandinavian rivers: the Nisa, now Nissan, in southwest Sweden; the Arne, now Arna, in Jutland and the Schoenus, now probably the Skjern, also in Jutland. (It may be said in passing that none of these names can be found in the Greek island of Crete, where some consider the present river Platanios to be Homer's Iardanos, without giving any precise arguments.[2]

If we have found Crete, what of famous Knossos? It seems fairly safe to say that 'wide Cnosus' (*Il.* XVIII, 591) was none other than the 'cap' of Jutland, the extreme north of Denmark, where there is a region and a hill with a name unique in Europe, Knösen. It is well established that the Celts lived in this area long before our own era, for archeologists found there one of the most celebrated of all Celtic works of art, the Gundestrup silver cauldron (called after the village where it was found). This cauldron is decorated with a frieze showing what seems to be a human sacrifice to a god (see Plate 6) and it is precisely to human sacrifice that Knossos owed its notoriety throughout the ages. However, it was not situated in the Mediterranean. It thus appears that the Celts had conquered Jutland already, before Homer's time, from more ancient peoples who had erected the many megalithic monuments found in the region. This may explain why Homer mentions various different peoples living in Crete:

> There dwell Achaeans, there great-hearted native Cretans, there Cydonians and Dorians of waving plumes and goodly Pelasgians. Among their cities is the great city Cnosus, where Minos reigned.
>
> (*Od.* XIX, 175-178)

The native Cretans must have been a pre-Celtic people. We have already discussed the Dorians earlier in this chapter. The Pelasgians, meaning 'sea people', (cognate with Greek *pelagos* = 'flat surface', both of land and sea) were everywhere in the lowlands of northern Europe in the Bronze Age and this name evolved to become 'Belgians', as we shall see in Part IV. The city of Cnosus, which is not the 'wide Cnonus' cited earlier, will also be identified in Part IV (Regiment 17). The Cydonians are no doubt the same people as the Sitones mentioned by Tacitus about 1,200 years after Homer, in his description of the extreme north of Europe.[3]

The only problem that remains to be solved is a passage in the *Odyssey* sometimes referred to as the 'lying tale' in which Odysseus pretends that he is a native of Crete, for fear of being recognized by his host. Some of the things he mentions during his tale do not correspond to the descriptions of Crete given elsewhere in Homer, and they are not all in accordance with reality. Odysseus does in fact seem to be making it up as he goes along – further evidence of Homer's supreme skill – but I was slow to realize this, and having extracted this 'evidence' for my researches I ran into a number of problems. Let readers of the *Odyssey* keep this in mind when they come to Book XIV.

Now that we know that Egypt was in Normandy and Crete was Scandinavia, it is easier to understand the part of the Odyssey where, on the return voyage from Troy to Sparta (from eastern England to southern Spain, as we shall discover in the following chapters), Menelaus was caught in a southerly storm which carried some of his ships to Egypt and others towards the coast of Crete:

> . . . as he passed over the wine–dark sea in the hollow ships, reached in swift course the steep height of Malea, then verily Zeus, whose voice is borne afar, planned for him a hateful path and poured upon him the blasts of shrill winds, and the waves were swollen to huge size, like unto mountains. Then, parting his ships in twain, he brought some to Crete, where the Cydonians dwelt about the streams of Iardanus. Now there is a smooth cliff, sheer towards the sea, on the border of Gortyn in the misty deep, where the Southwest Wind drives the great wave against the headland on the left toward Phaestus, and a little rock holds back a great wave. Thither came some of his ships, and the men with much ado escaped destruction, howbeit the ships the waves dashed to pieces against the reef. But the five other dark-prowed ships the wind, as it bore them, and the wave brought to Egypt.   (*Od.* III, 286–300)

The storm caught the two groups of ships when they were near a cape called Malea. It is most likely that they were in the western Channel, north of Brittany, in what is today the Gulf of St Malo, as it seems reasonable to equate Malea and Malo (but there is another Malea in the Odyssey that will be identified as Cape St Vincent in Portugal – see Part III, Chapter 5). If we assume the story begins in the Channel, the sequence of events becomes entirely logical, as the pattern of Channel storms is always the same, with the wind blowing at first from the southwest, then gradually veering northwest and intensifying. The ships were therefore driven on a course in the form of an arc, passing to the north of Cherbourg in the direction of the mouth of the Seine. Once the storm front has passed, the wind always backs southwest, remaining very strong. The second group of vessels, some distance behind the first, was then driven northeast before reaching the mouth of the Seine and on through the Strait of Dover (see Map 6, p.110).

Anyone unfamiliar with sailing boats might wonder why the second half of the fleet did not try to seek shelter near Calais. The answer is simple: a sailing boat caught in a storm cannot approach the coast under the wind without being driven aground and destroyed. What is more, the sailors would have known that there are dangerous sandbanks, not only off the French coast, but also off Belgium and Holland. Under such conditions, seamen will make every effort to keep away from land and ride out the storm at sea. In his book on the Channel, Nigel Calder reaffirms that the seafarer 'knows that the land, not the sea, is where the dangers lie',[4] and he mentions the recent case of a ship being carried by a storm from the Channel to Norway,[5] thus emulating Menelaus' ordeal 3,000 years later. After drifting for several days the crew had no idea where they were until they were picked up by the Norwegian coastguards. Menelaus was not so lucky, and his ships were lost on the rocky southwest coast of Norway, where Gortyn will be identified in Part IV, Regiment 17, while Phaestos has a name that is common enough in Norway (though the spelling differs), for example Fest-öy (Fest island) and composite names such as Hammar-fest. In this particular case we have to look for a place on the south coast of Norway, where the south wind is most likely to have driven Menelaus' ships on the rocks. And, indeed, there is today a place that corresponds entirely with Homer's description of Phaestus: Vestbygd (*bygd* = built-up area) situated precisely on the western promontory of a peninsula (see Map 14).

It is impossible for the shipwreck to have occurred in the Mediterranean, for to have carried the ships from Greece towards Crete and Egypt the storm would have to have been from the north, not from the south as Homer states.

Menelaus spends some time in Crete/Scandinavia, 'among men of strange speech gathering much livelihood and gold' (*Od.* III, 301), before once more setting out for his home in Spain as we will discover in Chapter 8. He returns first to Egypt (Seine-Maritime), then sails on, apparently in the direction of Cherbourg, as we read:

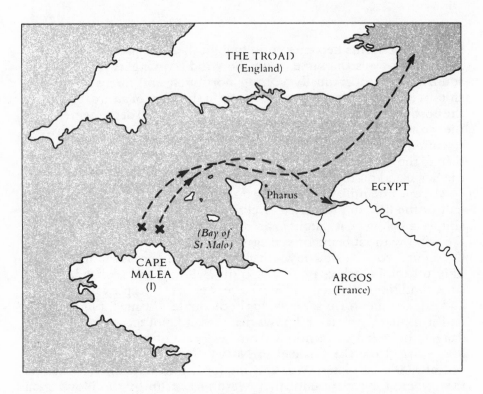

Map 6
Storm in the Channel.

> Now there is an island in the surging sea in front of Egypt, and men call it Pharos, distant as far as a hollow ship runs in a whole day when the shrill wind blows fair behind her. Therein is a harbour with good anchorage, whence men launch the shapely ships into the sea, when they have drawn supplies of black water. There for twenty days the gods kept me, nor ever did the winds that blow over the deep spring up, which speed men's ships over the broad back of the sea.   (*Od.* IV, 354-362)

The island of Pharos where Menelaus had another enforced stay is now known as Tatihou and lies off St Vaast (cognate with Pharos), about 20 km east of Cherbourg in Seine Bay. (It may be noted in passing that there is no island in the Mediterranean between Egypt and Greece off the Egyptian or Libyan coasts where a vessel could call). The distance covered by a sailing boat in a 'full day' of ten to twelve hours, corresponds perfectly to the distance of about 120 km between Le Havre and St Vaast. It is not surprising that he had to wait three weeks for a favourable wind to continue his voyage to Spain, for the east wind is much more infrequent in the Channel than the west wind. However, the sailors of the time thought that it was a god that held them back for some reason, so Menelaus went to consult Proteus, a minor sea-god:

> When the sun hath reached mid heaven, the unerring old man of the sea is wont to come forth from the brine at the breath of the West Wind, hidden by the dark ripple. And when he is come forth, he lies down to sleep in the hollow caves; and around him the seals, the brood of the fair daughter of the sea, sleep in a herd, coming forth from the gray water, and bitter is the smell they breathe of the depths of the sea. (*Od.* IV, 400–406)

The old sea god tells Menelaus he must first return to Egypt and make the proper sacrifices to the gods before he can continue his journey home:

> So he spoke, and my spirit was broken within me, for that he bade me go again over the misty deep to Aegyptus, a long and weary way. (*Od.* IV, 481)

The dark clouds driven by the west wind, the misty sea and the seals conjure up a picture more reminiscent of the Channel between Cherbourg and Le Havre than of the Mediterranean. As to the identification of Crete with today's Scandinavia, we shall identify dozens of towns in the list of Achaean regiments in Part IV.

Notes

1 M. Wood, *In Search of the Trojan War*, BBC Books, London, 1985, p. 177.
2 P. Faure, *Ulysse le Crétois,* Fayard, Paris, 1980.
3 Nigel Calder, *The English Channel*, Chatto & Windus, London 1986, p. 4.
4 Ibid. p. 216.

7

Ithaca

(Cadiz, southern Spain)

All readers of Homer know that Odysseus, one of the most popular commanders of the Achaean army before Troy, was king of Ithaca. Since his kingdom is such an important element of Homeric geography, we should try to locate it without further delay. Homer has Odysseus describe his person and his kingdom with a remarkable lack of modesty, as follows:

> I am Odysseus, son of Laertes, who am known among all men for my wiles, and my fame reaches unto heaven. But I dwell in clear-seen Ithaca, wherein is a mountain, Neriton, covered with waving forests, conspicuous from afar; and round it lie many isles hard by one another, Dulichium, and Same, and wooded Zacynthus. Ithaca itself lies close in to the mainland the furthest toward the gloom, but the others lie apart toward the Dawn and the sun – a rugged isle, but a good nurse of young men; and for myself no other thing can I see sweeter than one's own land.   (Od. IX, 19-28)

It is often believed that Ithaca was the island of Thiaki on the west coast of Greece, despite serious doubts of the scientific community. I had also myself hoped to locate Odysseus' kingdom in Greece if only to leave to the Greeks the honour of keeping the legendary hero for themselves. Unfortunately, Homer's descriptions of Ithaca do not correspond to Thiaki, nor to any other island in the vicinity, a problem which has led to many long and inconclusive academic disputes. What is more, the Trojan War was fought between Celts, and these peoples, in particular the Illyrians, had not yet settled in Greece in 1200 BC. For these reasons we must once again look elsewhere for the original place–names. In the case of Ithaca, the original place was already identified last century by Théophile Cailleux[1], a Belgian lawyer, born in Calais, France, who also identified most of Odysseus' ports of call in the Atlantic Ocean, as we shall see in Part III. According to him, ancient Ithaca is present Cadiz, a major port town in the extreme southwest of Spain. At first, this seems most unlikely, as the kingdom of Ithaca consisted of many islands according to Homer, whereas there are none to be found in southern Spain today. However, we can be sure that the geographical situation was entirely different 3,200 years ago, as the sea level was higher than it is today, resulting in the inundation of vast low-lying areas as far inland as Sevilla (see Map 16 at the end of Part IV). Since then, the landscape has changed considerably because of silting from the major rivers, land reclamation and the fall of the sea level (see Appendix Note 13, The Sea Level). A relief map showing low-lying land gives a good impression of the region in the Bronze Age.

It appears that the present peninsula of Cadiz was indeed an island at the time and surrounded by many other islands. Cadiz could therefore well have been the island of Ithaca as its characteristics meet Homer's descriptions which, at first, seem rather contradictory as the poet sometimes speaks of 'a rugged isle, not fit for driving horses' or 'a good land for goats' while saying elsewhere that 'there grows corn beyond measure'. It turns out that the name Ithaca refers sometimes only to Odysseus' island – and once even exclusively to the town – but sometimes to the entire archipelago, including the large island of Dulichium, the granary of the kingdom.

To support his theory that Ithaca was Cadiz, Cailleux provided too little evidence to be taken seriously although he identified a mountain and a source. The name of mount Neriton has disappeared long ago, but it can still be retraced thanks to Ptolemy, the Greek geographer of the second century AD, who mentions the 'Nertobriga' near Cadiz, where 'briga' is Celtic for 'mount' while 'Nerto' is a corruption of 'Neriton'. Homer also mentions a spring in Ithaca, the Arethusa where the Romans later build a temple to Heracles famous for its spring. The remains of this temple have been found near Chiclana de la Frontera, where there is a medicinal spring which is called today the Fuente Amarga.

Homer's description of the island of Ithaca itself is also contradictory: How can there be two mountains, Neion and Neriton, on a 'low and rocky' island? The only possible explanation is that these mountains were merely very low hills, hardly perceptible in modern Cadiz, which is now a high-rise town build on a rocky soil, the highest point of which does not rise more than 15 metres above sea level. Nevertheless, this modest height suffices to 'see the island from afar' as the skies in this region, called the Costa de la Luz (Coast of Light), are of an extraordinary limpidity. The harbour where Phaeacian sailors landed Odysseus after twenty years of absence is easily detected thanks to Homer's accurate description:

> There is in the land of Ithaca a certain harbour of Phorcys, the old
> man of the sea, and at its mouth two projecting headlands sheer to
> seaward, but sloping down on the side toward the harbour. These
> keep back the great waves raised by heavy winds without, but
> within the benched ships lie unmoored when they have reached the
> point of anchorage. At the head of the harbour is a long-leafed olive
> tree, and near it a pleasant, shadowy cave sacred to the nymphs that
> are called Naiads.   (*Od.* XIII. 96-104)

As the headlands are now for the most part submerged by the sea, the
harbour of Phorcys is not a port any longer while also the name has
disappeared. But from the boulevard surrounding the old city of Cadiz,
one can still distinguish at low tide the two long headlands projecting
westward into the Atlantic Ocean exactly as they still figured on a map
of Cadiz in Stieler's Atlas dating from 1862.

Ithaca's second harbour, Rheithron, where Athene arrived in the
disguise of the Taphian lord Mentes (*Od.* I, 186) can only have been on
the eastern shore of Cadiz, where we find today several modern ports.
On the island of Ithaca, Odysseus' swineherd Eumaeus used to herd his
pigs in the vicinity of the Ravens' Crag, or Corax, (Greek *Korakos petra,
Od.* XIII, 408). This onomatopoeic name is preserved in La Carraca, the
naval arsenal in nearby San Fernando.

As to the other islands of the kingdom, 'wooded' Zacynthus was
situated north of Cadiz, where the name is preserved by the Torre de
Jacinto at the mouth of the river Guadalquivir, which itself owes its
name to the only river mentioned in the region by Homer, the Cephisus
(Kephisos), the root *-quivi* being cognate with *kephi*, while *guada* is
derived from the Arab word for water. The river Guadalquivir thus
owes its name both to the Celts and the Moors.

To the east of Zacynthus lay a large fertile island where abundant
wheat was grown, presently the region around Jerez. As it was the
largest island of the kingdom, it must have been Dulichium, as it was
from here that nearly half of Penelope's suitors originated. The name
Dulichium has disappeared and was never transposed to Greece either.

As to the island of Samos or Same (not to be confused with Same of
Thrace in the Troad), it can be located from the following description:

> There is a rocky isle in the midst of the sea, midway between Ithaca
> and rugged Samos, Asteris, of no great size, but therein is a harbour
> where ships may lie, with an entrance on either side. There it was
> that the Achaeans tarried, lying in wait for Telemachus.
>   (*Od.* IV, 844-847)

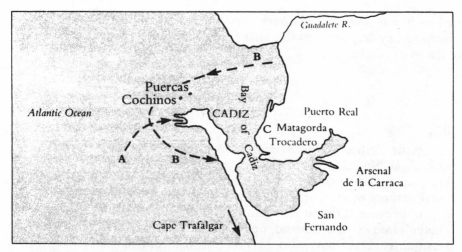

The Bay of Cadiz today. **A** *Odysseus' homecoming;* **B** *Telemachus' return from Pylos;* **C** *Ambush of the suitors.*

The islet of Asteris (never found in Greece), where the suitors laid an ambush for Telemachus, can be no other than Matagorda, in the Bay of Cadiz. In Homer's time ferrymen (*Od.* XX, 187) ran a service for travellers where we find today a bridge linking Cadiz via Matagorda to Porto Real, a town which is situated on another former island which must have been Homer's Samos. Finally, the rock Leukas must be the present islet of Sancti Petri to the south of Cadiz, where a lighthouse is built on the ruins of a Roman temple dedicated to Hercules.

Cadiz was usually said to have been founded by the Phoenicians as Gadir in 1100 BC – which would be later than Homer – but more recently traces of human settlements have been found dating from 1800 BC. What is more, not only objects of Phoenician art have been discovered in the region but lately also of a Mycenaean culture which may well be older than that of Greece.[2] This would imply that peoples from southern Spain penetrated into the Mediterranean as far as Greece and the Levant, giving new familiar names to the places they conquered, such as present Pilos and Sparta in Greece and Sidon, now Saïda in Lebanon, all names which existed already in southern Spain in Homer's time.

The beginning of the *Odyssey* recounts Telemachus' trip to Pylos and Sparta, the capitals of the neighbouring kingdoms of Nestor and Menelaus. Homer even indicates the travel times between these towns and Ithaca, which made it very easy indeed to identify these towns as well as Sidon. We will discover them in the following chapters thus removing any lingering doubts that Cadiz was once Odysseus' famous kingdom of Ithaca.[3]

Notes

1 Théophile Cailleux, *Pays Atlantiques décrits par Homère*, Paris, 1879.
2 *Archeologia*, No. 232, Dijon, France, Feb. 1988, p. 72-75.
3 The map of Greece on page 341 clearly shows that the present island of Thiaki cannot be ancient Ithaca as it is not situated 'furthest toward the gloom' because of the larger island of Kefalonia to the West; neither is Thiaki 'close in the mainland' nor is it 'flat' (as there are several high mountains). One looks also in vain for the islet of Asteris or the 'Pointed' islands in the vicinity of Thiaki. By contrast, Map 16 of South Spain on page 327 shows that Cadiz fully corresponds to these and other detailed descriptions of Ithaca and its surroundings in the Odyssey.

8

Pylos and Sparta

(Southern Spain)

When Odysseus goes off to the Trojan War, he leaves behind his wife Penelope and their infant son Telemachus. After the fall of Troy ten years later, the surviving Achaean warriors return home, except Odysseus, who is condemned by the gods to sail the Oceans for another ten years.

Among the commanders who return home immediately after the war, two are friendly neighbours of Odysseus: Nestor, king of Pylos, and Menelaus, king of Lacedaemon, whose capital is Sparta. As Telemachus, now an adolescent, becomes increasingly worried about the fate of his father, he decides – on the advice of Athene, disguised as the Taphian leader Mentes – to travel to Pylos and Sparta to enquire about his father. Without informing his mother or the suitors about his plans, he manages to obtain a boat and to hire some sailors. One evening he departs for 'sandy' Pylos, which is the name of both the kingdom and the capital of Nestor, surnamed 'the horseman of Gerenia'. It turns out that his kingdom was situated west of Seville and to the north of Cadiz, where is a large sandy region famous for its high-stepping Andalusian horses. Here Pylos is easily identified as the little town of Pilas while Gerenia is now called Gerena, another little town in the area.

Nowadays, Telemachus' journey to Pylos would lead over land, but in Homer's time the sea extended from Cadiz nearly as far as Pilas and Seville because of the higher sea level of the time, as a relief map shows. Part of this region is now dry land resulting from silting of the Guadalquivir and land reclamation, while other parts are still inaccessible marshlands. It is therefore not surprising that Telemachus and his crew had to board a ship for the voyage to Pylos. In order not to be detected by the suitors they set off at nightfall:

So they brought and stowed everything in the well-benched ship,
as the dear son of Odysseus bade. Then on board the ship stepped

> Telemachus, and Athene went before him and sat down in the stern
> of the ship, and near her sat Telemachus, while the men loosed the
> stern cables and themselves stepped on board, and sat down upon
> the benches. And flashing-eyed Athene sent them a favourable
> wind, a strong-blowing West wind that sang over the wine-dark
> sea . . .
> . . . So all night long and through the dawn the ship cleft her way.
>
> (*Od.* II, 414–434)

As can be seen on Map 16 at the end of Part IV, they travel first eastward
to round the island of Dulichium before heading straight north to Pylos
where they arrive the following morning, covering the distance of
some 100 km in ten to twelve hours, which perfectly corresponds to the
average speed of a sailing vessel.

Telemachus is cordially received by Nestor whose kingdom of Pylos
owes its name – due to migration – to a sandy region of the same name
situated on the left bank of the lower Rhine, close to the towns offered
by Agamemnon to Achilles as we will see in Chapter 12 (*see also*
Appendix Note 15, The Pylians). As Nestor unfortunately has no news
of Odysseus, Telemachus decides to enquire with Menelaus in Sparta,
which is a day and a half travel from Pylos. With a horsedrawn chariot
which Nestor puts at their disposal for this journey, Telemachus and
Peisistratus, Nestor's youngest son, set out in the early afternoon to
arrive in the evening in Pherae on the river Alpheus, now Seville near
the Huelva (on etymology, see Appendix Note 8). The next morning
they continue to Sparta, which must have been the present town of
Moron built at the foot of the Esparteros mountain to the southeast of
Seville. Apparently the Moors, who lived here for six centuries,
renamed the town of Sparta after themselves, but not the mountain.

The 60 km voyage through the plains from Seville to Moron can be
covered in a day by chariot. Today, driving along a virtually straight
road leading through fields of wheat – just as in Homer's time – one
soon distinguishes a cluster of mountain peaks standing close together
on the horizon, the highest being the Esparteros (585 metres).
Telemachus and Peisistratus arrive in Sparta, the capital of
Lacedaemon, at sunset:

> So they came to the wheat-bearing plain, and thereafter pressed on
> toward their journey's end, so well did their swift horses bear them
> on. And the sun set and all the ways grew dark.
> And they came to the hollow land of Lacedaemon with its many
> ravines, and drove to the palace of glorious Menelaus. (*Od.* III/IV)

Pylos and Sparta

It is not unlikely that this palace stood on the steep mountain where are today the ruins of a medieval fortress towering over the city of Moron.

In Greece, the voyage of Telemachus cannot be satisfactorily explained as the ancient Greeks already noted. Although both Pilos and Sparta are towns in the southern Peloponnese, and Alfios is a river in the centre of the peninsula, neither the distances nor the descriptions as given by Homer correspond to the terrain which is mountainous and rocky, not flat or sandy. The search for Nestor's Pylos in Greece can therefore be considered as abandoned although various alternative sites have been suggested.

Telemachus stays some time in Sparta, enjoying the hospitality of the opulent King Menelaus and the famous Queen Helen, but again there is no news of Odysseus, except that he is believed to be a captive of Calypso. On Telemachus' departure from Sparta, King Menelaus suggests that he take a different route overland back to Pylos:

> And if thou art fain to journey through Hellas and mid-Argos, be it so, to the end that I may myself go with thee, and I will yoke for thee horses, and lead thee to the cities of men. (*Od.* XV, 80–83)

At first sight, it now looks as if we are in serious trouble with our Bronze Age geography, which locates both Hellas and Argos in northwest Europe, as we will see in the following chapters (See Maps 17 and 15 respectively at the end of Part IV). But in Greece also, 'Menelaus' proposal would have made no sense at all, as such a trip would have meant an enormous detour for anyone travelling between Sparta and Pylos in the Peloponnese and therefore would not have suited Telemachus, suddenly eager to get home. We can therefore be sure that Homer's text has suffered a slight corruption at this point, clearly originating from the period of oral transmission of his epics, when 'Helus' became 'Hellas' while 'Argos' came to replace 'argos', a common noun meaning, among other things, 'untilled land' or 'plain' as the Greek geographer Strabo pointed out. Helus was therefore simply a town on the coast of Menelaus' Kingdom (see Helus B on Map 16 at the end of Part IV), the word itself meaning 'marshland' or 'water meadow'. Menelaus is thus merely suggesting an alternative route to Pylos passing through Helus and the coastal plain, which would at the same time give him a chance to show off some of his cities. But Telemachus prefers to take the shorter route back to Pylos from where he sails home again. He approaches Ithaca at sunset, pondering how to escape the murderous hands of the suitors:

Now the sun set and all the ways grew dark. And the ship drew near to Pheae, sped by the wind of Zeus, and on past goodly Elis, where the Epeans hold sway. From thence again he steered for the sharp isles, pondering whether he should escape death or be taken.

(*Od.* XV, 296–300)

Telemachus, aware of the ambush of the suitors who are waiting for him on the islet of Asteris (present Matagorda, east of Cadiz), cannot land in the harbour of Rheithron on the east coast of Ithaca without being seen and caught. He therefore decides to make a large detour around the northern tip of Ithaca to land on its west coast. After passing Elis, which according to Homer is opposite Dulichium (*Il.* II, 625 and Map 16), he heads toward the 'sharp' islands, an epithet for which no satisfactory explanation has ever been given in Greece[1]. But north of Cadiz there are indeed two groups of sharp rocks in the sea, called the Puercas and the Cochinos (see map of Cadiz in the previous chapter). By following a course around these islands which are like beacons in the sea, Telemachus' ship cannot be seen by the suitors from their ambush, the less so as the sun has already set on Telemachus' approach. We now also understand why the 'sharp' islands were given the unusual names of Puercas and Cochinos, both Spanish for 'swines', as they are reminders of the ancient legend of Telemachus sailing past these rocks on his way to the swineherd Eumaeus.

The sailors land Telemachus on the beach (which still runs all along the southwestern coast of Cadiz peninsula) before returning to the city. Telemachus then walks up to Eumaeus' hut where his father has arrived in the meantime. Here Odysseus reveals his identity to his son, who flings his arms around his father, both men being moved to tears by their long-awaited reunion. But they soon get down to business and start plotting the murder of the suitors.

Note

1 A.T. Murray, *The Odyssey II*, note p. 96, Loeb Classical Library.

9

The Honeymoon of Paris and Helen

(Isla Canela, southern Spain)

It was always believed that the Trojan War was caused by the kidnapping of Helen, the beautiful wife of King Menelaus of Sparta, by prince Paris (surnamed Alexander), a son of Priam, king of the Troad. Supported in this daring enterprise by Aphrodite, Paris sails from the Troad (England) to Lacedaemon (in southern Spain) continuing overland to its capital Sparta, a town we have already identified in Chapter 8. As soon as Paris has seduced Helen with the help of the goddess of love, the couple first travel to Sidon to acquire embroidered cloth before they embark for the journey to the Troad. Once they are seaborn, they pass their wedding night on the island of Cranae as Paris recalls when they are back in Troy:

> "But come, let us take our joy, couched together in love; for never yet hath desire so encompassed my soul – nay, not when at the first I snatched thee from lovely Lacedaemon and sailed with thee on my seafaring ships, and on the isle of Cranaë had dalliance with thee on the couch of love – as now I love thee, and sweet desire layeth hold of me."
> (Il. III, 443-446)

And elsewhere we read about the embroidered cloth bought in Sidon:

> But the queen herself went down to the vaulted treasure-chamber wherein were her robes, richly broidered, the handiwork of Sidonian women, whom godlike Alexander had himself brought from Sidon, as he sailed over the wide sea on that journey on the which he brought back high-born Helen. Of these Hecabe took one, and bare it as an offering for Athene, the one that was fairest in its broiderings and amplest, and shone like a star, and lay undermost of all.
> (Il. VI, 288-295)

The honeymoon journey of Paris and Helen can easily be retraced with the help of Map 16 at the end of Part IV: from Sparta (Moron near Esparteros mountain) in southern Spain, the town from which the couple elope, they travel in southwesterly direction to the coast, stopping at Sidon, today called Medina Sidonia, which is Arab for 'Town of the Sidonians'. At the coast they embark for the Troad, but as soon as they are safely outside the territories of Menelaus and his friendly neighbours Odysseus and Nestor, the young couple, impatient for love, pass the night on the island of Cranae, which is most likely the Spanish island of Isla Canela, situated near the border with Portugal (the dropping of the 'r' in Cranae being a very common sound change). It is unlikely that the name Cranae is derived from the Greek *kranaos* meaning rocky, as is often assumed, since Isla Canela is sandy, but rather from the Homerian word *Kraneia* which is the dogwood or cornel tree, which has a southern variety adapted to a subtropical climate as we saw in Part I, Chapter 4.

The honeymoon journey of Paris and Helen would not make any sense in the Mediterranean, for between Sparta in Greece and Troy in Turkey, the lovers would only have to cross the Aegean sea, so a visit to Sidon, now Saïda on the Lebanese coast, would mean an enormous detour, scarcely to be justified no matter how beautiful the Sidonian women's handiwork. Moreover, there is no island in the Aegean whose name recalls Cranae, only a Cretan peninsula.

As to Sidon, Homer also mentions the city in another context. In his lying tale to the swineherd Eumaeus, Odysseus, disguised as a beggar, recounts that he was landed in Ithaca by sailors on their way from Crete to Sidon (*Od.* XIII, 284). This story does not make sense in the Mediterranean either, where Ithaca (Thiaki) is not situated on the way from Crete to Sidon in Lebanon, but quite in the opposite direction. It is therefore obvious that Homer was speaking of sailors travelling from Crete (Scandinavia) via Ithaca (Cadiz) to Sidon (Medina Sidonia), a town situated to the southeast of Cadiz.

10

Nestor's Tale

(Lesbos – the Isle of Wight)

As we have seen, King Nestor has no news for Telemachus regarding his father, but he relates his own voyage back home from Troy. After leaving the theatre of war, Nestor and his fleet sail to Lesbos, where they stay for a while and Nestor discusses with Menelaus and Diomedes the best course to take from there on:

> ... and late upon our track came fair-haired Menelaus, and overtook us in Lesbos, as we were debating the long voyage, whether we should sail to sea-ward of rugged Chios, toward the isle Psyria, keeping Chios itself on our left, or to land-ward of Chios past windy Mimas. (*Od.* III, 168-172)

This discussion is without significance in the Mediterranean, but if we assume that Lesbos is the Isle of Wight (see Chapter 4 above) it becomes meaningful, for Nestor and Menelaus, en route for Spain, have first to cross the Channel, and their choice in modern terms is between:

(a) passing well to the west of Cap de la Hague (near Cherbourg) keeping Jersey on the port side, or
(b) taking a more easterly course, following the wind-swept coast of the Cotentin peninsula.

Today, yachtsmen in the ports of the Isle of Wight still discuss exactly the same choice of alternative routes to cross the sea towards the Channel Islands as Nestor and Menelaus once did, for the direction and speed of the tidal currents have to be considered in conjunction with the direction and speed of the winds. Map 7 shows us that course (b) is the more dangerous, not only because of the strong tidal currents in the Channel, which reach speeds of about 5 knots (10 km per hour), but also because a westerly wind will drive the vessel ashore on the west coast of Contentin which stretches 120 km from north to south. Even

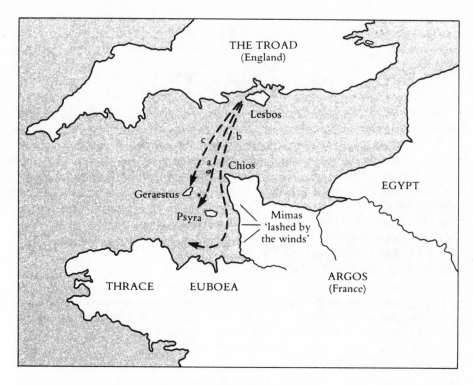

Map 7
Cross-Channel Routes.

for modern yachts the sea to the west of Cotentin is extremely dangerous because of very fast tidal currents which may reach speeds of up to 10 knots and occasionally create whirlpools. Option (a) is already much better as it gives more sea-room, but the two kings are still undecided and ask a god for a sign:

> ". . . and he shewed it us, and bade us cleave through the midst of the sea to Euboea, that we might the soonest escape from misery. And a shrill wind sprang up to blow, and the ships ran swiftly over the teeming ways, and at night put in to Geraestus. There on the altar of Poseidon we laid many thighs of bulls, thankful to have traversed the great sea. It was the fourth day when in Argos the company of Diomedes, son of Tydeus, tamer of horses, stayed their shapely ships; but I held on toward Pylos, and the wind was not once quenched from the time when the god first sent it forth to blow."
>
> (*Od.* III, 174–183)

Nestor's Tale

Not very surprisingly, the god's advice, course (c), is clearly the least dangerous. The island of Geraestus they stop at while on a heading for Euboea (northern Brittany, as we shall see) is Guernsey. From there, Diomedes returns home to Argos (France, as we shall see in Chapter 11), while Nestor and Menelaus sail on to Spain.

The name Chios seems to have disappeared from France, where the cape is now called La Hague, but survives in the town of Chichester (Chios castle) on the south coast of England, apparently built as a defence against raiders from across the Channel.

Such is the account of his voyage by Nestor, the old king of Pylos whom Homer also calls the 'horseman of Gerenia' (*Il.* II, 336) after a town in his kingdom, 30 km from Pylos, still called Gerena today. The different indirect clues we now have to show that Homer's Lesbos was indeed the Isle of Wight tend to confirm that the village of Mithimna on the island of Lesbos in Greece (*Méthumné* in ancient Greek) owes its name to the most important river on the Isle of Wight, now called Medina, after voicing of 'th' to 'd' and transformation of 'u' to 'i' as has occurred in many other names (e.g. *Mukéné* > Mycenae). However, it must be admitted that the name Methumna does not appear in Homer, as is the case with a number of other Celtic names transposed to Greece.

We can be absolutely sure that the place Homer called Lesbos was not the famous Greek island in the Aegean Sea, as it had an entirely different name in his time, as the Greek geographer Strabo explained long ago: 'Lesbos was formerly called Issa'.[1] So in the light of our findings we can now say with confidence that the Isle of Wight was formerly called Lesbos.

Note
1 Strabo, *Geography*, I, 3, 19.

11

Argos, Mycenae and Agamemnon, King of France

We read in Homer that the 'powerful' Agamemnon, commander-in-chief of all the Achaean armies, is 'lord of many isles and of all Argos' (*Il.* II, 107-8). It is therefore most important to know where his kingdom was located. Having first found the kingdom of his brother Menelaus in Spain, I tried to find Agamemnon's territories also in that country, using the names of several rivers mentioned in the list of armies. But my efforts were in vain (which should reassure those readers who imagine that one can prove anything one likes by playing with the etymology of names).

I still had not grasped the real significance of the Trojan War until I finally discovered, to my utter amazement, that Agamemnon's Argos corresponded approximately to the northern half of France, where there are still many place-names derived from Argos, such as the Argonne, a region west of Verdun, Argouges (Manche), Arromanches, ('Argos on the channel', Calvados), Argoeuvre (Somme) and Argueil (Seine-Maritime).

In the course of our analysis of the catalogue of armies (Part IV), we shall identify many more names of towns in Argos with present-day French towns and rivers such as the Orneia (Orne), Messeïs (Messei), Auros (Aure), Tarphe (Thar), etc., none of which can be found in Greece. However, the name of Agamemnon's capital, Mycenae, has disappeared. It is unlikely that he lived in the region where Paris now lies, for in Homer's time this region was known as 'broad Helice' (Elysée). Nearby was a place called Gonoessa (see Part IV, Regiment 9), which must be in the region of the present Gonesse, just north of Paris. It is generally thought that Paris itself was founded after Homer's time by the Parigii, a Celtic tribe who were still living there at the time of the Romans (who called the town Lutetia). According to some scholars, the name Paris is connected with sun worship, as dolmens have been found with images of a sun ship strikingly similar to the Egyptian sun ships. It seems that there were indeed certain links between the Druidic cult and that of the Egyptian goddess Isis. The sun ship, which is still found in the Paris coats of arms, gave its name to the city, via Barisis ('Barque d'Isis', or 'boat of Isis').[1] There can indeed be little doubt that Paris owes its name to Isis, as we also have written evidence that this goddess – usually associated only with the Egypt of the pharaohs – was venerated in northern Europe. This sounds so incredible that I cite my source in full, to avoid being suspected of misinterpretation. The authority in question is Tacitus, writing about the Germans in 98 AD:

> Above all other gods they worship Mercury (the Latin equivalent of Hermes) and count it no sin, on certain feast-days, to include human victims in the sacrifices offered to him. Hercules and Mars (Ares) they appease by offerings of animals, in accordance with ordinary civilized custom. Some of the Suebi (German: Schwaben) sacrifice also to Isis. I do not know the origin or explanation of this cult; but the goddess' emblem, being made in the form of a light warship, itself proves that her cult came in from abroad.[2]

Isis' boat, which had a symbolic meaning, the passage to the Other World, obviously does not 'prove' that she came in from the Land of the Pharaohs. The above passage proves only that we still know very little about the relationship between the cults of the Druids and those of the Near East. Isis was also worshipped in England, where the alternative name of the upper reaches of the Thames in Oxfordshire is the Isis. The Isis cult must have spread in Europe after Homer's time, as he never mentions her and her name figures neither in the Celtic nor the Nordic pantheon. The reverse has also happened, as the Celtic name Cleopatra 'migrated' to Egypt. The best known Cleopatra of mythology is the daughter of Boreas, the god of the North Wind, while Homer mentions a mortal Cleopatra, daughter of Marpessa.

As for the ancient capital of Argos, Mycenae, this could be a contraction of a name meaning Mysteries-on-Seine ('mystery' being cognate with the Greek *musterion* = secret), a place of Gnostic initiation. It is unlikely that this town, described by Homer as being 'opulent' and having 'broad streets', was the present Mussy-sur-Seine, a small village about 40 km southeast of Troyes, despite the phonetic resemblance of the names. It is much more likely that Mycenae changed its name after the Trojan War, to become Troyes, to commemorate for ever Agamemnon's victory. But both Troyes, the capital of the Champagne region, situated on the Seine, and Mussy-sur-Seine must have played a role in the Mysteries, as all ancient initiation ceremonies required that the initiate (*mustes*) make a voyage from the place of physical initiation to the place of teaching, this for symbolic reasons that will be explained in Part III.

If Homer's Argos was the northern half of France, it is not very surprising that the poet should call it a 'horse raising' country and qualify the kingdom as 'opulent', because it includes the richest land in France, a factor of vital importance in an age when a country's wealth depended almost entirely on agriculture. But let us return for a moment to the mysterious 'broad Helice'. It certainly seems to be the Paris region, for there is no other western European place-name resembling Gonoessa/Gonesse mentioned in the same context. It thus seems reasonable to assume that 'Helice' and 'Elysée' are one and the same, but what is more surprising is that the name of the Avenue des Champs Elysées has a different origin, though still from Homer, who speaks of an Elysian field or plain (Greek *Elusion pedion*). While Helice is a physical region, Elysion is an abstract one, the home of the souls of heroes and men of virtue. The description of Elysion by the sea-god Proteus is so ambiguous, as we shall see in a moment, that his listener, Menelaus, is not sure whether he is being promised a nice holiday or threatened with death. The scene takes place in Pharos (St Vaast, in the Channel) on his way home from Troy. Proteus tells him he must return to Egypt (Seine Maritime) and make the proper sacrifices before he can resume the voyage and continues:

'But for thyself, Menelaus, fostered of Zeus, it is not ordained that thou shouldst die and meet thy fate in horse-pasturing Argos, but to the Elysian plain and the bounds of the earth will the immortals convey thee, where dwells fair-haired Rhadamanthus, and where life is easiest for men. No snow is there, nor heavy storm, nor ever rain, but ever does Ocean send up blasts of the shrill-blowing West Wind that they may give cooling to men; for thou hast Helen to wife, and art in their eyes the husband of the daughter of Zeus.'

"So saying he plunged beneath the surging sea, but I went to my ships with my godlike comrades, and many things did my heart darkly ponder as I went. But when I had come down to the ship and to the sea, and we had made ready our supper, and immortal night had come on, then we lay down to rest on the shore of the sea. And as soon as early Dawn appeared, the rosy-fingered, our ships first of all we drew down to the bright sea, and set the masts and the sails in the shapely ships, and the men, too, went on board and sat down upon the benches, and sitting well in order smote the grey sea with their oars. So back again to the waters of Aegyptus, the heaven-fed

river, I sailed, and there moored my ships and offered hecatombs
that bring fulfilment. But when I had stayed the wrath of the gods
that are forever, I heaped up a mound to Agamemnon, that his
fame might be unquenchable. . . ." (*Od.* IV, 561-584)

Agamemnon's kingdom also included Egypt (Seine-Maritime), after
the victory over Thebes (Dieppe), and sandy Pylos (the Rhineland
Palatinate area of Germany, as we shall see in Chapter 12 and part of a
region called Phrygia, which covered what is now northern France and
western Belgium. The name Phrygia was also used for the present
Scotland, as we saw in Chapter 4, and the duplication of names is no
doubt due to the migration of peoples. It is strange that the dictionaries
or commentaries on Homer mention only one Phrygia, for it is clear
from the text that in addition to the one bounding the Troad there was
another on Achaean territory, according to what Priam says when
Helen points out Agamemnon to him from the walls of Troy:

"Ah, happy son of Atreus, child of fortune, blest of heaven; now
see I that youths of the Achaeans full many are made subject unto
thee. Ere now have I journeyed to the land of Phrygia, rich in vines,
and there I saw in multitudes the Phrygian warriors, masters of
glancing steeds, even the people of Otreus and godlike Mygdon,
that were then encamped along the banks of Sangarius. For I, too,
being their ally, was numbered among them on the day when the
Amazons came, the peers of men. Howbeit not even they were as
many as are the bright-eyed Achaeans." (*Il.* III, 182-190)

To try to find this second Phrygia (Greek *Phrugiê*) I looked for names
beginning with Phrug-, Frug- and, voiced, Brug-. It turns out that all
these names are grouped in the extreme north of France and western
Belgium, e.g. Fruges, Bruges, Bruay, Bruxelles and Bryas. The river
Sangarius has disappeared, which is not surprising, as in Homer's time
there were many islands and watercourses in the region, as is still the
case today in the Rhine delta further to the north. However, there are
still place-names beginning with Sang – in the region, such as Sangatte
and Sanghem near Calais. (The subsequent transposition of Homeric
names to the Mediterranean was very erratic, as we have noted already,
for the river Sangarios is to be found in Turkey, not in Greece.) It
appears that the Phrygians also inhabited the north of Holland, where
the name of a province, Frisia, and its capital, Leeuwarden, recall
respectively Phrygia and the village of Lewarde, near Douai in the
north of France.
But we still have to find the islands of Agamemnon's kingdom, for

according to Homer he was 'lord of many isles and all of Argos'. In the sixth century BC, this already posed a big problem for Thucydides, who tried to find them in Greece, for he writes:

> Homer mentions them, if the indications he gives are accepted as true . . . As regards islands, apart from those just off the coast, and they are not numerous, he, as a mainland dweller, would have had none under his rule, unless he had a substantial maritime force.[3]

Our search for Agamemnon's islands in western Europe is equally vain today, but the situation was quite different 3,000 years ago. We have already encountered the phenomenon of periodic higher sea levels in discussing the Troad and Ithaca, and they must also have affected parts of Agamemnon's territory. Much land has since been reclaimed, but still remains soft, to such an extent that new techniques had to be developed for the construction of the Calais-Lille motorway between the coast and St Omer, where there was once an arm of the sea. It is thus more than likely that there were indeed many islands in Agamemnon's kingdom, not only in northern France but also in western France.

In our analysis of the list of armies, we shall see that Agamemnon's Argos extended westwards to the Gironde, northwards to Brittany, and eastward to the far side of the Rhine. The extent of his territory does in fact seem enormous for the age, in view of the problems of communication, but we must not forget that 1,000 years later the Romans governed an empire that was very much larger still, despite the fact that communications had not changed at all since Homer. In fact, the horse was always the fastest means of land transport until just a few generations ago. Only military and administrative organization had really developed in the intervening period.

Agamemnon was commander-in-chief of the Achaean armies, so that even the greatest hero of the *Iliad*, Achilles, a native of the Rhine delta (as we shall see in Part IV, Regiment 21), owed him allegiance. Since Agamemnon was apparently freely chosen by the other peoples to be their leader for the duration of the war, he probably held no real power over the territory of other Celtic peoples on the continent of western Europe. But one thing that is highly confusing for the reader of Homer is that he uses the name 'Argos' not only for Agamemnon's kingdom, but also sometimes for a town, a province or even all the Celtic territories of Europe, with the possible exception of Crete (Scandinavia). Similarly, he refers to the Continental allies apparently indiscriminately as Achaeans, Danaans (a name deriving from Danaus, a king of Argos), or Argives, the people of Argos. However, the practice of using the same name for both the whole or part of a territory is still current today, for example, we very often refer to the Netherlands as Holland, the name of the biggest province of that country. In Homer, Argos in its broadest sense included all the Celtic territory down to the south of Spain, where there was the town of Ephyre in Elide, 'in the corner of Argos' (*Il.* VI, 152). Here was also the home of Helen of Argos. The present name of the region of Aragon in Spain is also a reminder of Celtic Argos. We shall see in Part IV that the northern limit of Argos was Holland, sometimes called 'Achaean Argos' and Belgium, 'Pelasgian Argos', Pelasgian being cognate with Belgian.

It might be asked why the two brothers, Agamemnon and Menelaus, ruled over kingdoms that were some 2,000 km apart. Homer gives us the answer to this question, discussed in Appendix Note 15, The Pylians. Suffice it to say here that the Celts from the north of France and the Netherlands had started to settle in the south of Spain just a few generations before the Trojan War. But despite the great distance between Mycenae in northern France and Sparta in southern Spain, the two brothers kept in personal contact, as we learn from Homer that Agamemnon visited Menelaus in Sparta before the war. They then travelled together to nearby Ithaca to request Odysseus' participation in the planned expedition against Troy. Homer mentions this in a scene taking place in the Underworld, where, long after the Trojan War, the ghost of Agamemnon recalls his long voyage, speaking to the ghost of Amphimedon, who was an Ithacan prince and one of Penelope's suitors slain by Odysseus:

> "Dost thou not remember when I came thither to your house with godlike Menelaus to urge Odysseus to go with us to Ilios on the benched ships? A full month it took us to cross all the wide sea, for hardly could we win to our will Odysseus, the sacker of cities." (*Od.* XXIV, 115-119)

With Argos and Ithaca situated wide apart in western Europe, it would indeed have taken a 'full month' to sail down the Seine river and cross 'all the wide sea' to Cadiz (see Map inside Front Cover). By contrast, in Greece it takes less that twenty four hours to sail from Argos in the northeast Peloponnese through the narrow Gulf of Corinth to Ithaca, present Thiaki, or at most three days if the trip were made around the Peloponnese. Having Greek geography in mind, the translator was clearly aware of the problem and assumed that the voyage had lasted so long *because* it took time to convince Odysseus. Consequently, he added the word 'for' to the above citation, although this word is absent in the Greek text which does not suggest any causality at all. (This is an example of translations being influenced by the context, see Appendix Note 4, Translation of Homer).

Argos was not only the name of a territory, but was also a common Celtic man's name and even Odysseus' dog was called Argos. It can be traced back to the very origins of the Indo-European languages, for it is derived, via 'argros', from the Sanskrit root 'rjra-', meaning 'bright', hence 'argent' (silver). In the Celtic era 'argos' meant 'white', particularly of oxen and geese, and 'swift', like lightning, but also 'plain' as we saw in Chapter 8.

As for the royal house of Argos, we know from ancient Greek literature, which must have drawn on Druidic tradition come from the north, that Agamemnon's family, the house of the Atreidae, had known a series of bloody dramas. In the *Odyssey*, Homer recounts the grisly end of Agamemnon himself, assassinated the very day of his triumphant return from Troy by his wife Clytemnestra and her lover Aegisthus. When Odysseus goes down to Hades to question the souls of dead warriors, the king's soul approaches him to tell how he was killed by his own wife:

"He [Agamemnon] knew me [Odysseus] straightway, when he had drunk the dark blood, and he wept aloud, and shed big tears and stretched forth his hands toward me eager to reach me. But no longer had he aught of strength or might remaining such as of old was in his supple limbs.

"When I saw him I wept, and my heart had compassion on him, and I spoke, and addressed him with winged words: 'Most glorious son of Atreus, king of men, Agamemnon, what fate of grievous death overcame thee?'"   (*Od.* XI, 390-398)

[Agamemnon replies:] "Ere now thou hast been present at the slaying of many men, killed in single combat or in the press of the fight, but in heart thou wouldst have felt most pity hadst thou seen that sight, how about the mixing bowl and the laden tables we lay in the hall, and the floor all swam with blood. But the most piteous cry that I heard was that of the daughter of Priam, Cassandra, whom guileful Clytemnestra slew by my side. And I sought to raise my hands and smite down the murderess, dying though I was, pierced through with the sword. But she, the shameless one, turned her back upon me, and even though I was going to the house of Hades deigned neither to draw down my eyelids with her fingers nor to close my mouth. So true is it that there is nothing more dread or more shameless than a woman who puts into her heart such deeds, even as she too devised a monstrous thing, contriving death for her wedded husband. . . ."   (*Od.* XI, 417-452)

132

Argos, Mycenae and Agamemnon

The son Agamemnon speaks of is Orestes, who is later to revenge his father by killing the murderer, Aegisthus. From Homer's text alone, it is difficult to understand why it is that Clytemnestra hates Agamemnon so much as to want to be personally involved in his murder. If she wants to be free to marry her lover Aegisthus, or if she fears her husband's wrath at her infidelity, she could use hired assassins. The fact is that she has a very good reason for nurturing her hatred of Agamemnon, a reason that Homer does not mention, because it was no doubt very well known to his audience. It is Aeschylus (born in Greece in 525 BC) who explains the background of the story in his drama *Agamemnon*. When the Achaean armies are assembled in Aulis, ready to attack Troy, the fleet is held in port for a long time by gales. The warriors start to get impatient and argue with one another, for stores are running low. Finally, Calchas, a seer, says that the situation is due to the goddess Artemis' anger at having had one of her goats killed by the Achaeans. According to him, the only way to calm the goddess, and hence the wind, is to sacrifice a royal virgin, Iphigenia, Agamemnon's elder daughter. He bows to the pressure put on him, and sends a messenger home to Argos to fetch his daughter, telling Clytemnestra that he has promised her in marriage to Achilles. But when Iphigenia arrives for what she thinks is to be her wedding, she is taken to the altar to have her throat cut. This gruesome episode is not related by Homer but by Aeschylus. (See Appendix Note 14, Iphigenia).

It is very unlikely that the sacrifice of Iphigenia took place in Aulis, where the Achaean fleet assembled (identified in the north of Jutland, see Chapter 15 in this section). If the fleet was unable to sail because of storm winds, it would not have been possible for a ship of that time, which could not make way against the wind (see explanation, Part III, Chapter 2), to make the round trip to Argos while these winds were still blowing. If, on the other hand, Iphigenia had accompanied her father to Aulis, she would already have known Achilles, which is apparently not the case. No, Clytemnestra's bloodthirsty revenge gives us grounds to think that the sacrifice of her daughter took place neither in the place nor for the reasons put forward by Aeschylus.

We can still find out when, why and even where, Agamemnon sacrificed his daughter. Before going off to war, this ambitious king, commander-in-chief of the Achaean armies, asked the gods to grant him the thing he wanted most of all, victory over the Trojans. In exchange he had to offer the person most dear to him, his daughter Iphigenia. She was therefore not sacrificed, as the Greeks later came to believe, for a minor problem of a killed goat and adverse weather, but for something much more important, victory in the greatest war the

133

world had ever known. The sacrifice must therefore have been made in Mycenae, before Agamemnon's army marched. It is fairly safe to say that the tragedy of Iphigenia took place where Troyes now stands, in the Bronze Age capital of France, and that the distraught mother was present at the horrifying spectacle. This would explain why she sought vengeance by personally and savagely killing her husband on his triumphant return from the war.

If Agamemnon's capital was renamed Troyes to celebrate the Achaean victory, why should his allies not have done something similar? Some of them did indeed do so, and we find the name of Troy in several places along the west coast of continental Europe: in southern Portugal is the Troia peninsula, in western France St Trojan (on Oleron island) and in the Netherlands the Berg van Troje ('Troy mountain'), a tumulus in the province of Zeeland. The little town called Troia in southern Italy must be of later date, as the Celts only arrived in that part of Europe many centuries after the Trojan War.

In conclusion, we can consider Argos and its capital Mycenae to be the cradle of modern France, and Agamemnon to be the first king of France of documented history, living in the twelfth century BC. The Trojan War thus turns out to have been a big war, between the king of England and his allies on the one side, and the king of France and his allies on the other. At stake was the access for continental Europeans to a raw material which was found virtually exclusively on the British Isles and which was as essential at the time as crude oil is in our time. In the Bronze Age this raw material was tin.

Notes

1 Marcel Moreau, *La Tradition celtique dans l'art roman*, Le Courrier du Livre, Paris, 1975.
2 Tacitus, *Germania*, 9, English translation by H. Mattingly, Penguin Classics.
3 Thucydides, *The Peloponnesian War*, I, IX, 4.

12

The Seven Towns
Offered to Achilles

(Rhineland Palatinate)

In the ninth year of the Trojan War, when the Achaeans are on the verge of being defeated, Agamemnon tries to reverse the military situation by wooing his estranged ally Achilles and his troops back into battle. In an attempt to persuade Achilles to forget his grievances, Agamemnon offers him many gifts, including seven towns which, according to the *Iliad*, are all situated 'near to the sea, on the furthest border of sandy Pylos' (*Il*. IX, 153 and 295). In fact there is more than one Pylos in Homer (see Appendix Note 15, The Pylians) and the one concerned here is clearly not that already identified as Pilas in the south of Spain (see Chapter 8 in this section) as Agamemnon could scarcely offer territory not belonging to him, and which in any case is too far from Achilles' own lands (identified as the Rhine delta in Part IV, Regiment 21) to be of use to him.

These towns can be found only by going back to the original meaning of the Greek *pulos*, 'gate', which according to Leaf and Usener[1] was the 'gate of Hell'. Now Hell, or Hades, the symbolic place of death and rebirth, was located in the great delta of the Rhine, Meuse and Schelde, on the Sea of Helle, as we shall see in Part III, Chapters 10 and 11). Further east there is a sandy area of Holland known as the Peel, a name that is clearly related to Pylos. Further upstream on the Rhine, Meuse and Moselle, the seven towns can still be identified today in the Rhineland Palatinate both names also being cognate with Pylos:

1	Cardamyle	Karden	(on the Moselle)
2	Enope	Ennepetal	(*−tal*=valley; on the Ruhr)
3	Hire	Irrel	(north of Luxemburg)
4	Pherae	Verviers	(east of Liège)
5	Antheia	Anthée	(west of Dinant)
6	Aipeia	Eupen	(east of Liège)
7	Pedasus	Pedenberg	(*−berg*=mount; north of Duisburg)

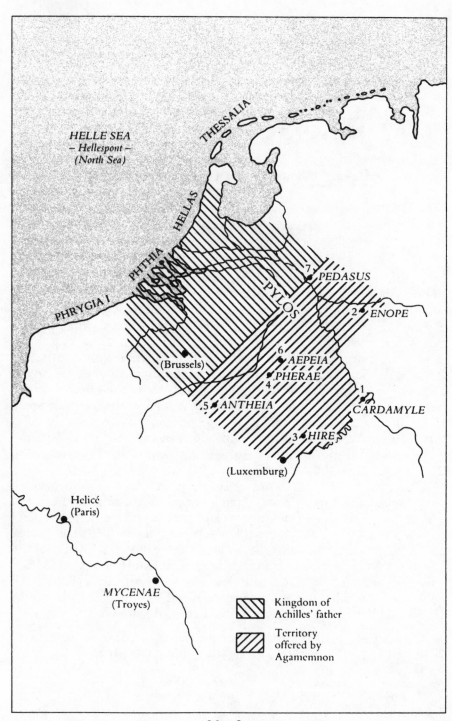

Map 8
Pylos I. The seven towns offered by Agamemnon to Achilles.

136

The Seven Towns Offered to Achilles

Map 8 shows that Agamemnon offers the northeastern part of his kingdom in exchange for Achilles' return to battle, thus doubling the latter's territory, in the hope that this will bring victory in the Trojan War. Confirmation that the Rhineland was once a Celtic territory is also provided by the name of the German town of Xanthen (Greek *Xanthos*), on the Rhine near the Dutch border, and Köln (Cologne, Greek *Colonos*), also on the Rhine (see Map 18, key No. 16 at the end of Part IV).

In Greece, there are several Kardamyles, but all far from Argos. There is an Iria in the northeast Peloponnese, but Pylos is in the southwest. None of the other five names are to be found. Some researchers claim to have identified a few other towns in the southwest Peloponnese, where there is a Kardamyle, but there are a number of basic objections to such identification. First, this area of Greece is mountainous and not sandy, which led the ancient Greeks themselves to say they did not know where Pylos was. Second, as already stated, Agamemnon could scarcely offer territory not belonging to him, and which in any case was too far from Achilles' own lands, believed to be in the northern part of Greece, to be of use to him. Third, in Greece, Agamemnon's offer is devoid of any logic or underlying argument.

Although the towns are easy to identify in western Europe, the intriguing question remains as to why a monarch would offer part of his territory – in addition to gold and other material benefits – to another state? This gesture is so unusual that at first sight it seems to owe more to poetic fantasy than to political reality, as such handsome gifts between even the closest of allies are rare if not totally unknown to history. But if we continue to believe that Homer is telling the truth, Agamemnon must have had a very particular reason for making such a unique offer – there must be something in it for himself and his country, but what? Achilles was apparently aware that Agamemnon's 'present' was a white elephant, as he turned it down without hesitation. A glance at Map 8, p.136, helps us to understand his attitude. The territory in question turns out to be almost entirely situated on the left bank of the Rhine, and thus undoubtedly exposed to incursions by tribes living on the eastern shore. Since time immemorial and up to our own era, peoples in central Europe have expanded westward (see Part IV, Regiment 28) and this must have made the Rhineland a strategic nightmare to Agamemnon, and no doubt very costly to defend. He may even have been afraid of losing this territory altogether, since his subjects – later called Gauls by the Romans – may not have been a match for the invaders if we can believe Caesar, whose armies a millenium later fought an alliance of Celts and Germans: 'They (the Gauls) do not even pretend to compete with the Germans in bravery'.[2] It is very likely that Agamemnon was already struggling with pressure on the eastern border of his kingdom. Therefore, as a cunning politician, he would have been anxious to create a buffer state on the Middle Rhine, to be ruled by the House of Achilles and defended by the latter's famous Myrmidons, the best warriors among the Achaeans. But Achilles refused and some time during the first millenium BC the whole territory between Luxemburg and the Rhine was conquered by tribes from the east. According to Caesar, they were the Treveri, Germanic by language, Celtic by religion, who gave their name to the present town of Trier (Trèves in French) (see also Appendix Note 16 , Celts and Germans).

The left bank of the Upper Rhine must also have been a trouble spot for the same reason, but here there was already a buffer state in Homer's day under the rule of Agamemnon's ally Agapenor, whose territory corresponded to the present Alsace (see Part IV, Regiment 12). As these 'Alsatians' obviously did not have a fleet, Agamemnon gave them sixty ships to carry their troops to Troy. This 'generosity' on Agamemnon's part must have been payment for Agapenor's services on the eastern border of Argos, since no other Achaean regiment received any special favours from the king. Agapenor protected Agamemnon's kingdom against attacks by tribes living in the Black Forest opposite Strasbourg.

Contrary to popular belief, many central European tribes were still of Celtic religion at the beginning of our era, in particular all those living south of the river Main, as was reported by Roman historians. Just like the Celtic seafarers, the Continental tribes were very dynamic, the Germans being, according to Tacitus, 'fond of travelling – and travelling fast'.[3] To protect his realm against such enterprising neighbours, it is perfectly understandable that Agamemnon should have considered the creation of another buffer state along the middle Rhine, where he was directly exposed to invasions. This, then, must have been the very special reason the king had for offering a large slice of land with seven towns to Achilles.

Notes

1 H. Usener, *Der Stoff des griechischen Epos*, Vienna, 1897.
2 Caesar: *The Conquest of Gaul*, VI, 24.
3 Tacitus, *Germania*, 46.

13

Back to Egypt

In Chapter 5 in this section we identified Homer's Egypt with the present French department of Seine-Maritime, surprising though that may seem. Since all the other major pieces of the jig-saw puzzle of *Iliad* geography are now in place, it is possible to add further arguments to support this finding.

We have already seen that Menelaus, on his way from Troy (England) to his home Sparta, (Spain), erects a monument in Egypt (Seine-Maritime) to his brother Agamemnon, assassinated on his return home to Mycenae (Troyes). None of this would make sense in the Mediterranean, where Egypt is too far away for anyone to visit on his way from Turkey to Greece. Besides, it would not only be illogical for a Greek king to erect a monument to his dead brother in a foreign country, but it is also highly unlikely that the local religious leaders would have allowed him to make offerings to gods which were unknown to them.

When Homer speaks of 'Thebes of Egypt' (*Il.* IX, 381) and 'Thebes of the Seven Gates' (*Il.* IV, 406), the town of Cadmus and the Cadmeians, it is clear that he cannot mean the Land of the Pharaohs, as none of them ever had the name of Cadmus or his descendents, such as Laius or Oedipus. Besides, the pharaonic Thebes, called Wase at the time, had no walls or gates. For this reason many scholars have assumed that Homer was referring to Thebes in Greece, a town in Boeotia, north of Athens. But Homer never mentions a Thebes in Boeotia, this famous name not even appearing among the Boeotian towns listed in the catalogue of ships. The Greek Thebes, like so many other places, must have taken its name from Homer at a later date. The poet knew only one Thebes on Achaean territory (there was another in the Troad) 'where treasures of great store are laid up in men's houses' (*Il.* IX, 381), and that was the Bronze Age Thebes of Egypt, the present Channel port of Dieppe. The riches are explained by the fact that Dieppe was the biggest port in northern France at that time, Le Havre (cognate with the English 'haven' as in Newhaven) being a very recent port, founded by François I in 1517.

The Oedipus Myth

In France, the name of the Cadmeians, subjects of King Cadmus, seems to be preserved by the town of Cabourg (Cadburgus in 1077), near the mouth of the Seine, and in Holland by the village of Cadzand ('Cadsands') near the mouth of the Schelde. It was the grandson of Cadmus, Laius, who was told by the Oracle that he would one day be killed by his new-born son Oedipus. In order to try to escape this fate, the father abandons the baby in the country, but he is found by a peasant and brought up by the royal family of a neighbouring country. When he has grown up, Oedipus nevertheless does kill his father, whom he does not know, during a dispute over the right of way at the intersection of three roads (see Appendix Note 17, Oedipus) near Delphi (identified in Part III as present day Delft). When Oedipus subsequently arrives before the walls of Thebes, he has to solve the riddle of the Sphinx (it was much later that the Greeks gave this name to the great stone figures in Egypt), or be killed by the monster. The question is, 'What animal has four legs in the morning, two in the afternoon and three in the evening?' Oedipus gives the correct answer, 'Man, because in childhood he crawls on hands and knees, as an adult he walks erect on two feet, and in old age he uses a stick.' The Sphinx kills itself on hearing the correct answer, and the Thebans, glad to be rid of it, proclaim Oedipus their king. This part of the story is told by Sophocles in his tragedy *Oedipus Rex*, but Homer tells us how Oedipus subsequently marries the queen Epicaste (Jocasta in Sophocles), widow of Laius, and hence his own mother. According to both sources the mother hangs herself when she learns the truth. In Homer, Oedipus remains king, but he 'suffers woes' (*Od.* XI, 275) and he finally dies in Thebes, 'Mecisteus . . . had come to Thebes for the burial of Oedipus, when he had fallen' (*Il.* XXIII, 678-9), while in Sophocles he puts out his eyes and wanders the world with his daughter Antigone, who remains faithful to him, finding refuge in Colonos. Very similar stories of incest are also found in later Celtic literature.

Oedipus had previously put a curse on his two sons, Eteocles and Polynices, predicting that they would fight one another for his throne. After his death, Polynices, exiled by his brother, takes refuge in Argos province (Calvados, see Part IV, Regiment 8), at the court of King Adrastus, whose daughter he marries. He persuades his father-in-law to raise an army to march on Thebes. One of the members of this expedition was Tydeus, the Aetolian (a native of Vendée in the west of France, see Part IV, Regiment 16).

[Agamemnon:] "So when they had departed and were got forth

upon their way, and had come to Asopus with deep reeds, that coucheth in the grass, there did the Achaeans send forth Tydeus on an embassage. And he went his way, and found the many sons of Cadmus feasting in the house of mighty Eteocles. Then, for all he was a stranger, the horseman Tydeus feared not, all alone though he was amid the many Cadmeians, but challenged them all to feats of strength, and in every one vanquished he them full easily; such a helper was Athene to him. But the Cadmeians, goaders of horses, waxed wroth, and as he journeyed back, brought and set a strong ambush, even fifty youths, and two there were as leaders, Maeon, son of Haemon, peer of the immortals, and Autophonus' son, Polyphontes, staunch in fight. But Tydeus even upon these let loose a shameful fate, and slew them all; one only man suffered he to return home; Maeon he sent forth in obedience to the portents of the gods. Such a man was Tydeus of Aetolia; howbeit the son that he begat is worse than he in battle, though in the place of gathering he is better."   (Il. IV, 382–400)

Asopus (not to be confused with Aesepus in the Troad, see Chapter 1 in this section) is no doubt the mouth of the Seine, as already suggested (see Chapter 5). The description of reeds and thick grass certainly indicates a marshy area, now the Vernier marshes which are to be found on the west bank of the Seine, near Aizier and Sainte-Croix-sur-Aizier nearby, reminders of the Bronze Age name of this river. Despite the disparaging remarks made by Agamemnon about Tydeus's son in the above passage, it was this son, Diomedes, who took Thebes, after a second siege, before setting out for the Trojan War:

"... [Sthenelus, speaking for himself and Diomedes:]we took the seat of Thebe of the seven gates, when we twain had gathered a lesser host against a stronger wall, putting our trust in the portents of the gods and in the aid of Zeus; whereas they perished through their own blind folly. ...."   (Il. IV, 406–409)

In his tragedy The Seven against Thebes, Aeschylus tells the story of the first siege, in which Polynices attacks the seventh gate of the town, defended by his brother Eteocles, after the Achaean commanders have drawn lots to decide who shall take his troops against which gate. The two brothers kill one another, as predicted by their father Oedipus, at the seventh gate. The city was saved on that occasion, and Tydeus lost his life there, as we learn in the Iliad, 'Tydeus, whom in Thebes the heaped-up earth covers' (Il. XIV, 114). Homer mentions the walls of Thebes and, in particular, the seven gates. There remains in Dieppe today only one ancient gate, known as 'Les Tourelles', but a plaque

141

informs visitors that this is the sole survivor of the six that the city's defences once counted. It is possible that in the very distant past there was a seventh, of which no trace has been found, or that the entrance to the port with its defences was counted as a gate. The enmity between the inhabitants of Egypt and the other Achaeans explains why Thebes did not participate in the Trojan War. According to Thucydides[1] the territory had in fact been occupied by Agamemnon after the fall of the city. This would have left the way clear for Menelaus to celebrate the rites for his dead brother in 'Egypt' without any difficulty.

The Io Myth

If Argos and Egypt were originally regions in northern France, it is also easy to understand the myth of Io, which is not recounted in Homer but in other ancient Greek texts, apparently based on Druidic tradition. Io is a young girl seduced by Zeus, whose consort, Here, as always, finds out about the affair. As a punishment, Here sends a gadfly to torment Io, who tries to escape by fleeing from Argos to Egypt. In the past, it has always been thought that she leaves Greece to go to Egypt, but in fact instead of sailing across the Mediterranean she simply swims across the Seine to get rid of the gadfly. However, this is no ordinary gadfly, and Io is so tormented that, according to Aeschylus in his *Suppliant Maidens*, she crosses the sea to try to escape: 'she crosses the stormy strait that separates the continents, going from the one to the other that faces it' (line 540). This is clearly the Strait of Dover, making Io the first Channel swimmer in recorded history. The Strait of Dover must have been the famous 'Pillars of Hercules', mentioned by Tacitus in northwest Europe,[2] before this name came to designate the Strait of Gibraltar after the migration of some Celts to the south. Since we know from Homer that Hercules was born in 'Egyptian' Thebes, Dieppe on the Channel, it is not even surprising that the promontories on either side of the Strait of Dover were once known as the Pillars of Hercules.

In England Io passes through many regions identified in this book. Her story is so bizarre that a brief explanation of its meaning is necessary, the more so as it is a very important myth. While the profane public rejoiced in the popular stories sung by the bards on the extramarital affairs of Zeus and the jealousy and vengeance of his wife Here, the initiates knew that the myth of Io was part of the story of Creation (*see also* Appendix Note 18, Creation).

According to R. Emmanuel, the key to understanding its esoteric meaning is the close resemblance of the name Io with the number 10, the number of Divine Perfection, as it is composed of the I (Zeus) and the O (the Cosmic Egg).[3] This indeed turns out to be the right key, although I was sceptical at first as in Homer's time numbers were not written in the same way as today. But we have evidence that ever since the Stone Age, a vertical line has always represented a unit, while the 'O' was known as an esoteric concept representing the never-ending cycle of Nature. The number 1, then, written as a vertical line connecting a point at the top (Heaven) with a point at the bottom (Earth) is the number of God manifested on earth. The O reflects God *not* manifested, the Divine Principle or the Universe, variously symbolized by the sacred stone circle, the curled-up snake biting its tail or the Cosmic Egg awaiting fertilization.

When Zeus (I) had fertilized the primordial material of the Universe (O), a human being, Io, was created. However, she still lacked Reason and the Consciousness enabling her to name things with words, a faculty which distinguishes humans from animals and therefore often dubbed the 'divine spark' in the human mind. But Reason, or the Word, was considered in all Indo-European religions as a female principle symbolized by the cow, as it was in pharaohnic Egypt by the celestial cow Mehet Ourt and still is in the Hindu religion by the goddess Vache, the name meaning 'cow' in French, which is not coincidental (see Appendix Note 19, Celts and Hindus).

It was therefore not the task of Zeus to give the Word to Io (as was made clear to the initiates by mentioning his vain enterprise of turning Io into a cow and visiting her in the shape of a bull), but clearly that of his consort Here, who sent a gadfly, symbol of the 'divine spark' to torment Io, and transform her into a dynamic being, gifted with reason and capable of giving names to things and places. The goddess Here is often described by Homer as 'ox-eyed' which was never flattering for any woman, let alone a goddess, and therefore unworthy of a great poet unless he has a particular reason to use this adjective.

Why then would the Word come from a cow and why would Zeus transform himself into a bull? Apparently because the myth of Io originated in the period when the sun stood in the zodiacal sign of Taurus (bull) at the spring equinox (21 March) which forebodes Nature's return to life. The bull was also a sun symbol as Taurus announced the period of the year when the days are longer than the nights. Since we know that the sun stood in the sign of Taurus between 4320 and 2160 BC, we may assume that the myth of Io dates from that period. (Later, when the sun subsequently moved into the sign of Aries, the bull symbol made place for the ram in all Indo-European religions, for instance in pharaonic Egypt and in the Celtic lands where the god Cernunnos was pictured with stag-horns, while our own era is that of Pisces, the symbol of the early Christians).

When the Io story reached Greece, its esoteric explanation was probably lost, judging by the wrong transcription of her name in the Greek alphabet, using the omega instead of the omicron, thus invalidating the argument that the name Io is related to the number 10. The names of Io's mythological parents, Inachus (a son of Oceanus) and Melia have been preserved by the villages of Incheville and Melleville, situated close together near Le Tréport on the French Channel coast, while the village of Jobourg, west of Cherbourg, may well owe its name to Io herself. Even the gadfly (*taon* in French) is eternalized in the old village of Thaon near Caen in Normandy. It would be here then that, according to ancient beliefs, Reason was first given to mankind.

Legend has it that Io returned to Egypt (northwest France) to be worshipped under the name Isis. This would explain why so many place-names in France and elsewhere in Europe (see Maps) still remind us of Isis worship, which was also practised around the Mediterranean, in particular of course in pharaonic Egypt where her effigy shows the sundisc, oxhorns and the serpent, all original attributes of Io. In southern France, the inhabitants of Eze on the Riviera also ascribe the name of their town to Isis and there can be little doubt that they are right as the municipal device, '*En mourant, je renais*' ('while dying I am reborn') is archetypal for a place of initiation into the Mysteries.

The Helle Myth

Knowing that Egypt and the Troad were in northwest Europe also makes it easier to understand the story of Helle and other Greek myths apparently of Celtic origin. We know the story of Helle, not from Homer, but from other Greek poets of the fifth century BC recounting the adventures of Jason and the Argonauts in the quest for the Golden Fleece. Helle and her brother Phryxos are the children of King Athamas, who has left his wife Nephele, to marry Ino, the daughter of King Cadmus of Thebes. Ino wants to get rid of Phryxos so that her own son can succeed the throne and schemes to produce a valid reason for having Phryxos sacrificed to the gods. However, just as his throat is about to be cut over the altar, the god Hermes intervenes in answer to Nephele's prayers. He sends a ram with a Golden Fleece to carry Phryxos and his little sister through the air to safety. As they are crossing the strait separating Thebes from Colchis, Helle falls into the sea and is drowned, giving her name to the sea, the Hellespont, as we saw in Chapter 4 in this section. Nephele was also the name of the goddess of the clouds, from the Greek word for 'cloud', *nephele*, cognate with Dutch *nevel*, Latin *nebula* and the English adjective 'nebulous'.

Back to Egypt

On his arrival in Colchis, Phryxos is well received by King Aëtes 'of the cruel thoughts', brother of Circe. To show his gratitude, he sacrifices to Zeus the ram that saved him and gives the precious Golden Fleece to Aëtes. Later on, Phryxos' uncle, the celebrated Jason, sets out with his Argonauts to find the Golden Fleece. They have a series of adventures at sea, comparable to those of Odysseus, who must have lived a generation later, for some of the heroes of the Trojan War are sons of the Argonauts. Although Homer mentions Jason, he does not tell the story of the Argonauts. According to C.G. Jung, these adventures symbolize the search for the impossible, and the final destruction of the vessel, the Argos, the loss of our illusions.[4]

Transposed to Greece, the story of Helle does not correspond with the geography of the country, for the Hellespont, now the Dardanelles, is a very long way from Thebes and Colchis, both of which are north of Athens, one on the mainland, the other on the island of Euboea. Let us therefore return once more to France. If Thebes is the present Dieppe, Colchis must be the region of Colchester in England, northeast of London.

In the preceding chapters, there has been much discussion of both Mycenae and Thebes as they play a very important role not only in Homer, but also in other works of classical literature. There can be little doubt that the two richest and most important towns in France in the Bronze Age were 'Golden' Mycenae, now Troyes, which was the home of the Atreides, the famous kings of Argos, and the great sea port of 'Egyptian' Thebes, now Dieppe, 'where treasures in great store are laid up in men's houses' (*Il.* IX, 381). This town was founded by 'Amphion and Zethus, who first established the seat of seven-gated Thebes, and fenced it with walls, for they could not live in spacious Thebes unfenced, however mighty they may be' (*Od.* XI, 262). They were the two sons of Antiope, daughter of Asopus (the god of the lower Seine, as we have seen), 'who boasted that she had slept in the arms of Zeus' (*Od.* XI, 261). Thebes was also the home of the blind seer Teiresias, the most celebrated prophet in Homer.

Notes

1 Thucydides, *The Peleponnesian War*, Book A, II, 1-2.
2 Tacitus, *Germania*, 34.
3 R. Emmanuel, *Pleins feux sur la Grèce antique*, Dervy-Livres, Paris 1982, p. 220.
4 C. G. Jung, *Introduction à l'essence de la mythologie*, 1968.

14

Celtic Territory
in 1200 BC

Now that we have identified the five key regions of Homeric geography, the Troad, Egypt, Crete, Ithaca and Argos, it is relatively easy to trace the orgins of the different combatants in the Trojan War, for Homer gives us a complete list of regiments, mentioning many rivers, mountains and towns situated in their respective home countries. There are twenty-nine Achaean regiments and seventeen Trojan regiments listed in Book II of the *Iliad* (plus one more Trojan ally named in the *Odyssey*). Though this list and the relevant explanations are vital to the thesis of this book, it does not make for easy reading and has therefore been consigned to a section of its own, Part IV. For the moment, I suggest that the reader should have a look at Map 9, showing the territories of the regiments concerned. The figures and letters correspond to the Achaean and Trojan regiments respectively, as set out in Part IV, the order being that in which Homer lists them. The full significance of this map can be seen if it is compared with Map 10, which shows the territory occupied by the Celts during the Hallstatt Period (roughly 600 to 400 BC), as established by archeologists. These two maps, with a period of about 600 years between them, seem to confirm that the combatants in the Trojan War must have been Celts, not only because of the names of the persons and places involved, but also because the two territories correspond to a large extent, bearing in mind that not necessarily all Celtic peoples were involved in the war.

As regards the Achaeans from continental Europe, it can be assumed that they were all Celts, in view of the apparent unity of language and religion, though there were some Celts, notably the Egyptians and the Libyans (from southwest France, see Chapter 16 in this section), who did not participate. In the Troad, however, the demographic situation was different. While the inhabitants of southeast England were Celts, their allies, mainly from Scotland, Wales and Cornwall, were probably pre-Celtic peoples (but already converted to Celtic religion) who spoke different and mutually incomprehensible languages, as Homer mentions on several occasions, for example:

146

> But for the Trojans, even as ewes stand in throngs past counting in
> the court of a man of much substance to be milked of their white
> milk, and bleat without ceasing as they hear the voices of their
> lambs: even so arose the clamour of the Trojans throughout the
> wide host; for they had not all like speech or one language, but their
> tongues were mingled, and they were a folk summoned from
> many lands.   (*Il.* IV, 433–438)

The pre-Celtic peoples are considered to be the builders of the
megalithic monuments found all over northern and western Europe.
They are also thought to be the first peoples to have been led by the
Druids, who worshipped the sun at sites such as Stonehenge in
England. It would appear that the Celts adopted and continued the
Druidic tradition, which was in fact a much more ancient Indo-
European tradition close to that of the Brahmins.

Through displacing or absorbing the neolithic peoples, the Celts
established themselves over the greater part of Europe during the
second and first millenium BC. A comparison of Maps 9 and 10
(overleaf) shows their expansion towards Ireland, the Celtiberic
peninsula, the southern half of France, Italy, the Balkans, Greece
(which during the Roman Empire was called the Prefecture of Illyricum
after the Celtic Illyrians), and even Turkey, while they lost ground in
Scandinavia and Germany. Not surprisingly, many western European
place-names were given to the new places to which Celts migrated. For
example, the Galates, originating in Gaul as their name indicates, who
invaded Turkey, must be at the origin of this country's present name,
taken from the village of Turkeije, near the left bank of the Schelde
mouth. The Gauls also gave their name to Galicia in northwest Spain
and Galicia in Poland. The expansion seems to be mainly due to their
population growth. The Celtic alliance dominated Europe in the way
the Roman Empire was to do much later, the difference being that the
Celts were united by a kind of confederation based on consensus, while
the Romans relied on centralized political and military power. The
Celtic alliance was nevertheless a force to be reckoned with, as the
Romans experienced, for example, when Rome was sacked by the
Celts in 387 BC. A few centuries later, the Druids of Gaul were to
conspire against the Romans with the Druids of the Galates in Turkey.
In view of the cohesion of the Celtic peoples and the efficiency of the
Druids in political and military coordination, it is not so difficult to
understand how it was possible to unite the peoples of western
continental Europe to wage war in England. It was certainly there that
the war took place, for according to Thucydides, as we have seen,
Greece at that time was inhabited by a great number of tribes, with little
or no contact with one another, living at mere subsistence level.

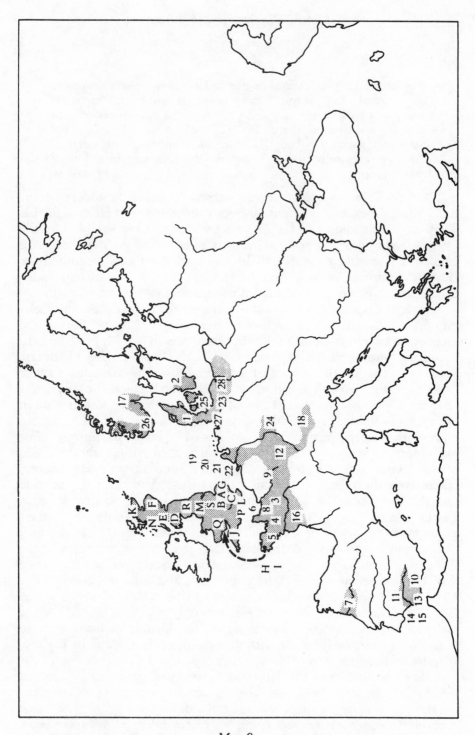

Map 9
Territories of the tribes participating in the Trojan War. (The letters and numbers correspond to the Trojan and Achaean regiments listed in Part IV.)

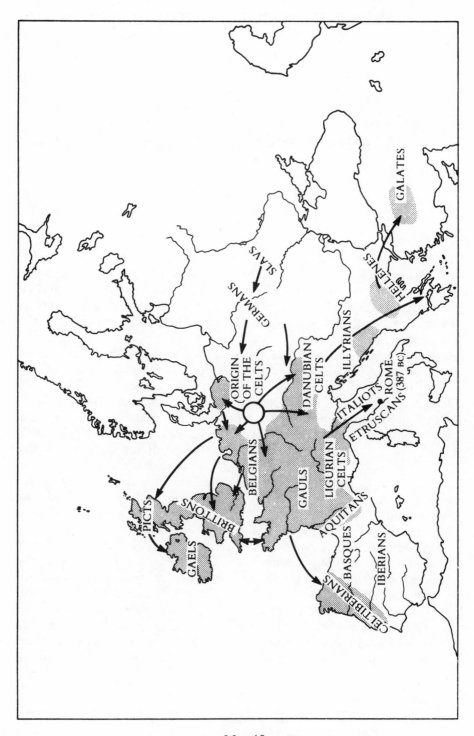

Map 10
Celtic territory during the Hallstatt period and subsequent migrations culminating in the sack of Rome in 387 BC.

15

Rendezvous in Aulis

(North Jutland)

It is easy to understand the need for the Achaean fleet to assemble somewhere before sailing to England to attack Troy, for if the ships were to arrive in small groups at different times the troops would be easy prey for the Trojan army. Homer tells us that the fleet was assembled in Aulis, which according to my analysis of the origins of the Achaean regiments, is in north Jutland, Denmark (see Part IV, Regiment 1 and Map 14). The question then arises, why did they meet in Denmark? At first sight it would seem more logical to choose the inland sea in Holland for the rendezvous. This choice would have had important advantages over Denmark for the Achaean armies, because of Holland's more central location between Spain and Scandinavia, and its proximity to England. However, the commanders had to reject this choice for a very important reason. As we shall see in analysing the *Odyssey* (Part III, Chapter 10 and 11), the Rhine delta was the religious centre of the Celtic world, and since the Trojans had the same religion as the Achaeans, their Druids must have frequently visited the Netherlands. The risk of the preparations for a great war being discovered by the enemy was thus too great if Holland was chosen for the rendezvous. The element of surprise has always been a major factor in warfare throughout the ages, and by opting for Denmark as the meeting place the risk of the fleet's being detected was certainly greatly reduced (*see also* Map inside the Front Cover). It was precisely in north Jutland, near the village of Nors and close to the waters where the fleet assembled, that one hundred small ships of goldleaf (length: 5 inches or 12 cm) were found.[1] Since this 'hecatomb' dates from around 1200 BC, there can be little doubt that it was offered by the Achaean fleet before sailing to Troy.

Note

1 C. Eluère, *L'Or des Celtes*, Bibliothèque des Arts, Paris, 1987. The treasure of Nors is in the National Museum, Copenhagen.

16

Libya

(Southwest France)

Homer mentions a country called Libya, situated on the sea, to the south of Crete and Argos, and apparently very fertile:

> . . . Libya, where the lambs are horned from their birth. For there the ewes bear their young thrice within the full course of the year; there neither master nor shepherd has any lack of cheese or of meat or of sweet milk, but the flocks ever yield milk to the milking the year through. *(Od.* IV, 85–89)

Unfortunately, Homer mentions no rivers or towns in this country. Although the Libyans were not involved in the Trojan War, they must have been Celts, for according to mythology their name comes from Libya, who was the daughter of Epaphus and the granddaughter of Zeus and Io, while Danaus, a king of Libya, fled to Argos where he became king and eventually gave his name to the Danaans, one of the names used by Homer for the attackers of Troy. We can assume that Libya was in southwest France, where the only four towns or villages in Europe whose names begin with Lib- are grouped together in the same region. The biggest is Libourne, on the Dordogne near Bordeaux. The other three place-names are Libos and Libousson in the department of Lot and Libaros in the Hautes-Pyrénées.

In the absence of river and place-names, we have to take our clue from the names of three tribes who, according to other ancient sources, were living in Libya. Normally tribal names are not the most reliable indication, but in this case we are lucky, as these tribes have left traces that can still be seen today in the same area of southwest France where we find the names with the Lib- prefix. First there were the Makai (village of Macaye near Biarritz), then the Nasamones (village of Naussannes, southeast of Bergerac) and the Machlues (Maillas, village still called Maglacum in the Church Latin of the early Middle Ages, situated northeast of Mont-de-Marsan (*see also* Map 15 at the end of Part IV).

17

The Isle of Syria

(Ireland)

Yet another case of a striking difference between the description of a country in Homer and the country known by the same name today is that of Syria:

> There is an isle called Syria, if haply thou hast heard thereof, above Ortygia, where are the turning-places of the sun. It is not so very thickly settled, but it is a good land, rich in herds, rich in flocks, full of wine, abounding in wheat. Famine never comes into the land, nor does any hateful sickness besides fall on wretched mortals; but when the tribes of men grow old throughout the city, Apollo, of the silver bow, comes with Artemis, and assails them with his gentle shafts, and slays them. *(Od.* XV 403–411)

This rich island cannot be the Syria we know today, nor can it be the tiny island of Syros in the Cyclades, for a variety of reasons, but mainly because we know by now that none of the action of the *Iliad* or the *Odyssey* took place in the Mediterranean. We learn from the above passage that the isle of Syria is situated north of Ortygia, there where the sun turns, and elsewhere we read that it is about six days' sail from there (*Od.* XV, 474).

The only place in Europe with a name resembling Ortygia is Ortigueira, a cape and town at the northwest tip of Spain. If we accept this identity, the isle of Syria must be Ireland, a country which, like Portugal, did not take part in the Trojan War, probably because the people were not yet Celts, but were of older origin and were subsequently chased from their land or enslaved by a Celtic people, the Gaels. Unfortunately, Homer mentions no towns or rivers in the island. The only geographical name that looks anything like Syria is the river Suir in the south of the country.

So far the evidence for identification is somewhat slim, but there are other clues. Homer mentions the absence of sickness, a feature also noted in Celtic poetry from Ireland:

Unknown are pain and peril,
Neither sorrow, nor mourning, nor death,
nor sickness, nor weakness,
here is the sign of Emain.
What a wonderful country, this country!
the young there never grow old.[1]

In the northwest of Ireland there is an Achill Island, Achill Point and a village called Achill, indications that Achilles is indeed a Celtic name. There is also a rocky peninsula in the southwest of Ireland called Sybil Point, which reminds us of the Sipylus of the legend of Niobe, recalled at the end of the *Iliad*:

> For even the fair-haired Niobe bethought her of meat, albeit twelve children perished in her halls, six daughters and six lusty sons. The sons Apollo slew with shafts from his silver bow, being wroth against Niobe, and the daughters the archer Artemis, for that Niobe had matched her with fair-cheeked Leto, saying that the goddess had borne but twain, while herself was mother to many; wherefore they, for all they were but twain, destroyed them all. For nine days' space they lay in their blood, nor was there any to bury them, for the son of Cronos turned the folk to stones; howbeit on the tenth day the gods of heaven buried them; and Niobe bethought her of meat, for she was wearied with the shedding of tears. And now somewhere amid the rocks, on the lonely mountains, on Sipylus, where, men say, are the couching-places of goddesses, even of the nymphs that range swiftly in the dance about Achelous, there, albeit a stone, she broodeth over her woes sent by the gods. (*Il.* XXIV, 602-617)

However, Celtic names in Ireland such as Achill Island and Sybil Point are of more recent date than Homer. The origin of the story of Niobe has to be sought elsewhere in a much older Celtic land, and it is in fact easy to identify three names related to the story situated close together in northern Denmark (see Map 14 Crete, key Nos. 32, 33, 34, at the end of Part IV).

Although Ireland did not participate in the Trojan War, the ancient history of the country is very closely linked with that of the other Atlantic countries, and the Mediterranean. For a start, Ireland is said to have been inhabited in ancient times by various peoples who were all conquerors come from overseas. From the deluge onward they were successively: the people of Parthelon, the Nemred, the Fir Bolg and the Thuata de Dannan.[2] The latter name means 'People of (the goddess)

Dana' who may well have been the legendary Danae of classical mythology, who was a daughter of Acrisius, a king of Argos which was a region we have identified in northern France. According to tradition, the king had his daughter put in a wooden chest together with her infant son, Perseus, and thrown into the sea because an oracle had predicted that he would some day be killed by his grandson. The legend does not tell where Danae came ashore, but this could well have been the coast of Ireland. But there is another possible link between Ireland and northern France: if Ireland was called the 'Isle of Syria' by Homer, it was after a certain Syrus (Greek *Suros*), who, according to some mythographers, was a brother of Cadmus, the legendary hero of Thebes, which we have also identified in northern France, in the town of Dieppe. It was generally believed that Syrus was the 'inventor of arithmetic'.[3] If Syria was the name of Ireland before designating ancient Aram in the Near East, we would have an indication that mathematics was developed in western Europe before it was transmitted by the Druids to Pythagoras, as was believed by some classical Greek authors (see Part I, Chapter 4).

Finally, there is still another country in the Near East which may well owe its name to an Irish legend: Lebanon, (Liban in French) which closely resembles the name of the Celtic heroine, Libane, who was said to be the sole survivor of her inundated city, to become a siren until she was baptised.[4]

It appears that various arguments can be found which tend to confirm that Homer's 'Isle of Syria' was in fact Ireland. This strengthens the impression that a number of countries in the eastern Mediterranean changed names in the Bronze Age or shortly thereafter to be henceforth called Syria, Lebanon, Egypt, Lybia, Crete, Lesbos and Cyprus, due to conquests by peoples from the Atlantic seabord, just as the descendants of these 'Sea Peoples' gave new names during the colonial era, only a few centuries ago, to a number of countries all around the world as distant as New Zealand.

Notes

1 Jean Markale, *Ancienne Poésie d'Irlande*, in Cahiers du Sud, No. 355.
2 J.C. Pichon, *Histoire universelle des sectes et des sociétés secrètes*, Laffont, Paris, 1969, Vol. I, p. 112.
3 P. Grimal, *The Dictionary of Classical Mythology*, Basil Blackwell, Oxford, 1986, p. 429.
4 J. Markale, *Petit dictionnaire de mythologie celtique*, ed. Entente, Paris, 1986, p. 139.

18

More Surprises

(i) Olympus

Since Homer's works did not originate in Greece, the name of Olympus, the home of the gods, often evoked in his poems, cannot be of Greek origin either. The ancient Greeks simply called their highest mountain, where they never actually built any temples, after the highest mountain on Celtic territory, Mont Blanc. This latter, consisting of a great massif with several peaks, corresponds better to the poet's descriptions, 'Zeus lived on the highest peak of Olympus of the many necks'. Elsewhere he calls Olympus 'snowy', 'vast' and 'steep', and he speaks of 'summits of Olympus' in the plural. In one passage he gives rather a surprising description, in which it is maintained that there is never wind, rain or snow – a claim that runs entirely counter to our experience of high mountains:

> So saying, the goddess, flashing-eyed Athene, departed to Olympus, where, they say, is the abode of the gods that stands fast forever. Neither is it shaken by winds nor ever wet with rain, nor does snow fall upon it, but the air is outspread clear and cloudless, and over it hovers a radiant whiteness. Therein the blessed gods are glad all their days, and thither went the flashing-eyed one, when she had spoken all her word to the maiden. (*Od.* VI, 41-47)

The explanation of this 'Olympian calm' is simply that in bad weather the summits of the massif cannot be seen, so that the observers of the time only saw them when conditions were good and they imagined that Olympus always remained as they saw it. At that time nobody climbed mountains, out of respect for the gods, an attitude that still exists, for example in parts of the Himalayas, where local populations do not climb for fear of angering the gods, and sometimes try to prevent expeditions from the outside world from doing so. Has the ancient name of Mont Blanc, Olympus, completely disappeared? Possibly not, because the name of the town of Chamonix could well come from Champs-Olympiques, subsequently contracted to Chamole, which was the name of the place at the beginning of the Middle Ages.

There is in Greece, northwest of Olympus, another mountain that also owes its name to Homer, and hence western Europe, Pieria, which was the name of the Pyrenees in the Bronze Age, the ending 'nees' being derived from *neve* = snow. In the *Odyssey* we read that the messenger of the gods, Hermes, stops there on his way from Olympus to the island of Calypso in the middle of the ocean to tell her that Odysseus is to be allowed to return home at last, after seven years on the island:

> So he [Zeus] spoke, and the messenger, Argeiphontes [Hermes], failed not to hearken. Straightway he bound beneath his feet his beautiful sandals, immortal, golden, which were wont to bear him over the waters of the sea and over the boundless land swift as the blasts of the wind. And he took the wand wherewith he lulls to sleep the eyes of whom he will, while others again he awakens even out of slumber. With this in his hand the strong Argeiphontes flew. On to Pieria he stepped from the upper air, and swooped down upon the sea, and then sped over the wave like a bird, the cormorant, which in quest of fish over the dread gulfs of the unresting sea wets its thick plumage in the brine. In such wise did Hermes ride upon the multitudinous waves. But when he had reached the island which lay afar, then forth from the violet sea he came to land, and went his way until he came to a great cave, wherein dwelt the fair-tressed nymph . . .   (*Od.* X, 43-58)

In Part III, Chapter 17, we shall identify the island of Calypso as being in the Azores, in the middle of the Atlantic, or in Homer's words, 'in the navel of the ocean'. That makes the description of Hermes' voyage entirely logical, as he leaves Olympus, flies overland to the western Pyrenees, then goes down to the Gulf of Gascogne where he transforms himself into a cormorant for the long flight over the ocean (see Map inside Back Cover). Once again, the description would not make sense transposed to Greece. If Hermes had left Olympus, stopped at Pieria to the northwest, he would not have been able to descend from there to the sea, but would have had to cross the whole continent of Europe if he continued on a straight line. What is more, there are in northern Spain, near the Pyrenees and the Bay of Biscay, two towns that remind us of Hermes' stopover: Hernani and Ermua (see Map 15, Key nos 108 and 109, at the end of Part IV).

(ii) Thrace

There seem to have been four different regions called Thrace in the Bronze Age, Homer's public understanding from the context which one was meant. The multiplicity of the name was probably not only due to migration, but also to the meaning of the adjective *thracus*, 'courageous', which must have been a popular epithet with many warrior peoples, who gave the name also to their respective regions. There was not only a Thrace in East Anglia, the Wash being called the Sea of Thrace (*Il.* XXIII, 230), as we have seen, but also in the west of Brittany, homeland of the Trojan allies who came from overseas (*Il.* XI, 222; see also Part IV, Regiment H). Furthermore, Homer tells us that the Achaean army in the Troad was supplied daily with shiploads of wine from Thrace (*Il.* IX, 71), a fertile country rich in flocks, which must have been the region of the present town of Drachten in the north of the Netherlands. The fourth Thrace, with its snowy mountains and high peaks, would have been in the French Alps, near the river Drac and the town of Draguignan. The latter place was visited by the goddess Here during her *Tour de France:*

> . . . but Hera darted down and left the peak of Olympus; on Pieria she stepped and lovely Emathia, and sped over the snowy mountains of the Thracian horsemen, even over their topmost peaks, nor grazed she the ground with her feet; and from Athos she stepped upon the billowy sea, and so came to Lemnos, the city of godlike Thoas. There she met Sleep, the brother of Death . . . (*Il.* XIV, 225-231)

Leaving Olympus (Mont Blanc), passing by way of Pieria (the Pyrenees) and Emathia (the Dordogne, where the towns of Eymeth and Eymouthiers are reminders of the name) and Thrace (the Alps) to Athos (near Cherbourg, see Part IV, Regiment 7) the last leg of the trip being over the sea to Lemnos (Lemmer in the Netherlands, see Part IV, Regiment 24), where she visits Sleep, the brother of Death.

(iii) The Phoenicians

The Phoenicians in Homer are likely to be the Venetians, whose name is phonetically close to Phoenicians. They were Celts who founded Venice. They lived not only in the north of Italy and in the south of Spain, at Sidon (now Medina Sidonia), but also on the Baltic coast of Germany, where they were probably engaged in the amber trade between the Baltic and the Mediterranean[1] and near the mouth of the Loire in France, where they were engaged in the tin trade between Cornwall and the Continent. There the Romans put an end to their activities by destroying their fleet in 56 BC. No descendents of the Venetians (Veneti in Latin) remain in western France because those unable to flee preferred suicide to Roman captivity, but the name of the region, Vendée, still reminds us of their presence.

It seems that the Phoenicians crossed the Atlantic some 3,000 years ago, as certain ancient inscriptions on stones in Brazil, appear to be of

Phoenician origin.[2] Other discoveries in the Americas also suggest that there had been visitors from the eastern side of the Atlantic at a very early date. This leads to the conclusion that the world was far better known at certain periods than in the following period, a view that is confirmed by the discovery that Odysseus' voyages also took place in the Atlantic, as we shall see in Part III.

(iv) The Pirates: Taphians and Thesprotians

Homer sometimes mentions a people of pirates, the Taphians, for example in the passage quoted above in Chapter 1 (*Od.* I, 178), where Athene, disguised as an iron merchant, tells Telemachus that she called at Ithaca (Cadiz) on her way to Temese (London). This means that she must have sailed from a port either in the Mediterranean or in West Africa. The second alternative is more likely for two reasons.[3]

First, there are several place-names cognate with Taphos (*Od.* I, 417; see Map inside Back Cover) beginning with 'Taf' in the same part of southwest Morocco, such as Tafilalet, Tafraoute and Cape Tafelney.

Second, there are substantial iron ore deposits in Morocco and, further south, in Mauritania. It is therefore probable that the Taphians inhabited the west coast of Africa in Homer's time, which helps us to understand that the northwest coast of Morocco was inhabited by Celts, as we shall see in Part III Chapter 5.

There is another race of pirates in Homer, the Thesprotians, who lived in a 'rich and fertile' land, which must have been situated in southwestern France, to the east of Bordeaux, where we find the village of Trespoux near Cahors on the river Lot. This region seems at first sight rather far inland for pirates to live, but in Homer's time the sea was much closer to the department of the Lot than it is today, due to the higher sea level (Appendix Note 13).

(v) Cyprus

The island we know as Cyprus was called Alasjia in Homer's time and later Makaria ('happy island') before the ancient Greeks gave it the name of Cyprus because they went there for copper (Greek *kupros*). Homer's Cyprus (which he never describes as an island) was (San) Ciprian on the northwest coast of Spain, a location also rich in minerals.

The poet tells us that, 'Aphrodite went to Cyprus, to Paphos, where is her demesne and fragrant altar' (*Od.* VIII, 362). According to legend, Aphrodite was born from the foam of the sea near there. If Homer's Cyprus was San Ciprian, Paphos would be the present Foz, a small town in the region, located on Escairo Bay.

(vi) Sicily

In the Odyssey, we find the name Sikele, which is usually translated as Sicily, although it is not certain that the Mediterranean island was meant. We know from classical authors that before Greek colonization of the island, Sicily was inhabited by two tribes, the Sicani in the west and the Siculi in the east, both of which had come from Spain. However, we do not know whether their migration had already taken place in Homer's time. It could well be that the 'Sicilian' woman living in Ithaca (*Od.* XXIV, 211) was a local inhabitant. If we go further back in time, it is even probable that the Siculi originated in southwest France, where we find many place-names starting with Sic- or Seg- (See Part IV, Regiment 9). This would be additional evidence that Celtic peoples migrated southwards along the Atlantic coast to Spain and Morocco and into the Mediterranean Basin. Pharaonic records mention the presence of 'Sea Peoples' in their area, already several centuries before Homer. It is likely that western Europeans have explored and colonized places in the Mediterranean at a very early date. It is known that the Sea Peoples attacked Egypt in the twelfth century BC.

The question arises why Homer does not mention a single other place in the Mediterranean. If seafarers from Cadiz knew their way in the Atlantic, they would certainly have been well acquainted with this inland sea, a fact which has been confirmed not only by archeological evidence, but also by the presence of identical place-names (such as Sidon) at both ends of the Mediterranean. The answer seems to be that the descriptions of places and routes in the Mediterranean were contained in another 'oral book' of the Druids, just as they almost certainly must have had oral literature on mathematics, religion, astronomy and medicine (this last based on their extensive knowledge of plants), all of which was lost due to the religious taboo on writing and the secrecy code of the initiates. We should therefore consider the *Iliad* (a history book) and the *Odyssey* (marine charts) just as accidental survivals of a much larger 'memorized databank' that were rescued thanks to the fact that they were written down in ancient Greece.

(vii) Ethiopia

Nowadays Ethiopia is a country in northeast Africa, but the ancients used this name for the entire African continent, and in particular the coasts of West Africa, apparently well known to Celtic seafarers, who went there for ivory and leopard skins, two products mentioned by the poet. As late as the last century, an area of the South Atlantic, extending roughly from the Ivory Coast to Angola, was still called the Ethiopian Sea.[4] Another name used to designate Africa was Hypereia. Homer calls the people of Africa by different names: Ethiopians ('those of the burnt faces'), Pygmies ('the thumb high'), or Cyclopes ('the round-eyed', see Part III, Chapter 4). I always wondered how Homer could have known about the existence of pygmies, who live in central and southern Africa, and found it difficult to imagine the Greeks crossing Africa overland for thousands of kilometres to seek ivory and leopard skins. But if we assume that Homer belonged to a seafaring people living on the Atlantic coast of Europe, the answer is obvious. Ships sailed great distances along the African coast, apparently even much further than Senegal, where Odysseus called, as we shall see in Part III.

Notes

1 P. Bosch-Guimpera, *Les Indo-Européens*, Payot, Paris, 1980.
2 'Hi, Columbus, like the trip?', in *Newsweek*, 28 September, 1978.
3 Moreover, in the Mediterranean "neither Taphos nor Temesa is otherwise known as a place-name and the many attempts, all failures, to identify them with one or another mining region illustrate once again the futility of such 'historicizing' of the Homeric poems" according to M. I. Finley in: *The World of Odysseus*, 2nd ed., p. 68, Penguin, 1979.
4 A. Stieler, Handatlas, Justus Perthes, Gotha, 1862.

Part III
The World of the *Odyssey*

*A new Ulysses leaves once more
Calypso for his native shore*

SHELLEY

1

The Odyssey:
Reality and Symbolism

Since the original purpose of this book was to demonstrate that the Trojan War took place in England, I could have left it at that, but if I have succeeded in whetting the reader's appetite, making him want to read or re-read Homer's works, he will almost certainly be curious to know the exact location of the places visited by Odysseus. Besides, some of these places are also extremely interesting for the history of western Europe. I shall therefore try to answer the main questions that arise regarding the fantastic sea voyages of Odysseus that lasted nine long years, during which he experienced the most extraordinary adventures. Many will remember, at least vaguely, that on his way home to Ithaca at the end of the Trojan War, Odysseus was caught in a storm that carried him off into the Ocean, and can recall one or two of the famous stories, such as his encounters with the Cyclopes and the Sirens.

But the ancient Greeks thought that there was no point in trying to identify Odysseus' ports of call with real places. Erathosthenes, a Greek philosopher who lived in Alexandria in the third century BC, was of the opinion that 'it will be as difficult to find the particular places of Odysseus' voyage as it is to find the man who made the leather bag containing all the winds for Aeolus!'. On the other hand, one must agree with Ernle Bradford when he says that:

> ... the main geographical descriptions in Homer's account of Ulysses' voyage are accurate. They read as if they were meant to be, and in fact they often bear an uncanny resemblance to our own *Admiralty Pilots* ... whenever the poet sets himself out to describe a harbour, an anchorage, or some navigational hazard, there is a remarkable air of authenticity – something quite different from a poet's invention.[1]

The *Odyssey*: Reality and Symbolism

In our era, researchers have therefore tried to trace Odysseus' travels in the Mediterranean. The best-known works are those of Victor Bérard[2] and Ernle Bradford (See Appendix Note 20, The Odyssey in the Mediterranean). More recently an unpublished manuscript was found by the Yugoslav writer A. Vucetic, who had devoted thirty years of his life to demonstrating that the action of the *Odyssey* took place in the Adriatic. However, all the researchers who have tried to locate the *Odyssey* in the Mediterranean have had to take considerable liberties with Homer's text. The distances covered by Odysseus' vessel in the number of days stated by the poet are often too great for this inland sea, and we now know that the point of departure assumed by these authors, 'Troy' in Turkey, is incorrect, as I was at pains to show in Part I of this book. Most other commentators have made no attempt to discover where Odysseus went, assuming that the entire story was a myth, so that such an enterprise would be doomed to failure.

I do not share this view. Let us not forget that Homer lived in a period when the problem of what to do with one's leisure time did not exist and life was too hard for there to be a culture that was pure luxury without any practical utility. I am strengthened in this opinion by the fact that Homer's topological descriptions are of astonishing precision, as we have seen in the *Iliad*. I therefore believe that we can have entire confidence in his text and that he will provide useful details about the places visited by Odysseus. It is true that some of his adventures belong to the realm of the mythical, even if there was once a king of Ithaca by the name of Odysseus, but this is explained by the fact that, first, the poems reflect a mystique connected with the Druidic religion that was partly understood by the Celtic public at large, and, second, they contain information that could be used as a maritime chart for use in the tin, gold, iron and amber trades in an age when tin was found virtually only in England, gold in Ireland and amber in the Baltic.

In order to make bronze, an alloy of roughly 90 per cent copper and 10 per cent tin, it was necessary to go to Cornwall for tin and then alloy it with the copper that the Mediterranean peoples had in Cyprus, the Gauls in France and the Scandinavians in the centre of Sweden. There was thus fierce competition from all sides on the sea routes leading to Cornwall. Phoenicians, Etruscans, Scandinavians, and others all met in the ports of Europe, where, as Homer says, 'all tongues are spoken'.

For the purpose of keeping their knowledge of sea routes secret, all the information required by Celtic navigators was contained in the *Odyssey* in such a way that it could not be understood except by those who knew how to interpret it. The *Odyssey* thus fulfilled the function of

163

a maritime chart, containing not only explicit information, but also hidden indications that have only recently begun to be decoded. On another level, the *Odyssey* also contains information of a totally different nature – a description of the stages of initiation into the Mysteries.

Notes

1 Ernle Bradford, *Ulysses Found*, Century Publishing, London, 1985, p. 48–49.
2 Victor Bérard, *L'Odyssée d'Homère: Les navigations d'Ulysse*, Armand Colin, Paris, 1928.

2

Navigation in the Bronze Age

Before starting to analyse Odysseus' voyages in the Ocean, it is necessary to mention briefly the navigational problems encountered by seafarers in ancient times. We know that people have sailed on the high seas since very early times in different parts of the world, sometimes over very great distances indeed, and we have archeological evidence that this was so in both the Atlantic and the Mediterranean. For example, jewels from the Egypt of the Pharaohs have been found in England, and, conversely, jewels and other objects from England and the continent have been found in Egypt.

The 'crescent-shaped' ships of the period were very rapid and seem to have been designed both for piracy and for carrying bulk cargoes. According to Homer, some carried 120 men, while others, like those commanded by Odysseus, had a crew of 52: captain, pilot and 50 sailors/oarsmen. The Greek *amphielissa* (*Il*. II, 181) is variously rendered in the translations, but the most likely meaning seems to be 'curved at both ends', i.e. they were symmetrical in shape, with the bow being identical to the stern, so that they were able to sail in either direction. They were therefore more like the Viking ships we know from the Middle Ages than the quite asymmetrical ancient Mediterranean vessels. Most ships were black, as Homer states, since they were covered with hides, according to Celtic custom. The mast was stepped, and secured by forestays, only at the moment of departure. The big sails were fixed on transverse beams, which meant that the vessel could not sail into the wind, as became possible later through the use of a triangular mizzen. It was therefore necessary to wait for a wind favourable for the chosen destination, i.e. one that would be within 45 degrees of the stern. In following Odysseus' course we are therefore sometimes given a rough guide by Homer's mentioning the wind direction.

In Homer there are only four winds: Boreas, Euros, Notos and Zephyr, the north, east, south and west winds respectively. It is as well to remember these names as they are frequently mentioned in both the *Iliad* and the *Odyssey*, and are sometimes simply retained in the translations.

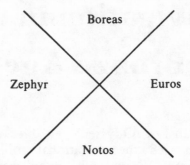

At night, sailors navigated by the stars, Homer calling the constellations by the names we still use today, such as the Great Bear, which is the only one of the constellations that 'has no part on the baths of Ocean' (*Od.* V, 275) (i.e. never dips below the horizon), Orion, the Pleiades, the Plough, etc. Where the direction to follow is not given explicitly by the direction of the wind, Homer uses other indicators, based on the zodiacal signs.[1] For example, if associated with a voyage there is an incident involving a bow or a hunter, the direction to take is North-North-East, where we find the zodiacal sign of Sagittarius (the Hunter). These indications of direction based on the zodiac will be very useful in helping us follow Odysseus.

Since the stars seem constantly to move due to the earth's rotation, it was necessary to agree on the position of the zodiac at a precise moment. The ancients chose sunset at the beginning of spring, when it was in the sign of Ares (the Ram). Ares therefore corresponds to the west and all the other signs are projected on the earth in an anticlockwise direction. In addition to the direction of the wind and the signs of the zodiac, Homer sometimes uses other methods of indicating the direction to take to get from one place to another.

It may be pointed out in passing that the twelve signs of the zodiac were not used for astrology in Homer's time. The Celts had designated thirty-six other constellations for this purpose, for their year was not divided into twelve months, but into thirty-six periods of approximately ten days each. Each of these periods was also associated with a specific type of tree.[2]

In order to estimate latitude (North-South position), the navigators of the time used a primitive kind of sextant, later known as a Jacob's stick. Estimating longitude (East-West position) was much more difficult and the problem was not solved until relatively recently. The only possibility in Homer's time was to estimate the distance covered, judging by the speed of the boat through the water and allowing for any North-South movement.

The sailors used their oars, even over great distances, if the wind fell or blew from an adverse direction, and, of course, to enter or leave port. When Homer says that ships arrived in port 'guided by a god', he simply means that the sailors used neither sail nor their oars, but allowed themselves to be carried by the rising tide for the final approach to a port. In the absence of any type of chart, this technique had the advantage of lessening the risk of damage when encountering sandbanks or rocks or any other shallow-water hazard when entering a port.

The ancients sailed only in the most favourable time of year. They took to the sea 'when the long days had returned', as Homer says more than once, when the constellation of the Pleiades was above the horizon, i.e. from May to October. They did not venture out in autumn and winter, because the bad weather conditions made sailing too risky.

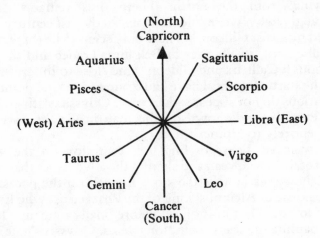

Notes

1 Jean Richer, *Géographie sacrée du monde grec*, Guy Trédaniel, Editions de la Maisnie, Paris, 1983.
2 Carol Carnac, *L'Astrologie celtique*, Sand, Paris, 1986.

3

Odysseus' Itinerary

To my knowledge, there have been few authors bold enough to seek Odysseus' itinerary in the Atlantic Ocean. In France, R. Philippe has written a thesis on the presence of Odysseus in Brittany,[1] while G. Pillot, in a very original book,[2] has tried to find all the places visited in the Atlantic, except for the first two (because Odysseus' point of departure is Turkey) and the last two (Corfu and Ithaca in Greece). Since he uses a 'key' based on Greek geography, he quickly goes off course in the Atlantic, to such an extent that he designates Iceland, a treeless Arctic island, as the luxuriant island of Calypso. What is more, he does not explain how it was that Odysseus could drift for nine days in an east to west direction in the Mediterranean, carried by a terrible storm blowing from the north. There thus remains only the interpretation given by Théophile Cailleux[3] in the last century, revised and corrected by Ernst Gideon.[4] (There only seem to be three copies of his work still extant, in libraries in Belgium, France and the United States.) Although Cailleux and Gideon came close to the truth, taking England as the starting point, I have had to amend several points where their explanations do not appear satisfactory. Odysseus' itinerary as set out in this Part III, and shown on the map inside the back cover, corresponds entirely to Homer's text.

Let us now leave Troy, in England, to follow in the wake of Odysseus, crossing the Ocean and sharing the adventures that carry his name, the *Odyssey*, as he tells the story himself on the occasion of a dinner in the house of Alcinous, king of the Phaeacians, who live in the island that is to be his last port of call before finally returning home to Ithaca after roaming the seas for nine long years. Odysseus' tale is found in Books IX to XIII of the *Odyssey*.

Notes

1 R. Philippe, *Ulysse est-il allé en Bretagne?*, in Planète, Paris, May, 1965.
2 G. Pillot, *Le Code secret de l'Odyssée*, Laffont, Paris, 1969.
3 Théophile Cailleux, *Pays atlantiques décrits par Homère*, Paris, 1879.
4 E. Gideon, *Homerus, Zanger der Kelten*, Ankh-Hermes, Deventer, 1973.

4

Ismarus,
Town of the Cicones

(Finistère, Brittany)

After their departure from Troy, Odysseus and his companions stop at Ismarus. They sack the town, situated on an island, then engage in a fierce battle with the Cicones, the inhabitants of the adjacent region. Odysseus himself relates what happened to King Alcinous:

> From Ilios (Troy) the wind bore me and brought me to the Cicones, to Ismarus. There I sacked the city and slew the men; and from the city we took their wives and great store of treasure, and divided them among us, that so far as lay in me no man might go defrauded of an equal share. Then verily I gave command that we should flee with swift foot, but the others in their great folly did not hearken. But there much wine was drunk, and many sheep they slew by the shore, and sleek kine of shambling gait. Meanwhile the Cicones went and called to other Cicones who were their neighbours, at once more numerous and braver than they – men that dwelt inland and were skilled at fighting with their foes from chariots, and, if need were, on foot. So they came in the morning, as thick as leaves or flowers spring up in their season; and then it was that an evil fate from Zeus beset us luckless men, that we might suffer woes full many. . . .   (Od. IX, 39-53)

According to Cailleux, Ismarus was the legendary town of Ys, which was situated in the extreme west of Brittany, near Douarnenez. After the town was engulfed by the sea, the French sang, 'Since Ys is no more, Paris is without rival'. In this town, the high priest, Hu, was said to be the custodian of the Holy Grail, the legendary chalice known from the writings of Chrétien de Troyes, among others. In Homer's time, the high priest was called Maro, as Odysseus recounts:

> . . . With me I had a goat-skin of the dark, sweet wine, which Maro, son of Euanthes, had given me, the priest of Apollo, the god

169

who used to watch over Ismarus. And he had given it me because
we had protected him with his child and wife out of reverence; for
he dwelt in a wooded grove of Phoebus Apollo. And he gave me
splendid gifts: of well-wrought gold he gave me seven talents, and
he gave me a mixing-bowl all of silver; and besides these, wine,
wherewith he filled twelve jars in all, wine sweet and unmixed, a
drink divine. . . .   (*Od.* IX, 196-205)

The explanation for the apparently unprovoked massacre is soon
found, for in the list of armies in Book II of the *Iliad*, we find a regiment
of Ciconian spearmen among the allies of the Trojans (see Part IV,
Regiment I). The little town of Sizun near Brest still reminds us of the
Cicones (see Map 15, no. 74 at the end of Part IV).

Odysseus finally gets away, after heavy losses, and embarks with the
survivors to continue towards his homeland, Ithaca, but shortly after
sailing they are caught in a northerly storm:

. . . But against our ships Zeus, the cloud-gatherer, roused the
North Wind with a wondrous tempest, and hid with clouds the
land and the sea alike, and night rushed down from heaven. Then
the ships were driven headlong, and their sails were torn to shreds
by the violence of the wind. So we lowered the sails and stowed
them aboard, in fear of death, and rowed the ships hurriedly
toward the land. There for two nights and two days continuously
we lay, eating our hearts for weariness and sorrow. (*Od.* IX, 67-75)

It is most probable that Odysseus wanted to hug the west coast of
France on his way to Spain, in order to avoid the dangerous crossing of
the Bay of Biscay. But they are caught by the storm shortly after
leaving Ismarus, while following the south coast of Brittany, which
runs west-east, rather than north-south. Their ships are unable to
advance with a wind from the beam, but they try nevertheless and their
sails are blown out, leaving them at the mercy of the wind and current,
which drive them to Spain. According to Cailleux, Odysseus arrives in
a bay on the northwest coast of Spain, where the river Ulla flows into
the sea. At the mouth of this river is the town of El Padron, whose
patron saint is San Iago (St James), who, according to legend, arrived
by sea with twelve companions (Odysseus with twelve ships), who on
arrival indulged in ceaseless lamentation. Thus the story told by Homer
is perpetuated in a Christian legend.

5

Cape Malea

(Cape St Vincent, southern Portugal)

Two days later, the storm dies down and Odysseus continues his voyage:

> . . . when now fair-tressed Dawn brought to its birth the third day,
> we set up the masts and hoisted the white sails, and took our seats,
> and the wind and the helmsmen steered the ships. And now all
> unscathed should I have reached my native land, but the wave and
> the current and the North Wind beat me back as I was rounding
> Malea, and drove me from my course past Cythera. (*Od.* IX, 76-81)

To sail to Ithaca (now Cadiz, see Part II, Chapter 7), the ships follow the Portuguese coast, helped by the currents that flow south off this coast. However, they are once again caught by a northerly storm, this time as they are about to round Cape Malea to sail west-east along the southern coast of Portugal, and Odysseus and his companions are driven south to Africa without seeing their homeland.

Cape Malea is now Cabo de Sao Vicente in the extreme southwest of Portugal. How do we know this? Elementary, says Cailleux, because in Homer's time this cape was named after Malios, an alternative name for Heracles or Hercules (see Appendix Note 25, The Principal Gods), the hero who became a god and was renowned for his twelve labours, among which was the construction of the Pillars of Hercules, the mountains on either side of the Strait of Gibraltar, that separates Europe from Africa. He was long venerated as the principal god of Spain, where he was considered to be the founder of Sevilla and Bajadoz (which has the Pillars of Hercules on their coats of arms) and was the patron of Toledo. As we have seen, a famous temple was dedicated to him in Cadiz. The Iberians called him 'Il Vinzente', ('the victorious'), whence the present name of Cape St Vincent.

Odysseus seems to regret having missed Cythera, mentioned only this once in the *Odyssey*, but called 'sacred Cythera' in the *Iliad* (XV, 432), and we can assume that the Celtic public would understand the importance of this place. Cailleux confirms that in Homer's time the north of Morocco was also inhabited by Celts, who had a Druidic religious centre near the present Rabat. According to him, the name Cythera, like the Spanish name Cotarro, was connected with religious festivals known as Floralia. Although the name Cythera has disappeared today, a seventeenth-century map by Blaeuw shows a town with a very similar name in northwestern Morocco, situated on a river flowing into the Atlantic: Cititheba, meaning 'inner-Cythera'.

The high mountains of northwest Africa are called the Atlas Mountains, a name that has not been transposed to Greece. There has in the past been considerable speculation as to why a 'Greek' god should give his name to a region so far away from Greece, but it is perfectly understandable now that archeological research has proved that 3,000 years ago Celtic peoples were living not only in the south of Spain, but also in the north of Morocco. This explains why the mountains on either side of the Strait of Gibraltar are called the Pillars of Hercules – they were named after the god that was particularly revered in this region – and confirms, if further confirmation were necessary, that the Greek gods were Celtic.

Although the name of the Atlas Mountains was not transposed to Greece, the Homeric names of other Iberian mountains were. Examples are Espartero/Sparta, as we have already seen, Mount Ossa, east of Lisbon, which gave its name to the Ossa Mountains in northern Greece and, probably, the Sierra Bermeja in Spain, which has become Mount Parnassus in Greece.

6

The Land of the
Lotus-eaters

(Senegal)

Thence for nine days' space I was borne by direful winds over the teeming deep; but on the tenth we set foot on the land of the Lotus-eaters, who eat a flowery food. There we went on shore and drew water, and straightway my comrades took their meal by the swift ships.   (*Od*. IX, 82-86)

The land of the Lotus-eaters cannot be the small island of Hierro in the Canaries, as suggested by Cailleux and Gideon, for the great distance covered in nine days of running with the northerly storm would mean that they no doubt ended up on the beach north of Dakar, probably in the fertile region of the river Senegal, a 'rich land' (*Od*. XXIII, 311). They are well received by the natives of this place, who give them the lotus to eat. This cannot be the Egyptian lotus, which is a water-lily, but a variant of the Provençal micocoulier. In English the three variants of this tree are named the nettle tree, hackberry and lotus tree, this last clearly being the one Homer is talking about. The fruit of the lotus tree resembles the black olive in looks, but not in taste. As the fruit has an intoxicating effect, Odysseus, who wisely abstains from eating it, has great difficulty in getting his euphoric companions back on board:

So they went straightway and mingled with the Lotus-eaters, and the Lotus-eaters did not plan death for my comrades, but gave them of the lotus to taste. And whosoever of them ate of the honey-sweet fruit of the lotus, had no longer any wish to bring back word or to return, but there they were fain to abide among the Lotus-eaters, feeding on the lotus, and forgetful of their homeward way. These men, therefore, I brought back perforce to the ships, weeping, and dragged them beneath the benches and bound them fast in the hollow ships; and I bade the rest of my trusty comrades to embark with speed on the swift ships, lest perchance anyone should eat of the lotus and forget his homeward way. So they went on board straightway and sat down upon the benches, and sitting well in order smote the grey sea with their oars   (*Od.*.IX., 91-104)

The lotus flower and fruit – a variant of the Provençal micocoulier.

Odysseus thus forces his companions to continue the voyage, but strangely enough not to return home. They could have waited for a southerly wind to carry them home to Spain, which would have been the normal thing for anyone driven off course by a storm to do. This supports my theory that the Odyssey was composed partly for the use of seafarers sailing in the Atlantic. The poem serves as a chart, showing ports of call and distances and describing the known limits of the ocean.

On another level, the visit to the land of the lotus-eaters is the start of a series of trials for Odysseus. He successfully passes the first test in having the strength of character to refuse to eat the 'forbidden fruits' that had such a euphoric effect on his companions that they forgot their purpose.

Curiously enough, I had a very similar experience when, several years before identifying Senegal as Homer's land of the lotus-eaters, I spent a holiday in this fascinating country. Even without tasting the lotus, I was as reluctant as Odysseus' crew to leave its spontaneous and friendly inhabitants who so closely resemble the description of their remote ancestors.

The next port of call, not far away, is to be the island of the Cyclopes.

7

The Land of the Cyclopes

(Cape Verde Islands)

As we shall soon see, Homer lets us know by means of a code that Odysseus has sailed west:

> Thence we sailed on, grieved at heart, and we came to the land of the Cyclopes, an overweening and lawless folk, who, trusting in the immortal gods, plant nothing with their hands nor plough; but all these things spring up for them without sowing or ploughing, wheat, and barley, and vines, which bear the rich clusters of wine, and the rain of Zeus gives them increase. . . .   (*Od.* IX, 105-111)

Homer's description of the land of the Cyclopes tells us that it was made up of islands, rainy and warm, where everything grows without the inhabitants having to make any effort. In the Atlantic, 280 miles west of Senegal, we find the Cape Verde islands, which enjoy a tropical oceanic climate, since they are far out at sea and only 15 degrees north of the Equator. Admittedly, the islands are now not as fertile as the poet describes them. They have very little rainfall, which may well be due to a climatic change in the region related to the rapidly progressing desertification of West Africa.

In the Cape Verde archipelago there is the small Fogo ('fire') island with a volcano 2,829 metres high. On the west coast of this island there is today the port of San Felipe, facing the smaller island of Brava. It is on the west coast of the latter that Odysseus landed:

> Now there is an isle overgrown with brush that stretches aslant outside the harbour, neither close to the shore of the land of the Cyclopes, nor yet far off, a wooded isle.   (*Od.* IX, 116)

The reason why Odysseus chooses to land on the west of a westward

175

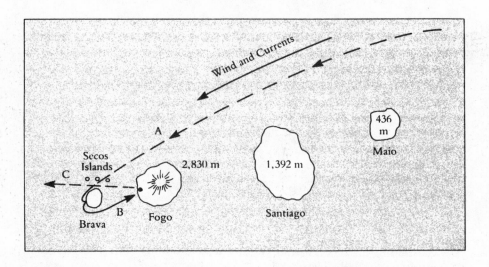

Odysseus' course in the Cape Verde Islands.

island is that the currents and the winds (for the most part) come from the northeast, so that it would be dangerous for a sailing vessel to approach the east coast of these islands. The sketch map shows how Odysseus and his men, coming from the east, round the islands to land on the west coast of Brava, and later row to the west coast of Fogo.

Homer tells us that among the Cyclopes there is one, Polyphemus, who is much bigger than the others:

> For he was fashioned a wondrous monster, and was not like a man
> that lives by bread, but like a wooded peak of lofty mountains,
> which stands out to view alone, apart from the rest. (*Od.* IX, 190–92)

And if this were not enough, he has only one eye. Many hear at school how Polyphemus shuts Odysseus and his men in a cave and eats two of them at each meal before Odysseus manages to blind him by piercing his eye with a glowing pointed stick while he is asleep. The other Cyclopes come to the closed entrance to the cave when they hear his cries of pain and rage, and ask who is injuring him. Polyphemus replies 'Noman', the false name Odysseus had given him on arrival, so the others go away reassured. Cailleux explains that we have here one of Homer's plays on words that the Celts so enjoyed. The Greek *outis* means 'no-one', but to the Celts it also meant 'pointed stick'. The same radical is also found in the Dutch noun *hout*, meaning 'wood' and in the Greek verb *outazein* meaning 'to injure with wood'. This again

A painting by Rembrandt depicting Aristotle contemplating the bust of Homer. (The Metropolitan Museum of Art, New York.)

The maze represented on the floor of
Ely Cathedral. The cathedral was built
on an important pagan religious site,
that of the tomb of Ilos, ancestor of
Priam, founder of the Troad (England).

An aerial view over Cambridgeshire of
the Devil's Dyke, one of the two giant
war dykes in the East Anglian plain.

Wandlebury Ring, a prehistoric hill fort
on the Gog Magog hills.

A modern replica of Triton, found on
the town hall at Middelburg. His
father, Poseidon, also appears on the
town hall at Zierikzee.

Present-day Zierikzee, Netherlands.
Once the site of Circe's Mystery
School.

Charon's boat to the Other World,
commemorated in the town of Veere,
Netherlands.

The Gundestrup silver cauldron (late second to early first century BC). A man is put head down into a vessel of liquid in a ceremony with attendant cavalry and infantry.

Stonehenge on Salisbury Plain, the biggest stone circle of all.

Homer was born and died a stone's throw from Middelburg town hall. The town, in the centre of Hades' island, was originally built in a perfect circle.

The Land of the Cyclopes

illustrates the proximity of the Greek and Celtic languages in Homer's time.

Odysseus and his men cannot escape until Polyphemus removes the boulder blocking the entrance to the cave, but the Cyclops knows that to escape his wrath they will try to get out at the same time as his sheep, so he runs his hand over the sheep as they pass. However Odysseus once again outwits him by attaching his men and himself under the bellies of the sheep.

In this story, Homer places great emphasis on the rams. Normally they are left outside the cave, but on the fateful night Polyphemus brings them inside. Odysseus himself hides under the biggest ram, that he keeps back till last. Polyphemus talks to this ram. Why? The reason was to draw the attention of those for whom the message was intended to the zodiacal sign of the Ram (Ares), which as we saw in Chapter 2, in this section, was the sign for a due westerly direction. Navigators would know that they had to sail west from the land of the lotus-eaters, first to the land of the Cyclopes, then on to their next destination, the island of the god of the winds, Aeolus.

There is a widespread mistaken belief that the Cyclopes were a one-eyed people, but nowhere does Homer say this. Only Polyphemus, son of Poseidon 'the earth-shaker', was one-eyed, and he had fire thrust into this eye, and he threw huge rocks into the sea that caused huge waves. If we add all this to the lines quoted above that describe him as being like a peak that stands out alone, he must very clearly be a volcano, and the story is in part camouflage and in part a device to introduce the rams and hence the navigational directions. The other Cyclopes certainly had two eyes, otherwise Homer would have called them Monopes. Cyclopes means the 'round eyed' and is intended to describe the black Africans, by contrast with the Achaeans, who are 'oblong eyed', again without giving the game away to those not intended to understand.

In this episode, Odysseus is able to save himself and most of his companions by using guile against an adversary of much greater physical strength.

8

The Aeolian Isle

(Saba, Netherlands Antilles)

Having escaped the wrath of Polyphemus, the Cyclops, Odysseus and his surviving crew sail on to the island of Aeolus, the god of the winds:

> Then to the Aeolian isle we came, where dwelt Aeolus, son of Hippotas, dear to the immortal gods, in a floating island, and all around it is a wall of unbreakable bronze, and the cliff runs up sheer. Twelve children of his, too, there are in the halls, six daughters and six sturdy sons, and he gave his daughters to his sons to wife.
>
> (*Od.* X, 1-8)

Why does the poet attract attention to this incestuous family? It is likely that these twelve children of the god of the winds represented the twelve directions corresponding to the signs of the zodiac. The name of his daughter Alcyone, for instance, still figures on modern celestial maps as the brightest star in the constellation of the Pleiades, situated in the zodiacal sign of Taurus. In fact, half the Celtic pantheon can be found on celestial maps of the northern hemisphere, as the ancients gave names to the stars as a navigation aid for their seafarers, whose success and survival depended on accurate navigation by night. But also wind force and direction were obviously of the utmost importance to seafarers, which may be the reason why many of Homer's heroes claim descent from Aeolus, the god of the winds, such as Jason the Argonaut, Nestor and Odysseus himself (see the genealogies in Appendix Note 25, page 362).

As Odysseus and his companions had left the cave of the Cyclops clinging to the rams (Aries) we can be sure that they continued their voyage in a westerly direction. In this part of the Atlantic they are aided by the prevailing wind and currents, to the northeastern Caribbean, where, according to Gideon, they dropped anchor off Saba, a small volcanic island in the Netherlands Antilles. Gideon was able to identify this island from Homer's description, though his starting point was in the Canary Islands, whereas Cailleux was off course somewhere in the Azores. It must be admitted, however, that both these authors were severely handicapped by not knowing about the zodiacal 'compass', which, as Jean Richer discovered, was known to the ancient Greeks and which apparently was a borrowing from the Celtic navigators, for the indications given in Homer's text fit perfectly in the Atlantic Ocean (but not in the Mediterranean). Saba does indeed have cliffs, and is the only Atlantic island surrounded by a bank containing copper in such high concentrations that people are advised not to eat too much fish caught in the vicinity. Odysseus is well received by Aeolus who promises to help him return home and as a parting gift stows in his ship a bag containing all the winds:

> He gave me a wallet, made of the hide of an ox nine years old, which he flayed, therein he bound the paths of the blustering winds; for the son of Cronos had made him keeper of the winds, both to still and to rouse whatever one he will. And in my hollow ship he bound it fast with a bright cord of silver, that not a breath might escape, were it never so slight. But for my furtherance he sent forth the breath of the West Wind to blow, that it might bear on their way both ships and men. Yet this he was not to bring to pass, for we were lost through our own folly. (*Od.* X, 19-27)

After nine day's sailing, with Odysseus constantly at the helm, they see the fires of Ithaca. Believing himself to be home at last, Odysseus finally falls asleep, and his men open the bag, thinking it must be full of treasure, thus unleashing the winds, which drive them back to the Aeolian isle, where this time Aeolus is not so generous:

> "'Begone from our island with speed, thou vilest of all that live. In no wise may I help or send up on his way that man who is hated of the blessed gods. Begone, for you comest hither as one hated of the immortals.'
> "So saying, he sent me forth from the house, groaning heavily."
> (*Od.* X, 72-76)

The sack of winds symbolizes the cyclones that are frequent in the Caribbean area. The place where the god of the winds has his home is therefore most appropriate and sailors are well-advised to avoid this region.

The voyage from the Aeolian isle (Saba) to the waters off Ithaca (Cadiz) and back seems quite futile and incomprehensible at first sight, and in his attempt to trace Odysseus' vogages in the Mediterranean, Victor Bérard even had to leave it out altogether, because between his Aeolian isle, to the north of Sicily, and Ithaca in Greece, there is the 'boot' of Italy, which makes such a voyage impossible (see Appendix Note 20, The Odyssey in the Mediterranean). Of course, Odysseus could have passed through the Strait of Messina, separating Sicily from Italy, which was often believed to be the famous Scylla and Charybdis, but these rocks are not mentioned by Homer in this particular context.

In the Atlantic Ocean, however, the voyage is entirely feasible, and this indeed seems to be the precise reason why Homer introduces it. The purpose is to tell seafarers that there is no land in the middle of the Atlantic, so that there is a shorter route from Spain to the Caribbean than that described in the Odyssey, but that this shorter route is inadvisable because of the unreliable winds.

The other purpose of this story is a further lesson in life on Odysseus' path to initiation. His unfortunate experience with his over-curious companions teaches him that it is no good relying on others, and that one must oneself keep full control in any important undertaking.

9

The Land of the Laestrygonians

(Cuba)

After the unpleasant encounter with Aeolus, Odysseus continues his voyage in northwesterly direction, as we will soon find out:

> Thence we sailed on, grieved at heart. And worn was the spirit of the men by the grievous rowing, because of our own folly, for no longer appeared any breeze to bear us on our way. So for six days we sailed, night and day alike, and on the seventh we came to the lofty citadel of Lamus, even to Telepylus of the Laestrygonians, where herdsman calls to herdsman as he drives in his flock, and the other answers as he drives his forth. There a man who never slept could have earned a double wage, one by herding cattle, and one by pasturing white sheep; for the outgoings of the night and of the day are close together. When we had come thither into the goodly harbour, about which on both sides a sheer cliff runs continuously, and projecting headlands opposite to one another stretch out at the mouth, and the entrance is narrow, then all the rest steered their curved ships in, and the ships were moored within the hollow harbour close together; for therein no wave ever swelled, great or small, but all about was a bright calm. But I alone moored my black ship outside, there on the border of the land, making the cables fast to the rock. (*Od.* X, 77-96)

According to Cailleux there is but one port in the world that exactly fits Homer's description – Havana, the capital of Cuba (see Map 11). When the Spaniards first landed there five centuries ago, they found to their astonishment that this port was already called by a name close to 'Havana', a word cognate with the English 'haven'. But in Homer's time it was called Lamus, with the most appropriate epithet Telepylus, which simply means 'the far-remote port'.

It is unlikely that Homer ever visited any of the more distant ports he

181

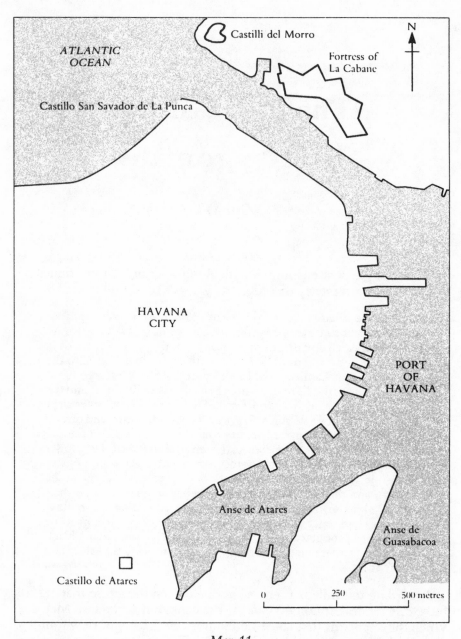

Atlantic Ocean

Castilli del Morro

Fortress of La Cabane

N

Castillo San Savador de La Punca

HAVANA CITY

PORT OF HAVANA

Anse de Atares

Anse de Guasabacoa

Castillo de Atares

0   250   500 metres

Map 11
The entrance to the port of Havana corresponds perfectly with the description of the
port of Lamus in the Odyssey. *The entrance to the basin is very narrow, and was*
even narrower in Homer's day, before it was canalized for modern shipping.
Note the Guasabacoa, bottom right.

182

describes in the *Odyssey* but his descriptions are very clear as regards their aspect from the sea, the type of harbour and whether fresh water is available, all matters of vital interest to seafarers, and it is likely that he had heard this information directly from sailors in Ithaca (Cadiz), which appears to be indicated as a necessary port of call for vessels visiting Africa or venturing across the Atlantic. This supports the theory that Homer may have lived in Cadiz.

But let us return to the text quoted above, which states that 'a man who never slept could have earned a double wage, one by herding cattle, and one by pasturing white sheep; for the paths of night and day are close together'. The meaning is not obvious, and going back to the Greek does not immediately elucidate it. A number of commentators have thought that it was a reference to a northern land where the sun virtually never sets in summer. However, it is also possible to interpret the passage as meaning that the *lengths* of day and night are close together, which is certainly the case with Cuba, where there is a difference of only two hours between the longest and shortest day. But there still remains the problem of the 'double wage'. The answer may lie in the translation of the Greek *mélon*, which is in fact a generic term for 'smaller livestock', which has usually been translated as 'sheep', but could also mean goats or, even more appropriate, llamas, which will never graze at night, even if they have not eaten during the day. Herdsmen could therefore take out one type of animal in daytime, and another for an equal length of time during the night.

Near the port of Lamos (cognate with Llama?) there is the 'fair-flowing spring of Artacia' (*Od.* X, 108), a name that could be translated as 'therapeutic water'. The Cubans of today call it Guasabacoa, which has a similar meaning. In our century a residential district has been built around the medicinal springs of Havana which attract many tourists who come to take the waters.

Homer describes the wife of King Antiphates as being 'huge as the peak of a mountain' (*Od.* X, 113). She symbolizes the island itself, the name of which, Cuba, is derived from the saxon *chub*, meaning 'big head'.

The Laestrygonians scarcely welcome Odysseus and his companions as they would have wished. The king ate one of them and the population, 'not like men but like Giants' (*Od.* X, 120), threw rocks from the cliffs to crush their ships. All were lost except Odysseus and his own crew.

However, there is one person who seems normal and friendly:

> And before the city they met a maiden drawing water, the goodly
> daughter of Laestrygonian Antiphates, who had come down to the
> fair-flowing spring Artacia, from whence they were wont to bear
> water to the town . . . And she showed them forthwith the high-
> roofed house of her father. (*Od.* X, 105-111)

Here we have the Water-Carrier, Aquarius, showing the way to
Lamus (Havana), and a little later, in a less pleasant context, we read
'spearing them like fishes they bore them home' (*Od.* X, 124), so here is
Pisces showing the way. The conclusion must be that the direction to
take from the Aeolian isle to Lamus is between Aquarius and Pisces, i.e.
northwest. This corresponds perfectly with the sailing direction from
Saba to Havana.

But why describe the way to such a distant island and stress the fame
and safety of its harbour, if it turns out to be such a terrible trap for any
sailor foolish enough to enter the port? The logical answer would seem
to be that the Druids wanted to show the way to the Celtic sailors,
discouraging any others from going there, where the Celts were
probably buying gold, for Cuba had gold mines which were exhausted
only a few centuries ago. It is also possible that Mexican gold was
traded there. It is by no means certain, then, that there was actually
cannibalism in Cuba in Homer's time, though we know that it existed
in several other Carribean islands until just a few centuries ago. The
most famous victim of this gruesome practice was Giovanni da
Verrazano, a Florentine explorer who, in 1528, was eaten virtually
before the eyes of his crew, who had stayed aboard the ship. The
victim's name lives on in New York's longest suspension bridge, the
Verrazano Narrows Bridge between Brooklyn and Richmond.

The moral of Homer's story is simply that one must always be
prudent and never rush into an unknown situation blindly. Odysseus
keeps his ship outside the harbour and it is the only one to be saved.

10

Aeaea,
The Island of Circe

(Schouwen, southwest Netherlands)

With just one ship remaining out of the original twelve, Odysseus sails away from Lamus:

> Thence we sailed on, grieved at heart, glad to have escaped death, though we had lost our dear comrades; and we came to the isle of Aeaea, where dwelt fair-tressed Circe, a dread goddess of human speech, own sister to Aeetes of baneful mind; and both are sprung from Helius, who gives light to mortals, and from Perse, their mother, whom Oceanus begot. Here we put in to shore with our ship in silence, into a harbour where ships may lie, and some god guided us.
> (*Od.* X, 133-141)

After a voyage about which Homer says not a word, neither duration nor wind direction, Odysseus allows the tide, considered at the time to be the breathing of a sea god, to carry him into a port on the island of Circe, Aeaea. The location of this island and the purpose of the voyage are totally obscure for the modern reader, although it has been understood throughout the ages that the story of Odysseus is basically about initiation, as is the case with the myth of Heracles and his twelve labours. As we shall see, after proving himself a man by passing through all the harsh trials imposed upon him by the gods, Odysseus is now ready for initiation into the Mysteries, to be performed in the holy of holies of the Gnostic religion (Greek *gnosis* = knowledge) of that time, the island of Circe, the high priestess of the cult. Judging by the detailed descriptions of the region, Homer himself must have been initiated here. In the next three chapters we will locate this island and investigate what takes place on it and the neighbouring island of Hades, as this is essential to a full understanding of the *Odyssey*.

Since we have no explicit information about the voyage from Lamus

185

to the island of Circe, we must look for an encoded indication of the course sailed, and the first action of Odysseus on arrival on Aeaea provides the clue:

> But when, as I went, I was near to the curved ship, then some god took pity on me in my loneliness, and sent a great, high-horned stag into my very path. He was coming down to the river from his pasture in the wood to drink, for the might of the sun oppressed him; and as he came out I struck him on the spine in the middle of the back, and the bronze spear passed right through him, and down he fell in the dust with a moan, and his spirit flew from him. (*Od.* X, 156-163)

Here we see Odysseus the sailor in the unusual role of hunter and this is precisely the purpose of this little episode. The hunter is associated with the zodiacal sign Sagittarius, which, as we saw in Chapter 2, indicates a northeasterly direction, the course to be sailed from Lamus (Cuba) to Aeaea (see Map inside Back Cover).

One has the impression that Homer reinforces the mystical nature of the isle by saying absolutely nothing about the inhabitants. But we can be sure there were inhabitants because there was a port and because Odysseus' companions hid their belongings before going to Circe's house. Most translations say they hid their things in a cave, but it will turn out that there are no caves on the island, and the Greek word used is indeed not *speleos* but *speos*, a generic word for any kind of hollow or cavity.

We are told that Odysseus arrives at a flat island, where there are tides and that he visits another similar island close by. He is therefore probably in the delta of a river, close to the sea. Many estuaries of great rivers, such as the Nile, the Euphrates and the Ganges, have always been religious centres and the great delta of the Rhine in the Netherlands must have had a very similar function in the pre-Christian era, as Cailleux and other authors have suggested in the past, identifying even a dozen place-names with those mentioned by Homer. We also know that the Celts attached a particular religious importance to three major European rivers: the Rhine (Celt *rene* = rebirth), which was the symbol of birth, the Meuse (Celt *moza* = to moult), symbol of transformation, and the Schelde (from an old Indo-European root *skeid* = to separate), symbol of death. These three rivers together form a vast estuary in the province of Zeeland, southwest Netherlands. Among the many islands of this estuary, there is one called Schouwen whose quaint little capital is Zierikzee, a name that has no meaning in Dutch, but the explanation was given four centuries ago by Justus Lipsius (Joost Lips, a professor at the University of Leyden) who said that if the 'c' in Circe is pronounced like a soft 'z', the name sounds the same as Zierikzee. This was always considered to be an academic joke, but with our advanced knowledge of ancient languages and the discovery of a number of other clues found in the area, it is possible to confirm that Circe and Zierikzee are one and the same name.

First, let us examine the linguistic explanation. According to the *Oxford Dictionary of English Etymology*, the word 'church' comes from Old English *cirice* or *circe*, a word that clearly seems to be cognate with Circe. We also know that the dialectal form of Circe (also found in Greek) was *Kirke* and etymologists are agreed that the Dutch word for 'church', *kerk*, the German *Kirche* and the Scots *kirk* all come from the Old Saxon *kirika*, another word cognate with Kirke or Circe.

If Zierikzee, for which many different spellings can be seen on old maps, such as Ziericxzee, Sierckzee, or Zircze was also the same word as *circe* meaning 'sacred place' or 'church', then Circe, the goddess whose name was Church with a capital 'c', must have been the highest authority of the Gnostic religion. In the Bronze Age, Zierikzee must then have been the religious centre of the Gnostics, invariably associated with initiation into the Mysteries, the knowledge of the universe that surrounds us. Therefore the most important Gnostic school of Homer's time must also have been located here.

The name of the island, also sometimes attributed to Circe herself, Aeaea, can be explained as follows: *Aia* or *Aiaie* is the most ancient version of *Gaia*, the Earth Mother, source of all life who sprang from Chaos and was the mother of Uranus, the heavens and Pontus, the sea, amongst others. On arrival at the isle of Circe, Odysseus enters a harbour 'where ships may lie', but the Greek could also mean a port 'where ships may be repaired'. This detail has its importance, for where Odysseus probably landed there is a port called Brouwershaven (from the Middle Dutch *brouwen* or *breeuwen* = to repair and *haven* as in English). Here Odysseus and his men rest for two days, then on the third Odysseus goes to see the lie of the land:

> For I climbed to a rugged point of outlook, and beheld the island, about which is set as a crown the boundless deep. The isle itself lies low, and in the midst of it my eyes saw smoke through the thick brush and the wood. (*Od.* X, 194-197)

It is hardly likely that a low island will be 'rugged', nor, as other translations have it, will there be a 'rocky height'. The Greek actually speaks of a lookout point in an undulating place, so it looks very much as if the point in question was simply the top of a sand dune. Today there is a dyke at Brouwershaven, but, according to a history of the island, there used to be dunes, the sand of which was transported for use elsewhere. Just outside Brouwershaven, old maps show the Uitkijkpolder ('look-out polder'). Since a polder is flat by definition, this name could well refer to the adjacent look-out dune of Odysseus. The fact that the dunes of Zeeland are not very high would explain why Odysseus sees the smoke *through* the trees. He decides to send his second in command, Eurylochus, with half his men to investigate:

> Within the forest glades they found the house of Circe, built of polished stone in a place of wide outlook, and round about it were mountain wolves and lions, whom Circe herself had bewitched; for she gave them evil drugs. Yet these beasts did not rush upon my men, but pranced about them fawningly, wagging their long tails.
>
> (*Od.* X, 210-215)

Gideon suggested that the house of Circe stood in the vicinity of Zierikzee where, in the Christian era, the monastery of Syon was built on foundations of large dressed stones that fitted together without cement, thus revealing a very ancient origin, possibly Bronze Age. The monastery was destroyed in the Napoleonic wars and these prehistoric foundations are unfortunately no longer accessible because houses have since been built on the spot.

The rest of the above citation is incomprehensible if one does not know where the episode is taking place. Apart from other symbolic meanings, the wolves and lions that seem domesticated also symbolize the tidal waters that surround the islands and sandbanks of Zeeland with their 'long tails'. They do no harm to the people because they are held back by dykes, which already existed in Homer's time (see Part I, Chapter 4). The names of two villages still remind us of Circe's animals: Wolfaartsdijk (Wolves' dyke) and Lewedorp (Lion-village).

If the wild animals are not dangerous, Circe is. She drugs the men's food and drink and turns them into swine and puts them in a pig pen. Curiously enough, marine charts show a sandbank in the vicinity of Zierikzee, called Berendam, meaning 'pig pen', which must be the place where Odysseus' companions were imprisoned. The only one to escape this fate is Eurylochus, who suspects a trap and remains at a safe distance. When he sees what has happened, he returns to the ship to tell Odysseus, who sets off to see what he can do. On his way to Circe's house the god Hermes comes to him in the guise of a young man and offers to help him by giving him an antidote to Circe's potions:

So saying, Argeiphontes [Hermes] gave me the herb, drawing it from the ground, and showed me its nature. At the root it was black, but its flower was like milk. Moly the gods call it, and it is hard for mortal men to dig; but with the gods all things are possible. Hermes then departed to high Olympus through the wooded isle, and I went my way to the house of Circe.

(*Od.* X, 302-306)

This plant, for which both Greeks and translators ·have always retained the original (probably Celtic) name, moly, is none other than madder, found in temperate climates. It has whitish-yellow flowers and very long roots making it indeed very hard to dig up (see illustration). It was formerly cultivated in Zeeland in order to produce alizarine, a red dye, whence the botanical name of this plant, *rubia tinctorum*. It has

The roots of the madder:
'Moly the gods call it,
and it is hard for
mortal man to dig;
but with the gods
all things are possible'
(Od. X, 304).

become a rare species since the advent of synthetic dyes. The encounter between Odysseus and Hermes is eternalized by the present village of Beldert in the centre of the island, the name meaning 'image land' (*beeld* = image, *ert* = earth), a reminder of the fact that Hermes had taken the image of an adolescent. Although Hermes' name has disappeared, at least in this part of the Netherlands, that of his mother, Maia, was preserved until the sixteenth century in the village of Maye, near the northeastern shores of the island, which has been engulfed by the sea since then.

Thus armed with the 'moly', Odysseus is able to resist the drug that Circe had used to turn his men into pigs. Although the poet does not specify which drug it was, we can assume that it was the indigenous plant that still bears Circe's name in botanical parlance, *Circaea lutetiana*. This plant has been associated with witches and is therefore more commonly known as 'enchanter's nightshade'. To heighten the effect of her potion, the goddess may well have added the very toxic *Colchicum automnalis*, better known as meadow saffron or autumn crocus, which French peasants call *tue-pourceau*, 'pig-killer'. With its white, pink or violet flowers, it must have grown in abundance in the damp meadows of Circe's island, as no doubt also small scabious (*Scabiosa columbaria*), which gave its name to the adjacent island, Duiveland, 'Land of the Dove(weed)', this plant having a symbolic meaning in the ancient Mysteries. This potion, then, was one of the arms of the 'dread goddess, Circe of the many drugs' (*Od.* X, 276), whose name was also related to the word *circos*, not only meaning sparrowhawk, as we have seen, but also hawk-weed (*Hieracium asteraceae*), no doubt another plant in her collection. (See illustration)

We have thus already several indications that the low island of Aeaea, 'where dwelt fair-tressed Circe, a dread goddess of human speech', daughter of Helius (the sun) and granddaughter of Oceanus, was in fact Schouwen. As Oceanus gave his name to the sea to the west of the island and far beyond, perhaps her father too was the source of a geographical name? The first places to look were the waters to the north and the east of the island on which the ports lay, and indeed a historical atlas of the Netherlands shows us that in the Roman era they were called Helinium, clearly a latinized version of Helion, a reminder of Circe's father Helius. The atlas is no doubt based on the writings of Pline, who states that Helinium is the southern branch of the Rhine. Today it is called Krammer and Grevelingen. The names of Circe's illustrious ascendants Helius and Oceanus are preserved in the village of Zonnemaire (Sun-Sea), situated precisely on the river Helion/Grevelingen.

Some indigenous plants in the collection of Circe 'of the many drugs': (a) Circaea (enchanter's nightshade): (b) Colchicum (meadow saffron); (c) Achillea (milfoil); (d) Scilla (wild hyacinth); (e) Scabiosa ('doveweed'); (f) Rubia tinctorum (madder, Homer's moly).

On Aeaea, Odysseus soon comes to terms with 'fair-tressed' Circe and persuades her to free his companions from the spell she has put on them:

> So I spoke, and Circe went forth through the hall holding her wand in her hand, and opened the doors of the sty, and drove them out in the form of swine of nine years old. So they stood there before her, and she went through the midst of them, and anointed each man with another charm. Then from their limbs the bristles fell away which the baneful drug that queenly Circe gave them had before made to grow, and they became men again, younger than they were before, and far comelier and taller to look upon. They knew me, and clung to my hands, each man of them, and upon them all came a passionate sobbing, and the house about them rang wondrously, and the goddess herself was moved to pity. (*Od.* X, 388-399)

A place in Zeeland still recalls this event. In the above translation, it says that the noise made by the newly-released 'pigs' (the uninstructed, the neophytes) was such that the house 'rang wondrously', but the Greek *konabos* can also mean 'trembling'. Near to Zierikzee, there is still today a village called Schuddebeurs, 'trembling of pigs'.

Circe transforms Odysseus' men into pigs with the aid of a magic wand, an instrument frequently mentioned in Celtic myths and fairy stories. Not only certain gods, such as Hermes, carried wands, but so did the Celtic wizards and the Druids themselves. We saw above that Hermes helps Odysseus by giving him an antidote for Circe's drugs. At the same time he gives him some advice:

> Here, take this potent herb, and go to the house of Circe, and it shall ward off from thy head the evil day. And I will tell thee all the baneful wiles of Circe. She will mix thee a potion, and cast drugs into the food; but even so she shall not be able to bewitch thee, for the potent herb that I shall give thee will not suffer it. And I will tell thee all. When Circe shall smite thee with her long wand, then do thou draw thy sharp sword from beside thy thigh, and rush upon Circe, as though thou wouldst slay her. And she will be seized with fear, and will bid thee lie with her. Then do not thou thereafter refuse the couch of the goddess, that she may set free thy comrades, and give entertainment to thee. But bid her swear a great oath by the blessed gods, that she will not plot against thee any fresh mischief to thy hurt, lest when she has thee stripped she may render thee a weakling and unmanned. (*Od.* X, 287-301)

192

Aeaea, the Island of Circe

Needless to say these lines are also an allegory, not only because a heroic king is unlikely to assault a lady, but also because the lady in question was a mere symbol of the Gnostic religion. The key to interpretation of this text is the sword brandished by Odysseus as it was a symbol of knowledge since the earliest times, probably because the shape of the two-edged blade has a certain similarity with the tongue which expresses the Word. The same symbolism of the sword is also found in the Bible and in the medieval story of King Arthur with his famous sword, Excalibur, as the Arthurian cycle was, much like the Homerian epic, an initiation story where Elaine – a corruption of the name Helen in the *Iliad* – was the initiatrice. The same symbolism of the sword has remained alive until today. For instance, the members of the Académie Française, the intellectual élite of France who call themselves the 'Immortals', have a beautifully decorated sword. As to Odysseus, he was obviously eager to obtain wisdom by 'sharing the couch of the goddess' at the advice of Hermes. He even takes a bath at Circe's house, as Homer tells us, which in itself is quite a normal thing to do, but in this particular case also a symbolic gesture, as it is well known that an initiate had to be pure, mentally and physically, before initiation.

Odysseus and his companions stay a year on Aeaea, 'but when a year was gone . . . and the long days were brought in their course' (X, 469) the men remind Odysseus that they should be on the way home and he asks Circe to send them back to Ithaca. She agrees on one condition:

> "'but you must first complete another journey, and come to the house of Hades and dread Persephone, to seek soothsaying of the spirit of Theban Teiresias, the blind seer, whose mind abides steadfast. To him even in death Persephone has granted reason, that he alone should have understanding; but the others flit about as shadows.'
>
> "So she spoke, and my spirit was broken within me, and I wept as I sat on the bed, nor had my heart any longer desire to live and behold the light of the sun. But when I had had my fill of weeping and writhing, then I made answer, and addressed her, saying:
>
> "'O Circe, who will guide us on this journey? To Hades no man ever yet went in a black ship. . . .'" (*Od.* X, 490-502)

Hades is generally spoken of as a place, but for Homer Hades was the god of the Underworld and the human subconscious, while he was also the god of the new life through cyclic rebirth. Odysseus is extremely frightened by what awaits him, for he has to go through the harsh ceremony of initiation. This is to occur on another island in the same region, the home of Hades, whose name means the 'Invisible One'.

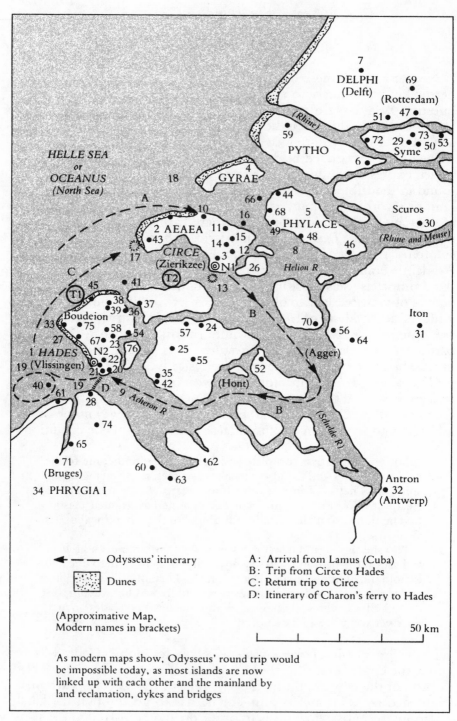

Map 12
*Phthia in the Zeeland Estuary, southwest Netherlands. (Bronze Age.)
Modern names in brackets.*

Key to Map 12

In the Bronze Age, Europe's religious centre was in 'deep-soiled', 'fertile' Phthia, once the name of the vast delta of the Rhine, Meuse and Schelde in the present province of Zeeland and adjacent regions in Holland and Flanders. Phthia was also the kingdom of Peleus, father of Achilles.

N1   Nol – Sacred circle dedicated to Circe near Zierikzee. Called Lokker Nol on older maps; name disappeared in the seventeenth century.

N2   Nol – Sacred circle dedicated to Hades near Vlissingen. Today called Nolle at Dishoek ('Corner of Dis' or 'Hades').

T   Sites where altars of Nehalennia (Circe) were found in the sea: T1, near Domburg; T2, near Colijnsplaat.

In the Odyssey we find:

1 Hades	Near village of Dishoek (Place of Dis or Hades) on the island of Walcheren★, name cognate with 'Valkyries' and Homer's 'Ker' (Fate)
2★ Aeaea (Greek *Aia* or *Aiaie*: 'Mother Earth')	The island of Circe, today called Schouwen
3★ Circe (Greek *Kirke*)	Name preserved by the town of Zierikzee and many place-names ending in -kerke
4 Gyrae (Greek *Gure*) (*OD.* IV, 500)	The island of Goeree. Probably also the legendary island 'whence nobody returns', Gore in Celtic vernacular literature
5 Phylace (Greek *Phulake*)	The island of Flakkee (Overflakkee on modern maps)
6 Pytho (Greek *Puthon*)	The island of Putten. (Pytho was the oracle of Apollo)
7 (Delphi)	Delft, situated close to its port Kirra (see no. 47). Homer calls Delphi only by its older name, Pytho
8★ (Helion)	River named after Helios, the sun god and Circe's father; called Helinium in the Roman era; today it is Krammer and Grevelingen
9★ Acheron	River whose name split into two local names, Agger and Hont in our era; today called Honte or Westerschelde

Names related to the Odyssey, but not explicitly mentioned in the epic

10★ Brouwershaven	Port of first arrival of Odysseus on the island of Circe
11★ Zonnemaire	Village whose name is an allusion to Circe's ancestors, Helios and Oceanus (Sun-Sea)
12★ Syon	Village, possible site of Circe's 'sacred' house

195

13*	Berendam ('Pig pen')	Site of the neophytes' stay, now a sandbank
14*	Schuddebeurs ('Trembling of pigs')	Neophytes' village
15*	Beldert ('Image land')	Village; reminder of Odysseus' encounter with Hermes disguised as a youngster
16*	Maye	Village (engulfed by the sea in the seventeenth century); eponym of Maia, Hermes' mother
17*	Banjaard ('Boneguard')	Burial place of Elpenor, today a sandbank
18	Renesse ('Rebirth').	Village; reminder of initiations
19*	Vlissingen	Town named after Ulysses/Odysseus
20	Rammekens ('Flock of rams')	Name of beach (and fortress) near Vlissingen where Odysseus landed the sacrificial rams
21	Vijgeter ('Fig-eater')	Former hamlet; reference to hierophants in charge of initiations
22	Souburg ('Under-burg')	Town, likely reference to the Underworld
23	Middelburg	Capital of Zeeland, the most likely site for the 'town of the Cimmerians'
24*	Wolfaartsdijk ('Wolf's dyke)	Village; reminder of Circe's animals
25	Lewedorp ('Lion-village')	Village; reminder of Circe's animals
26	Duiveland ('Land of doves')	Part of Circe's island; symbolically: 'Land of Souls'
27	Biggekerke ('Pig-church')	Village; 'pigs' were neophytes but also sacrificial animals and chtonic symbols in the Mysteries
28	Breskens ('Tribe of Bres')	Town, eponym of Persephone (Part III, Chapter 11)

In the Iliad we find:

29	Syme (Greek *Sumetha*)	Village of Smitshoek, home of Nireus, commander of Regiment 19 (see Part IV)
30	Scuros (*Il.* XIX, 326)	Schuring, hamlet, home of Achilles' father, Peleus (there is another Scuros in Troad)
31	Iton (*Il.* II, 696)	Etten, village
32	Antron (*Il.* II, 697)	Antwerp ('wharf of Antron'), situated 'near the sea'
33	Boudeion (*Il.* XVI, 572)	Boudinkercke on old maps, hamlet now called Boudewijnskerke
34	Phrygia I (*Il.* III, 184)	Flanders
35	(Berg van Troje) 'Mount of Troy'	Tumulus near the village of Borssele. Possible memorial for the Trojan War. (Not in Homer)

Names related to classical mythology

36	Veere	Town, eponym of Persephone (Phere-phassa) (see Part III, Chapter 11)
37	Kamperland (Campe on old maps)	Village, eponym of the female monster Campe, guardian of Hades, slain by Zeus
38	Serooskerke	Village, eponym of Cerberus, the three-headed watchdog of Hades, slain by Heracles
39	Hondgem (*Hond* = dog)	Twin hamlet of Serooskerke (38)
40	Romedorp 'Village of Rome'	Named after Romus, eponymous founder of the city of Rome in Italy, a legendary son of Odysseus and Circe. Village (and island) engulfed in the fourteenth century
41	Roompot	Waters off Veere, usually explained as 'Roman Port' because of coins found; more likely to be an older name: Port of Romus (see 40)
42	Borssele (or Borsele)	Village, eponym of the monster Porce, a seasnake that killed Laocoon, priest of Apollo in Troy. A twin village was called Monster until the seventeenth century
43	Haamstede (or Haemstede)	Village, 'town of Haemus'; a son of Boreas, god of the Northwind. (For the other sons, Calais, see Map 15, and Zetes, Map 17 at the end of Part IV)
44	Melissant	Village; eponym of Melissa, high priestess of Demeter who had a shrine further north (Map 17, note 13 at the end of Part IV)
45	Domburg	Village; likely eponym of the Cretan leader Idomeneus, who was banished from his country after the Trojan War
46	Galatese Sluis (Galatea on old maps)	Former hamlet named after 'illustrious Galatea', legendary mother of the Celts
47	Kirra	For the Ancients, Kirra was the port of Delphi (Delft); today Kralingen, a district of nearby Rotterdam
48	Coredijk ('Dyke of Core')	Village; Core (Greek *Kore*) was a surname of Persephone; cognate with English *corn* and Dutch *koren*
49	Herkinge(n)	Village, eponym of Hercyne (Greek *Herkuna*), a companion of Persephone
50	Carnisse	Rotterdam suburb, eponym of Carneus, son of Zeus and Europa
51	Kethel	Rotterdam district, ('Keto-lo' = 'Place of Ceto'), a Nereid, daughter of Nereus and Doris, grand-daughter of Pontus

52	Ierseke (or Yrseke)	Village, eponym of Iresia, also a Nereid.
53	Briene	Legendary village founded by one of the Amazons who lived further north (see Map 17 at the end of Part IV). The only – unexpected – reminder is a twelve-lane bridge east of Rotterdam: the Van Brienenoordbrug ('Bridge of Briene's place')
54	Arnemuiden	Village, eponym of Arne, a consort of Poseidon and daughter of Aeolus, god of the winds
55	Nisse	Village; eponym of Nyssa, a nymph and nurse of Dionysus, god of the vine. (For viticulture, see Appendix Note 23)
56	Halsteren	Village; Hals was a servant and companion of Circe; 'hals' means both 'salt' and 'sea'
57	Sabbinge	Village, eponym of Sabbe, a priestess believed by Pausanias to have been a Babylonian oracle (for nearby Babylonia, see Map 17, 47)
58	(St) Laurens	Village; Laurentium's king was said to be loved by Circe.
59	Brielle	Town; possible eponym of Prylis, who predicted that Troy would only be taken with the help of the Trojan Horse
60	Assenede (Asene on old maps)	Village; eponym of Asine, a minor mythological figure, grandson of Zeus
61	Cadzand ('Cadsands')	Village, eponym of Cadmilus, patron of seafarers, and the Cadmeans
62	Axel (or Axele)	Town; eponym of Axiierus, also a patron of seafarers
63	Zelzate	Village; with nearby Zele, eponym of Zelus, son of Oceanus and Styx
64	Heerle (Here–lo = 'place of Here')	Village, eponym of Zeus' consort
65	Damme	Village; likely eponym of Damia, whose cult was dedicated to Persephone
66	Roxnes	Village; eponym of Roxane, a minor mythological figure.
67	Triton	Former hamlet, named after a son of Poseidon. Triton's effigy is on nearby Middelburg town hall
68	Griisort	(Name disappeared since seventeenth century), region; eponym of Chrysaor ('the man with the golden sword'), son of Poseidon and the Gorgon, brother of the winged horse Pegasus, whose name means 'source' (of knowledge)

69	Rodenrijs	Rotterdam suburb; eponym of Rhodus, a daughter of Poseidon, married to Helios, the father of Circe (-rijs = twigs or shrub)
70	Tholen (contraction of Thoe-land)	island and town; Thoe was a Nereid, granddaughter of Pontus
71	Brugge (Brugis on map of around 1300)	Town of the Brugi, seafarers who waged war against the Thesprotian pirates (Map 15, note 100) according to Hesiod (Telegony, 1)

Names that migrated with the Celts to Southern Europe

72	Poortugaal	Rotterdam suburb (Portugal)
73	Lombardijen	Rotterdam suburb (Lombardy, Northern Italy)
74	Turkeije	Village; (Turkey)

Names associated with the person of Homer

| 75 | Meliskerke | Village; eponym of Meles, which was the original name of Homer and his father. |
| 76 | Ios | Formerly the island of Joosland, today part of the island of Walcheren and named Nieuw and St Joosland. Place of birth and decease of Homer. |

*Place names already identified by Cailleux, Gideon and other authors.

N.B. On some older maps of Zeeland appear the names Cocycx and Stryx designating waters near Breskens (Key 28), a likely reminder of the Cocytus and the Styx, the rivers of hell mentioned by Homer in this region (see Chapter 11).

11

Hades

(The Island of Walcheren, southwest Netherlands)

It goes without saying that Hades was frightening, but the ancients also associated him with rebirth and cyclical renewal through his wife Persephone who joined her husband in the Underworld for only three or four months of the year, during winter when nature, dead with cold, sleeps under the earth waiting for the renewal of springtime.

The island of Hades is found in the extreme southwest of Zeeland, and is now known as Walcheren, a name cognate with the German Walküren and English Valkyries, the handmaidens of Odin (Wodan), who in Nordic mythology, rode through the air and picked out the heroes who were to fall in battle, and accompanied the dead into the world beyond. In the *Iliad*, this was the task of the Ker (often translated as Fate, e.g. *Il*. XVIII, 535), and if we combine this word with the Old Norse *Val* meaning both 'battlefield' and 'dead warrior', we get Valker, plural Valkeren, clearly the same as Walcheren (the island) and Valkyries (the dreaded goddesses), who took the spirits to Hades, as Homer explains: 'He had fallen to Ker and gone down to the house of Hades' (*Od*. VI, 11).

Near the island of Hades, Homer mentions the river Acheron, which is now called the Westerschelde (western Schelde), but not so long ago part of this river was called the Agger while another part is still called the Hont, and phonetically Agger + Hont = Acheron, the mythological river of death mentioned by Homer (see Map 12 in the previous chapter). In addition to the name of Walcheren, and that of the river Acheron, the third piece of evidence pointing to the identification of this island as Homer's Hades is provided by the Roman historian Tacitus (approximately 55-120 AD), who tells us that in his day it was believed that Ulysses (a dialect version of the name Odysseus) had visited northern Europe:

> The Germans, like many other peoples, are said to have been
> visited by Hercules and they sing of him as the foremost of all the

heroes when they are about to engage in battle. Ulysses also, in all those fabled wanderings of his, is supposed by some to have reached the northern sea and visited German lands, and to have founded and named Asciburgium ("town of acceptance"!), a town on the Rhine inhabited to this day. They even add that an altar consecrated by Ulysses and inscribed also with the name of his father Laertes was discovered long ago at this same place, and that certain barrows with monuments upon them bearing Greek inscriptions still exist on the borders of Germany and Raetia. I do not intend to argue either for or against these assertions; each man must accept or reject them as he feels inclined.[1]

It is not surprising that the Romans confused the Rhine and the Schelde, for the two rivers do in fact mix their waters close to the sea in this region. The town mentioned by Tacitus must have been the port on the Schelde that still carries the name of Odysseus/Ulysses: Vlissingen which is a corruption of Ulyssingen, the U and the V having been identical in Latin, while the Y was still used in the old spelling of the name. The suffix -gen means 'creation' or '(re)-birth' as in the word 'genesis'.

After three millenia it is still possible to trace Odysseus' course between the island of Circe and that of Hades by carefully reading Homer's verses, where Circe gives him hidden, but very precise instructions for his descent in the Underworld:

> "'But when in thy ship thou hast now crossed the stream of Oceanus, where is a level shore and the groves of Persephone – tall poplars, and willows that shed their fruit – there do thou beach thy ship by the deep eddying Oceanus, but go thyself to the dank house of Hades. There into Acheron flow Periphlegethon and Cocytus, which is a branch of the water of the Styx; and there is a rock, and the meeting place of the two roaring rivers. Thither, prince, do thou draw nigh, as I bid thee, and dig a pit of a cubit's length this way and that, and around it pour a libation to all the dead. . . .'"
>
> (Od. X, 508-518)

> " 'Then the seer [Teiresias] will presently come to thee, leader of men, and he will tell thee thy way and the measures of thy path, and of thy return, how thou mayest go over the teeming deep.'
>
> "So she spoke, and straightway came golden-throned Dawn. Round about me then she cast a cloak and tunic as raiment, and the nymph clothed herself in a long white robe, finely-woven and beautiful, and about her waist she cast a fair girdle of gold, and upon her head she put a veil. . . ." (Od. X, 538-545)

But when we were on our way to the swift ship and the shore of the sea, sorrowing and shedding big tears, meanwhile Circe had gone forth and made fast beside the black ship a ram and a black ewe, for easily had she passed us by. Who with his eyes could behold a god against his will, whether going to or fro? (*Od.* X, 569-574)

She [the ship] came to deep-flowing Oceanus, that bounds the Earth, where is the land and city of the Cimmerians, wrapped in mist and cloud. Never does the bright sun look down on them with his rays either when he mounts the starry heaven or when he turns again to earth from heaven, but baneful night is spread over wretched mortals. Thither we came and beached our ship, and took out the sheep, and ourselves went beside the stream of Oceanus until we came to the place of which Circe had told us.

(*Od.* XI, 13-22)

Part of the information contained in the above lines is in the form of an implicit play on words. We have already seen that the river to the north of Aeaea was called the Helion, after Circe's father, the god of the sun. By saying that Dawn came as Odysseus was preparing for departure, Homer is in fact telling us that not only was the sun (Helios) rising, but also the tide was rising in the river Helion. As the goddess goes 'to and fro', Homer gives us two encoded sailing directions, the first being: 'the nymph clothed herself in a long white robe, finely-woven and beautiful, and about her waist she cast a fair girdle of gold, and upon her head she put a veil', which is a perfect picture of Virgo, the zodiacal sign indicating a southeasterly direction, and as Circe precedes the men to the ship, this is clearly the way to go. But there is also a ram (Ares) in the ship, thus indicating a westerly direction. The resolution of this apparent contradiction is simple: Odysseus and his men first sail southeast, helped by the rising tide and the north wind for six hours, then sail west with the falling tide and the current of the river Acheron (Schelde) for another six hours, arriving at their destination just after sunset (see Map 12 at the end of the previous chapter). The voyage takes place in early spring, when the days are already slightly longer than the nights, thus lasting about twelve hours for a distance of about 120 km, which corresponds to a reasonable average speed for a sailing vessel. Homer indicates the place where they beach the ship as being by 'deep-flowing Oceanus, at the edge of the earth', which must have been near present-day Vlissingen, while the 'stream of Oceanus' designated the broad tidal waters of the Westerschelde.

Already the Greek geographer Strabo wondered how Odysseus could '*leave* the riverstream of Oceanus while still *going to* Oceanus', as he rightly pointed out that 'it is not possible for a man to leave the whole and still be in the whole'.[2] Homer's text is quite puzzling indeed for an ancient Greek unfamiliar with the Ocean and the movement of the tides in an estuary. However, for someone knowing that Odysseus was travelling in Zeeland, Homer's lines are not contradictory at all. Map 12 clearly shows that Odysseus, on his way to Hades (the island of Walcheren) sailed down the tidal waters of the Acheron, several miles wide, (the Westerschelde), described by the poet as 'the riverstream of Oceanus', in the direction of the open sea, called 'Oceanus', to beach his ship at 'the edge of the earth' near 'deep-flowing Oceanus' close to the present port of Vlissingen. Where he disembarked the sacrificial rams, the beach is still called 'Rammekens' (Flock of rams). For the ewes, Homer employs the word *'ois'* which is virtually identical to modern Dutch *'ooi'*.

Odysseus' Initiation

Odysseus thus does not take the much shorter North Sea route passing to the west of the islands, not only because this route may be difficult for a vessel sailing in the north to south direction, due to the prevailing southwesterly winds, but also for symbolic reasons, as Gideon explained: 'Odysseus has now to tread the thorny path where his old personality is to die to make place for a new, free man'.[3] To this end, the hero is carried by the rising tide up the river Helion to commence his voyage to the places of initiation into knowledge, and knowledge is enlightenment, symbolized by the rising of the sun, Helios. The moment of his departure is symbolized in the coat of arms of the village of Zonnemaire (Sun-Sea) which also shows the levels of high and low tide (see page 204). But before he can be enlightened, Odysseus must pass the ordeal of the Druidic rites that simulate death. These rites are performed on the island of Hades, where he has to cross the boundaries that separate the world of the living from that of the dead, symbolized by the poet as the 'edge of the earth' (the land of the living) and the 'deep-flowing Oceanus' (the Underworld), respectively. It is for this initiation that he needs the advice of Circe, head of the Gnostic religion.

Homer does not describe these rites in detail as they were certainly secret and known only to those who had actually been through them, but from literature on the subject, we can now have a very good idea of these rituals.[4] The person to be initiated into the Mysteries had to pass through a state that resembled death. This could be achieved through ritual contact with one of the four elements, depending on the place or culture: ordeal by fire (whence the Phoenix symbol), immersion in water (the Celtic custom),[5] air (the Nordic practice of hanging head

Veere

Middelburg

Vlissingen

Zonnemaire

LUCTOR ET EMERGO

Zeeland

Serooskerke

Terneuzen

ZIERIKZEE

Zierikzee

Breskens

Armorial devices from Zeeland, Netherlands, clearly of pagan origin.

down from a tree[6] or the earth (the live burial of Lazarus/Saint John). There were thus various rituals in the Gnostic schools, which were found until the fifth century AD, not only in Greece and the Land of the Pharaohs, but also in western Europe, where Moreau[7] mentions, in addition to the island of Walcheren (here identified as Hades): the isle of Anglesey off the coast of Wales, the isle of Sein in Brittany; the isle of Tombelaine, ('Tomb of Elaine or Hellen') near the Mont-Saint-Michel; Heligoland, in the North Sea near the mouth of the Elbe, the isle of Fehmarn, between Germany and Denmark; the island of Gotland in the Baltic; and Aquilèia, between Venice and Trieste. By choosing islands as places of teaching the Druids and their pupils were less exposed to the relentless warfare on the continent, but there was also a symbolic reason: the Mystery Schools considered themselves as islands of knowledge in the sea of ignorance.[8]

The ancient rites were thus very hard to withstand, and Odysseus' anguish as he wept and asked Circe for guidance (*Od*. X, 501) is understandable. His temporary visit to the kingdom of the dead was comparable to the state of 'clinical death' nowadays being studied in some hospitals, in particular in the United States. But what was the objective of Gnostic initiation? According to Joseph Campbell who described the very similar Vedic Mithra cult performed around 1400 BC in southeastern Europe, 'The mystic was led by degrees to an experience, in his final stage, of the transcendent reality of his own being'.[9] The rites were intended to purify carefully selected candidates of their imperfections and to deliver them from their prejudices and their past errors, before they had access to the higher knowledge required to find the Cosmic Truth. It was believed that the soul of the initiated was immortal and could count on a privileged place in the Other World, as we read in Hesiod's *Homeric Hymns*:

> Happy is he among you upon earth who has seen these mysteries;
> but he who is uninitiated and has no part in them never has lot of
> like good things once he is dead, down in the darkness and gloom.
>
> (Hymn to Demeter, 480-82)

During his stay on the island of Hades, Odysseus was obviously in some kind of second state, because his environment such as the poet describes it does not exist in reality. The eternal darkness, 'never does the bright sun look down . . . but baneful night is spread over wretched mortals' (*Od*. XI, 15) describes the world of the subconscious. The three rivers are also symbolic, as their names suggest: the Periphlegethon (river of Flaming Fire), the Cocytus (river of

Lamentation) and the Styx (the Terrifying One, river of irrevocable oaths by which the gods swore). The rock at the meeting place of the rivers is also imaginary for there are only dunes in the area, so that Odysseus is able to dig a big hole in the sand with his sword:

> Here Perimedes and Eurylochus held the victims, while I drew my sharp sword from beside my thigh, and dug a pit of a cubit's length this way and that, and around it poured a libation to all the dead, first with milk and honey, thereafter with sweet wine, and in the third place with water, and I sprinkled thereon white barley meal. And I earnestly entreated the powerless heads of the dead, vowing that when I came to Ithaca I would sacrifice in my halls a barren heifer, the best I had, and pile the altar with goodly gifts, and to Teiresias alone would sacrifice separately a ram, wholly black, the goodliest of my flocks. But when with vows and prayers I had made supplication to the tribes of the dead, I took the sheep and cut their throats over the pit, and the dark blood ran forth. Then there gathered from out of Erebus the spirits of those that are dead, brides, and unwedded youths, and toil-worn old men, and tender maidens with hearts yet new to sorrow, and many, too, that had been wounded with bronze-tipped spears, men slain in fight, wearing their blood-stained armour. These came thronging in crowds about the pit from every side, with a wondrous cry; and pale fear seized me.   (*Od.* XI, 23-43)

Hades, in the concrete sense, is thus nothing but a hole in the sand into which Odysseus pours the blood of the sacrificial animals provided by Circe for this ritual. These animals are black, as Homer repeats, because only black animals were offered to the gods and spirits of the Underworld.

Persephone

Now that we have found Hades on the island of Walcheren, where is his wife and niece Persephone? At first, it seemed as if she had disappeared in the Underworld forever, until it finally turned out that she left a trace in the name of the ancient town of Veere (also spelled Veer, Verr or Vere on old maps), which is a port on the northeast coast of the same island. The locals believe that Veere simply means 'ferry' ('*veer*' in Dutch). However, since there are countless island ports having ferry links with other places, but only a single Veere, this explanation of the name can only be correct if it refers to a very particular ferry, in other words: the interpretation is incomplete, the full story being, in my view, the following: Veere owes its name to Persephone via the well-known dialect forms of her name, which were: Phere-phatta and

Pher(r)e-phassa, meaning '(she who) carries doves' which is symbolic language for 'ferries souls' because for the ancients, a particular type of immaculate white dove represented the part of a human being that is ever-lasting: the soul. (This also explains the name of the region near Zierikzee which is called Duiveland, not only meaning 'Land of doves', or 'doveweed', but foremost 'Land of souls'). Persephone was indeed the goddess responsible for sending the souls to Hades in attendance of their resurrection to a new life. For this voyage she embarked them on Charon's boat or 'ferry' just as Isis was believed to send the souls of the dead by boat to the Other World.

Charon's boat can still be seen on the coats of arms of Veere, passing under a shield which hangs between two pillars guarded by warriors armed with clubs and holding snakes in their hands. This phantom ship, which has neither mast nor oars, seems to cross a frontier which must be the dividing line between life and death (see Plate 5). Persephone was often called by her surname Core (Greek *Kore*) which relates to the Dutch *koren* and the English *corn* as she was the goddess of renewal of Nature in springtime in general and the growth of wheat in particular. But even more important was her role in the resurrection of the human soul, as R. Emmanuel has pointed out.[10] Classical mythographers tell us that the young Persephone had a companion who was abducted by Hades while the two girls were having a picnic. The name of her friend, Hercyne (Greek *Herkuna*) has been preserved by the village of Herkinge(n) on the island of Flakkee (Homer's Phulake) to the north. In turn, the town of Veere gave its name to Pheraea ('She from Pherae' or Veere, the Greek alphabet lacking the 'V'), who was a daughter of Aeolus the god of the winds and a granddaughter of Poseidon and Arne, the latter name being preserved by Arnemuiden and Arnestein situated a few miles away from Veere. Pheraea was the mother of the well-known goddess Hecate, whose surname was also 'Pheraea', as she had been brought up by a shepherd from Pherae. Hecate was originally considered a beneficient goddess who was believed to provide fishermen with abundant draughts of fish and people in general with all sorts of riches until later mythographers described her as a rather frightful patron of sorcerers.

On the southern shore of the Scheldemouth, just opposite Vlissingen, we find the little town of Breskens. The suffix '-kens' is derived from the Gothic *kunna*, meaning 'tribe' or 'family' (cognate with English *kin*), while 'Bres' poses a problem as it could be a corruption of either Perse, (via Bers or Bres), a daughter of Oceanus, or Perses, the brother of Circe, if not Perseus, the legendary hero from Argos and ancestor of Heracles, or else Persephone, the wife of Hades.

This dilemma would have remained unsolved if the coats of arms of Breskens had not provided the clue: it shows a two-headed eagle (see page 204) which symbolizes not only vegetation (H. Beyer) but also the kingdom of the Two Worlds (C.G. Jung), both attributes of Persephone. After all, it is not even surprising that Breskens also owes its name to Persephone for the following reason: in antiquity, it was believed that Persephone sent the dead by boat across the river Acheron to Hades as we have just seen. Charon, their ferryman, was an unpleasant old man who made them row the boat themselves, although the trip was already paid for with the obole, a coin they carried under their tongues as a last gift from relatives or friends. The shortest crossing of the Acheron to Hades is exactly there where today a car ferry links Breskens to Vlissingen over the Westerschelde, Homer's Acheron. The souls departing from Breskens arrived where Vlissingen now stands and where also Odysseus came ashore for his temporary visit to Hades. At the time, there was no town here but only 'a level shore and the groves of Persephone, tall poplars and willows that shed their fruit' according to Homer. But the poet does mention the 'Town of the Cimmerians' (*Odyssey*, XI, 4) whose most likely site is present Middelburg, the provincial capital, as it was ideally located on the leeward side of the island with direct access to the sea until last century. The city's arms, which show the gates of Hades and the Phoenix symbol, speak for themselves and confirm that it was always the most important town of the island (see page 204). The ancient Greeks believed that the Cimmerians were a legendary people living somewhere in the extreme west or north of Europe. In fact, they were a people that really existed and whose name has been preserved by a town and confluent of the Rhine in Germany: Simmern. That Zeeland was inhabited long before Homer's time has been confirmed by archeologists who have found traces of human settlement here as early as 7000 BC.

Other Clues

As we know, Hades, the Underworld, was guarded by several monsters (which symbolize the monsters in our own subconscious), such as Cerberus and Campe (Greek *Kampe*) who can also be retraced on the island of Walcheren. At the entrance of the port of Veere, there is a medieval building called the 'Campveersetoren' meaning 'Tower of the monster Campe'[11] which looks out over an adjacent island across the waters where we find Kamperland (Land of Kampe) which, on older maps is shown as Campe(n), after the female monster which was slain by Zeus. Also the terrifying three-headed dog Cerberus, the best known among the guardians of Hades, is still recognizable in the name of the village of Serooskerke (via Sérbrus and Sérwrs) and the adjacent hamlet of Hondgem (*hond* = dog), both situated in the vicinity of Veere. It was Heracles, the archetypal initiate, who killed Cerberus during one of his Twelve Labours, the descent into Hades. The dog's three heads symbolize, according to Alice Bailey: desire, sensation and good intentions, the latter 'paving the way to hell' as we still say.[12] The three dog heads figure until today on the coats of arms of Serooskerke, two on the upper half of the shield with the third underneath, as the latter represents 'desire' which is the underlying impulse of both 'sensation' and 'good intentions' (see page 204). On the adjacent island of Schouwen (Aeaea) there is a second village called Serooskerke which happens to have exactly the same arms. There can therefore be no doubt that 'Cerberus' became 'Seroos' over time.

Once the rites in Hades are accomplished, Odysseus returns to the isle of Circe, this time via the North Sea route to the west of the islands:

> Straightway then I went to the ship and bade my comrades themselves to embark, and to loose the stern cables. So they went on board quickly and sat down upon the benches. And the ship was borne down the stream Oceanus by the swelling flood, first with our rowing, and afterwards the wind was fair.   (*Od.* XI, 636–640)

> Now after our ship had left the stream of the river Oceanus and had come to the wave of the broad sea, and the Aeaean isle, where is the dwelling of early Dawn and her dancing-lawns, and the risings of the sun, there on our coming we beached our ship on the sands, and ourselves went forth upon the shore of the sea, and there we fell asleep, and waited for the bright Dawn.   (*Od.* XII, 1-7)

We can see from Map 12 at the end of Chapter 10 that Odysseus and his men had to row from Vlissingen far into the open sea before hoisting sail to take advantage of the prevailing southwest wind and the tide that runs in the south to north direction for six hours and then turns and runs in the opposite direction. But the voyage of Odysseus from the 'dark' island of Walcheren (Hades) to the 'island of the sunrise', Schouwen (Aeaea) also has a symbolic meaning: the initiate passes from ignorance (darkness) to knowledge (light). This both real and symbolic voyage was a common feature of all ancient Mysteries.

The morning after their return to Aeaea, they burn the body of their young comrade Elpenor, who died in a fall just before their departure from Circe's island, and bury it on the furthermost promontory of the island. Today marine charts show a submerged sandbank before the west coast of Schouwen, called Banjaard, (or Banigert on older charts), the meaning of which is 'bone guard', so this could be where Odysseus and his men built the burial mound over Elpenor, who symbolized Odysseus' own old personality before the initiation.

Travelling around Zeeland in search of clues, I found several indications that a pre-Christian initiation site must indeed have existed near the town of Vlissingen. By following the boulevard running along the coast from the old port to the northwest, which was the direction taken by Odysseus ('we went beside the stream of Oceanus until we came to the place of which Circe had told us'), there is after about two kilometers a beach called Nollenstrand, edged by dunes covered by trees, the Nollenbos.

The word *nol* meant 'zero' in Middle Dutch but before it was used as a mathematical concept it was known to the ancients as an esoteric notion, the 'sacred circle' symbolizing the cyclic renewal of nature. In several places in the Netherlands, whether near the sea or in forests, there is a 'nol', which was the place for Druidic rites, a series of stones arranged in a circle as Homer confirms: 'the elders were sitting upon polished stones in the sacred circle' (Greek *hieros kuklos, Il.* XVIII, 504).

A few hundred metres from the 'nol', a little inland, I was surprised to see a road sign pointing the way to Dishoek (Dis Corner or Place of Dis), which is the name of a hamlet and a public park behind the dunes of the 'nol'. None of the local residents questioned about this name knew who Dis was, which is just as well, as they may sleep less soundly if they knew that they lived near to the gates of Hell! For Dis is none other but Hades, the god of the Kingdom of the Dead, but also of Life through Rebirth. This is confirmed by Cicero (see Appendix Note 21, Cicero on the nature of the gods) and Caesar, who writes that, 'the Celts believed that they all descended from Father Dis, claiming that it was the tradition preserved by the Druids'.[13] (Knowing that the Trojans had the same religion as the Achaeans, it is not surprising that there is also a town called Diss in East Anglia). It must have been here on the 'Beach of the Sacred Circle' (Nollenstrand) near Dis Corner (Dishoek) that Odysseus had his ritual contact with death through the dangerous Gnostic baptism.

This would explain why the name of Odysseus is perpetuated in the town of Vlissingen (Ulyssingen). But the name Asciburgium mentioned by Tacitus has disappeared, unless it is preserved by an avenue (Assumburg) between Dishoek and a peripheral town called Souburg ('under-burg') which is most likely to be another reference to the Underworld.

The Grail

Thus far, we have found many clues of various sorts – such as place-names, tides, sailing directions, travel times and a mention by Tacitus – which confirm the presence of Odysseus in Zeeland, but how can we be absolutely sure that Vlissingen is named after the hero of the Odyssey? The town is not evocative of a very ancient past as it was rebuilt many times in history. Because of its strategic situation at the entrance of the Schelde river, which gives access to the port of Antwerp, Vlissingen was destroyed in almost every major European war. In these circumstances, the only evidence of Odysseus' visit to remain intact over a long time span would be the coats of arms, which I hoped to be of pre-Christian origin, as is the case with those of several other municipalities in Zeeland. The first impression of the arms was rather disappointing, as it merely shows a white vase with a gold mask. While I was still in doubt about its heraldic significance, my wife was already convinced that it symbolized the Grail and for good reason: it turned out that the local population calls the vase simply 'the bottle' because of an ancient legend about Saint Willibrord having 'twelve beggars' drink from his bottle, the contents of which did not diminish.[14]

This story leads us into the realm of the supernatural and has indeed much in common with that of the Grail, which is probably the most ancient, abstract and elusive symbol in European civilization. In the Christian version, the Grail was a very popular theme for medieval authors like Chrétien de Troyes and Wolfram von Eschenbach. In the Middle Ages, the Holy Grail was believed to contain the blood of Christ, thus symbolizing the Divine Grace given to His disciples. But it is well known that the theme of the Grail is much older than Christianity, its origin being lost in the mists of time. For the Celts, the Grail was a vase with magic powers, such as the cauldron of the god Dagda in Ireland. If ever there was a Grail in the physical sense, it might have looked like the Danish vase of Gundestrup, dating from the second century BC, which was used for initiation ceremonies, judging by its decorations (see Plate 6). But ever since C.G. Jung, the father of the psychology of the subconscious, the Grail is considered to be the symbol of interiorization leading to communication with the divinity which is simultaneously in ourselves and in Heaven. The vase, which is open at the top, perfectly symbolizes both interiorization and communication. However, the most important aspect of the Grail is not the unattainable object itself, but the *quest* for it, which requires a very difficult spiritual voyage of the initiates. We may therefore assimilate the quest of the Grail with an initiation experience as J. Markale confirms: 'it is certain that all versions of the quest are initiation stories'.[15] Conversely, the *Odyssey*, being an initiation story, is clearly a quest for the Grail, thus explaining the vase on the arms of Vlissingen. The *Odyssey* is therefore the oldest epic about the Grail, which was to be found exactly where, in the Bronze Age, the initiation rites were performed: on the Nolle beach between Dishoek and Vlissingen, the latter name meaning: 'the Rebirth of Ulysses', after its founder, the archetypal initiate of Homer's time.

It is not surprising to find the Grail also in nearby Middelburg as this town was the centre of Hades' island. (Plate 8) The city was originally built in a perfect circle, which is still evident today from the layout of the streets. In the eleventh century, a large abbey was built in the town centre around a sculpture of the Grail standing in the large inner courtyard. The present sculpture is modern, as the abbey was destroyed by air raids in the Second World War, but since rebuilt. The Grail's transition from a Gnostic to a Christian symbol is described by Paul Le Cour, according to whom the first and last patrons of the Grail were Poseidon and St John, who were considered as the patrons of the initiates.[16] This provides us not only with the explanation of why, of all Olympians, it is precisely Poseidon, god of the Ocean and the subconscious whose golden statue is maintained on top of the town hall of Zierikzee, once the site of Circe's Mystery school, but also why the tallest church tower of Middelburg, which was built close to the Grail, is called Sint Jan (St John).

The Key to the Underworld

In the figurative sense, Hades, the Underworld, is simply our own subconscious, source of our creative and destructive forces.[17,18] The goddess Circe held the key to the Underworld which gives access to our subconscious. According to an old tradition, the three bits of the key each had a different colour: red, white and blue, which have been retained in the national flags of the countries in northwest Europe – the United Kingdom, France, the Netherlands, Norway and Iceland – which are situated on the ancient Sea of Helle or Hellespont, symbol of the Underworld and the subconscious for their distant ancestors, whether they were of Celtic or Nordic religion. According to Guillaume Postel, an initiate of the sixteenth century, this 'key' represents a doctrinal synthesis of the occult sciences. The bits of the key, as completed by Eliphas Levi,[19] are illustrated on page 213.

The symbolism of the key is as old as the object itself which apparently was already part of everyday life in the Bronze Age as we learn from Homer that Penelope 'climbed the high stairway to her chamber and took the bent key in her strong hand – a goodly key of

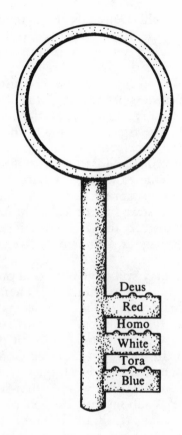

Deus
Red
Homo
White
Tora
Blue

bronze, and on it was a handle of ivory' (*Od.* XXI, 5-7).

It is well known that the ancients attached great importance to self-knowledge, i.e. knowledge of the subconscious. We are all familiar with the expression 'know thyself' (Greek *gnôthi séauton*), and we often need the 'key' (the knowledge) to solve a problem. The rites that were performed at Dishoek, the entrance to the Underworld, were therefore certainly intended to lead to the rebirth of the personality through knowledge acquired after contact with the subconscious.

Delphi and Delft

In addition to Aeaea and Hades, there was a third sacred island in the region, Pytho (Greek, *Puthon*), today called Putten, which gave its

213

name to the oracle at Delphi. Delphi itself was the old name for Delft, a town to the north of the Rhine mouth. At first, this may seem surprising, especially when we think of the famous oracle, where intoxicating vapours emanating from a fissure in the rock put the sibyl in a state of trance. But such a place never existed in reality as it is an allegory of a priestess consulting the 'emanations' of her subconscious.[20] There is further circumstantial evidence that Delft was called Delphi in the Bronze Age: according to the ancients, the port of Delphi was called Kirra, which corresponds to present-day Kralingen, a district of nearby Rotterdam. Moreover, Delphi was considered to be the 'navel of the world' where the link was between Heaven and Earth. This link is still symbolically preserved by the coats of arms of Delft, which merely shows a straight vertical column, linking the very bottom of the shield to the very top. At some later date, not only a town in Greece, but also a village in Connemara, Ireland, would be called Delphi by the Celts.

The sceptical reader may still have doubts about the explanation of certain geographical names in Zeeland. There is of course the possibility of pure coincidence, though this seems unlikely because, of old, places were certainly named in a religious context. The fact that many names are clearly Germanic and not Celtic or Greek is explained by later occupation of this land by Celticized Germanic peoples, who simply translated the names already existing, as is still common practice in bilingual countries like Belgium, where, for instance, the same town is called Mons by the Walloons and Bergen by the Flemings, both names meaning 'mountains'. (It should be noted in passing that people living in the plains of northern Europe call anything higher than a moleheap a mountain, and so does Homer). In conclusion, we may say that Zeeland was the sacred land of the Celts and that Walcheren was indeed the Hades of the ancients, although the visitor will find nothing on this charming island to be frightened of.

Hades

Notes

1 Tacitus, *Germania*, 3, translated by H. Mattingly, Penguin Classics.
2 Strabo, *Geography*, Book A, 1, 7.
3 E. Gideon, *Homerus, Zanger der Kelten*, p. 114.
4 See Bibliography.
5 W. Rutherford, *The Druids*, Aquarian Press, Wellingborough, 1983, p. 63.
6 R. Boyer and E. Lot-Falck, *Les religions de l'Europe du Nord*, Fayard-Denoël, Paris, 1974, p. 565.
7 M. Moreau, *La tradition celtique dans l'art roman*, Le Courrier du Livre, Paris, 1975.
8 J-P. Persigout, *Dictionnaire de mythologie celtique*, ed. du Rocher, Monaco, 1985.
9 J. Campbell, *Occidental Mythology*, Penguin London, 1987, p. 256.
10 R. Emmanuel, *Pleins feux sur la Grèce antique*, Dervy-Livres, Paris, 1982, p. 260.
11 'Veer' in 'Campveersetoren' is derived from the substantive *pher(os)* = monster, not from the verb *pherein* = to carry, as in the name of Veere itself as we saw above.
12 Alice A. Bailey, *The Labours of Hercules*, Lucis Trust, 1981.
13 J. Caesar, *The Conquest of Gaul*, VI, 18.
14 Willibrord was a British evangelist of the Low Countries (658–739) whose tomb is in Echternach, Luxemburg.
15 J. Markale, *Le Graal*, ed. Retz, Paris, 1982, p. 257.
16 P. Le Cour, *L'Evangile ésothérique de Saint Jean*, Dervy-Livres, Paris, 1987, p. 191.
17 P. Diel, *Le Symbolisme dans la Mythologie Grecque*, Payot, Paris, 1966.
18 W. Bauer et al., *Lexikon der Symbole*, Fourier, Wiesbaden, 1980, p. 148.
19 E. Levi, *The Mysteries of the Qabalah*, Aquarian Press, Wellingborough, 1984.
20 Paul Le Cour, op. cit.

12

Circe
(Nehalennia)
in Zeeland

There are very few remains of the Bronze Age in Zeeland, which is unfortunate, but not surprising in a region that has been devastated by wars and submerged by the sea over large areas on many occasions. It is nevertheless possible, as we saw in Chapter 10, that the prehistoric foundation stones of the Sion (or Syon) monastery were those of Circe's house, for the early Christians preferred to build their temples on the sites of the pagan rites that they replaced. There are no other remains of Bronze Age temples for the simple reason that the places of worship consisted of a number of big stones arranged in a 'sacred' circle and the linguistic link between 'Circe' and 'circle' has already been noted (Part II, Chapter 3). Ceremonies were held in the open air, for the people of the time were profoundly attached to the nature that surrounded them, as borne out by Homer's works.

By contrast, there are many reminders of the Roman era: various objects, traces of habitation, foundations of fortifications (castelli) and the remains of several temples, the first of which was discovered in 1647, when the sea was whipped up by a severe storm that swept away the dunes near Domburg on the island of Walcheren, exposing a sanctuary dedicated, according to the Latin inscriptions on the votive altars, to the goddess Nehalennia. The slabs of the forecourt of the temple of Domburg were last seen on the occasion of a particularly low tide in 1736. The traces of many trees indicated that this temple had been surrounded by a wood according to Celtic custom. On some of the altars there is also the image of the sea god Poseidon (Neptune) with his trident. A second important discovery was made quite by chance in 1970, when a fisherman hauled in two stone altars from a depth of twenty-five metres off Colijnsplaat in the Eastern Schelde close to Zierikzee. These, too, were from the Roman era and also dedicated to Nehalennia. Since then, more than hundred altars and three statues

Votive altars (second century AD) dedicated to Nehalennia, identified as Circe.

have been found in the same place and these, or copies of them, are now to be seen in the Archeological Museum of Leyden and the Zeeuws Museum in Middelburg. Several of these altars have an image of Nehalennia in a niche (see page 217). She was worshipped not only by the local people, but also by seafarers, Roman traders and by people from Germany and France, who had engraved their names on the stones. Judging by the many coins of different origins, Zeeland was involved in flourishing maritime trade with the Rhineland, England and the coastal regions of the Roman empire.

Nehalennia is a particularly mysterious goddess, for her name does not appear in the Celtic, Nordic or Roman pantheons, or in the encyclopedias. Recent literature has rejected a number of tentative explanations of her name without proposing a credible alternative. Under these circumstances, I would suggest that 'Nehalennia' means 'Initiatrice' as 'Nehal' comes from the Greek *ne-elos*, meaning 'neophyte', while *'ennia'* is simply the Greek number nine, symbol of perfection for the ancients. Nehalennia is therefore the goddess responsible for the initiation of neophytes to knowledge which is the way to perfection. But education requires the presence of a school, and as we have seen, there was indeed a Gnostic school in Zeeland, and Circe was its supreme authority. It is therefore reasonable to assume that Nehalennia and Circe are one and the same, Nehalennia being the name or title by which Circe was locally known in the Roman era. It is likely that by that time the name of Circe designated a place of worship or 'church' in Germanic languages, through the dialect form of her name, Kirke. This would explain why so many villages in Zeeland have a name ending in '-kerke' such as Aagtekerke, Biggekerke, Grijpskerke, Meliskerke, Serooskerke, and so on.

Nehalennia is often portrayed with her foot resting on the prow of a boat, with underneath the letters DB which, according to de Grave, meant 'Dood Baere' ('bier of the dead'), a reference to Charon's boat which took the souls to Hades.[1] On the bas–reliefs, Nehalennia is often accompanied by a dog, an animal that in mythology is associated with the Underworld, although it is also man's friend and protector who was believed to have healing powers, judging by the many prehistoric ex-votos of dogs found near medicinal springs in France and England.[2] For the latter reason, the dog was also associated with Asclepius (or Aesculapius) a god of healing, who was originally a god–mole, who has also left his trace in Zierikzee, as we shall see shortly.

Nehalennia is also often portrayed with a basket of fruit, especially pomegranates, symbol of fertility, but also of the afterlife and for this purpose given by Hades to Persephone. In ancient cultures fertility goddesses were as important as the gods of the sun and the sea as the survival of man depends upon the fertility of his land, his flocks and himself, while the sun and the sea (water) make a vital contribution to the growth of plants and animals. The fact that life would not exist at all without water, whether coming from the sea, lakes, rivers or wells, explains why the Celts cast their offerings to the gods into water. On the abstract level, the fertility of the human mind, its creativity, springs from the subconscious, which is the reason why the ancients considered water, and in particular the sea, to be the symbol of the subconscious.

The effigy of Poseidon, god of the ocean, is found in various places in present-day Zeeland. There are golden statues of him and his son Triton on the towers of Zierikzee and Middelburg town halls, complete with their tridents (see Plate 4b). At first, one wonders what 'Greek' gods are doing in Zeeland, and assume that they were adopted for decorative purposes during the Renaissance. But since Poseidon's image has been found on Nehalennia's votive altars dating from the very beginning of our era, it is clear that he was already very much at home in Zeeland in the Roman era. But was he already worshipped there more than a thousand years earlier, in Homer's time?

The answer is affirmative, for several reasons. First, let us suppose for a moment that the temples built in Zeeland were of Roman origin. In this case, they would have been dedicated to an 'imported' Roman goddess, instead of Nehalennia, who was totally unknown to the Romans. Besides, the archeologists state categorically that, not-withstanding the Roman style of the statues, Nehalennia was not a Roman goddess but a local one, for she sometimes wears shoes, not sandals, and a short cape, unknown on Roman statues, but still part of the traditional dress of the Zeeland women. Furthermore, on the altars, Nehalennia is often seen with other gods, not only Poseidon (Neptune), but also Zeus (Jupiter) Heracles (Hercules) and Nike (Victory). On one statue she wears a sun wheel, a symbol already known in the Bronze Age or else a sun disc, further clues to indicate that she could be Circe, whose father was Helius, the sun god. She shares this symbol with Zeus, who was worshipped under this name in Celtic lands, as we have seen. As for Heracles, we know that he was worshipped on the Atlantic coast, especially in Germany and Spain, before the arrival of the Romans. As regards Nike, Victory, it is very likely that she was worshipped in Zeeland before the Roman era, for she symbolized not only victory in war, but also the victory of life over death, an extremely important facet, for the pair Circe-Hades in Zeeland was concerned precisely with rebirth into a second life, judging by the words of Circe: 'Rash men, who have gone down alive to the house of Hades to meet death twice, while other men die but once' (*Od.* XII, 21). As regards Poseidon, he was the god of the ocean, 'the river that surrounds the world' according to the ancient Greeks, meaning the real ocean with its tides, its dark colour and its enormous waves – the Atlantic. There can therefore be no doubt that Poseidon was already worshipped in the Bronze Age on the Atlantic seaboard, where he watched the battles of the Trojan War from a piece of high ground (*Il.* XIII, 10). Besides, Poseidon has left many other traces in northern Europe (see Map 12 in Chapter 10, and Maps 15 and 17 at the end of Part IV).

Nehalennia must have been a goddess of the very highest rank, for on all the votive altars found so far there is a shell over her head, which is an exclusive symbol that she shares only with the greatest gods of the pantheon, such as Here, Aphrodite, Apollo and Heracles. The question then arises how a local goddess could count among the coryphae? The inevitable answer must again be that it is because Nehalennia is Circe, symbol of the Earth Mother, the Great Initiatrice and the highest authority of the Gnostic religion.

Homer calls Circe the 'dread goddess of human speech' (*Od.* XI, 8), an expression that may make us smile today, but knowing that the poet always chooses his words very carefully, we must try to find an explanation for this curious epithet.

Circe was certainly not a 'witch' as is often believed, and Homer never calls her a sorceress as he knew of course that she was a far more important personality: the symbolic head of the Gnostic religion in Europe in the Bronze Age.

Her Mystery school in Zierikzee was a place of teaching comparable to a school or university of our days, the main difference being that science and religion were inseparable, because research into the functioning of the world that surrounds us was considered as an effort to discover the metaphysical laws of the universe which are of divine making.

Just as in schools and universities today, the Mystery schools counted many drop-outs. Caesar recounts that the Druids had many pupils but that very few made it to the end. The reason for this was not only that the teachings in the higher grades were increasingly difficult, but also because the final degree – the initiation at Hades – was a dangerous ritual. No wonder then that Circe was a 'dread goddess of human speech', the latter epithet being a reference to the Word which, as we have seen in the myth of Io, confers consciousness to human beings, which is a prerequisite to discovering the transcendental reality behind the apparent world.

Symbols and Numbers

But there is no initiation without symbolism, which is the key to the Truth and at the same time the means to hide the Truth of the Mysteries from the profane. Fortunately, much of the symbolism has been preserved by the coats of arms of several municipalities in Zeeland which are manifestly of pre-Christian origin. The arms of both the town of Zierikzee and the province of Zeeland still remind us of the existence of the Gnostic school here, for they show the water below symbolizing the subconscious, with a lion emerging from it that represents the power and domination obtained through knowledge, this last usually symbolized by a key which has unfortunately disappeared from these armorial devices but has been retained in others such as that of the town of Terneuzen (see page 204). The arms of Zierikzee are crowned by a tetrad which is composed of a cross and a square and, as the word indicates, associated with the number four (Greek *tetra*). This number has several meanings for the Gnostics. Thus, four stages of initiation lead the neophyte through the four gates that he must pass on the mystic path, each gate corresponding to one of the four elements, in the order: air, fire, water, earth. The tetrad also encompasses the universe in its entirety and the four paths that man must take to understand both the physical and spiritual worlds.[3] It also symbolizes the four corners of the earth from which the four winds blow, and the four great Kingdoms that embrace the history of the world in the pre-Messianic era.[4] The tetrad is also connected with the tetraktys (the series of the first four numbers whose sum is ten), associated by Pythagoras with the oracle at Delphi, and the system of numbering called in the Qabalah (the Jewish esoteric tradition) the ten Sefiroth.

It appears that all numbers have their importance for our research, because the map of Zeeland and of the area northwards to Delft shows that the numbers from one to ten – and even beyond – are found in place-names. It is impossible to know whether all these names existed in Homer's time, but the fact that there are so many villages whose names begin with a number is just one more small piece of evidence that Zeeland was once a Gnostic centre and a sacred land for the Celts, as in all Gnostic systems numbers are considered to be the most profound expression of Divine Wisdom. Plato even thought that numbers led to the highest degree of knowledge and to both cosmic and internal harmony. In our era of computers, we tend to forget that each number had an esoteric significance for the ancients. It would take too long to describe all of them here, but let us nevertheless consider the number nine, which is most frequent in Homer's works, often with an esoteric meaning. Nine being a triple triad it is the holy number of renewal and perfection. As nine is the last digit in the series, it announces both an end and a new beginning. For example, we are all born after nine months of gestation, birth itself being the end of one phase in life and the beginning of another. It was also thought that there were nine caverns in the subconscious, corresponding to the creativity of the nine Muses, who were born of Zeus and Mnemosyne after nine nights of love. It seems that there were nine steps on the ladder of initiation as Odysseus was away for nine years after the end of the Trojan War, although the more usual number was seven, corresponding to the seven metals, the highest degree being associated with the only non-corrosive, ever-lasting metal: gold. Homer evokes this ladder of initiation in the story of young Elpenor, who, on the morning of the departure to the island of Hades, missed the steps in Circe's house and fell to his death:

> He heard the noise and the bustle of his comrades as they moved about, and suddenly sprang up, and forgot to go to the long ladder that he might come down again, but fell headlong from the roof, and his neck was broken away from the spine, and his spirit went down to the house of Hades. (*Od.* X, 556-560)

To the initiates among Homer's public, the story was crystal clear: the ladder symbolizes the link between the sky and the earth. The example best known to modern readers is, of course, Jacob's Ladder. Going down a ladder that leads underground symbolizes the descent into the depths of the subconscious in search of esoteric knowledge. Climbing a ladder symbolizes the progress made in earthly, esoteric and divine knowledge.[5] In the *Odyssey*, young Elpenor's falling to his death is simply Odysseus' *alter ego*, his own old personality which he had to abandon to become a new personality after his initiation on the island of Hades.

The number nine has a similar significance in cultures as diverse as that of the Maya or the Chinese and, of course, of the Nordic neighbours of the Celts who also lived on the shores of the Helle Sea. In the books of Nordic mythology, we learn how the god Odin (Wodan) had to suffer himself, hanging from the Tree of Knowledge for nine nights, for his initiation into the Nordic writing, the Runes (the name itself meaning 'Mysteries'):

> I [Odin] know that I hung
> From the tree whipped by winds
> Nine whole nights through
> Injured by a spear

Circe in Zeeland

And given to Odinn
Myself to myself given
. . .
I picked up the runes
Howling picked them up
(Hávamál, poem V)

Thus in the old Nordic tradition knowledge had also to be obtained through confrontation with the self, through suffering and contact with death, here through hanging head down from an oak for nine nights, 'to better understand the roots of the Tree of Knowledge'. Like the Celts, the Nordics also believed that Hell, which they also called Hela or Niflheim, had nine compartments.

In the centre of Zierikzee there is a street sign with the name Mol (the Dutch word for mole), which is another reminder of the ancient history of this place. The mole was associated with the forces of Mother Earth and the initiator into the mysteries of the earth, an initiation which, once attained, preserves one or cures illnesses. Precisely for this reason, Asclepius, god of healing, is thought to have been originally a god-mole. From the physical level, that of the animal of the fields, the symbol leads at the spiritual level to the master who guides the spirit through the darkness of the subconscious and cures it of its passions and troubles.[6] There is also a 'rue Mole' in the centre of the old town of Troyes (France), which I suggested in Part II, Chapter 11 was ancient Mycenae, the name meaning 'Mysteries-on-the-Seine' and hence an important centre of initiation. It is very likely indeed that the Dutch 'Mol' and the French 'Mole' are one and the same word. The street name 'Mol' in Zierikzee is yet another indication that we are on the track of Circe, the Initiatrice into the secrets of the Earth, and more particularly of the subconscious, the realm of Hades.

As can be seen on a thirteenth-century plan of Zierikzee (see page 224), this small town had no less that six monasteries, a Beguine convent with a church, and a basilica whose tower was originally planned to reach a height of more than 200 metres, by far the highest ever conceived for a church anywhere. The only possible explanation for the Christian Church being present in such force here is that this town was earlier the most important religious centre of Europe in the Bronze and Iron Ages, which must have been in regular contact with Britain. Were this not the case, the Achaean army would have assembled their fleet for the attack on Troy in the Netherlands, which is so much closer to England than is Denmark, where we discovered Aulis (see Part II, Chapter 15). The fact that the army commanders

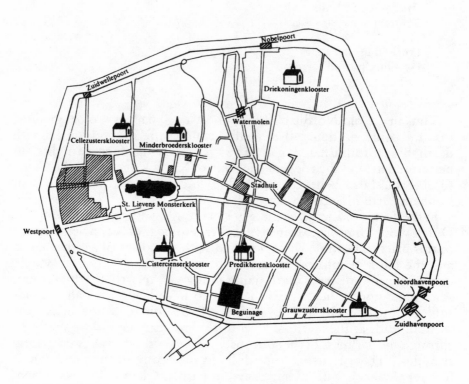

A plan of Zierikzee in the thirteenth century when the town was a stronghold of Christianity, with a huge basilica, three monasteries, three convents and a beguinage.

opted for Denmark to avoid detection by the enemy is a further, indirect, indication that the Rhine delta was the religious centre of all the Celts in Homer's time, whether they lived in England or on the Continent.

It would appear that Zeeland was at the same time the cradle of the Celts. Not only is their name cognate with that of the river Schelde (Scelt on old maps) as some researchers already suspected, but more importantly there was, until a few centuries ago, also a village in the delta named after the legendary mother of the Celts: Galatea ('Milkwhite') who was a daughter of Nereus, the seagod (see Map 12, Key No. 46). The fact that her name is mentioned by Homer, who calls her, very respectfully, 'glorious Galatea' (*Il.* XVIII, 45), confirms that the poet's works are of Celtic origin. What is even more surprising is that Galatea was Achilles' aunt. (see Appendix, Note 25, 'The Origin of the Celtic Peoples' page 360). The peoples founded by Galatea's sons. Galas, Celtus and Illyrius subsequently migrated to other parts of Europe and the Near East: the Gauls to Gallia (France), Galicia (Spain), Galicia (Poland), Galatia (Turkey) and Galilea (Near-East). The Celts moved to England, southern Scandinavia, Germany and northern Italy (Latinus being a legendary son of Odysseus and Circe), while the Illyrians settled in Yugoslavia and Greece, the only country where Homer's orally transmitted epics would survive in writing.

Notes

1 C.J. de Grave, *République des Champs Elysées ou monde ancien*, P.F. de Goesin-Verhaeghe, Gent, 1806.
2 A. Hondius-Crone, *The Temple of Nehalennia at Domburg*, Meulenhoff, Amsterdam, 1955.
3 J. Chevalier and A. Gheerbrant, *Dictionnaire des Symboles*, Laffont, Jupiter, Paris, 1982.
4 The Bible alludes to these significations in Daniel 2:37 and 7:17 and in Apocalypse 7:1 and 20:8.
5 J. Chevalier and A. Gheerbrant, op. cit.
6 J. Chevalier and A. Gheerbrant, op. cit.

13

The Tin Route

(Sirens, Scylla and Charybdis, Thrinacia)

After his visit to Hades, Odysseus returns to Circe to report his experiences, then Circe gives him instructions for the next stage of the voyage, making it clear to him that there are many dangers still to be faced, 'you may yet reach Ithaca, though in evil plight' (*Od.* XII, 138), and explaining in detail how to deal with some of the dangers. First, he has to resist the song of the Sirens, the two temptresses so dangerous to seafarers, then pass Scylla and Charybdis, two rocks with a dangerous whirlpool between them, to go to Thrinacia, the isle of Helios, the sun god, whose cattle must on no account be harmed, for fear of dire consequences.

Although this new series of trials seems even more enigmatic than the first, it turns out that in fact they contain hidden information about one of the most important sea trades of Homer's day. Odysseus left Troy and sailed from the Wash but, about eighteen months later, he is almost back where he started. In order to return home to Ithaca he once again has to sail through the Dover Straits and down the Channel. We have seen that on the first occasion he sailed to Ismarus (Finistere) to take vengeance on the Cicones. The voyage through the Channel was uneventful and nothing is said about it, but we can assume that the ships kept fairly close to the French coast to give themselves plenty of sea-room to the north in case a storm should blow up from the southwest. This time, however, we shall see that Odysseus, following Circe's instructions, takes the more dangerous route along the south coast of England all the way to Land's End. Just off Land's End are the Scilly Isles, which the Greeks, according to Herodotus,[1] called the Kassiterides, from *kassiteron* meaning 'tin', for this is where they obtained their supplies of the metal. As we have seen, (Chapter 1 in this section), tin was absolutely vital in the Bronze Age and virtually the only source of supply was Cornwall. It is likely therefore that the part of the Odyssey that describes the dangers of the Sirens, Scylla and Charybdis and Thrinacia is at the same time a description, to those who knew how to decode it, of the sea route leading to the tin mines.

A first clue of an occult nature that might indicate that we are about to sail on the tin route is the mere fact that it is Circe who shows the way. In order to reach Circe's island, Odysseus had to sail northeast, following the sign of Sagittarius, but Circe herself is also associated with this same sign, and so is tin. This could be coincidence, but the more one studies Homer the more one is impressed by the way that every detail counts and that all the different levels of meaning are woven together in a web like that of Circe: 'a great imperishable web, such as is the handiwork of goddesses, finely-woven and beautiful, and glorious.'

The description of this route has been wrapped in mysterious stories, perhaps to prevent competitors from understanding if they should hear Celtic bards or seafarers quoting Homer's lines, for competition was fierce for this commodity. Even a statue of the Pharaoh Pepi (2300 BC), made in an early bronze, contains tin from Cornwall, as was determined from the traces of other substances typical of Cornish tin that had not been removed by the primitive refining technique.

As we shall see, however, the three adventures that Odysseus has to experience after leaving the isle of Circe – the encounter with the Sirens, Scylla and Charybdis, and the isle of Helios, not only describe the tin route, but also and simultaneously describe the 'near death' experience of Odysseus during his initiation. Homer thus tells us once again in esoteric fashion about the initiation of his hero, but the message hidden in this series of adventures could have been understood only by the initiated themselves in Homer's time. Thanks to recent research into clinical death and the near death experience, it is now possible to reconstitute and understand the double meaning of these stories, even though the concept of clinical death did not exist in the Bronze Age. In Homer's time, death was considered to be a state close to sleep and, conversely, sleep was considered to be a kind of death, and in ancient mythology Hypnos and Thanatos (Sleep and Death) were twin brothers, as Homer himself reminds us: 'the twin brethren, Sleep and Death' (Il. XVI, 672), and: 'sweet sleep fell upon his eyelids, an unawakening sleep, most sweet, and most like to death' (Od. XIII, 79–80).

Although Circe gives Odysseus very detailed instructions about how to avoid or deal with the dangers on his voyage, she gives no explicit indication of the direction he is to take. However, we now know that in such a case we must look for a direction encoded in the form of a zodiacal sign. Here the direction is given first by the two Sirens, twin sisters, an allusion to the sign of Gemini, indicating a southwesterly direction, and subsequently by the insistence on the importance of Helios' cattle grazing on the isle of Thrinacia. Although the translations usually speak of 'kine' or 'cattle', the Greek *bous* also means 'bull', and this gives us our second direction. The sign Taurus indicates a west-south-westerly direction, which is that to take from Zeeland to Cornwall.

Notes
1 Herodotus, *The Histories*, III, 114.

14

The Siren's Song

(The Solent, southern England)

Here is Circe's warning to Odysseus about the first of the trials he will have to face:

> To the Sirens first shalt thou come, who beguile all men whosoever comes to them. Whoso in ignorance draws near to them and hears the Sirens' voice, he nevermore returns, that his wife and little children may stand at his side rejoicing, but the Sirens beguile him with their clear-toned song, as they sit in a meadow, and about them is a great heap of bones of mouldering men, and round the bones the skin is shrivelling. But do thou row past them, and anoint the ears of thy comrades with sweet wax, which thou hast kneaded, lest any of the rest may hear. But if thou thyself hast a will to listen, let them bind thee in the swift ship hand and foot upright in the step of the mast, and let the ropes be made fast at the ends to the mast itself, that with delight thou mayest listen to the voice of the two Sirens. (*Od.* XII, 39-52)

Odysseus follows Circe's instructions scrupulously:

> Meanwhile the well-built ship speedily came to the isle of the two Sirens, for a fair and gentle wind bore her on. Then presently the wind ceased and there was a windless calm, and a god lulled the waves to sleep. But my comrades rose up and furled the sail and stowed it in the hollow ship, and thereafter sat at the oars and made the water white with their polished oars of fir. But I with my sharp sword cut into small bits a great round cake of wax, and kneaded it with my strong hands, and soon the wax grew warm, forced by the strong pressure and the rays of the lord Helios Hyperion. Then I anointed with this the ears of all my comrades in turn; and they bound me in the ship hand and foot, upright in the step of the mast, and made the ropes fast at the ends to the mast itself; and themselves sitting down smote the grey sea with their oars. (*Od.* XII, 166-180)

If we accept the hypothesis of the tin route, then according to Cailleux and Gideon the most logical place to situate the Sirens is the Solent, the strait separating the Isle of Wight from England. This would indeed explain why the wind drops when they are approaching the Sirens. The 'fair wind' they had enjoyed from Circe's island of Aeaea, Schouwen in the Netherlands, must have been easterly, so that they are deprived of the wind from the moment they enter the Solent heading northwest in the direction of the present Southampton. Since Odysseus does not need to sail through the Solent if he is on the way to Cornwall, the only point of this episode seems to be to warn seafarers that the Solent is more dangerous than it looks (because of sandbanks and currents) unless, as some scholars think, some of the Cornish tin was carried overland to Southampton and shipped from there. The fact that Homer does not mention the name Lesbos (Isle of Wight – see Part II, Chapters 4 and 10) confirms the secret nature of the story.

15

Scylla and Charybdis

(Mount's Bay, Cornwall)

Having been able to resist the temptation of the Sirens, thanks to Circe's advice, Odysseus sails on to face the next trial, Scylla and Charybdis, again with Circe's words in mind:

> "'Now on the other path are two cliffs, one of which reaches with its sharp peak to the broad heaven, and a dark cloud surrounds it. This never melts away, nor does clear sky ever surround that peak in summer or in harvest time. No mortal man could scale it or set foot upon the top, not though he had twenty hands and feet; for the rock is smooth, as if it were polished. And in the midst of the cliff is a dim cave, turned to the West, toward Erebus, even where you shall steer your hollow ship, glorious Odysseus. Not even a man of might could shoot an arrow from the hollow ship so as to reach into that vaulted cave. Therein dwells Scylla, yelping terribly. Her voice is indeed but as the voice of a new-born whelp, but she herself is an evil monster, nor would anyone be glad at sight of her, no, not though it were a god that met her. Verily she has twelve feet, all misshapen, and six necks, exceeding long, and on each one an awful head, and therein three rows of teeth, thick and close, and full of black death. . . .'" (*Od.* XII, 73-92)

> "'But the other cliff, thou wilt note, Odysseus, is lower – they are close to each other; thou couldst even shoot an arrow across – and on it is a great fig tree with rich foliage, but beneath this divine Charybdis sucks down the black water. Thrice a day she belches it forth, and thrice she sucks it down terribly. Mayest thou not be there when she sucks it down, for no one could save thee from ruin, no, not the Earth-shaker. Nay, draw very close to Scylla's cliff, and drive thy ship past quickly; for it is better far to mourn six comrades in thy ship than all together.'" (*Od.* XII, 101-110)

According to Cailleux, these fearful rocks and the whirlpool between them are to be found in Mount's Bay in the extreme southwest of

Cornwall. Near to the coast in this bay is a rock now called St Michael's Mount, which could well be Homer's Scylla, this name being preserved in that of the Scilly Isles off Land's End, while the facing rock on the mainland would be Charybdis. Arriving from the east, Odysseus does not pass between the rocks, which Circe says only Jason and the Argonauts were able to succeed in, and then only thanks to Here (*Od.* XII, 69–72). Instead, he passes to the south of Scylla, and rounding this rock has on his left hand Charybdis, who 'sucks down the black water thrice a day', which could well have been true, as we shall see.

There is a difference of about 5 metres between high and low tide in Mount's Bay, rendering the narrow channel between Scylla and Charybdis really very dangerous. So what is Odysseus doing in a place that any sailor in his right mind would avoid like the plague? The answer has been given already, he is there for tin. And what is this monster with twelve uneven feet and six long necks with terrible heads? A row of primitive cranes to load the ships, the legs of the cross-trees being of uneven length to fit the rocks. And the yelping that seems so incongruous for such a fearful monster? The squealing of the ropes and pulleys. All this sounds most plausible, but why are the ships loaded from a rock island rather than from the mainland? It was long thought that Cornish tin was sent to the region of Southampton for export, and indeed this looks likely, since we have seen that Odysseus' ordeal with the Sirens took place in the Solent, the approach to Southampton Water, another vital place in the tin trade. However the overland route from Cornwall was long, difficult, dangerous and expensive, so if ships could be loaded near the mines, so much the better. But it was too dangerous to moor ships alongside this south-facing coast, open to the ocean swell and the prevailing wind and with the additional complications of big tides and fast currents. It was therefore better to transport the tin to Scylla, which was perfectly possible at low tide and store it in the cave, then to load ships at high tide as rapidly as possible, using six cranes rather than one.

Unfortunately for Odysseus, the price for this tin, or his knowledge, is high – he loses another six men:

> So we looked toward her [Charybdis] and feared destruction; but meanwhile Scylla seized from out the hollow ship six of my comrades who were the best in strength and in might. Turning my eyes to the swift ship and to the company of my men, even then I noted above me their feet and hands as they were raised aloft. To me they cried aloud, calling upon me by name for that last time in anguish of heart. (*Od.* XII, 244-250)

Scylla and Charybdis

Is there a rational explanation for this? It may be that these men, 'who were the best in strength and in might', had to be handed over as slaves to the people running this ingenious system, for Circe has warned Odysseus that: 'no sailors yet may boast that they have fled unscathed in their ship, for with each head she carries off a man' (*Od.* XII, 98). Being a crane operator on Scylla would be no easy job.

Circe mentions a 'great fig-tree' over Charybdis. Fig trees are unusual in England, but not unheard of, and Homer mentions another just outside Troy, 'the wind-waved wild fig-tree' (*Il.* XXII, 146). Fig trees are also found today in England, for example as a free-standing species in St James' Park or as a shrub in front of the National Gallery in London, so this cannot be taken as counter-evidence for Scylla and Charybdis being in Cornwall. However, in this precise context, Circe speaks of it because for the ancients it was a mystical tree whose leaf was associated with the North-South axis, and a seafarer like Odysseus wanting to sail from Cornwall to Spain would have to head due south. Here is a third type of indication of direction, after the obvious wind direction and the less obvious zodiacal sign.

For the ancients, both in Europe and the Near East, the fig tree was a symbol of the Gnostic religion. This is also borne out by the words of Jesus to Nathaniel, a scholar: 'I have seen you under the fig-tree' (John 1, 48) meaning 'You believe that your redemption will come with knowledge' (instead of faith). No wonder then, that Odysseus, a Gnostic, held firmly on to the fig tree when he found himself between Scylla and Charybdis:

> All night long was I borne, and at the rising of the sun I came to the cliff of Scylla and to dread Charybdis. She verily sucked down the salt water of the sea, but I, springing up to the tall fig-tree, laid hold of it, and clung to it like a bat. (*Od.* XII, 428-433)

Even the fruit had a special meaning for the ancients, who believed the fig to be the preferred food of hermits. There must be something to it, because an old map of Walcheren (Hades) shows a hamlet called Vijgeter (fig-eater) very close to Dishoek, where was most probably the residence of the hierophants in charge of the initiation ceremonies.

Not so surprisingly for Homer, there still remains an unexpected problem to be solved. The attentive reader of the *Odyssey* will discover a passage implying that Scylla was situated very close to the island of the Sirens, while in reality there is still a long way to sail between the Isle of Wight and Land's End:

We had no sooner put this island (the Sirens) behind us, when I saw
a vapour ahead and a raging surf, the roar of which I could already
hear [Scylla].   (*Od.* XII, 201-202)

These lines are in obvious contradiction with our geography, but
there is a logical explanation for them, to which we will return in
Chapter 17, where we will discover that Homer not only describes the
tin route, but also tells an allegory, where the way from the Sirens to
Scylla is very short indeed.

16

Thrinacia, the Island of Helios

(Land's End, Cornwall)

Odysseus cannot leave for Ithaca and home immediately after his adventure with Scylla and Charybdis because he has to wait for a north wind, so with his remaining companions he lands in Thrinacia, the isle of Helios, in the immediate vicinity. The name of Thrinacia is often taken to mean that the land is triangular, but according to the German philologist Ehrlich, it could also be derived from the Greek *thrinax*, meaning extreme point[1] – a most appropriate explanation if we accept the theory of the tin route, which leads us to Land's End. But there is a problem, for Homer specifically states that Thrinacia is an island, whereas Land's End is not. However, the situation may have been different 3,000 years ago, for we know that the level of the sea was higher then than it is now, and Land's End, the extreme southwest tip of England, could have been separated from the mainland by a narrow strait, where the river Hayle now runs right across the peninsula except for a narrow neck of land in the south, low-lying and now a golf course (see Map 13, page 236).

If Land's End was an island in Homer's day, it would have been counted among the Scilly Isles, whose name must certainly come from Scylla. The river Hayle we just mentioned flows into St Ives Bay, on which lies the village of Carbis Bay, a reminder of Charybdis (via Carybdis > Carbdis > Carbis).

And the whirlpool? There are many off the south and west coasts of England, some of them particularly dangerous, but there is no such phenomenon in Mount's Bay. (See Appendix Note 22, Whirlpools and Waves) However, the situation could have been different when Land's End was still an island, for this would have complicated the movements of tides and currents in the area. In any case Homer does not specifically speak of a whirlpool, but rather of a water being sucked down and regurgitated three times a day, and there are indeed places not far from Mount's Bay where there are today three or even four tides a day instead of the usual two, because of the peculiar configuration of the

235

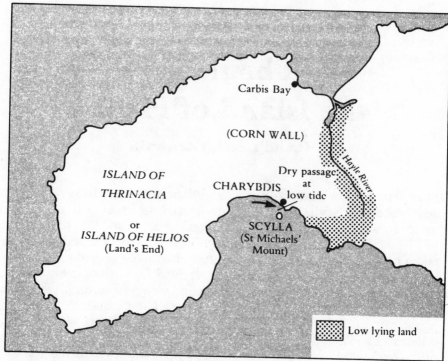

Map 13
Thrinacia, the Island of Helios, Land's End Peninsula.

coast and the sea bed. It is possible that there were three tides in Mount's Bay when Land's End was still an island, whereas today there is only an agger, i.e. a temporary reversal in the movement of the tide.

There is thus considerable evidence in favour of identifying the western tip of Cornwall, where the tin mines were, as Homer's Thrinacia, and, as we shall see, Odysseus has not abandoned his idea of taking some tin home to Ithaca with him. However, for the moment he is stranded on Thrinacia, waiting for the north wind, and Circe has given him dire warnings about the consequences of harming Helios' cattle:

> "'And thou wilt come to the isle Thrinacia. There in great numbers feed the kine of Helios and his goodly flocks, seven herds of kine and as many fair flocks of sheep, and fifty in each. These bear no young, nor do they ever die, and goddesses are their shepherds . . . If thou leavest these unharmed and heedest thy homeward way, verily ye may yet reach Ithaca, though in evil state, after losing all thy comrades. . . .'" (*Od.* XII, 127-141)

Thrinacia, the Island of Helios

Odysseus, who had tried to prevent his men even landing on the island of Helios, makes them swear not to harm any animals they might find, but they have to wait a whole month for a north wind, and:

> "Now so long as my men had grain and red wine they kept their hands from the kine, for they were eager to save their lives. But when all the stores had been consumed from out the ship, and now they must needs roam about in search of game, fishes, and fowl, and whatever might come to their hands – fishing with bent hooks, for hunger pinched their bellies –" (*Od.* XII, 327-333)

After going off to pray to the gods for advice, Odysseus falls asleep, and Eurylochus takes advantage of his absence:

> "'Hear my words, comrades, for all your evil plight. All forms of death are hateful to wretched mortals, but to die of hunger, and so meet one's doom, is the most pitiful. Nay, come, let us drive off the best of the kine of Helios and offer sacrifice to the immortals. . . .'"
> (*Od.* XII 340-344)

But what are these animals that 'bear no young, nor do they ever die'? The answer is that they are ingots of tin. Archeological research has shown that, in the Bronze Age, copper ingots were cast and stored in the shape of ox-hides, often stamped with the mark of their owner. At the time, people must have spoken of 'ox-hides' to mean a certain amount of money in the same way that a modern punter might use the term 'poney' (£25). This throws light on a line in the *Iliad*: 'it was not for a bull's hide that they strove, as is normally men's prize for swiftness of foot'(*Il.* XXII, 160). Odysseus and his companions are severely punished for stealing these ingots, as Circe had predicted, for when they finally leave the island:

> . . . straightway came the shrieking West Wind, blowing with a furious tempest, and the blast of the wind snapped both the fore-stays of the mast, so that the mast fell backward and all its tackling was strewn in the bilge. On the stern of the ship the mast struck the head of the pilot and crushed all the bones of his skull together, and like a diver he fell from the deck and his proud spirit left his bones. Therewith Zeus thundered and hurled his bolt upon the ship, and she quivered from stem to stern, smitten by the bolt of Zeus, and was filled with sulphurous smoke, and my comrades fell from out the ship. Like sea-crows they were borne on the waves about the black ship, and the god took from them their returning.
> (*Od.* XII 408-419)

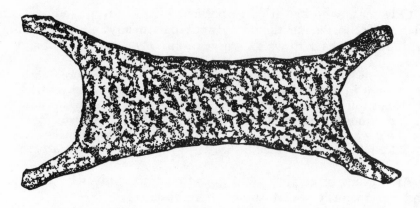

A prehistoric copper ingot in the form of an ox hide.

Odysseus has lost his last ship and all his companions, but he manages to cling to the wreckage, and after being swept back to Scylla and Charybdis and saving himself by hanging on to the fig tree, he drifts for another nine days, ending up on the island of Calypso.

Notes

1 Ehrlich, *Untersuchungen über die Natur der griechischen Betonung*, Berlin, 1812, p. 140.

17

Ogygia,
the Island of Calypso

(St Miguel, Azores)

Odysseus finally arrives at the isle of 'Ogygia, where the fair-tressed Calypso dwells, dread goddess of human speech, who gave me welcome and care' (*Od.* XII. 447-50). He is to stay there seven years, under the spell of Calypso, daughter of Atlas, who gave his name to the Atlas Mountains in Morocco and to the Atlantic Ocean. She hopes to marry him, but Odysseus' heart is still in Ithaca, where his wife Penelope and their son Telemachus are waiting for him. However, Odysseus has no boat in which he can leave the island.

According to Cailleux, Ogygia is St Miguel, an island in the Azores, the Portuguese archipelago in the middle of the Atlantic Ocean, nearly half way between Lisbon and New York or, as Homer has it, 'where is the navel of the sea' (*Od.* I, 50), a very apt figure of speech, but also of symbolic significance as we shall see in Chapter 19.

Cailleux also suggests that the Azores owe their name to the Celt *soore*, meaning 'dried out' (and close to the Greek *sauros*, an animal that moults or sheds its skin, such as the lizard), for according to the legends quoted by him, the Azores were a far-off country where the mummies of the just were taken to await their resurrection. This is therefore an appropriate place for Odysseus to await his return to the everyday world of men.

As to the explanation of the name Ogygia, according to von Wilamowitz[1] it simply means 'land situated in the ocean', since it contains the words *okeanos* (ocean) and *gaia* (earth). All the evidence of Homer's text point to the island being far out in the ocean, so it can scarcely be the island of Peregil, at the foot of the Atlas Mountains, in the Strait of Gibraltar, as suggested by V. Bérard (see Appendix Note 20, The *Odyssey* in the Mediterranean), who overlooked the remark already made by Plutarch that Calypso's Ogygia was in the Atlantic, five day's sail from the Isle of Brittany.

There is also a directional clue in the text, as we have now come to expect. When Odysseus finally gets away from Scylla, he recounts:

> Thence for nine days was I borne, and on the tenth night the gods brought me to Ogygia, where fair-tressed Calypso dwells, dread goddess of human speech. . . .   (*Od.* XII, 447-450)

If this description of Calypso sounds familiar, this is because precisely the same words are used by Homer to describe Circe. So they sound like twin sisters, Gemini, the zodiacal sign for a southwesterly direction. Together with the sailing time of nine days from Thrinacia (Cornwall) this is strong additional evidence in favour of identifying Ogygia as an island in the Azores.

However, it is very unlikely that Odysseus had managed to hang on to a piece of wreckage for nine days and not only survive but reach the island of Calypso. For one thing it would appear physically impossible to survive so long under such conditions, and for another the Atlantic currents would not carry drifting spars from Cornwall to the Azores. But if we assume that the ship was unharmed and had a normal crew, the distance of about 2,000 kilometers could quite feasibly be covered in nine days as this means an average speed of less than 5 knots. It appears that Homer is again telling us two things at once: first, the location of various Atlantic ports and islands, hence sailing instructions for physical voyages; and, second, a description of the initiation experience, an intellectual and spiritual voyage. If the poet tells us that Odysseus was borne along or drifted, this is a description of his state of mind after his visit to Hades. His ports of call and his ordeals in the first part of the *Odyssey* before he reaches the isle of Circe symbolize the trials of a neophyte. After his physical initiation in Hades, Odysseus in fact returns to the isle of Circe to the Druids' school for another seven years, but at the same time as describing the experiences of this initiate, Homer goes on describing sea routes through the adventures of a seafarer also called Odysseus. He does this through a very skilful blend of reality and fiction, which would not have been disconcerting for the Celts, who in any case did not see any sharp divide between the material and spiritual worlds.

The initiates among the audience would have understood that the story of the Sirens symbolized the irresistible call of the Other World,[2] experienced by Odysseus as he was entering the state of 'clinical death' (not a state of intoxication by drugs as Homer has stated explicitly that Hermes had provided him with an antidote).

Ogygia, the Island of Calypso

The ancients represented the Sirens as composite beings who had the head and breasts of a woman and a body either of a fish, in the case of the Atlantic peoples, or of a bird, in the case of Mediterranean peoples, notably the Egyptians. The significance was the same in both cases, for both sea and air refer to the domain of an infinite element, water or air, and as we have seen, these elements represent the collective subconscious. The song of the Sirens that none can resist is the seduction of the Other World.[3] The Sirens are thus the psychic forces that pull the individual towards disaster and death, so that they later became the image of the *femme fatale*, in particular for sailors. Odysseus' encounter with the Sirens corresponds to the first phase of death, when the victim is losing consciousness due to lack of air and is overcome by a feeling of deep peace, symbolized by Homer by the wind dropping to complete calm as the ship enters the Solent. Odysseus is the only one to hear the song of the Sirens, for he has plugged his companions' ears with wax, but he is unable to surrender himself to them because he cannot break the links attaching him to the reality of the physical world, symbolized by the ropes tying him to the mast of his ship, the ship itself being the symbol of the individual spirit. The Sirens' song corresponds to the strange sounds reported by survivors of the near-death experience described by Moody. As for Odysseus, we have seen that he had his temporary contact with death on the Nollenstrand beach on the island of Walcheren. It is precisely there that a modern structure has been built on a mole extending out in the sea. From a distance, one sees a large number of pipes cast vertically in a concrete base, while on approaching one hears an eery noise caused by the wind blowing in the pipes. This monument is claimed to be the biggest wind organ in the world and is called 'The Sirens'. Its name and location constitutes a most amazing coincidence – if it is a coincidence.

According to Moody's patients, the Sirens' song is followed by the impression of passing through a dark tunnel or spiral, which corresponds well with Homer's description of the whirlpool between Scylla and Charybdis. The victim then arrives at the final stage of clinical death, symbolized by Thrinacia, land of the sun god, Helios. The adventure on this island corresponds to the last phase that those who have returned from clinical death describe as entry into a brilliant light. Thus the true meaning of Thrinacia, is not 'triangular land', as was always thought, but rather 'Land of the Triangle', for the triangle has for time immemorial been the symbol of the sacred trinity, hence of God (see Part I, Chapter 4 and Appendix Note 2, Trinities). Thrinacia is thus man's final destination, Paradise (from the Sanskrit *paradesha*, 'supreme region'), where even the sheep and cattle are immortal and have goddesses for shepherds: Helios' daughters, Lampetia ('the Illuminating') and Phaetousa ('the Shining One'). They each have a flock of 350, which seems to correspond to the number of days in a year of twelve lunar months.

However, Moody's studies on the clinical death phenomenon insist on the fact that survivors of suicide attempts did not see this light, but had the impression of floating in darkness and unhappiness.[4] Apparently one is not free to choose the moment of one's death, just as one cannot decide the day of one's birth. We are all obliged to live our lives of joys and sorrows, no matter how terrible the latter may be. Homer, in his great wisdom, also knew that one should not try to approach the Country of Light on one's own initiative:

> ". . . and upon my mind fell the words of the blind seer, Theban Teiresias, and of Aeaean Circe, who very straitly charged me to shun the island of Helios, who gives joy to mortals. Then verily I spoke among my comrades, grieved at heart:
> "'Hear my words, comrades, for all your evil plight, that I may tell you the oracles of Teiresias and of Aeaean Circe, who very straitly charged me to shun the island of Helios, who gives joy to mortals; for there, she said, was our most terrible bane. Nay, row the black ship out past the island.'" (*Od.* XII 266-276)

The Celts and the Ancient Greeks believed that Paradise was in the far North, probably for the following reason: they thought that there was another sun in the Other World of the spirits of the dead. While the sun shines at midday at its 'Zenith', situated in 'our' world of Europe above the southern horizon, the 'nocturnal' sun was thought to shine at midnight in the 'Nadir' to the north. If we think of the sun as revolving round the earth, this concept becomes coherent and intelligible. The Nadir is in fact on the other side of the earth below the northern horizon, at least for people living in the northern hemisphere. On the concrete level, Odysseus needs a northerly wind to carry his ship home to Spain from Cornwall. But also, on this other level, since Paradise is in the north, he needs a wind from the north to take him back to the world of the living.

Odysseus and his men have scarcely put to sea to sail for home, when they are caught by a violent storm in which the ship founders and all the men are lost, bar Odysseus himself who is swept, clinging to the wreckage, back to the whirlpool of Scylla and Charibdis, where he saves himself by hanging on to the fig tree while the remains of his ship are sucked down into the sea and then returned to him. Odysseus thus has to pass by way of the terrible Scylla and Charibdis both before and after his visit to Thrinacia, the isle of the sun god. This is confirmation that Homer is describing a near–death experience, for those who have survived the last stage of clinical death say that they passed twice through the same 'tunnel' or 'spiral', the first time to arrive in the land of light and the second time to return to life.

Odysseus continues his way, but in a state of mind that can be described as 'drifting', and when he is so hospitably received by Calypso he is not even grateful. This, too, can be understood now that research has been carried out in hospitals into the reactions of people resuscitated from the last stage of clinical death, for in the majority of cases they are not at all pleased with the medical team's efforts to save them, no longer having any desire to return to life. Likewise Odysseus remains in a state of depression throughout the seven years he spends on the isle of Calypso, whose name means 'spell-binding' or 'enveloping', and she is, like Circe, connected with the Underworld (and the opposite, 'apo-calypse' means literally 'discovery' or 'revelation'), a further indication that on the initiation level of the story, Odysseus is still at the Druidic school.

There is a further indication in the text that Odysseus is still continuing his initiation into knowledge: the mention of the fountains in Calypso's garden (*Od.* V, 70), for fountains, whether in the garden of a goddess, at the foot of the Tree of Life or in the middle of Paradise, were always the symbol not only of youth and regeneration, but also of teaching.[5] There are many instances of the importance attached to fountains by the ancients, for example in the Irish epic of the battle of Mag Tured there is a regenerative fountain that heals the wounded in a day; in the Arthurian romances there is frequent mention of the fountain of youth in the forest of Paimpont (Brittany); while in Nordic mythology the fountain of Mimir contained the water of learning that was so precious that Odin (Wodan) sacrificed an eye to have the privilege of drinking the water of knowledge, prophecy and poetry. This sacrifice by the novice is by no means unique, for it is found in other mythologies of Indo–European origin. Hephaestus, for example, the god of fire, was lame because this was the price he had had to pay for the knowledge necessary to master fire and become the blacksmith and armourer of Olympus..As for Calypso's fountains, Homer states that there were four, sending their waters in various directions, and, as we saw in Chapter 12, the number four was the symbol of universality. There can thus be no doubt that Homer is here speaking of the fountains of wisdom, so that it is pointless to look for an island with four real fountains as some researchers have done in the past.

During his stay on the isle of Calypso, Odysseus often goes down to the beach and weeps on the shores of the ocean. This is hard to understand for the modern (male) reader who could ask for nothing better than to live on a sub-tropical island waited on hand and foot by a loving and beautiful goddess.

But it is well known that anyone confronted with his subconscious through harsh initiation rites is likely to be subject to a state of depression which much resembles that of the mid-life crisis. In both instances, the psychological phenomena are caused by a physical process, either of a violent or hormonal nature, as the case may be. Particularly depressing is the realization to have lost one's youth: Odysseus' 'alter ego', Elpenor, whose name can be understood to mean 'the Young Man', has died for good to make place for a spiritually 'reborn' personality. This personality change was so profound that initiates even used to change their names.

After Odysseus has been on the island for seven years, the goddess Athene takes pity on his plight and asks Zeus to intercede on his behalf. Zeus agrees, and sends the messenger, Hermes, to tell Calypso that she must let Odysseus go, and that he will finally be allowed to return home, but only after suffering more difficulties.

Hermes leaves Olympus (Mont Blanc, see Part II, Chapter 18), steps on Pieria (the Pyrenees) and, like a sea-gull, flies over the ocean to Ogygia to wonder at the garden paradise of Calypso in the Azores, situated 'far out at sea' (*Od.* VII, 244):

> . . . and he [Hermes] found her within. A great fire was burning in the hearth, and from afar over the isle there was a fragrance of cleft cedar and juniper as they burned. But she within was singing with a sweet voice as she went to and fro before the loom, weaving with a golden shuttle. Round about the cave grew a luxuriant wood, alder and poplar and sweet-smelling cypress, wherein birds long of wing were wont to nest, owls and falcons and sea-crows with chattering tongues, who ply their business on the sea. And right there about the hollow cave ran trailing a garden vine, in pride of its prime, richly laden with clusters. And fountains four in a row were flowing with bright water hard by one another, turned one this way, one that. And round about soft meadows of violets and parsley were blooming. There even an immortal, who chanced to come, might gaze and marvel, and delight his soul; and there the messenger Argïphontes [Hermes] stood and marvelled.
>
> (*Od.* V, 58-75)

The gods' decision to allow Odysseus to return home is obviously bad news for Calypso, who had so wanted to keep him for herself, so she reacts violently against poor Hermes, who is only the messenger:

Ogygia, the Island of Calypso

... Calypso, the beautiful goddess, shuddered, and she spoke, and addressed him with winged words: "Cruel are ye, O ye gods, and quick to envy above all others, seeing that ye begrudge goddesses that they should mate with men openly, if any takes a mortal as her dear bed-fellow. Thus, when rosy-fingered Dawn took to herself Orion, ye gods that live at ease begrudged her, till in Ortygia chaste Artemis of the golden throne assailed him with her gentle shafts and slew him. Thus too, when fair-tressed Demeter, yielding to her passion, lay in love with Iasion in the thrice-ploughed fallow land, Zeus was not long without knowledge thereof, but smote him with his bright thunder-bolt and slew him. And even so again do ye now begrudge me, O ye gods, that a mortal man should abide with me. . . ."

Then again the messenger Argeïphontes answered her: "Even so send him forth now, and beware of the wrath of Zeus, lest haply he wax wroth and visit his anger upon thee hereafter."

So saying, the strong Argeïphontes departed, and the queenly nymph went to the great-hearted Odysseus, when she had heard the message of Zeus. Him she found sitting on the shore, and his eyes were never dry of tears, and his sweet life was ebbing away, as he longed mournfully for his return, for the nymph was no longer pleasing in his sight. By night indeed he would sleep by her side perforce in the hollow caves, unwilling beside the willing nymph, but by day he would sit on the rocks and the sands, racking his soul with tears and groans and griefs, and he would look over the unresting sea, shedding tears. *(Od.* V, 116-158)

Since the gods give her no choice, Calypso helps Odysseus to find the trees to build a raft, and she weaves the sails he needs. A few days later Odysseus sails, aided by a warm and gentle wind provided by Calypso:

Gladly then did goodly Odysseus spread his sail to the breeze; and he sat and guided his raft skilfully with the steering-oar, nor did sleep fall upon his eyelids, as he watched the Pleiads, and late-setting Bootes, and the Bear, which men also call the Wain, which ever cirles where it is and watches Orion, and alone has no part in the baths of the Ocean. For this star Calypso, the beautiful goddess, had bidden him to keep on his left hand as he sailed over the sea. For seventeen days then he sailed over the sea, and on the eighteenth appeared the shadowy mountains of the land of the Phaeacians. . . .
(Od. V, 269-280)

The raft is not like his 'swift ship', but he makes headway, sailing east for Calypso has told him to keep the Bear, which circles closely round the Pole Star, on his left, but when Odysseus eventually comes in sight of land he is seen by the sea god Poseidon on his way back from a visit to the Ethiopians (Africa). Poseidon sends a terrible cyclone as revenge for Odysseus blinding his son, the Cyclops, Polyphemus. The raft is wrecked and Odysseus is close to drowning, but fortunately he receives the aid of Ino 'of the fair ankles' who had become a goddess under the name of Leucothea:

> "Strip off these garments, and leave thy raft to be driven by the winds, but do thou swim with thy hands and so strive to reach the land of the Phaeacians, where it is thy fate to escape. Come, take this veil, and stretch it beneath thy breast. It is immortal; there is no fear that thou shalt suffer aught or perish. But when with thy hands thou hast laid hold of the land, loose it from thee, and cast it into the wine-dark sea far from the land, and thyself turn away."
>
> (*Od.* V, 343–350)

This story of Leucothea's veil is another indication of the link between Odysseus and the south of Spain, for Leucothea's name is perpetuated in Spain in Saint Leucadia, patron saint of Toledo and a number of other towns.

Odysseus once more escapes death and manages to swim ashore on the isle of the Phaeacians, and, naked and exhausted, falls asleep on a bed of leaves under some bushes.

The tale of Calypso was meant to give precise travel directions to and from her island, as the Azores were—and still are—a port of call for all vessels sailing from Cadiz to England during late spring and summer when northerly winds near Portugal prevent sailors from heading north. In the following Chapter we will find that Odysseus does sail in a northerly direction from the Canaries to his native Cadiz, but this is only possible in early spring. For this reason, sailors are informed by Homer that Odysseus slew the suitors of Penelope on the holy feastday of the archergod Apollo (*Od.* XXI, 258) which was approximately on May, 1st.

Notes

1 V. von Wilamowitz, *Homerische Untersuchungen*, Berlin, 1884.
2 J. Chevalier and A. Gheerbrant, *Dictionnaire des Symboles*, p. 950.
3 J. Chevalier and A. Gheerbrant, op. cit., p. 888.
4 A. Moody, *Life after Life*, Mockingbird, Covington, Georgia, 1975.
   Reflections on Life after Life, Mockingbird, St Simon Island, Georgia, 1975.
5 J. Chevalier and A. Gheerbrant, op. cit., p. 950.

18

Scheria,
the Island of the Phaeacians

(Lanzarote, Canary Islands)

Odysseus' adventure on this island is one of the most charming stories of the *Odyssey*. The goddess Athene helps him by arranging for him to meet Nausicaa, the daughter of Alcinous, king of the Phaeacians. She does so by going to Nausicaa's room, in the guise of her best friend, while she is asleep:

> "Nausicaa, how comes it that thy mother bore thee so heedless? Thy bright raiment is lying uncared for; yet thy marriage is near at hand, when thou must needs thyself be clad in fair garments, and give other such to those who escort thee. It is from things like these, thou knowest, that good report goeth up among men, and the father and honoured mother rejoice. Nay, come, let us go to wash them at break of day, for I will follow with thee to aid thee, that thou mayest with speed make thee ready; for thou shalt not long remain a maiden. Even now thou hast suitors in the land, the noblest of all the Phaeacians, from whom is thine own lineage."
>
> (*Od.* VI, 25-35)

Nausicaa's father, Alcinous, lets the girl and her handmaidens have a mule waggon, 'high and stout of wheel and fitted with a box above' (*Od.* VI, 69-70) and they go to the river mouth to wash the linen. While the clothes are drying on the beach, the girls play with a ball:

> then the goddess, flashing-eyed Athene, took other counsel, that Odysseus might awake and see the fair-faced maid, who should lead him to the city of the Phaeacians. So then the princess tossed the ball to one of her maidens; the maiden indeed she missed, but cast it into a deep eddy, and thereat they cried aloud, and goodly Odysseus awoke . . .   (*Od.* VI, 112-117)

Odysseus breaks off a good leafy branch to give himself a little covering and goes to meet the girls. He considers whether to throw himself at Nausicaa's feet, but decides to speak from a slight distance:

> so straightway he spoke a gentle word and crafty: "I beseech thee, O queen, – a goddess art thou, or art thou mortal? if thou art a goddess, one of those who hold broad heaven, to Artemis, the daughter of great Zeus, do I liken thee most nearly in comeliness and in stature and in form. But if thou art one of mortals who dwell upon the earth, thrice-blessed then are thy father and thy honoured mother, and thrice-blessed thy brethren. Full well, I ween, are their hearts ever warmed with joy because of thee, as they see thee entering the dance, a plant so fair. But he again is blessed in heart above all others, who shall prevail with his gifts of wooing and lead thee to his home. For never yet have mine eyes looked upon a mortal such as thou, whether man or woman; amazement holds me as I look on thee. Of a truth in Delos once I saw such a thing, a young shoot of a palm springing up beside the altar of Apollo – for thither, too, I went, and much people followed with me, on that journey on which evil woes were to be my portion; – even so, when I saw that, I marvelled long at heart, for never yet did such a tree spring up from the earth. And in like manner, lady, do I marvel at thee, and am amazed, and fear greatly to touch thy knees. . ."
>
> (Od. VI, 148-168)

For reasons not only of logic and aesthetics but above all for the symbolism contained in these verses, I should like to alter the usual translations while remaining faithful to the Greek, as follows:

> "in Delos once I saw such a thing, a young *phoenix rising* up beside the altar; . . . when I saw that, I marvelled long in my heart, for never yet did such *majesty* arise from the earth."

Translators have always rendered the Greek *phoinix* as 'palm tree' instead of the bird Phoenix, because there is the word *doru* in the second phrase, and this, like *drus* means, among other things 'tree trunk', but by extension it could also mean 'power' (Dru-ids), while for the image of the beautiful bird I have preferred 'majesty' to 'power'. What is more, the reference to the phoenix, the mythical bird that is reborn from its ashes, is most appropriate here, as Odysseus, shortly to return home to Ithaca at last, has emerged a new man after all his ordeals. The symbol of the phoenix was known in different civilizations. In the land of the Pharaohs its name was Bennou. The end of Odysseus' trials is also symbolized a few lines later when he washes off the salt from his body in the clear waters of the river. Here Homer kills two birds with one stone: salt not only has a complex symbolic meaning in most civilizations, but it has also been the mainstay of the economy of the island of Lanzarote.

Delos

When Odysseus compares Nausicaa with the majestic phoenix, he says that he saw this at Delos, but where is Delos? Many translators have added the word 'island', which does not appear in the Greek text, to help their readers situate the action in Greece. However, since we know that there were neither Celts in Greece nor temples of Apollo on this Aegean island in Homer's time, we have to look in western Europe. The only place-name that closely resembles Delos is Deelen, a village north of Arnhem, a town on the right bank of the Rhine in the Netherlands. It is quite possible that Odysseus visited the region of Deelen, now covered with forests and fields of heather and called Veluwe. This would be further evidence that Odysseus sailed up the Rhine, as was believed in the time of Tacitus, 2,000 years ago. This hypothesis would also confirm the opinion of the most ancient Greek authors that Delos was a fabulous and distant country situated in the extreme northwest, there where the sun sets at the June solstice. It is possible that this is how the Netherlands looked, through the eyes of an ancient Greek, the country being 'fabulous' because of its extremely fertile soil. In the Veluwe region there are many indications that it could have been the prehistoric Delos, and it is even possible to identify the precise place where Odysseus would have seen the phoenix.

The first thing that struck me when visiting the region was the name of an hotel at Bennekom, Keltenwoud (Celt wood). On its own this name obviously proves nothing, but it might nevertheless be a first indication that there is some dim collective memory on the part of the local population of their very distant ancestors and that this area was once occupied by the Celts or at least a Celticized tribe. The people in question would have been the Dorians, who gave their name to nearby Doorn (see Part II, Chapter 6). Other reminders of the Dorians are: Doorwerth, on the Rhine, Duurstede, which was called Dorestad (Dori[an] town) in the Middle Ages, and Apeldoorn, a modern town with a very ancient name, for while its etymology is considered to be 'obscure', i.e. lost in the mists of time, it becomes very clear if we assume it was once a centre for the worship of Apollo of the Dorians (Apol-Dorion) and perhaps even his birthplace, for according to the myths he was from Delos.

We find here indeed the forests and a royal palace called Het Loo (The Place, in Celtic; pronounced 'low'), while the coats of arms of Apeldoorn show not only the phoenix, but also the key to knowledge:

Furthermore, there is a nearby village with the name of Apollo's oracle, Putten (become *Puthoon* in Greek), the same name we have already found in Zeeland, where there must have been another oracle on the island of Putten. (Apollo was, of course, worshipped in other parts of Europe, and his name has left traces elsewhere, for example in Alsace, where the historians tell us that the village of Grand owes its name to Apollo-Granus.) Another god whose name is found in the region of Deelen is Hermes, the village of Ermelo having derived its name from Hermes-lo (Hermes' place). Pallas Athene herself was worshipped not only in France and England (see Part IV, Regiment 6), but also in the Netherlands under the old name by which she was also known by the early Greeks, (Pallas) Okke, and we find a village about 20 kilometres east of Apeldoorn called Okkebroek (Okke's brook), north of Deventer. As for the towns of Arnhem and Dieren, their names are to be found in Homer in a different context (see Appendix Note 15, The Pylians). Aeschylus tells us that there was a lake at Delos, probably a site used for initiation by submersion, and in the Hoge Veluwe National Park there is indeed a lake called Deelense Was (Deelen water, *was* being Old Saxon for 'water', akin to The Wash, Homer's bay of Ilion). The only 'sacred' circle in the Netherlands outside the province of Zeeland, so far as I know, is the Nol in't Bos (Circle in the Wood), southwest of Deelen, near the present village of Bennekom (Valley of Benne, or Bennou, the ancient name of the phoenix). Nol in't Bos would therefore be the place Odysseus is referring to when he tells Nausicaa that he saw the phoenix at Delos (see Map 17, key 26, at the end of Part IV).

What he actually saw was an initiation ceremony, for the phoenix rising from his ashes is clearly a symbol of rebirth, but it was not Odysseus' own initiation, for we have seen that he was initiated by Circe on Aeaea. According to the custom of the time, Odysseus mentions this event to let Nausicaa know that he is not an ordinary man, but an initiate. For example, when a Druid visited the land of the Pharaohs he let it be known that he was an initiate and his hosts then let him into the Mysteries of their own religion. In the present case, hearing that Odysseus is an initiate, Nausicaa decides to present him to her father, King Alcinous.

Scheria, the Island of the Phaeacians

One question that might arise in connection with the identification of Delos as Deelen and its surroundings, the present Veluwe, is whether there is any evidence that the region was in fact already inhabited in the Bronze Age. The answer is affirmative without a shadow of a doubt, for archeologists have found objects belonging to a people of hunters and gatherers of the late paleolithic age (14000 BC), and the most ancient pottery dates from 2450 BC, while there are bronze swords and axes as old as 1600 BC, i.e. even long before Homer. It is thus entirely possible that the Veluwe was a sacred place for the Druids of the Celts, but apparently not for their Stone Age predecessors, who built their megalithic monuments (Hunnebedden) about 100 km further north, in the province of Drenthe.

Like Pallas Athene, Apollo was worshipped not only in the Netherlands and the north of France in the Bronze Age, but also in England, to the extent that Homer says that he was one of the gods who gave the Trojans most support in their war against the Achaeans (see Part I, Chapter 4). As for the Dorians, there is reason to think that, like the Pelasgians, they lived on both sides of the Helle Sea, for there are a number of place-names beginning with Dor- in the south of England, for example, Dorset, Dorchester and Dorking. In theory, then, we should also expect to find a place whose name recalls Apollo-Dorion or Apeldoorn, and in fact there are two small towns called Appledore, one in Kent and the other in Devonshire. These names are thus likely to have nothing to do with apples or thorns (the Dutch *doorn* is related to 'thorn') and everything to do with Apollo and the Dorians. That Apollo was worshipped in England is confirmed by Hecates, a Greek geographer of the fourth century BC, who wrote a *History of the Hyperboreans*, which has unfortunately not survived, but is quoted by another ancient Greek writer, Diodorus Siculus, who lived in Rome in the time of Caesar and compiled a historical encyclopedia. Long fragments of Diodorus' forty volumes survive, among them a passage taken from Hecates, in which he speaks of Hyperborea, which is clearly England, and the veneration of Apollo in that country. To allow the reader to judge the evidence for my theory of the northern origin of Apollo, I quote the entire passage from Diodorus Siculus:

> Among the historians who have consigned in their annals the traditions of Antiquity, Hecates and certain others claim that there is beyond the Celtic land, in the ocean, an isle that is no less in size than Sicily. This isle, situated to the north, they say, is inhabited by the Hyperboreans, so-called because they live beyond the point from where Borea [the north wind] blows. The soil of this island is excellent, and so remarkable for its fertility that it produces two

crops a year. It is there, according to this same account, the birthplace of Leto [mother of Apollo], which explains why the islanders particularly revere Apollo. They are all, so to speak, the priests of this god. Every day they sing hymns in his honour. There is also to be seen in this isle a huge enclosure consecrated to Apollo, and a magnificent temple, round in shape and decorated with many offerings. The town of these islanders is also dedicated to Apollo; its inhabitants are for the most part players of the cithara, who ceaselessly celebrate in the temple the praise of the god, accompanying the singing of the hymns on their instruments. The Hyperboreans speak a language of their own; they are very hospitable towards the Greeks and especially towards the Athenians and the Delians, and this attitude goes far back in time. It is even said that several Greeks went to visit the Hyperboreans and that they left rich offerings bearing Greek inscriptions, and that in return, Abaris the Hyperborean in the old days travelled to Greece to renew with the Delians the friendship that exists between the two peoples. It is also added that the moon, seen from this island, appears to be at a very little distance from the earth, and that one can distinctly see the contours of its terrain. Apollo is said to descend to this isle every nineteen years. It is also at the end of this period that the stars are, after their revolution, returned to their point of departure. This period of nineteen years is designated by the Greeks by the name of BIG YEAR. This god is seen, during his apparition, to dance every night accompanying himself on the cithara, from the spring equinox to the rising of the Pleiads, as if rejoicing for the honours paid to him. The government of this isle and the guarding of the temple are entrusted to kings called Boreads, the descendents and successors of Borea.[1]

No satisfactory explanation has ever been found for this text, and it has therefore been discarded as devoid of any scientific value. However, in the light of the various discoveries we have made in this book, this negative judgement appears unjustified. Although there are many observations in the text that are hard to reconcile with the facts – England is not beyond the origin of the north wind and the moon is not specially close – Hecates does provide concrete and valuable clues. For example, if Apollo was the most venerated god in England (and the staunchest supporter of the Trojans in the *Iliad*), then it is likely that the 'magnificent temple, round in shape' was the biggest 'sacred' circle in the country, the megalithic monument of Stonehenge, which would thus still have been in use in the seventh century BC (see Plate 7).

As for the 'big year', I found no evidence that stars are in the same position every nineteen years as Diodorus states, but modern astronomers speak of the period of Saros, meaning the period of eighteen years and ten days between two total eclipses of the sun. This phenomenon thus occurs in the nineteenth year. The 'big year' obviously had a special significance for the ancients, since not only was Apollo said to visit England every nineteen years, but also because both Odysseus and Helen are away from home for nineteen years.

According to the ancient source quoted above, England (the isle 'beyond the Celtic land' – Gallia) was the birthplace of Leto, so it is also possible that Delos, the birthplace of her son Apollo, was in the region of Deelen in the Netherlands. (The Delos in the citation is obviously the Mediterranean Delos, since Hecates lived several centuries after the transposition of names to Greece.)

However unfamiliar it may still sound to the reader, the nordic origin of Apollo is indirectly confirmed by many other classical authors, such as Aelianus, Alcaeus and Hesiod. The first left a poem mentioning the swans in the big temple of the Hyperboreans (presumably Stonehenge) which must have been the Nordic, singing swan because they join in with the choirs singing in honour of the god Borvon (another name for Apollo, see Appendix Note 25, The principal gods). Alcaeus, who lived in Marseilles about 600 BC, recounts how Apollo went to Delphi in a chariot drawn by swans, which again were not the silent swans so familiar to us, but the wild singing swans. Hesiod, (eighth century BC) is also very specific on this point in his *Shield of Heracles*, line 316: '. . . the swans were calling loudly'. Since the singing swan was definitely unknown in the Mediterranean, as Wernsdorf noted a few centuries ago, (see Part I, Chapter 1), there can be no doubt that Apollo was born in the Netherlands and venerated in England. We have thus also found confirmation that the Delphi of the Bronze Age was the Dutch town we call Delft today (see Map 12 in Part III, Chapter 10).

Odysseus on Scheria

But let us return to Odysseus and his adventures on the island of Scheria. After his bath, Nausicaa gives him food and clothing and directs him to the town, but will not go with him for fear of gossip:

> "Rouse thee now, stranger, to go to the city, that I may escort thee to the house of my wise father, where, I tell thee, thou shalt come to know all the noblest of the Phaeacians. Only do thou thus, and, methinks, thou dost not lack understanding: so long as we are passing through the country and the tilled fields of men go thou quickly with the handmaids behind the mules and the waggon, and I will lead the way. But when we are about to enter the city, around which runs a lofty wall, – a fair harbour lies on either side of the city and the entrance is narrow. . . . " (*Od.* VI, 254-62)

According to Cailleux, Scheria is the island of Lanzarote in the Canaries, the Spanish archipelago in the Atlantic to the west of Morocco. Odysseus, shipwrecked once again, landed on the northwest coast, near La Caleta, driven by the north wind. He fell asleep near to the mouth of the Rada de Penedo. The capital of the isle of the Phaeacians is on the east coast where Arrecife now stands.

Until the last century, one of its ports was called Puerto del Cavallo ('port of the horse' in Spanish), while the other is still called Puerto de Naos ('port of the boat', in Portuguese). Both these names are connected with the *Odyssey*. The Puerto del Cavallo is a reference to the speed with which the Phaeacian ship that takes Odysseus home to Ithaca leaves the island, as is clear in Homer's imagery:

> And as on a plain four yoked stallions spring forward all together beneath the strokes of the lash, and leaping on high swiftly accomplish their way, even so the stern of that ship leapt on high, and in her wake the dark wave of the loud-sounding sea foamed mightily. . . .   (*Od.* XIII, 81-85)

We have already seen that Poseidon is still hostile to Odysseus because he defeated his son Polyphemus. When Poseidon discovers too late that the Phaeacians have taken Odysseus back home to Ithaca safe and sound, he takes vengeance on them by turning their ship to stone when they return. Puerto de Naos owes its name to a rock resembling a ship off the east coast of the island:

> Now when Poseidon, the earth-shaker, heard this he went his way to Scheria, where the Phaeacians dwell, and there he waited. And she drew close to shore, the seafaring ship, speeding swiftly on her way. Then near her came the Earth-shaker and turned her to stone, and rooted her fast beneath by a blow of the flat of his hand, and then he was gone.
>
> But they spoke winged words to one another, the Phaeacians of the long oars, men famed for their ships. And thus would one speak, with a glance at his neighbour:
> "Ah me, who has now bound our swift ship on the sea as she sped homeward? Lo she was in plain sight"   (*Od.* XIII, 159-69)

And why does Homer tell us the charming story about the meeting on Scheria between Odysseus and the young princess Nausicaa? It is once again an indication of direction. Since it is stressed that Nausicaa is

Scheria, the Island of the Phaeacians

still a virgin, we have here the zodiacal sign Virgo, indicating the southeasterly direction to take from Calypso's isle in the Azores to the Canaries. We already knew that Odysseus had to sail in an easterly direction, for Calypso told him to keep the constellation of the Bear on his left, and the sign Virgo gives more precision.

The name of the land of the Phaeacians, Scheria, originally meant 'series', and the map shows that the Canary Islands are strung across the sea like a string of pearls. The Canaries were also the legendary Hesperides of the ancients, named after the daughters of Atlas, the guardians of the golden apples.

Lanzarote must once have been a very fertile island, but it is now extremely dry and there are few trees, which was apparently not the case 3,000 years ago. It is likely that the population made the common mistake of cutting down too many trees, causing erosion of the soil and reducing the capacity to retain water, as happened in parts of the Spanish mainland. Alternatively the trees may have been destroyed by volcanic eruptions, not infrequent in this area (Poseidon was not called the earth-shaker for nothing). Such eruptions completely devastated the island in the eighteenth and nineteenth centuries. The inhabitants of the Canary Islands were close to the Celts of Southern Spain as evidenced not only by the fact that their local bard sings about the Trojan War, but also by the absence of a linguistic barrier between Odysseus and his hosts, who, besides, receive him amicably. These people could well be the ancestors of the Guanches, who lived here in the Middle Ages and were described by Iberian explorers of the islands as a 'tall, fair people'. But the Phaeacians did not come from Spain, but rather from West Africa, where Celts must have lived before Homer's time, as the poet reminds his public that:

> These [the Phaeacians] dwelt of old in spacious Hypereia [Africa], hard by the Cyclopes [the round-eyed, black Africans], men of overweening pride, who plundered them continually and were mightier than they. From thence Nausithous the godlike [Nausicaa's grandfather] had removed them and led and settled them in Scheria, far from men that live by toil. (*Od.* VI, 4-8).

Hypereia literally means 'high land' and refers to the high mountains of northwest Africa which still bear the name of Atlas, the father of Calypso (*Od.* I, 52), who also gave his name to the Atlantic Ocean and the legendary continent of Atlantis.[2] When Homer recalls the origin of Nausicaa's lady-in-waiting, he designates Africa with yet another name which was never identified either:

> There a fire was kindled for her by her waiting-woman,
> Eurymedusa, an aged dame from Apeire. Long ago the curved
> ships had brought her from Apeire . . . She it was who had reared
> the white-armed Nausicaa in the palace. (*Od*. VII, 7-12).

Since Apeire (-gaia) means 'limitless (land)', it is another obvious
reference to Africa, the present name of this huge continent being even
directly derived from it (via Apire-ga, and Afir-ca).

During the dinner that Odysseus takes with King Alcinous, the blind
minstrel Demodocus sings of the end of the Trojan War, since when
nine years have gone by:

> and the minstrel, moved by the god, began, and let his song be
> heard, taking up the tale where the Argives had embarked on their
> benched ships and were sailing away, after casting fire on their
> huts, while those others led by glorious Odysseus were now sitting
> in the place of assembly of the Trojans, hidden in the horse; for the
> Trojans had themselves dragged it to the citadel. So there it stood,
> while the people talked long as they sat about it, and could form no
> resolve. Nay, in three ways did counsel find favour in their minds:
> either to cleave the hollow timber with the pitiless bronze, or to
> drag it to the height and cast it down the rocks, or to let it stand as a
> great offering to propitiate the gods, even as in the end it was to be
> brought to pass; for it was their fate to perish when their city should
> enclose the great horse of wood, wherein were sitting all the best of
> the Argives, bearing to the Trojans death and fate. (*Od*. VIII, 499-513)

The Trojans' fate is sealed because they are faced with something new
and, being unable to deal with the problem, go off to sleep on it rather
than remaining vigilant. What has come to be known as the Trojan
Horse is Homer's superb image for the Trojans bringing defeat upon
themselves by their own hands. Troy falls not because of attacks
coming from without, but because of weaknesses within.

Seeing that the minstrel's song is making Odysseus weep, Alcinous
tells Demodocus to stop. He promises Odysseus that a Phaeacian ship
will take him home, but asks him to first tell his own story. It is at this
point that Odysseus begins to tell the *Odyssey* in the words that have
been quoted so often in this Part III. The next day rich gifts are stowed
in the ship that is to take Odysseus home, sacrifices are made to the
gods, and there is a banquet with speeches, before the ship sets sail at
nightfall. Odysseus sleeps throughout the voyage and does not even
wake up when the Phaeacians put him and his gifts ashore in Ithaca. It is

therefore clear that this is not an account of an actual voyage, but another allegory. Sunset is a strange time to sail, and the distance of about 1,000 km between the Canary Islands and Cadiz is too great to be covered by a ship in a single night. Homer in fact tells us that the ship is going so fast that 'not even the circling hawk, the swiftest of winged things, could have kept pace with her' (*Od*. XIII, 86). This announces the end of Odysseus' period of initiation into knowledge, for as we saw in Chapter 11, the sparrow hawk, Greek *kirkos*, is certainly associated with Circe, *Kirke*. We are therefore to understand that Odysseus has finally earned his freedom from the influence of Circe, for he is now going faster than her:

> [The ship] sped on swiftly and clove the waves of the sea, bearing a man the peer of gods in counsel, one who in time past had suffered many griefs at heart in passing through wars of men and the grievous waves; but now he slept in peace, forgetful of all that he had suffered. (*Od. XIII, 90-92*)

Notes

1 Diodorus Siculus, *Bibliotheca Historica*, II, 47, English translation by C. H. Oldfather, Loeb Classical Library.
2 'Atlantos' is the genitive, meaning 'of Atlas'.

19

Odysseus Finally Returns to Ithaca

(Cadiz, southwest Spain)

After his last voyage from the land of the Phaeacians Odysseus wakes up, surrounded by the gifts of his late hosts, on the shores of his own country, though he does not recognize it immediately. Once again Athene helps him, advising him not to go directly and openly to his palace, but first to go and see his old swineherd, Eumaeus, to hear what has happened during his long absence, but Athene first disguises him:

> Athene touched him with her wand. She withered the fair flesh on his supple limbs, and destroyed the flaxen hair from off his head, and about all his limbs she put the skin of an aged old man. And she dimmed his two eyes that were before so beautiful, and clothed him in other raiment, a vile ragged cloak and a tunic tattered garments and foul, begrimed with filthy smoke. And about him she cast the great skin of a swift hind, stripped of the hair, and she gave him a staff, and a miserable wallet, full of holes, slung by a twisted cord. So when the two had thus taken counsel together, they parted; and thereupon the goddess went to goodly Lacedaemon to fetch the son of Odysseus. (*Od.* XIII, 429–40)

The swineherd welcomes the disguised Odysseus most hospitably, using the traditional formula 'from Zeus are all strangers and beggars', and gives him a meal, complaining all the time about the behaviour of Penelope's suitors and saying how much he regrets that his master Odysseus had never returned from the Trojan War. Even though the 'beggar' swears on oath that Odysseus will soon return, Eumaeus refuses to believe him, because so many others in the past have claimed to have news of Odysseus in the hope of reward from Penelope. He is so upset at being reminded of Odysseus, that he asks the 'beggar' to tell his story to take his mind off the subject. Odysseus then tells a tale that is part invention, but he claims to have had news of the king of Ithaca.

Odysseus Finally Returns to Ithaca

Odysseus stays with Eumaeus and the two go on swapping tales over bowls of wine, but on the fourth day, Telemachus, Odysseus' son, on his way back from a journey to Pylos and Sparta to try to get news of his father (see Part II, Chapter 8), calls at Eumaeus' hut. The swineherd goes to tell Penelope that her son is safe, and Athene restores Odysseus his normal looks so that he can reveal himself to Telemachus. Father and son discuss how they can get rid of the suitors. Telemachus says there are so many of them that direct attack is out of the question, so they agree that Odysseus will go to the palace disguised as an old beggar, and put up with whatever treatment is meted out until the time comes for vengeance.

Telemachus goes to the palace first, but does not tell Penelope that Odysseus is near. When he arrives, Odysseus is recognized only by his aged dog Argos, who dies immediately afterwards. Odysseus is insulted and hit by one of the suitors and has to fight with another beggar, but Penelope arrives in the hall and tells Telemachus to take better care of the stranger, whose identity she still does not know.

The suitors finally leave for their own homes and Odysseus tells Telemachus to hide all the arms in the palace except for those they will need themselves. Penelope asks the 'beggar' to tell his story, and though he does not tell the truth he convinces her that he has indeed seen Odysseus. The old nursemaid, Eurycleia, is summoned to wash Odysseus' feet. She recognizes him through a scar on his thigh, but he makes her keep silent.

Penelope tells of a dream in which Odysseus returns in the form of an eagle and kills all the fat geese she is feeding, but she also says she can put off the evil day of remarriage no more (her famous trick of unpicking her weaving at night was long ago found out) and is going to arrange a contest to see who can string Odysseus' bow and shoot an arrow through the hole formed by twelve axes leaning on one another like the props that hold up a beached ship, as Odysseus used to do.

The next day, the suitors all fail even to string the bow, but are most indignant when the still-disguised Odysseus wants to try. However, Telemachus says only he can decide who is allowed to join the contest. Odysseus of course succeeds, kills the most overbearing of the suitors, Antinous, then reveals to the others who he really is. They offer to make amends, but, aided by Telemachus, Eumaeus and Philoetius, Odysseus kills them all bar the minstrel Phemios and the herald Medon. Telemachus also hangs twelve of the servant girls who had become mistresses of the suitors.

The old nurse, Eurycleia, goes to tell Penelope what has happened, but she is still unable to believe that he really is Odysseus until he describes the bed chamber whose form was known only to the two of them and one servant girl.

The next day, Odysseus goes to see his father Laertes, but meanwhile news of the slaughter has got out and the relatives of the dead come to attack Odysseus. A fierce battle starts, but Athene puts an end to it:

"Refrain, men of Ithaca, from grievous war, that with all speed you must part, and that without bloodshed."

So spoke Athene, and pale fear seized them. Then in their terror the arms flew from their hands and fell one and all to the ground, as the goddess uttered her voice, and they turned toward the city, eager to save their lives.   (*Od.* XXIV, 531-36)

The *Odyssey* ends with Odysseus being told to fight no more for fear of angering the gods, and Homer tells us nothing about what happens to Odysseus later on, but all was foretold by the seer Teiresias when Odysseus visited him in the Underworld:

"'But when thou hast slain the wooers in thy halls, whether by guile or openly with the sharp sword, then do thou go forth, taking a shapely oar, until thou comest to men that know naught of the sea and eat not of food mingled with salt, aye, and they know naught of ships with purple cheeks, or of shapely oars that are as wings unto ships. And I will tell thee a sign right manifest, which will not escape thee. When another wayfarer, on meeting thee, shall say that thou hast a winnowing-fan on thy stout shoulder, then do thou fix in the earth thy shapely oar and make goodly offerings to lord Poseidon – a ram, and a bull, and a boar that mates with sows – and depart for thy home and offer sacred hecatombs to the immortal gods who hold broad heaven, to each one in due order. And death shall come to thee thyself far from the sea, a death so gentle, that shall lay thee low when thou art overcome with sleek old age, and thy people shall dwell in prosperity around thee. In this have I told thee sooth.'"   (*Od.* XI, 119-36)

Could it be that already 3,000 years ago the ideal place to retire, for those who could afford it, was a certain prosperous and mountainous country in the centre of Europe?

As we have seen, Odysseus does not reveal his true identity until he proves himself to be the only one capable of stringing the bow. This famous story was to remind sailors of the time that Ithaca (Cadiz) was in the zodiacal sign of Sagittarius, represented by a centaur with bow and arrow, i.e. in a north-northeasterly direction with respect to the last port of call, the island of Scheria (Lanzarote in the Canaries).

260

Odysseus Finally Returns to Ithaca

The last major episode in the work, the massacre of the suitors and the hanging of the servant girls, seems at first sight to be a rather unpleasant ending to a beautiful poem. However, we now know that there is a lot more to Homer than blood and thunder, and there must be a hidden meaning, probably connected with initiation. In fact this ending is not only perfectly logical, but is also the realization of the warning given to the suitors by Telemachus in Book I of the *Odyssey*:

> "depart from these halls. Prepare you other feasts, eating your own substance and changing from house to house. But if this seems in your eyes to be a better and more profitable thing, that one man's livelihood should be ruined without atonement, waste ye it. But I will call upon the gods that are forever, if haply Zeus may grant that deeds of requital may be wrought. Without atonement, then, should ye perish within my halls." (*Od.* I, 376-80)

However, there is good reason to believe that this massacre never took place in reality, but is an allegory, a warning to weak-willed men. Reference has already been made to the famous story of Penelope weaving during the day and unpicking her work at night so that she will never finish her work and will not have to choose a new husband from among the suitors, for she still hopes for the return of Odysseus. Now the loom, also associated with Circe and Calypso, was of great symbolic significance to the ancients, as is still the case in North Africa, for example, where the upper beam of the loom is called 'the Sky' and the lower one 'the Earth', while the threads weave 'Destiny'. When the piece of cloth is finished, the women intone the same formula of benediction as the midwife when she cuts the umbilical cord of the new-born baby.[1] This is an indication that the nature of the loom resembles the spider, which uses a kind of umbilical cord to weave his web. In its turn the spider's web resembles the labyrinth, as shown by those in Amiens Cathedral illustrated below and on page 262. (*See also* Plate 3).

261

Labyrinth from Amiens Cathedral.

Both the spider's web and the labyrinth have centres that can be approached only at the risk of becoming a prisoner for ever. As regards the loom, the woman who uses it has been initiated into the art of weaving. She is therefore a holder of knowledge and is considered to be 'the woman who teaches'. The common characteristic of the loom, the spider's web and the labyrinth is knowledge. The Greek language itself makes this link, for the same word *histos* is used for both 'loom' and 'cloth', while the related word *histor* is used for 'he who holds knowledge', hence our word 'historian'. In Homer's day, women were the holders of wisdom and knowledge, for they carry the fruit, which, in the figurative sense, is knowledge. The concept of woman in the role of teacher was not specifically Celtic, or Indo-European in general, for in the Land of the Pharaohs too the woman was the initiatrice who opened the path to knowledge: 'Isis unveiled is the naked truth, revealed only to the Masters'.[2] The most important holders of knowledge were goddesses and nymphs like Circe and Calypso. In Ithaca, the woman teacher was Penelope, whose wisdom is praised many times by Homer. Her erring servant girls were twelve in number, and this number is associated with accomplishment and completed cycles (as the year has twelve months). In this precise case this number announces the end of Odysseus' twelve trials, which were so many lessons of life. Symbolically these twelve servants are priestesses, each

262

of whom possesses a fraction of Penelope's knowledge. Just as Odysseus had to join with Circe to acquire knowledge, the suitors approach Penelope to the same end, but are unable to unite with her because they are not ready for initiation. They thus make do with the servants/priestesses, who are subsequently punished by death for having shared their knowledge with the common people, 'common' in the sense of 'uninitiated', for there were princes among them. Homer tells us that there were 108 suitors (*Od*. XVI, 247-56) in Odysseus' palace, a number considered 'exaggerated' by most commentators, for the refectories of the time could not seat more than about fifty people. For this reason these lines have sometimes been dismissed as not authentic. On the symbolic level, however, the number is significant, for 108 is the product of 12 times 9, the symbols of the accomplished cycle and of renewal, respectively.

This explanation leads us to the conclusion that Circe, Calypso and Penelope represent one and the same personality, or more precisely a trinity, three aspects of the same goddess, the Great Initiatrice into knowledge (*see also* Appendix Note 2, Trinities). This makes it easier to understand why the suitors were punished so severely: they had tried to approach Penelope the Initiatrice without having followed the proper path. Homer tells us through this allegory that the way to God is not easy and salvation cannot be achieved through luxury, arrogance and a life of feasting. Only the path that Odysseus has followed, that of perseverance in passing through the trials necessary to win knowledge can lead to the wisdom of Zeus. The very name of our hero, Odysseus, tells us this, for it could well come from *Hodos Zeus*, 'the path to God'. This at any rate is my interpretation, but there are other explanations, including 'child of wrath' and 'he pursued by the wrath of the gods' (from the Greek verb *odussomai*), in line with Homer's own suggestion, apparently intended for the uninitiated (*Od*. XIX, 405-409). The reader may be disappointed to learn that the famous couple Odysseus and Penelope never existed as described by Homer. Nor did their son, Telemachus. We can be sure of this also, because of this last name, which means something like 'He who battles in a distant place', an obvious epithet of Odysseus himself, but given as the name of an imaginary son. But how do we reconcile this conclusion with the description of the physical appearance of our hero in the *Iliad*? Apparently, the allegory of the *Odyssey* was composed in honour of a real city-king of Ithaca who lived under a different name. Later Hellenistic tradition has it that Odysseus married Circe, who bore him many children. But these stories are more recent than Homer and show clearly that the oral explanation of the hidden message in the *Odyssey* was never given to the Greeks (as I suspected in Part I, Chapter 5), who must have considered the epic to be simply a fairy-tale to be taken at face value.

Now that we know a lot more about the geography of the *Odyssey*, the esoteric meaning of the labyrinth and of Odysseus' name, we also understand why this kings' realm was called Ithaca, a name derived not from Greek but from Hebrew, meaning 'Island in the middle', which was present-day Cadiz in southern Spain. Its port was called on by all ships travelling back and forth between northern Europe and the Mediterranean, as it lies about mid-way on the sea lanes, but more significantly, it was situated in the centre of the world, as it was known to the seafarers of the time, which stretched from Scandinavia to Senegal and from Cuba to the Levant. But this is not all: the name Ithaca has also a particular meaning at the esoteric level. We have already seen that 'Odysseus' means 'The path to God', the thorny way that leads to illumination and redemption, which is found, symbolically speaking, in the centre of the labyrinth which was also called the 'Island in the middle'. The name of Odysseus and that of his kingdom, Ithaca, are therefore inseparable, the latter being only a surname which cannot be found on a map. In Antiquity, Cadiz was known as Gadir, while Ithaca must have been a nickname for sailors who considered it the 'island in the middle' on their long trips over the high seas. Only to Homer and other initiates the name Ithaca had a double meaning.

Not only numbers had an esoteric meaning for the ancients, but colours were also significant.[3,4] As white encompasses all other colours, it symbolized love and knowledge, the two prerequisites for humanity to advance to ever higher levels, as was taught by the early 'Gnostic' Christians, in particular St John, who perpetuated the ancient traditions of the West.[5] The centre of a labyrinth or mandala – whenever represented in colour – is therefore always white, and so is the Grail on the arms of Vlissingen, as white is the colour of Divine Light.

Notes

1 J. Chevalier and A. Gheerbrant, *Dictionnaire des Symboles*, p. 950.
2 Michel Mirabail, *Dictionnaire de l'ésotérisme*, Privat (Marabout), 1981.
3 J. Prieur, *Les Symboles universels*, Fernand Lanore, Paris, 1982.
4 R-L Rousseau, *Le language des couleurs*, Dangles, St-Jean-de-Braye, 1977.
5 P. Le Cour, *L'Evangile ésotérique de Saint-Jean*, Dervy-Livres, Paris, 1987.

20

The Destiny of the Gods

It has never been possible to explain the *Iliad* or the *Odyssey* logically and coherently while locating the action in the Mediterranean, even by taking considerable liberties with the texts. For this reason it has often been though that Homer's original texts had been greatly modified by minstrels who wanted to please a particular king or public and altered names and descriptions accordingly.

It now seems that this is not the case at all, and that the poems have survived with so few changes that it is still possible to locate virtually all the places mentioned by Homer in western Europe and the Atlantic and follow the action without deviating from the text in the slightest. This adds a lot of interest for the modern reader, since the poems are now no longer entirely in the realm of myth, but describe the way of life on the Atlantic shores of Europe over 3,000 years ago, and the horrors of the Trojan War.

We have seen that the pieces of the Homerian puzzle fit logically and easily together in western Europe and the Atlantic, which they never did in the Mediterranean, and that anyone can confirm this by reading Homer together with the maps and explanations presented in this book. But we have been so conditioned by the classical tradition in Western education that we have difficulty in believing that there was any civilization or culture worthy of the name in western Europe before the Romans came. The reason for this is, of course, that there are so few traces of this earlier civilization (though each year now brings new archeological finds). And the fault lies very much with the Druids' religious taboo on writing. The conquerors of Celtic territories only had to get rid of a few leaders who held all the knowledge in order easily to hold the annexed lands, and this is precisely what happened according to a well-established pattern that has been repeated throughout history and even very recently in different parts of the world. The Celtic territories were occupied by the Roman army for 400 years, though there was fierce resistance and a real guerilla war on the part of the Gauls, often aided by their allies from the right bank of the Rhine. However, there were cruel reprisals by the occupiers, and Julius Caesar himself admits to having his men cut off the hands of the defenders of Uxellodunum (now taken to be Puy d'Issolu, Lot, in the south of France).[1] The Roman military machine was too much for the ill-disciplined Gauls, the occupation lasted too long for resistance to continue and the survivors of Caesar's genocide naturally enough ended up by not just collaborating with the enemy but by virtually forgetting that there had been a time before the Romans came. Unfortunately, militarism and foreign cultures have never got on well together, and the occupiers had a very destructive influence from one end of the Empire to the other. For example, in the extreme northwest, the Romans destroyed the Druids' school on Anglesey (off North Wales, where the Gallic Druids also used to complete their studies), and in the east they destroyed the temple of Jerusalem. They were also responsible for the destruction of Carthage and the decline of the universities of Marseille and Alexandria.

There can be no better summing up of the Roman occupation than the words of the Roman historian Tacitus, who would today be called a 'dissident'. In his memoirs, written in secret in his country house outside Rome, he has this to say about the activities of the Roman army in western Europe: 'They pillage, massacre and rape, and they call that "governing"; they create a desert, and they call that "peace"'.[2]

In the light of what we have discovered in this book, we have to agree with Tacitus' judgement, and researchers are only just beginning to realize that a thriving Celtic culture was destroyed first by the Roman army, then by the churchmen, who did all they could to eliminate anything that recalled the Gnostic past. In these circumstances it is an irony of history that a Celt, Lleyn, son of a British king, succeeded St Peter to become the first bishop of Rome, thus opening the long list of popes under the Latinized name of Linus. When the Roman Empire, and with it Roman culture, collapsed in its turn about 400 AD, Europe plunged into the darkness of the Middle Ages, and the decline was such that it took almost a thousand years to recover. There was a great cultural revival with the Renaissance, but then almost everything had to start from scratch again. The sea route to the Americas was rediscovered (Columbus, Amerigo Vespucci, Verrazano), astronomy was redeveloped (Copernicus, Galileo, Brahé, Keppler), and the subconscious was rediscovered (Freud, Jung), to mention just a few examples. But western Europe has still not recovered the memory of its illustrious Bronze Age past.

Recent archeological and linguistic discoveries are making us reconsider much of the received wisdom. For example, it would appear that the oldest geographical names in Europe go right back to the neolithic age and are found in the plains of northwest Europe, in particular the frontier region between Germany, the Netherlands and Belgium, which is not so surprising as we now know that farming was practised on a large scale several millenia before Christ, and it would be only natural if this occurred on the best land first.[3] We have concrete evidence of this very early cultivation in the form of tools, traces of farms and dykes, these last indicating long-term planning of the work. Homer confirms the existence in his era of dykes, fields of wheat, orchards and vineyards (see Appendix Note 23), houses (generally of wood, as is often the case still today in northern latitudes, wood being warmer than stone), 'well-built' towns and citadels, fine ramparts, streets and roads. All this existed long before the Romans, for contrary to popular belief they were not the first to build roads, and in fact there are examples in England and France of Roman roads being built over a more ancient one, for instance in Cambridgeshire.[4]

It is not true either that these ancestors of ours were clothed only in animal skins, though skins were indeed used for special effects. For example, Gallic orators sometimes wore lion skins to underline their eloquence, which was an efficient arm for impressing an illiterate audience.[5] The Germans wore wolf skins in time of war, to frighten the Romans (the German *Wehrwulf* simply means 'wolf of defence or resistance'), and perhaps also for mystical reasons, believing that the skin could transfer some of the qualities of the animal, such as aggressiveness, to the wearer. At home, though, they wore tunics and undergarments.[6] The Celts also produced very high quality cloth, samples of which have recently been found in the tomb of a Celtic chief discovered near Stuttgart, Germany, dating from about 700 BC.

We are taught that the ancient peoples of the Rhine used to spend their days drinking and playing dice, with their wives as stakes. This, too, appears to be a fabrication of history if we read Tacitus, a contemporary, who says exactly the opposite: 'their marriage code is strict and no aspect of their morality deserves more praise'.[7] The Dutch are taught that their ancestors had come down the Rhine in hollow tree trunks. This too is nonsense, as we have seen, since more than a millenium before Christ the peoples living near the sea were able to build 'well-balanced ships' capable of sailing great distances over the ocean. As to the Gauls, and in particular the Aquitains, Timagenus of Alexandria wrote that: 'nowhere in the country does one see men or women dirty or dressed in rags, however poor they might be', and Pline and other historians tell us that Gallic women used not only soap, but also perfumes and cosmetics.

The destruction of Celtic culture and society by outside forces was facilitated by their own weaknesses. Although everyone, including women, had in principle access to education after careful selection, society was highly inegalitarian as all power was concentrated in the hands of a very small élite class of initiates, who did not share their knowledge with the population at large, and even prohibited writing for other purposes than administration. The great majority of the population was thus barred from decision-making, even in affairs of general interest. What was even more serious, the Druids left their subjects in a spiritual void by refusing to explain their religion and philosophy to outsiders. It seems that their philosophy was very advanced indeed, not to say of great complexity and therefore incomprehensible for ordinary man anyhow. The common public was therefore given only the empty shells: a series of fairytales called 'mythology', devised by the Druids to hide and pass on their philosophy in space and time to other initiates, while keeping the masses happy with simplistic, popular stories. But with the evolution of society, this policy could not last indefinitely. Already from late classical literature, one has the impression that the Greeks and Romans did not really believe in all those gods which they now appear to have inherited from the Celts. The fate of the gods, who once were such lively concepts of the fertile Celtic mind, was to die after a long agony on the shores of the Mediterranean, where they would be turned into marble forever.

Notes

1 Caesar, *The Conquest of Gaul*, VIII, 44.
2 Tacitus, *Agricola*, 30.
3 *The Times Historical Atlas*.
4 H.C. Coppock, *Over the Hills to Cherry Hinton*, Plumridge, Linton, Cambridge, 1984, p. 103.
5 N. Chadwick, *The Celts*, Penguin, 1985.
6 Tacitus, *Germania*, 17.
7 Ibid, 18.

21

Who was Homer?

This question has been the subject of speculation ever since classical antiquity. Since the earliest times, the Greeks considered Homer as their greatest poet and they believed that he had personally written the *Iliad* and the *Odyssey* on papyrus in Ionian Greek around the eighth century BC. Despite the many legends about Homer, nothing was known with much certainty about his person, his parents, his birthplace, his life or even his place of death, so that many Greek towns vied for the honour of being the guardian of his tomb.

In the nineteenth century it was widely believed that the *Iliad* and the *Odyssey* were amalgams of poems composed by different people at different times. More recent studies however, including detailed analysis of the language and style, have convinced most scholars that the epics are in fact the work of a single poet, though a number of changes and later additions have been identified. We can be confident that such changes were relatively slight because certain characteristics not typical of Greece were not modified. For example, the Greek bards could have easily substituted cypress and olive trees for poplars and willows.

According to some, Homer was in fact the blind bard Demodocus, who sings the end of the Trojan War at the court of Alcinous, king of the Phaeacians, in Book VIII of the *Odyssey*. This would amount to Homer having 'signed' his work. However, there is so little description of Scheria, the isle of the Phaeacians, that it is unlikely that Lanzarote was his home, and it is also unlikely that he was blind because of the wealth of visual detail in the poems. For the ancients, the mention of blindness merely referred to the capacity of clairvoyance of many seers and poets, for it was believed that the blind could 'see' the future because they were more receptive than other people.

There has also been considerable speculation about the meaning of the name Homer itself. According to Hesiod, it was precisely the Aeolian nickname of the blind, while other ancient Greeks noted that *homer* simply meant 'hostage', because only hostages have the time to compose long poems while a war is going on. This argument seems so absurd that we must look elsewhere, and in any case, since he was not

Greek, we should consider other Indo-European languages where we find a Gothic root *omer-*, which, like its Latin counterpart *amar-*, means 'to love'. If there is indeed a linguistic relationship between *omer* and *Homer*, his name would simply be an epithet meaning the 'Well-loved one'.

We have seen in this book that Homer's cradle must have stood far from classical Greece in space and time and that he was in fact a Celt, living in the Bronze Age and describing a war between Celts, Celtic trade routes and the Gnostic religion. He must have been an eyewitness of the Trojan War to judge by the detail of his descriptions. But this does not mean that he composed the *Iliad* during the war itself. It is even certain that the epics date from at least one generation after the war, because of the following observation about a strong warrior before Troy, lifting a heavy rock:

> But the son of Tydeus grasped in his hand a stone – a mighty deed –
> one that not two men could bear, such as mortals now are; yet
> lightly did he wield it even alone. (*Il.* V, 302-304)

Homer would not be the last war-veteran to look down on the younger post-war generation as weaklings! But this time-lag implies that Homer has composed the *Iliad* around his fifties at the earliest. Since the Trojan War presumably took place around 1200 BC, the poet lived in the twelfth century BC, much earlier than assumed hitherto. Subsequently, his epics were transmitted orally for about four centuries until they were written down in Greece in the eighth century BC.

While it is relatively easy to situate Homer in time, it is much less so to retrace the region of origin of this bard who travelled widely with his lyre. He was unquestionably a Celt, but the Celtic lands of the time stretched from Scandinavia to Morocco. A first clue of his origin is of course his name which may have been fairly common as it is also found in a number of towns in northwest Europe. Most appropriately, there is a Homersfield in East Anglia, close to the battlefields of Troy. In the northern Netherlands there is the little town of Hommerts and in northern France we find St Omer-en-Chaussée (northwest of Paris) and St Omer (near Calais). We must rule out England as the poet's homeland, for he was much less informed about the Trojans than the Achaeans, as the lists of regiments clearly show (see Part IV). On the Continent, there are only two regions that are described in great detail, including trees and plants: the province of Zeeland in the Netherlands and the province of Cadiz in Spain. The former was the home of the greatest hero of the *Iliad*, Achilles, while the latter was the kingdom of Odysseus, the central figure of the *Odyssey*.

Who was Homer?

When Cailleux identified Cadiz with Ithaca in the last century, he concluded – too quickly – that Homer was also from Cadiz, as he considered it very likely that the poet had dedicated his epics to the greatest hero of the *Odyssey*, the king of Ithaca.[1] I shared this view for many years, the more so as it can be backed up by several arguments which we will discuss first.

To start with, Homer often compares warriors with lions and he seems to be familiar with the behaviour of these animals both when they attack their prey and when they are attacked themselves. There were indeed lions in northern Morocco and probably also in southern Spain in Homer's time so that the poet was able to observe them if he had lived there. Frequent contact between Celtic peoples of northern and southern Europe would also explain how the lion as a symbol of power came to figure so frequently on the armorial devices of countries, provinces and towns of northern Europe long before the colonial era.

Another indication that Homer lived in southern Spain is the fact that he often describes Troy, Mycenae and Athens, the towns we identified in northern Europe, as having 'broad streets'. If this particularity struck him, he must also have been familiar with southern towns with very narrow streets, so constructed to provide a maximum of shade as protection against the summer heat.

A third argument in favour of Spain is provided by Homer's viewpoint that 'Thessaly is beyond Euboea', as Lasserre reminds us. For this reason, many Greeks believed that the poet was from southwest Turkey. Seen from there, Thessaly in northern Greece is 'beyond' Euboea, the large island on Greece's east coast. But if that were the case, Homer, living on 'Trojan' territory, would have been part of the Trojan camp. By contrast, if he lived in Spain, this problem is entirely solved, for in Part IV we have identified Thessaly in the northern Netherlands (Map 17) and Euboea in western France (Map 15) so that for Homer, composing his epic in Spain, Thessaly was indeed 'beyond Euboea', while the poet himself was firmly on the Achaean side of the conflict.

If we combine the following two legends, we are even made to believe that Odysseus was not only a countryman of Homer but also his grandfather, by his son Telemachus. According to a legend ascribed to Hesiod, Telemachus had a son by a daughter of King Nestor:

> So well-girded Polycaste, the youngest daughter of Nestor, Neleus' son, was joined in love with Telemachus through golden Aphrodite and bare Persepolis.[2]

271

When, nine centuries later, the Roman emperor Hadrian inquired with the Sibyl about the origin of Homer, he received a very similar message, the priestess answering him in Greek verse:

> Do you ask me of the obscure race and country of the heavenly siren? Ithaca is his country, Telemachus his father, and Epicasta, Nestor's daughter, the mother that bare him, a man by far the wisest of mortal kind.[3]

The mother's name is not identical in the two legends, but this is not unusual in ancient texts. (For instance, the mother of Oedipus has also different names depending on the source). As to Persepolis, it cannot be excluded a priori that it refers to Homer, as the latter name was a mere epithet as we have seen. (Persepolis was, of course, also the capital of the Persian Empire at the time of Darius, as it is a very ancient Indo-European name).

Although there are thus several indications that Homer was from southern Spain, there still appear to be flaws in the argument. If it is certain that Homer lived in Cadiz, this does not necessarily imply that he was also born there. Besides, as legends are not the most reliable source of information, we may doubt that Homer was a grandson of the king of Ithaca, the more so as Homer was an eyewitness of the Trojan War, who was even surprised to see the sons of Dares on the battlefield. For this reason the poet must have been of the same generation as the king of Ithaca.

We are thus confronted with a problem that cannot be solved unless we examine the other side of the coin: the *Iliad*. As neither Cailleux nor Gideon (a century later) had identified the origin of any of the Achaean and Trojan regiments (with the exception of Odysseus' regiment), he could not retrace either the origin of Homer in case he was a compatriot of the greatest hero of his *Iliad*, Achilles, who turns out to have been a prince of the present provinces of Holland and Zeeland in the Netherlands and Flanders in Belgium (see Part IV, Regiment 21). In 'The Origin of Homer and Hesiod, and of their Contest', which in its present form dates from the second century AD, although it is certainly based on a much older tradition, we find that the most likely name of Homer's father, and of himself, was Meles. During the contest, Hesiod even addresses him as 'Homer, son of Meles'. Although the same source mentions four different names for his mother, it is certain that she was from the island of Ios. Once, when travelling as a minstrel from city to city, Homer came to Delphi (Delft) where he asked the Pythia who he was and from what country. The priestess replied:

Who was Homer?

> The isle of Ios is your mother's country and it shall receive you dead; but beware of the riddle of the young children.[3]

There is only one island along the Atlantic coast whose name resembles Ios. On ancient maps of Zeeland it is marked as Joosland (Land of Ios became Joos in Dutch spelling), situated east of Vlissingen. Because of land reclamation, this tiny island has become part of Walcheren where we find today a village called Nieuw en St Joosland (New and Saint Joosland). Homer's original name and that of his father, Meles, is preserved not only by a village situated only a few miles distant, Meliskerke (Map 12, 75 and 76), but also by many families on Walcheren whose surnames are Melis or Melisse ('Son of Melis').

This is a first indication that Homer was from Zeeland, the region he describes in so much detail. Judging by his profound knowledge of symbolism, history, geography and mythology, he was certainly initiated at the Mystery school in Zierikzee, where he became befriended with the Trojan priest Dares and with the king of Ithaca. It is most likely that he composed the *Iliad* first, in which he glorifies the local prince Achilles. He then set off to live in southern Spain, where he composed the *Odyssey*, describing the routes over the Atlantic Ocean based on information from the seafarers of Cadiz, at the same time glorifying his host under the name Odysseus. But, according to the 'Contest', at the end of his life, Homer travelled to Argos (Normandy, France) where he stayed for a while. He then 'crossed over' to Delos (Deelen, the Netherlands) where he attended an important gathering. After the meeting he went to Ios (Joosland in the nearby province of Zeeland):

> The poet sailed to Ios, after the assembly was broken up, to join Creophylus, and stayed there some time, being now an old man. And, it is said, as he was sitting by the sea he asked some boys who were returning from fishing:
> 'Sirs, hunters of deep-sea prey, have we caught anything?'
> To this they replied:
> 'All that we caught, we left behind, and carry away all that we did not catch.'
> Homer did not understand this reply and asked what they meant. They then explained that they had caught nothing in fishing, but had been catching their lice, and those of the lice which they caught, they left behind; but carried away in their clothes those which they did not catch. Hereupon Homer remembered the oracle and, perceiving that the end of his life had come composed his own epitaph. And while he was retiring from that place, he slipped in a clayey place and fell upon his side, and died, it is said,

273

the third day after. He was buried in Ios, and this is his epitaph:
   'Here the earth covers the sacred head of divine Homer, the glorifier of hero-men.'[3]

Since it is certain that Homer lived for some time in southern Spain, one may wonder why he travelled to northern Europe in his latter days. The reason must be that, like so many elderly people, he yearned after his native land. Apparently, he wanted to see for a last time the familiar surroundings of his youth. After a long life of wandering Homer thus returned to die where he was born: on the islet of Ios, today Nieuw and St Joosland which is now part of the larger island of Walcheren, the Hades of the ancients. Although we may never find his remains here as the islet of Joos was submerged by the sea for a long period during the Middle Ages, the crescent on the coats of arms of the village (shown below) is likely to have been a homage paid by the Druids to the great poet, as it is far too exclusive a symbol to be attributed to just any rural community. For the ancients, the crescent was associated more in particular with Artemis, the daughter of Zeus who was in charge of the succession of births, symbolized by the ever-returning crescent of the moon. In the classical era, Artemis was therefore pictured with a crescent in her hair. But also Isis and the Virgin Mary were often portrayed with the crescent, the symbol of resurrection and eternity. Although Homer's ashes have disappeared, truly eternal monuments remain: the *Iliad* and the *Odyssey* that have fascinated mankind for over 3,000 years. In this respect, Homer's fate resembles that of Shakespeare and Mozart. It is as if these giants of creative genius do not need a tomb like lesser mortals, as they remain forever alive in our hearts.

> On this theme, then, we shall endeavour to make our reputation; the more so, since we observe how greatly historians are admired: it is for the same reason that Homer has been honoured in life and death by all mankind. Let us then thank him thus for his playful entertainment; and as for his origin and the rest of his poetry, let us hand them down through the gift of accurate memory for the common possession of those Hellenes who aspire to be Lovers of the Beautiful.[4]
> (Alcidamas, *On Homer*)

Notes

1 Th. Cailleux, *Poésies d'Homère faites en Ibérie et décrivant non la Méditerranée mais l'Atlantique*, Théorie nouvelle, Paris, 1879.
2 Hesiod, *The Catalogues of Women*, 12. Translation H. G. Evelyn-White, Loeb Classical Library.
3 *The Origin of Homer and Hesiod, and of their Contest*, translation by H. G. Evelyn-White, Loeb Classical Library.
4 J.G. Winter, (Michigan Papyri, 2754), *Transactions and Proceedings of the American Philological Association*, LVI, 1925, p. 120.

Part IV The Catalogue of Ships

(Supplement to Part II: The World of the *Iliad*)

A list of all Achaean and Trojan Regiments with Maps

1

Where did all the
Warriors come from?

The main elements of Homeric geography that I have tried to sketch in the previous chapters will be completed in this section, which is devoted to the list of the Achaean and Trojan armies, as set out in Book II of the *Iliad*, and referred to since antiquity, somewhat inappropriately, as 'The Catalogue of Ships'. The reader of the *Iliad* will thus now be able to situate not only the theatres of action, but also the origins of the principal actors in the drama. This considerably adds to the interest of the *Iliad*, which no longer belongs solely to the realm of myth, but can be seen as an account of a war that really did take place. (Maps 14–19 are grouped at the end of Part IV).

What is more, knowing the geographical origin of the warriors in the *Iliad* gives an added dimension to the description of their respective characters, so brilliantly portrayed by Homer. It seems to be possible to recognize certain characteristics shared by the inhabitants of particular regions of Europe, even if they are not strictly the same peoples from the ethnic standpoint, since it is indeed generally recognized that climate has a definite influence on human behaviour. We are struck, for example, by the contrasting characters of the two main Achaean heroes, Achilles and Odysseus, who come from the Netherlands and the south of Spain respectively (see Regiments 21 and 15).

Achilles exhibits a somewhat Nordic character still recognizable today in northern Europe, especially in the country. He is a man of action rather than words, a very stubborn introvert, quick-tempered and belligerent if provoked, but with a very profound sense of justice, loyal to the end and very generous towards those to whom he feels deeply attached.

In contrast, Odysseus has a more Mediterranean character, like his neighbour, the famous orator Nestor (Regiment 11) 'from whose tongue flowed speech sweeter than honey' (*Il.* I, 249). Having the gift of the gab he always first tries to resolve the problems by clever negotiation, if not by trickery, before resorting to force. He is

277

physically smaller than Achilles, which may be a further indication of his southern origin.

Agememnon, commander-in-chief of the Achaean armies fighting against Troy, and king of the northern half of France and the Rhineland (Regiment 9), exhibits the qualities that the French still much admire in their leaders: he attaches great importance to glory, prestige, and material and spiritual power. Agamemnon is an egoist and extrovert, who likes making speeches to impress, manipulate and dominate his subjects. However, it must not be forgotten that eloquence was much admired among the Celts and was also the only means by which to influence an illiterate public. It was thus of vital importance to any head of state.

As for the Trojans, it is not possible to discern any traits that are typical of the English of today – except perhaps, one might unkindly mention Priam's tendency to hark back to the good old days rather than face up to present problems (Il. II, 796). Homer was in fact not in a good position to describe the characters of the people living in the enemy camp in detail, but he shows great respect for the old king Priam and speaks with admiration of his eldest son Hector, and gives tender descriptions of the relations between Hector and his wife Andromache and son Astyanax, but he mistrusts Priam's other sons and, in particular, has nothing good to say about Paris, who had caused the war by abducting Helen, the wife of his host Menelaus.

If I have been able to convince the reader of the validity of the many arguments put forward in Part II in identifying the five key areas of Homeric geography: the Troad, Egypt, Crete, Ithaca and Mycenae/ Argos as England, Seine-Maritime, Scandinavia, southwest Spain and northern France, respectively, he will have no difficulty in following the identification of the regions of origin of all the Achaean and Trojan regiments. It was in fact relatively easy to put all the other pieces of the puzzle in their proper places once these five key pieces had been found. For me, this is confirmation that this identification must be basically correct. Once again, the names of rivers were the main clues and turned out to be most helpful and reliable, while the identification of some city names may be erroneous and some could not be found at all.

Even the most recent studies show that only a minority of the place-names cited in the catalogue of ships can be found in Greece. Two thousand years ago, the Greek geographer Stabo gave up the search altogether, writing that 'it is difficult to find these places today, and you would be no better off if you did, because no one lives there'. Besides, Homeric names found in Greece are spread over the country in such a haphazard way that it is very difficult to assign a regiment to a particular territory. What is more, the outcome of such an exercise is most puzzling because, for example, the four main kings, Agamemnon, Odysseus, Achilles and Menelaus, would have held very small territories, quite out of keeping with their supposed power. Conversely, it was always incomprehensible that the regiment from Athens, the Greek capital, should play such an insignificant role in the *Iliad*.

For nine out of the twenty-nine Achaean regiments, not even a single name can be found in Greece. Of the twenty-nine place-names listed by Homer for Regiment 1 from Boeotia, only ten were transposed to Boeotia in Greece, whereas all but one can be found in Jutland, Denmark (the only region in Europe where the roots of all the names of Regiment 1 can be found together), taking into account language and sound changes over time. In some cases there is even a choice to be made between various possibilities. For example Hyle (Greek *Hule*), which is not found in Greece, is the name of many places in Scandinavia, two of which are situated in Jutland: Hyllebjerg (Hylle mountain) and Hyllested (Hylle town). The former is situated on a lake, the latter inland. In this particular case the context provides the answer, for Homer states that Hyle was on a lake, so it must be the village of Hyllebjerg.

It is even more difficult to find Trojan place-names in Turkey. The number of Homeric names transposed to that country being so small that a well-known researcher wrote in despair that a Trojan regiment must have come from the moon! By contrast, in western Europe almost all the names in both Achaean and Trojan territory can be found and, with the notable exception of Troy, they are nearly all still inhabited, though probably not by the descendants of the Bronze Age heroes. Similarly, in this new context, the names of all the tribes, many of which were formerly a complete mystery, can now be explained. The remaining gaps and errors in the identification of place-names may be remedied in due course, possibly with the help of readers familiar with particular regions and the etymology of local names. In many cases it suffices to go back to the medieval name to find a close resemblance with the corresponding Homeric name. For example, we can identify Homer's Tyrins with Thury-Harcourt in France only because we know that the latter town was still called Tirins in the Middle Ages (and, of course, because other names associated with the same regiment are found in the same region).

In the following pages, the description of each of the regiments is preceded by a summary table for each of the two armies in order to give the reader a quick overview of the composition. The *Iliad* does not list the regiments in a logical geographical order, either because of the prestige attached to particular numbers, or because later transcriptions of the text attempted to fit it to the geography of Greece and Turkey, but I keep to the order as it figures in Book II. Within the territory of a given regiment, Homer gives place-names in random order, no doubt governed by the dictates of meter. The regiment numbers (for the Achaeans) and letters (for the Trojans) correspond to those appearing on Map 9 in Part II, Chapter 14.

2

The Achaean Army

(*Il.* II, 494–759)

Résumé of the list of regiments and their identification
Commander-in-chief: Agamemnon, king of Mycenae
(Argos)

(See Map inside Front Cover)

	Name of region, town or people	Name of chief	No. of ships	Present region and country
1	Boeotians	Peneleos	50	Jutland, Denmark
2	Aspledon	Ascalaphus	30	Halland, Sweden
3	Phocians	Schedius	40	Beauce, France
4	Locrians	Aias of Oileus	40	St Lô, France
5	Euboea	Elephenor	40	North Brittany, France
6	Athens	Menestheus	50	Cherbourg, France
7	Salamis	Aias of Telamon	12	Salamanca, Spain
8	Argos (town & region)	Diomedes	80	Arromanches and Calvados, France
9	Mycenae (Kingdom of Argos)	Agamemnon	100	Northern France
10	Lacedaemon	Menelaus	60	Southwest Spain
11	Pylos	Nestor	90	Southwest Spain
12	Arcadia	Agapenor	60	Vosges, France
13	Buprasium Elis	Amphimachus Eurytus	40	Southwest Spain
14	Dulichium	Meges Echinae	40	Southwest Spain
15	Ithaca	Odysseus	12	Southwest Spain
16	Aetolians	Thoas	40	Western France
17	Crete	Idomeneus Meriones	80	Southern Norway
18	Rhodes	Tlepolemus	9	Switzerland/Austria
19	Syme	Nireus	3	Western Holland

20	Nisyrus, Crapathus,			
	Casos, Cos, and	Pheidippus	30	Northern Holland
	Calydnian Isles	Antiphus		
21	Pelasgian Argos,	Achilles	50	Flanders, Zeeland
	Phthia and Hellas			Western Holland
22	Phylace and	Protesilaus	40	Western Holland
	Pyrasus	Podarces		
23	Pherae	Eumelus	11	Schwerin, East Germany
24	Methone and	Philoctetes	7	Eiffel, Taunus, Odenwald
	Thaumacia			West Germany
25	Tricca and	Podaleirius	30	Langeland, Fünen,
	Ithome	Machaon		Sjælland, Denmark
26	Ormenius	Eurypylus	40	Western Norway
27	Argissa	Polypoetes	40	Schleswig-Holstein, West
				Germany
28	Cyphus	Gouneus	22	Pomerania, East Germany
29	Magnetes	Prothous	40	Pomerania, East Germany
				and Poland

Regiment 1

Of the Boeotians Peneleos and Leïtus were captains, and Arcesilaus and Prothoënor and Clonius; these were they that dwelt in Hyria and rocky Aulis and Schoenus and Scolus and Eteonus with its many ridges, Thespeia, Graea and spacious Mycalessus; and that dwelt about Harma and Eilesium and Erythrae; and that held Eleon and Hyle and Peteon, Ocalea and Medeon, the well-built citadel, Copae, Eutresis, and Thisbe, the haunt of doves; that dwelt in Coroneia and grassy Haliartus, and that held Plataea and dwelt in Glisas; that held lower Thebe, the well-built citadel, and holy Onchestus, the bright grove of Poseidon; and that held Arne, rich in vines, and Mideia and sacred Nisa and Anthedon on the seaboard. Of these there came fifty ships, and on board of each went one hundred and twenty young men of the Boeotians. (*Il.* II, 494-510)

Homer begins the list of regiments of the Achaean army with the Boeotians, apparently out of politeness towards the population of the country playing host to the entire fleet assembled for the invasion of the Troad. The host country was in fact the present Denmark (see Part II, Chapters 6 and 15), where virtually all place-names of Regiment I can still be identified (see Map 14 at the end of Part IV). That Denmark was once a Celtic country is well attested, both by archaeological finds and by the Danish language, which has a curious way of counting, different from that of its neighbours and reminiscent of the French system, where, for example, 'ninety-two' is 'quatre-vingt-douze', literally 'four (times) twenty (plus) twelve'. In Old Danish this same number is 'tooghalvfemsindstyve', literally 'two and half of the fifth twenty' – a Celtic method of counting.

In the north of mainland Denmark, Jutland, the Limfjord links the North Sea with the Baltic through a series of big lakes and forms the ideal place for the secret rendezvous of the great fleet of 1,186 vessels. Homer calls this place Aulis, a name preserved in that of a number of towns on the shores of the fjord, such as Ålborg (Ål is pronounced like English awl), Oland, Ålum and Ålestrup. Other names mentioned by Homer are still to be found in the same region: Hyria (Hjørring, the region north of Ålborg), Scoinos (Skjern, a town southwest of Limfjord), Scolos (Skjoldborg, in the extreme northwest of Jutland, while in the northeast is the famous Cnossus, now Knösen. This whole region of northern Jutland was already an important religious centre long before the Bronze Age, as evidenced by the presence of many megalithic monuments. Closely connected with Cnossus is the story of Icarus, who escaped from the labyrinth on wings that he made himself. His names is preserved in the present town of Ikast in the centre of Jutland (from Ikar-sted = town of Icarus). Homer mentions the Icarian Sea once (*Il.* II, 145). This must have been part of the North Sea, most probably the waters between Oslo and Jutland, where the 'south and east winds whip up the sea', against the coast, that is. It should be noted in passing that this description makes little sense in the Mediterranean, where the Icarian Sea is just off the southwest coast of Turkey, not between Crete and mainland Greece as one would expect.

Homer rightly calls Denmark 'a land exceeding rich', apparently because of its first-rate agricultural land. A region called by Homer 'spacious Mycalessus' was eastern Jutland, where we find Mygind and Mylund. He mentions Graea (Grærup), 'grassy' Haliartus (Halling), Hyle (Hyllebjrg). Other recognizable names are: Harma (Harnorup), Medeon (Madum), Thisbe (Thisted), Arne 'rich in vines' (near the river Arnå). The epithet is not so surprising, since there were vineyards in Scandinavia in the Bronze Age (see Part I, Chapter 4, Vegetation, in particular in the south of Jutland, where we find Pramne (now Bramming), where Circe got her wine from (*Od.* X, 235). An interesting Scandinavian name found in Homer is Scandeia, a town and region in east Jutland now Skanderborg (*Il.* X, 268). Eutresis ('good' Tresis) was probably Dreslette, Copae (Copenhoved – a name also found further east: Copenhagen = port of Copae), Nisa (Nissum, but also the name of the river Nissan in southwest Sweden) and Anthedon 'on the seaboard' seems to be Andkaer, while Eilesium could be Elsö. For more names, see Map 14 at the end of Part IV.

Regiment 2

> And they that dwelt in Aspledon and Orchomenus of the Minyae
> were led by Ascalaphus and Ialmenus, sons of Ares, whom in the
> palace of Actor, son of Azeus, the honoured maiden, Astyoche,
> conceived of mighty Ares, when he had entered into her upper
> chamber; for he lay with her in secret. And with these were ranged
> thirty hollow ships. (*Il*. II, 511-16)

Aspledon and Orchomenus are difficult to identify, but by combining
the scant information available, it seems probable that this is the southwest of Sweden, where Aspledon might be the region of Astorp (*torp* =
village) near Hälsingborg, and Orchomenus (the name of three different regions in Europe) the region of Örkelljunga and Örkened.

To try to verify the identification of Sweden as the country of origin
of Regiment 2, I made the assumption that the commanders were given
the name of their town or region, which was often the case in Homer's
time (for example, Thessalos seems to have been king of Thessaly – see
Regiment 20). In this case the chief warriors Ascalaphus and Ialmenus
would have come from Ask and Halmstad respectively, both places in
southwest Sweden.

A further clue is that near Halmstad we now find the River Nissan,
no doubt the Celtic name Nisa mentioned in the description of Regiment 1, which has apparently migrated east with the Celts invading
southern Sweden (see Map 14 at the end of Part IV).

Regiment 3

> And of the Phocians Schedius and Epistrophus were captains, sons
> of great-souled Iphitus, son of Naubolus; they held Cyparissus and
> rocky Pytho, and sacred Crisa and Daulis and Panopeus; and dwelt
> about Anemoreia and Hyampolis, and lived beside the goodly river
> Cephisus, and held Lilaea by the spring of Cephisus. With these
> followed forty black ships. And their leaders busily marshalled the
> ranks of the Phocians, and made ready for battle hard by the
> Boeotians on the left. (*Il*. II, 517-26)

The Phocians, as their name indicates, were the inhabitants of the
Beauce, the broad region southwest of Paris. 'Sacred Crisa' was
Cressely in the Chevreuse valley (the suffix -*ly* meaning 'place'). The
name of the river Cephisus seems to have disappeared, unless it was
preserved by the town of Sées, on the upper Orne, Homer's Orneia (see
Regiment 9). Daulis seems to correspond to Dollon east of Le Mans.

Hyampolis was Janville, between Paris and Orléans, called Hiemivilla in the Middle Ages (*polis* = ville). 'Rocky Pytho' would be Putanges, also on the Orne. Cyparissus was Civry (Siveriacum in 1250), east of Châteaudun; Panopeus corresponds to Panon, southeast of Le Mans; Anemoreia was Amné, west of Le Mans, and Lilaea was the present Lilly (Liliacum in 1157), which, however, seems to have been rebuilt on the right bank of the Seine (see Map 15 at the end of Part IV).

Regiment 4

> And the Locrians had as leader the swift son of Oileus, Aias the less, by no means as great as Telamonïan Aias, but far less. Small of stature was he, with corselet of linen, but with the spear he far excelled the whole host of Hellenes and Achaeans. These were they that dwelt in Cynus and Opus and Calliarus and Bessa and Scarphe and lovely Augeiae and Tarphe and Thronium about the streams of Boagrius. With Aias followed forty black ships of the Locrians that dwell over against sacred Euboea.   (*Il*. II, 527-535)

Homer tells us that the Locrians 'dwell over against (or opposite) sacred Euboea', the latter being for him a region on the mainland, and certainly not an island as some translators who have added the word would have us believe, apparently trying to help the reader situate the place in Greece. Euboea is easy to locate (see Regiment 5) on the Channel coast north of Rennes, in the region of Dinard and St Malo. Opposite, on the far shore of the Mont St Michel bay, was the land of the Locrians, whose name is still preserved in the town of St Lô. Tarphe was the Thar, a river to the south of Granville and the Boagrius the river Oir, near Avranches (where we also find the village of Buat-sur-Oir). Cynus corresponds to Cigné, while Opus (Greek *Opoenta*) was Pontaubault ('bridge on the Opoenta'). Calliarus would be present Carolles (inversion of l/r), while Bessa was Beslon (-lon being a later suffix from the Old Norse *lundr* = grove). I did not find the river Scarpe in the region, but the name is certainly Celtic and preserved by the river Scarpe, a confluent of the Escaut (Schelde) in northern France and by the river Scorffe in central Brittany. Thronium was Trugny (Trungei in 1040), southwest of Bayeux (see Map 15 at the end of Part IV).

Regiment 5

> And the Abantes, breathing fury, that held Euboea and Chalcis and Eretria and Histiaea, rich in vines, and Cerinthus, hard by the sea, and the steep citadel of Dios; and that held Carystus and dwelt in Styra, – all these again had as leader Elephenor, scion of Ares, him that was son of Chalcedon and captain of the great-souled Abantes.

> And with him followed the swift Abantes, with hair long at the back, spearmen eager with outstretched ashen spears to rend the coreselets about the breasts of the foemen. And with him there followed forty black ships. (*Il.* II, 536–45)

Euboea, literally 'good Boea' has its name preserved in that of two tiny islands before St Malo roads, Grand Bé and Petit Bé, as well as by the Porte des Bés in St Malo. The mainland was also called Euboea, for Homer, unlike some of his translators, nowhere mentions that it is an island. We have already seen, in Nestor's Tale (Part II, Chapter 10) on his return home from Troy, that Euboea must lie to the southwest of the Isle of Wight, on the shores of the Channel. Cerinthus, 'hard by the sea', was Cap Guerin, on the coast to the west of Dinard and the 'steep citadel of Dios (Greek *Dion* was Dinan.) Chalcis would be Caulnes and Eretria possibly Ernée. Histieia was present Hédé (via Hestié – Hêtié), northwest of Rennes, while Carystus would be the village of Carnet, southeast of Pontorchon. Styra (Greek *Stura*) seems to have been rebuilt further east in the department of the Eure, where we find Etreville, still called Sturie in 1069. The tribe of the Abantes seem to have migrated to northern France, where we find the town of Abbeville, 'Town of the Abantes' (see Map 15 at the end of Part IV).

Regiment 6

> And they that held Athens, the well–built citadel, the land of the great-hearted Erechtheus, whom of old, Athene, daughter of Zeus, fostered, when the earth, the giver of grain, had borne him; and she made him dwell in Athens, in her own rich sanctuary, and there the youths of the Athenians, as the years roll on in their courses, seek to win his favour with sacrifices of bulls and rams; – these again had as leader Menestheus, son of Peteos. Like him was no other man on the face of the earth for the marshalling of chariots and of warriors that bear the shield. Only Nestor would vie with him, for he was the elder. And with him there followed fifty black ships. (*Il.* II, 546–556)

The 'well–built citadel' of Athens must have been on or near the site of the present Cherbourg. Unfortunately, Homer gives few clues to help us confirm this, but the reasoning is set out fully in the following paragraphs.

First, in Homer's list of regiments, the Athenians appear between their neighbours to the south and west, the Locrians (Regiment 4) and the Abantes (Regiment 5), and, to the southeast, the people from around the town of Argos, the present Calvados (Regiment 8).

Furthermore, there is a district of Cherbourg, Octeville, the origin of whose name is 'uncertain' according to the etymologists, but which could well stem from another name for Pallas Athene, Okke or Onka, frequently used in ancient times. For example, Aeschylus always calls this goddess Pallas Onka. There are also several places called Ocqueville, no doubt sites where Athene was worshipped, in Seine–Maritime. (Since the Trojans were of the same religion as the Celts of the continent, there should also be traces of Athene worship in England. There is in fact a London suburb of Ockendon, just north of the Dartford Tunnel.)

According to the Odyssey there is a place called 'holy Sunium, the cape of Athens' (*Od.* III, 278), which could be the cape to the east of Cherbourg, before which we find today the Basses de Sen (= Sun[ion]). Between Cherbourg and this cape is Théville, which possibly owes it name to [A]the[ne], which is indeed a pre-Greek name according to explanatory dictionaries.

To the south of Cherbourg there is Martinville, whose name could come from Marathon, for in the *Odyssey* we read that Athene 'came to Marathon and broad-wayed Athens, and entered the well-built house of Erechtheus' (*Od.* VII, 80–81). As we see in the description of this Regiment, Athene had given the town, where there was a temple dedicated to her, to Erechtheus. Later, in Greece, the reverse happened: the Greeks dedicated a temple to Athene in the town that subsequently became their capital, Athens. Athene was worshipped throughout the Celtic countries, however, in the Troad as well as on the Continent, where we find, in France, Athéville, while in central Germany we find Athenstedt, 'Town of Athene' (see Map 18, (32) at the end of Part IV).

Through the House of Athens, there was a close link between Cherbourg and Calais (see genealogy at the end of Appendix Note 25, page 361), the northernmost seaport of France, very appropriately named after Calais, the son of the god of the North Wind, Boreas. It should be noted, however, that Calais is not mentioned by Homer, but by other ancient sources (see Map 15 at the end of Part IV).

Regiment 7

> And Aias led from Salamis twelve ships [and stationed them where the battalions of the Athenians stood].　　　　(*Il.* II, 557-8)

The Aias in question is the son of Telamon, one of the most celebrated Achaean warriors, 'Aias that in comeliness and deeds of war was above all the other Danaans next to the peerless son of Peleus (Achilles)' (*Il.* XVII, 279–80), who says himself 'I was born and reared in Salamis' (*Il.*

VII, 199). It is strange that Homer tells us nothing about his country of origin, and unfortunate for us, because trying to identify a single geographical name is extremely hazardous. However, Homer's Salamis may well be Salamanca in northwest Spain, for no other name in western Europe resembles it. Salamanca has access to the Atlantic via the rivers Tormes and Douro, which flow into the sea near Porto in northern Portugal.

The fact that this regiment is listed between those of Athens and Argos (both in northern France) may be explained by the fact that in Greece the island of Salamine in Piraeus bay lies between Athens and Argos in the northeast Peloponnese. The part of the quotation in brackets is missing from some manuscripts and was disputed by some ancient Greek critics. Strabo thought that these words had been added at a later date to justify the Athenians' claim to the possession of Salamine. But the first Athenians, who were Pelasgians (Sea Peoples) according to Herodotus, had not yet arrived in Greece!

Regiment 8

> And they that held Argos and Tiryns, famed for its walls, and Hermione and Asine, that enfold the deep gulf, Troezen and Eïonae and vine-clad Epidaurus, and the youths of the Achaeans that held Aegina and Mases, – these again had as leaders Diomedes, good at the war-cry, and Sthenelus, dear son of glorious Capaneus. And with them came a third, Euryalus, a godlike warrior, son of king Mecisteus, son of Talaus; but leader over them all was Diomedes, good at the war-cry. And with these followed eighty black ships. (*Il.* II, 559–68)

The region near the town of Argos (as opposed to Agamemnon's kingdom, also often called Argos) corresponds approximately to the present Calvados, which 'enfolds the deep gulf' now known as Seine Bay, which was the theatre of the allied landings in Normandy in June 1944.

On the coast was the town of Argos (Arromanches, 'Argos on the Channel'). Homer mentions two other coast towns, to the west Asine (Asnières, on Omaha Beach) and to the east Hermione (Hermanville-sur-Mer, north of Caen). On the Orne (Orneia in Homer, see Regiment 9), we find Tiryns (Thury-Harcourt, still called Tirins in the Middle Ages, situated south of Caen) and Mases [Greek *Maseta*] (Maizet, southeast of Caen). Epidaurus must be a town on the river Aure (*epi* being Greek for 'on') and therefore could be the present Bayeux. Troezen could be Troarn (to the east of Caen). Eïonae was Yainville and Aegina Aignerville (see Map 15 at the end of Part IV).

Regiment 9

> And they that held Mycenae, the well-built citadel, and wealthy
> Corinth, and well-built Cleonae, and dwelt in Orneiae and lovely
> Araethyrea and Sicyon, wherein at first Adrastus was king; and
> they that held Hyperesia and steep Gonoessa and Pellene, and that
> dwelt about Aegium and throughout all Aegialus, and about broad
> Helice, – of these was the son of Atreus, lord Agamemnon,
> captain, with a hundred ships. With him followed most people by
> far and goodliest; and among them he himself did on his gleaming
> bronze, a king all-glorious, and was pre-eminent among all the
> warriors, for he was the noblest, and led a people far the most in
> number. (*Il.* II, 569–580)

It is possible today to have a good idea of the extent of the territory of
which Mycenae was the capital and Agamemnon, commander-in-chief
of the Achaeans, was king (see Map 15 at the end of Part IV).

To the west, Agamemnon's kingdom included the region of Orneiae
(the southern part of the Orne valley) and the town of Cleonae (Cléon,
on the Seine, southeast of Rouen). Pellene would be the present
Bellême, between Alençon and Chartres. In the centre of the kingdom
was Gonoesse (Gonesse, just north of Paris) and 'broad' Helice
(Elysée), the region where the Celtic tribe of the Parigii later built Paris.
The Greek *helikè* meant 'willow', these two words in fact being
cognate, as is perhaps more apparent in the case of the Dutch equivalent
wilg. Hellenists therefore think that Helice was originally a willow
forest, which is not so surprising now that we have situated it in the
plain where Paris was built. A central quarter of the city is indeed called
the Marais, meaning 'marshland', a typical place for willows to grow.

As to Gonesse, there are several suburbs north of Paris of this name
(whose origin was thus far unknown), such as Garges-les-Gonesse and
Tremblay-les-Gonesse. This would mean that the name referred to a
region. But it seems also to have been the name of a town situated on a
hill, as the poet speaks of 'steep' Gonoessa which then must have
designated the steepest hill in the north Paris region: the famous Butte
Montmartre.

Hyperesia could be present Suèvres (via *Suvieres, 'hyper' and
'super' being interchangeable), Araethyrea was either Artres near
Valenciennes or Ardres near Calais, both in the extreme north of
France, while Corinth was Courances (Corintia in the Middle Ages),
between Etampes and Fontainebleau. To the east, near the sources of
the Seine, was Aegialus, the present Eguilly-sous-Bois, 30 km
southeast of Troyes and Aegium, now Aigny-le-Duc, halfway
between Troyes and Colombey-les-Deux-Eglises.

Agamemnon also seems to have held territory in the southwest of France, separated from his other territories by La Beauce, for the only names that resemble Sicyon are Sciecq near Niort, Siecq to the west of Angoulême, and Sigogne and Segonzac to the west of Poitiers. It is not clear whether this area was obtained by force or inheritance, Homer telling us only that 'at the first Adrastus was king'. This Adrastus, an earlier king of Argos province, with a curious name meaning 'He who cannot escape (his fate?)' is not to be confused with the Trojan Adrastus, commander of Regiment D or two other Trojans of the same name. He gave one of his daughters in marriage to Tydeus, son of Oileus, king of Calydon in neighboring Aetolia, the region in which we just identified Sicyon. Tydeus was the father of Diomedes, commander of Regiment 8, from Argos province, the present Calvados to the north.

The name of the capital of Agamemnon's kingdom, Mycenae, did not mean mi-Seine ('half way down the Seine') but Mystères-sur-Seine ('mystery' or 'mystère' being related to Greek *musterion* meaning 'secret ceremony'), an allusion to an important Celtic place of initiation. The name, but not the town, has disappeared, very probably because the city was renamed Troyes after the victory over Troy in England.

One may wonder why the Regiment of the supreme commander was only ninth in the list instead of being number 1. Since numbers had a mystical value in the Bronze Age (as we saw in Part III, Chapter 12), it is likely that Agamemnon's regiment had been allocated number 9, the number of perfection, for reasons of prestige. This would also explain why the regiment of Agapenor, his neighbour and closest ally, had the next most prestigious number, 12, thus being listed in the catalogue among the regiments from Spain. By contrast, the list of Trojan regiments seems straightforward, possibly because Homer did not know the rankings in the enemy camp.

For Agamemnon's genealogy, see Appendix Note 25, The Principal Gods and the table of the House of Mycenae on page 361.

Regiment 10

And they that held the hollow land of Lacedaemon with its many ravines, and Pharis and Sparta and Messe, the haunt of doves, and that dwelt in Bryseiae and lovely Augeiae, and that held Amyclae and Helus, a citadel hard by the sea, and that held Laas, and dwelt about Oetylus, – these were led by Agamemnon's brother, even Menelaus, good at the war-cry, with sixty ships; and they were marshalled apart. And himself he moved among them, confident in his zeal, urging his men to battle; and above all others was his heart fain to get his requital for his strivings and groanings for Helen's sake.
(*Il.* II, 581-90)

Lacedaemon, the kingdom of Menelaus, king of Sparta, was identified in Part II, Chapter 8 as being in the southwest of Spain. Pharis is probably the present Paradas, and 'lovely Augeiae' Algar in the valley of the Machaceite. For the most likely sites of other places, see Map 16, page 327.

Regiment 11

> And they that dwelt in Pylos and lovely Arene and Thryum, the ford of Alpheius, and fair-founded Aepy, and that had their abodes in Cyparisseïs and Amphigeneia and Pteleos and Helus and Dorium, where the Muses met Thamyris the Thracian and made an end of his singing, even as he was journeying from Oechalia, from the house of Eurytus the Oechalean: for he vaunted with boasting that he would conquer, were the Muses themselves to sing against him, the daughters of Zeus that beareth the aegis; but they in their wrath maimed him, and took from him his wondrous song, and made him forget his minstrelsy; – all these folk had as leader the horseman, Nestor of Gerenia. And with him were ranged ninety hollow ships. *(Il.* II, 591-602)

Pylos, the kingdom of Nestor, was identified in Part II, Chapter 8 in the southwest of Spain, Pylos being Pilas, Gerenia Gerena and the river Alpheius the Huelva (see Map 16 at the end of Part IV). Other names are more difficult to identify since many of them must have changed during the occupation by the Moors, but Arene could be Mairena, west of Seville, and Pteleos could be San Telmo. The immigrants in this region seem to have come from the Netherlands where all ten names are easy to identify (see Map 17, page 330).

The bard Thamyris the Thracian (but unfortunately we do not know from which Thrace he came), sang at the court of the king of Oechalia, now Sjællerup in Sjælland, Denmark (see Regiment 25).

Regiment 12

> And they that held Arcadia beneath the steep mountain of Cyllene, beside the tomb of Aepytus, where are warriors that fight in close combat; and they that dwelt in Pheneos and Orchomenus, rich in flocks, and Rhipe and Stratia and wind-swept Enispe; and that held Tegea and lovely Mantineia; and that held Stymphalus and dwelt in Parrhasia, – all these were led by the son of Ancaeus, lord Agapenor, with sixty ships; and on each ship embarked full many Arcadian warriors well-skilled in fight. For of himself had the king of men, Agamemnon, given them benched ships wherewith to cross over the wine-dark sea, even the son of Atreus, for with matters of seafaring had they nought to do. *(Il.* II, 603-14)

Arcadia should be in a different place in the list of regiments unless the number 12 was given it for reasons of prestige (see Regiment 9). It could equally well have been moved to his position by the ancient Greeks because in their country this region is in the Peloponnese, near Pilos and Lacedaemon. However, in western Europe in the Bronze Age, with which we are concerned, it was not in Spain, near Pilas and Esparteros (where it is impossible to identify it), but in northeast France and more particularly Alsace and the region to the southwest of the Vosges. The name Arcadia is in fact related to Argos (via *Argadia). The name of mount Cyllene has been preserved in the nearby town of Sélestat ('Séle/ Cylle town'). Stratia is Strasbourg, whose name in the sixth century AD was Strateburgo ('Strate fortress'). Pheneos is now Fénétrange, Rhipe Ribeauville and 'wind-swept Enispe' Ensisheim in the Rhine valley, indeed exposed to the wind. Parrhasia would be Barr to the southeast of Strasbourg. As for Orchomenus, a name frequently found in Celtic territory and used to designate several regions in Europe, in the present case it was probably the region 'rich in flocks' on the river Doubs, where we now find Orchamps (Orchens in the Middle Ages). 'Lovely Mantineia' was the upper Saône region between Dijon and Besançon, where the village of Mantoche near Gray reminds us of Mantineia, the suffix –oche coming from –usca, of non-Celtic origin. Ancient Tegea is now Tagsdorf ('Village of Tag – Teg') near Altkirch, while Stymphalos could be Staffelfelden (a case of phonetic adaptation, since the two names have entirely different meanings).

Since Arcadia was so far from the sea, it is not surprising to find that the Arcadians 'with seafaring had naught to do' and that their neighbour, Agamemnon, had to give them sixty ships to cross the sea (see Map 15, page 320).

Regiment 13

> And they that dwelt in Buprasium and noble Elis, all that part thereof that Hyrmine and Myrsinus on the seaboard and the rock of Olen and Alesium enclose between them, – these again had four leaders, and ten swift ships followed each one, and many Epeians embarked thereon. Of these some were led by Amphimachus and Talpius, of the blood of Actor, sons, the one of Cteatus and the other of Eurytus; and of some was the son of Amarynceus captain, even mighty Diores; and of the fourth company godlike Polyxeinus was captain, son of king Agasthenes, Augeias' son.
>
> (*Il.* II, 615–24)

Elis is easy to locate, for Homer tells us that it was opposite Ithaca (already identified in Part II, Chapter 7).

Buprasium is a neighbouring region, where the 'rock of Olen' is now the Sierra de Ojèn in the extreme south of Spain, while Alesium is the Rio Guadalete ('River of Alese' > Alete), the northern boundary. Elsewhere, Homer mentions the 'well-peopled land of Sidon' (*Od.* XIII, 285) near Elis, thus confirming our earlier identification of Sidon as Medina Sidonia. On the other hand, the names of Hyrmine and Myrsinus seem to have disappeared (see Map 16, page 327).

Regiment 14

And those from Dulichium and the Echinae, the holy isles, that lie across the sea, over against Elis, these again had as leader Meges, the peer of Ares, even the son of Phyleus, whom the horseman Phyleus, dear to Zeus, begat – he that of old had gone to dwell in Dulichium in wrath against his father. And with Meges there followed forty black ships. (*Il.* II, 625-30)

Dulichium is one of the islands of Odysseus' kingdom, Ithaca, already identified in Part II, Chapter 7, and it was no doubt the biggest of these islands as it is referred to several times as being rich in wheat. It now forms part of the Spanish mainland in the Guadalquivir delta. In addition to the Echinae, there were other islands, called the 'Sharp' or 'Pointed Isles', situated close to Ithaca (see Map 16, page 327 and map of Cadiz on page 115).

Regiment 15

And Odysseus led the great-souled Cephallenians that held Ithaca and Neritum, covered with waving forests, and that dwelt in Crocyleia and rugged Aegilips; and then that held Zacynthus, and that dwelt about Samos, and held the mainland and dwelt on the shores over against the isles. Of these was Odysseus captain, the peer of Zeus in counsel. And with him there followed twelve ships with vermilion prows. (*Il.* II, 631-37)

Odysseus' kingdom, Ithaca, was identified in Part II, Chapter 7. The name of the warriors, the Cephallenians, must come from the name of their region, and since regions in Homer often take the name of the river running through them, this could well be Cephisos (Greek *Kèphisos*), now the Guadalquivir ('River of Quivir', Quivi and Kephi being phonetically very close). The first part of the name is Arab for 'river' (cognate with the more familiar wadi). The Celtic immigrants of southern Spain apparently brought the name Cephisus from northern Europe, where it designates a lake in Boeotia, the Sebbesund in Denmark (*Il.* V, 709) and a river in Phocia, France, probably the upper

Orne, near the town of Sées (*Il.* II, 522). The names of Crocyleia and Aegilips on the mainland seem to correspond to (Nuevo) Rocio and the region of the mountain Gibalbin northeast of Jerez (see Map 16, page 327).

Regiment 16

> And the Aetolians were led by Thoas, Andraemon's son, even they that dwelt in Pleuron and Olenus and Pylene and Chalcis, hard by the sea, and rocky Calydon. For the sons of great-hearted Oeneus were no more, neither did he himself still live, and fair-haired Meleager was dead, to whom had commands been given that he should bear full sway among the Aetolians. And with Thoas there followed forty black ships. (*Il.* II, 638-44)

The name of the region of Aetolia is preserved in that of the small town of Etaules in southwest France, on the right bank of the Gironde not far from the sea. Further north, on the coast, we find Olenus (Olonnes) and, to the northwest of Nantes, Pylene (Blaine). The Gironde must have marked the southern boundary of Aetolia, for beyond it lay Libya, whose people did not take part in the Trojan War (see Part II, Chapter 16).

The northwestern boundary of Aetolia was marked by Pleuron, now Ploëren, between Auray and Vannes. Chalcis (there is another Chalsic in Euboea, North Brittany) seems to be Challans, though this town is no longer 'hard by the sea' but separated from it by marshland, and 'rocky Calydon' would be La Caillère, in the hills southeast of Nantes. It would appear that the Aetolians kept alive the memory of their victory over Troy through the name of Trojan on the isle of Oléron (St Trojan since the Christian era) (see Map 15, page 320).

Regiment 17

> And the Cretans had as leader Idomeneus, famed for his spear, even they that held Cnosus and Gortys, famed for its walls, Lyctus and Miletus and white Lycastus, and Phaestus and Rhytium, well-peopled cities; and all they beside that dwelt in Crete of the hundred cities. Of all these was Idomeneus, famed for his spear, captain, and Meriones, the peer of Enyalius, slayer of men. And with these there followed eighty black ships. (*Il.* II, 645-52)

There is no doubt that this regiment came from South Norway where we had already identified approximately the region of Phaestus where part of Menelaus' fleet was thrown on the rocks (Part II, Chapter 6). Phaestus was described as a western promontory near the region of Gortys. Today there is still a large region of South Norway called Hordland, a name derived from Gort[ys]. On the southwest coast there is indeed a large promontory with a little town called Vestbygd, phonetically close to Phaest[us]. From the text cited above, it seems that there was not only a region but also a town of Gortus (or Gortyn) which seems to be Horden, a town located at the entrance of the Oslo fjord.

'White' Lycastus could well be the region around the Lisefjord, which is surrounded by high snow-covered mountains, Lyctus could be Liknes in the Lista region and Miletus possibly Meling, while Rhytium was either Ryen near Kristiansand ore Ryfylke ('County of Ry') near Stavanger. There remains the problem of Cnosus. Since it is unlikely that warriors of Regiment 17 came from the Cnosus identified in Jutland, the region of Regiment 1, there must have been a second Cnossus, a town most probably situated in the Oslo region, where the Minnesund ('Sound of the Minne or Minoians, so called after King Minos of Cnossus, son of Zeus and Europa) is a reminder of the Minoians (see Map 14, page 316).

The famous 'Gordian knot' owes its name to Gortys on the coast of Norway, not to Gordes in inland Turkey, for its is seafarers, not peasants, who use complicated knots for different purposes.

Regiment 18

> And Tlepolemus, son of Heracles, a valiant man and tall, led from Rhodes nine ships of the lordly Rhodians, that dwelt in Rhodes sundered in three divisions – in Lindos and Ialysus and Cameirus, white with chalk. These were led by Tlepolemus, famed for his spear, he that was born to mighty Heracles by Astyocheia, whom he had led forth out of Ephyre from the river Selleïs, when he had laid waste many cities of warriors fostered of Zeus. But when Tlepolemus had grown to manhood in the well-fenced palace, forthwith he slew his own father's dear uncle, Licymnius, scion of Ares, who was then waxing old. So he straightway built his ships, and when he had gathered together much people, went forth in flight over the sea, for that the other sons and grandsons of mighty Heracles threatened him. But he came to Rhodes in his wanderings, suffering woes, and there his people settled in three divisions by tribes, and were loved of Zeus that is king among gods and men; and upon them was wondrous wealth poured by the son of Cronos.　　　　　　　　　　　　　　　　(*Il.* II, 653–70)

Although the translations usually state that the Rhodians 'dwelt in Rhodes', the Greek says that they 'lived round about Rhodes' which is a curious expression if we think of the Greek island instead of a region. In western Europe, the region concerned is in the northeast of Switzerland, in the canton of Appenzell, which is divided into Outer and Inner Rhoden. Close by, on the shores of Lake Constance, we find Lindos (Lindau, in Germany) and a river Argen, which has the same root as Argos, Aargau and Argovie. Ialysus is the present St Gallen (via *Galus), a town in northeast Switzerland (see Map 18, page 334).

'Cameirus, white with chalk', the usual rendering, is a further example of translators being influenced by the conviction that the Achaeans were Greeks and that this regiment came from the chalk hills of Rhodes. There is, in fact, no mention of chalk in the Greek text. It seems likely that 'white' Cameirus was at some distance from the other places mentioned, in the centre of Austria, in the region of Salzkammergut. *Salz* means 'salt', and I suggest that *kammer* comes from Cameirus and has nothing to do with *Kammer* the German for 'room'. Homer calls it white not because of chalk or the snows of Mount Dachstein, but because of the abundant salt still to be found in the region, another reminder of which is the name of Salzburg, 'salt fortress'. In Homer's time, salt was a rare commodity, especially in places far from the the sea, and commanded a high price. This explains why the poet says of the Rhodians that 'upon them was wondrous wealth poured by the son of Cronos (Zeus)', for their riches would certainly not come from the quality of the soil in this mountainous region. We know that the Celts of the period exploited salt mines, for in 1734 the body of a man who lived 2,500 years ago was found, well preserved by the salt in which he was accidentally buried. In the centre of the Salzkammergut region is the village of Hallstatt, situated on a lake of the same name. This place is famous among students of the Celts, for it has given its name to the oldest known Celtic civilization (seventh to fifth century BC), because of the many objects found in excavations there, such as iron weapons, horses harnesses, beautiful bronze cauldrons, and pottery, some bearing decorations believed to be of Greek and Etruscan origin.

Tlepolemus was originally from Ephyre, a town already identified in the southwest of Spain, where Heracles was in fact particularly revered (see Part III, Chapter 5). After murdering his uncle, he fled as far as possible, apparently following the Atlantic coasts to the present Netherlands, then going up the Rhine as far as Switzerland. Tlepolemus and his followers must have settled this region and given it the name that became Helvetia. It was certainly seafaring Celts who gave the name to Switzerland, as it is the only place-name in Europe beginning with Hel- that lies so far from the Helle sea, the Hellespont (see Map 5 in Part II, Chapter 4). It is also known that the Swiss are the descendants of a Celtic tribe, the Helvetii, mentioned by Roman historians. The founder of Helvetia was thus Tlepolemus, 'the tall and handsome son of Heracles', who was wounded in the Trojan War (*Il.* V, 627). His genealogy is as follows:

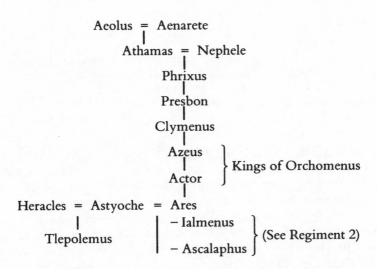

Regiment 19

> Moreover Nireus led three shapely ships from Syme, Nireus was
> son of Aglaïa and Charops the king, Nireus the comeliest man that
> came beneath Ilios of all the Danaans after the peerless son of
> Peleus. Howbeit he was a weakling, and but few people followed
> him. (Il. II, 671-5)

Since we have only a single place-name, it is hazardous to say where
Nireus' troops came from, and to make matters worse, no place-name
in western Europe even remotely resembles Syme, *Sumetha* in the
Greek text. This latter name must have contracted over time in the same
way as Phulake – Flakkee, i.e. the first syllable being unstressed, the
vowel disappeared, leaving Smet(h) or Smit. Even so, the atlas does not
reveal any promising names with the consonants smt. However, a
book of postcodes was more helpful, for there is a hamlet Smitshoek,
very appropriately situated near the mouth of the Rhine between two
southern suburbs of Rotterdam, Poortugaal and Lombardije (two
names that have left their mark in southern Europe, following the
subsequent southward migration of the Celts). Smitshoek would
normally be taken to mean 'blacksmith's corner', but in this case the
original meaning could be 'Sumetha corner'. The fact that Nireus'
regiment precedes three other regiments from the Netherlands is an
additional clue indicating that he was a native of the Rhine mouth (see
Map 17, page 330).

Regiment 20

> And they that held Nisyrus and Crapathus and Casus and Cos, the
> city of Eurypylus, and the Calydnian isles, these again were led by
> Pheidippus and Antiphus, the two sons of king Thessalus, son of
> Heracles. And with them were ranged thirty hollow ships.
>
> (*Il.* II, 676–80)

Assuming that the territory of King Thessalus was called Thessaly,
then this name is preserved in the island of Tessel in the north of
Holland. The five place-names mentioned by Homer can all still be
traced in that area. Nisyrus is Niezijl on the Lauwerszee, now drained,
between the provinces of Friesland and Groningen. Cos is Kooy, a
suburb of Helder. Homer calls it a 'well-situated' place (*Il.* XIV, 255
and XV, 28), as well it might be, for it controlled the sea traffic between
the North Sea and the inland sea, and indeed still does, Helder being a
navy base. Crapathus is Krabbendam ('crab dyke') 20 km south of
Helder. Casus is Castricum, a deceptively Latin-looking name, located
in the dunes 20 km northwest of Amsterdam. The Calydnian isles are
the archipelago running along the north coast of Holland, the present
Wadden islands. The one from which they took their name, Calydnia,
is the present Callandsoog, now part of the mainland south of Helder
(see Map 17, page 330).

Regiment 21

> Now all those again that inhabited Pelasgian Argos, and dwelt in
> Alos and Alope and Trachis, and that held Phthia and Hellas, the
> land of fair women, and were called Myrmidons and Hellenes and
> Achaeans – of the fifty ships of these men was Achilles captain.
> However they thought not about evil war, since there was no man
> to lead them forth into the ranks. For he lay in idleness among the
> ships, the swift-footed, goodly Achilles, in wrath because of the
> fair-haired girl Briseïs, whom he had taken out of Lyrnessus after
> sore toil, when he wasted Lyrnessus and the walls of Thebe, and
> laid low Mynes and Epistrophus, warriors that raged with the
> spear, sons of king Evenus, Selepus' son. In sore grief for her lay
> Achilles idle; but soon was he to arise again. (*Il.* II, 681–94)

We have already seen, in Part II, Chapter 11, that the Pelasgians were
the Belgians and that their territory, Pelasgian Argos, was in today's
northern France and Belgium.

The Achaean Army

We can still identify some of the places mentioned in this passage. Alos is now Alost (in French) or Aalst (in Dutch), to the west of Brussels. Alope is Halluin, near Lille, which was still called Alp-heim in the Middle Ages, while Trachis is Treizennes, called Trachina in the Middle Ages. The region of 'deep-soiled Phthia, mother of flocks' (Il. IX, 479), can be identified from other evidence in Homer as the present provinces of Zeeland and South Holland to the Old Rhine, where Delphi (Delft) 'the centre of the world' for the Druids, was located (see Part III, Chapters 10 and 11). (This role of the centre of the world has now been taken over by the London suburb of Greenwich, situated on the 0 Meridian).

Hellas, whose name means 'land on the Helle sea', was Holland (<Helle-land), the centre-west region of the Netherlands. Curiously enough, the Dutch often say that their most beautiful women come from the region of Haarlem, a town situated in Homer's 'Hellas, the land of fair women'.

Achilles' subjects were called the Myrmidons ('the ants'), and their name is to be found in many villages in the Netherlands, such as Mirdum and Mirns (Friesland), Merm (between Arnhem and Nijmegen), De Meern (near Utrecht), Merum (near to Roermond), Moerdijk (north of Breda) and Moermont Castle in Zeeland (see Map 17, page 330).

Homer tells us here that Achilles has taken the girl Briseïs, whose loss causes him to stop fighting in the Trojan War, from Lyrnessus, one of the towns sacked by him, identified in Part II, Chapter 1 as King's Lynn (see Map 2).

Achilles' father who lived in Scuros (Schuring, see Map 12, Note 30) was king of Phthia. His 'divine' descent, from the gods Oceanus and Zeus, is set out below:

$$
\begin{array}{c}
\text{Oceanus} = \text{Tethys} \\
| \\
\text{Aesepus} \\
| \\
\text{Aegina} = \text{Zeus} \\
| \\
\text{Aeacus} \\
| \\
\text{Peleus} = \text{Thetis} \\
| \\
\text{Achilles}
\end{array}
$$

(For Achilles' Celtic origin, see Appendix, Note 25, page 360.)

Regiment 22

> And they that held Phylace and flowery Pyrasus, the sanctuary of
> Demeter, and Iton, mother of flocks, and Antron, hard by the sea,
> and Pteleos, couched in grass, these again had as leader warlike
> Protesilaus, while yet he lived; but the black earth already held him
> fast. His wife, her two cheeks torn in wailing, was left in Phylace
> and his house but half established, while, for himself, a Dardanian
> warrior slew him as he leapt forth from his ship by far the first of
> the Achaeans. Yet neither were his men leaderless, though they
> longed for their leader; for Podarces, scion of Ares, marshalled
> them, he that was son of Phylacus' son, Iphiclus, rich in flocks,
> own brother to great-souled Protesilaus, and younger-born; but
> the other was the elder and the better man, even the warrior, valiant
> Protesilaus. So the host in no wise lacked a leader, though they
> longed for the noble man they had lost. And with him there
> followed forty black ships.   (*Il.* II, 695-710)

Phylace (Greek *Phulakê*) is the island of Flakkee, recently renamed
Overflakkee, in South Holland, while Pyrasus is Brasem (via *Pras <
*Bras), the name of a lake in the middle of the flower-growing region of
the western Netherlands. It was evidently already 'flowery' in Homer's
time, no doubt due to the damp climate and the exceptional quality of
the soil. It is thus not surprising that Demeter, goddess of agriculture
and fertility, should have her sanctuary here. She was in particular the
goddess of corn, and is hence sometimes called 'fair-haired' Demeter by
Homer (e.g. *Il.* V, 500). 'Iton, mother of flocks', is now Etten, west of
Breda, a green region in the west of Brabant, while 'Pteleos, couched in
grass' is probably Tiel, on the Rhine, where there are lush meadows on
the low, well-watered land near the two main branches of the Rhine.
'Antron, hard by the Sea' is Antwerp, the etymolgy being *Antron-
werf or werp ('Antron wharf or height'). In Homer's time this town
was closer to the sea than it is now, as at that time the greater part of
Flanders was covered by the North sea, as can be seen on old maps (*see
also* Appendix Note 13, The Sea Level).

Elsewhere in the *Iliad*, Homer mentions the small town of Scuros,
where Achilles' son was raised (*Il.* XIX, 326), now the hamlet of
Schuring, south of Rotterdam, and the 'heaven-fed river Spercheius'
(*Il.* XVI, 174), the present Bergse Maas (via *[s]Berch[ios]).

The present name thus has nothing to do with *berg* meaning
'mountain' – understandably enough, as there is not even the slightest
hill in this region (see Map 17, page 330).

Regiment 23

> And they that dwelt in Pherae beside the lake Boebeïs, and in
> Boebe, and Glaphyrae, and well-built Iolcus, these were led by the
> dear son of Admetus with eleven ships, even by Eumelus, whom
> Alcestis, queenly among women, bare to Admetus, even she, the
> comeliest of the daughters of Pelias.   (*Il.* II, 711-15)

Boebe is probably the present town of Bobitz in Mecklenburg in East
Germany, but the lake Boebeïs is now called Lake Schwerin, after
another town on its shores. Glaphyrae corresponds to Glave, on the
southern shore of Lake Krakow, about 80 km east of Schwerin. Iolcus
would appear to be Golwitz on the island of Poel in the Baltic to the
north of Wismar. Pherae seems to have disappeared, unless it is
Behlendorf, near the western shore of Lake Schwerin (see Map 18, page
334).

Regiment 24

> And they that dwelt in Methone and Thaumacia, and that held
> Meliboea and rugged Olizon, these with their seven ships were led
> by Philoctetes, well-skilled in archery, and on each ship embarked
> fifty oarsmen well skilled to fight valiantly and with the bow. But
> Philoctetes lay suffering grievous pains in an island, even in sacred
> Lemnos, where the sons of the Achaeans had left him in anguish
> with an evil wound from a deadly water-snake. There he lay
> suffering; yet full soon were the Argives beside the ships to bethink
> them of king Philoctetes. Howbeit neither were these men
> leaderless, though they longed for their leader; but Medon
> marshalled them, the bastard son of Oïleus, whom Rhene bare to
> Oïleus, sacker of cities.   (*Il.* II, 716-28)

The key to the identification of the region concerned is Meliboea. This
unique name is found in West Germany, just south of Frankfurt, near
the right bank of the Rhine, and is today Mount Melibocus. Thaumacia
is thus the mountainous region of Taunus, to the north of Frankfurt.
On the left bank of the Rhine in the Eiffel region, opposite Taunus, we
find Methone, now Mettendorf (*dorf* means village) and Olizon, now
Olzheim (-heim is equivalent to '-ham' in English) (see Map 18 at the
end of Part IV). Homer tells us that the leader of this Regiment had been
left 'in an island, even in sacred Lemnos' suffering from a snake bite.
This must be Lemmer in Friesland (Netherlands), located in the sandy
southern part of this province. In Homer's time the land surrounding

this place was no doubt under water, leaving it an island. What is more, Lemmer is on the shipping route between the Rhine and the North Sea via a branch of the Rhine now known as Ijssel (Isla in the Roman period). Elsewhere, Homer tells us that the son Jason, leader of the Argonauts, lived in Lemnos: 'And ships full many were at hand from Lemnos, bearing wine, sent forth by Jason's son, Euneüs' (*Il.* VII, 468).

The name of Medon's mother, Rhene, is most puzzling: is the poet referring to a river goddess? The question arises because Medon's troops come from the mid-Rhine region, while his mother's name seems precisely to be a reminder of the Rhine (see Map 18, page 334).

Regiment 25

And they that held Tricca and Ithome of the crags, and Oechalia, city of Oechalian Eurytus, these again were led by the two sons of Asclepius, the skilled healers Podaleirius and Machaon. And with these were ranged thirty hollow ships. (*Il.* II, 729-33)

Tricca is probably the small town of Tryggelev on the island of Langeland in Denmark, while 'Ithome of the crags' would be Tommerup on the neighbouring island of Fyn, where there is an elevation near the town. Oechalia, is Skaelskör on the island of Sjaelland (see Map 14 on page 316). It is interesting to note that there is also a village called Korinth on this island. The name is also found in France, where Homer mentions it (*Il.* II, 570); although the modern name is Courances, the medieval name was Corintia (see Map 15, page 320).

Regiment 26

And they that held Ormenius and the fountain Hypereia, and that held Asterium and the white crests of Titanus, these were led by Eurypylus, the glorious son of Euaemon. And with him there followed forty black ships. (*Il.* II, 734-37)

This regiment seems to come from western Norway, the 'white crests of Titanus' being the Tind, which is generally known as the Glittertind, since its crests are always glittering with snow. The assumption that Tind and Titanus is the same word is allowed by etymologists who explain that the latter name contains a repetition, or rather a mix, of the two syllables tin and tan. If the Tind was indeed the Titanus, this is a reminder of the Titans, the giant children of Heaven and Earth (Uranus and Gaea). It is not so surprising that ancient man should have considered the grandiose landscape of Norway, with its high mountains and deep fjords, to be the playground of the Giants. One of the Titans was Cronus, the Creator and father of Zeus. His name is also preserved in Scandinavia by a large province in southern Sweden (where we have already noted the presence of the Celts in Regiment 2) called Kronoberg ('Mountain of Kronos'). The English 'crown', German *Krone* and French *couronne* all seem to be derived from Cronus, since at the human level the crown is the symbol of the highest authority. The Tind mountain, rising to 2,470 metres, is situated near the sources of the Sognefjord, the largest in Norway. South of the entrance to the fjord, near the sea, we find Austrheim, which could well be Homer's Asterium. Ormenius, seems to have disappeared, unless it is the present Hermanssverk (via Ormen > *Erman) situated on the southern shore of the Sognefjord, half-way between the North Sea and the Tind mountain.

Regiment 27

> And they held Argissa, and dwelt in Gyrtone, Orthe, and Elone, and the white city of Oloosson, these again had as leader Polypoetes, staunch in fight, son of Peirithous, whom immortal Zeus begat – even him whom glorious Hippodameia conceived to Peirithous on the day when he got his vengeance on the shaggy centaurs, and thrust them forth from Pelion, and drove them to the Aethices. Not alone was he, but with him was Leonteus, scion of Ares, the son of Caenus' son, Coronus, high of heart. And with them there followed forty black ships. (*Il*. II, 738-47)

Homer uses the name Pelion to designate two different rivers, the second being in the region of Regiment 29. Today there are also two rivers called Plöne, one in northern Germany and the other in Poland. It therefore seems reasonable to believe that Pelion and Plöne are identical, particularly as the identification of another river (Peneius/ Peene, see Regiments 28 and 29) confirms this hypothesis. Regiment 27 would therefore be from the region around Kiel and Lübeck, where a river, a lake and a town are all called Plöne. The name Orthe is found in the village of Orth on the island of Fehmarn, off the coast. Elone would be the village of Ellund, to the west of Flensburg. Gyrtone could be Kiel, the name having undergone two mutations frequent in etymology: g > k and r > l. The 'white city of Oloossson could be the present Olderup, and would suggest that the habit of painting houses white, as is often done, especially in Denmark, started a very long time ago indeed. Argissa would be the village of Arkebek. These last two villages are west and southwest of Rendsburg, respectively (see Map 18, page 334).

We read in the *Iliad* that Achilles had a lance made of ash from the 'peak' of Pelion, now called the Bungsberg, situated near Lake Plöne. This is in fact the only elevated point in a broad region of coastal plain. 'Achilles alone was skilled to wield it, even the Pelian spear of ash, that Cheiron had given to his dear father from the peak of Pelion' (*Il.* XVI, 142-4).

Regiment 28

> And Gouneus led from Cyphus two and twenty ships, and with him followed the Enienes and the Peraebi, staunch in fight, that had set their dwellings about wintry Dodona, and dwelt in the ploughland about lovely Titaressus, that pours its fair-flowing streams into Peneius; but it does not mingle with the silver eddies of Peneius, but flows on over its waters like oil; for it is a branch of the water of Styx, the dread river of oath.   (*Il.* II, 748-55)

The region of origin of this regiment can easily be identified thanks to the name of the river Peneius, now the Peene, in the northern part of East Germany, and the region does indeed have a harsh climate. The name of a confluent of the Peneius, the Titaressus, is preserved in the town of Teterow, located close to a lake and rivers that flow into the Peene. Cyphus (Greek *Kuphos*) seems to be the present Kieve, near to lake Muritz, while an ancient religious site marked by the Maron stone is found near a lake in Neuendorf forest. In the age of Homer, Maron was the name of one of Apollo's priests (see Part III, Chapter 4). The Styx is the imaginary river of Hades (see Part III, Chapter 11 and Map 18 at the end of this section).

Dodona was a large region, where three villages still remind us of the name, in particular Dodow in the territory of present Regiment 28, another Dodow is that of Regiment 23 and Dodendorf (*dorf* = village) near Magdeburg on the Elbe. According to a story that was already a myth in Homer's time, Dodona was the original territory of the Pelasgians (Belgians), which would confirm that migrations in Europe have generally been in the east to west direction right throughout the ages. Dodona was also a very important religious centre for the Celts, the home of Zeus himself according to Achilles' prayer:

> 'Zeus, Oh king, Dodonaean, Pelasgian who dwellest afar, ruling over wintry Dodona, – and about thee dwell the Selli, thine interpreters, men with unwashed feet that couch on the ground. In

former times thou didst indeed hear my word, when I prayed: thou
didst me honour, and mightily smote the host of the Achaeans;
even so now also fulfil me this my desire. . . .'   (*Il.* XVI, 233-238)

Before the Belgians start thinking that Zeus was a compatriot, it
should be explained right away that the ancient name of the Belgians,
Pelasgians, is related to *pelagos*, meaning both 'sea' and 'flat surface'.
The Pelasgians were thus the people living on coastal plains, which was
true of all the Celts in Homer's epic. 'Zeus, . . . Pelasgian', therefore
simply means 'God of the peoples living near the sea'.

The name of the priests of Zeus, the Selli, has been preserved by the
village of Sellin on the Baltic island of Rügen, just off the East German
coast. If Zeus himself was called 'Dodonaean', he should have left a
trace somewhere near, and it could well be that the town of Zeuthen, a
Berlin suburb, bears his name.

Dodona was also a place of pilgrimage, to judge by the following:

'. . . But Odysseus, he said, had gone to Dodona, to hear the will of
Zeus from the high-crested oak of the god. . . .'
                                        (*Od.* XIV, 327 and XIX, 296)

This famous oak most probably stood in present Dodendorf, which
was of easy access for seafarers sailing up the Elbe, and is located
precisely in the heart of Germany, which archeologists consider to have
been the birthplace of the Celts. We have thus here a second link-up
with archeological evidence, after that of Hallstatt in Austria (see
Regiment 18, and also Map 18, at the end of Part IV, and Map 10 in Part
II, Chapter 14). We can be absolutely certain that there were not only
'coastal' but also 'continental' Celts, living in the heart of Europe,
where many Celtic place-names are still to be found. A good example is
the river Neisse, which flows northward from Czechoslovakia and is
now the border between the German Democratic Republic and Poland.
On old engravings, this river was called the Nissa, a typical Celtic name
as we have seen with Regiments 1 and 2.

Homer is the first, but not the only source to suggest that the Celts,
or at least the seafarers, originated from the area of the North Sea and
the Baltic coast. Timagenus of Alexandria (first century BC) quoted by
Ammianus Marcellinus (fourth century AD) wrote that 'the Druids
reported that part of the population (of Gaul) was indigenous, but that
others had come from remote islands and regions beyond the Rhine'
(*Drusidae memorant revere fuisse populi partem indigenam, sed alios quoque ab
insulis extremis confluxisse et tractibus transrhenanis*), the reason for their
migration being that 'they were expelled by warring neighbours and

305

flooding by the sea' (*crebritate bellorum et alluvione fervidi maris sedibus suis expulsos*).

If the Celts originated in northern Europe, which is also borne out by Map 5, (Part 2, Chapter 4) the Helle Sea, we can better understand the difficulty stressed by the Greek geographer Posidonius (first century BC) and other classical authors in physically distinguishing between Celts and Germans, although there was of course a difference in language and often of religion. The Celts were more superstitious, had more gods and made more sacrifices.

Regiment 29

> And the Magnetes had as captain Prothous, son of Tenthredon. These were they that dwelt about Peneius and Pelion, covered with waving forests. Of these was swift Prothous captain; and with him there followed forty black ships. (*Il*. II, 756–59)

The Magnetes lived in the region around the river Peneius, the present Peene, and a second river Pelion (see Regiment 27 for the first), the present Plöne, or Plona in Polish, southeast of the Baltic port of Stettin, Polish Szczecin (see Map 18, page 334).

3

The Trojan Army

(*Il.* II, 816–877)

Résumé of the list of regiments (see Map 19 at the
end of Part IV)
Commander-in-chief: Hector, son of Priam,
king of Troy

Name of region, town or people	Name of chief	Present region
A Trojans	Hector	Cambridgeshire
B Dardanians	Aeneas	Cambridgeshire
C Zeleia	Pandarus	Cambridgeshire
D Adrasteia	Adrastus	Strathclyde (southwest of Glasgow)
E Pityeia	Amphius	Stirling (north of Glasgow)
F Percote Practius Arisbe	Asius	Perth, Angus (Central Scotland)
G Pelasgians Larisa	Hippothous Pylaeus	Suffolk, East Anglia
H Thracians	Acamas	Allies from Finistère, France
I Ciconians	Peirous Euphemus	
J Paeonians	Pyraechmes	Devon, southwest England
K Paphlagonians	Pylaemenes	Northern Scotland
L Halizones	Odius, Epistrophus	Cornwall
M Mysians	Chromis, Ennomus	Leicestershire, central England
N Phrygians	Phorcys, Ascanius	Eastern Scotland
P Maeonians	Mesthles, Antiphus	Hampshire, southern England
Q Carians	Nastes, Amphimachus	Wales
R Lycians	Sarpedon, Glaucus	Westmorland, northwest England
S Ceteians	Eurypylus	Northamptonshire, eastern England

N.B. The Ceteians are mentioned only in the *Odyssey* (*Od.* XI, 521)

Regiments A and B

> The Trojans were led by great Hector of the flashing helm, the son
> of Priam, and with him were marshalled the greatest hosts by far
> and the goodliest, raging with the spear.
>
> Of the Dardanians again the valiant son of Anchises was captain,
> even Aeneas, whom fair Aphrodite conceived to Anchises amid the
> spurs of Ida, a goddess couched with a mortal man. Not alone was
> he; with him were Antenor's two sons, Archelochus and Acamas,
> well skilled in all manner of fighting. (*Il.* II, 816-23)

Homer tells us that Ida is in the region of Troy, so the Dardanians lived
in what is now Cambridgeshire, the town of Troy having been
localized in Part II, Chapter 2 on the Gog Magog Hills. The name of this
people comes from Dardanus, founder of the Troad and an ancestor of
King Priam, whose genealogy is, according to the *Iliad*, (XX, 215 f):

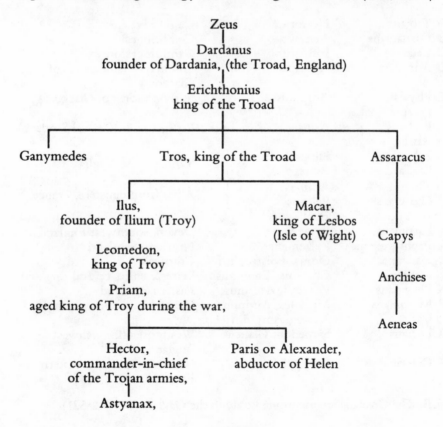

Zeus
|
Dardanus
founder of Dardania, (the Troad, England)
|
Erichthonius
king of the Troad

Ganymedes — Tros, king of the Troad — Assaracus

Ilus, founder of Ilium (Troy)

Macar, king of Lesbos (Isle of Wight)

Capys

Leomedon, king of Troy

Anchises

Priam, aged king of Troy during the war,

Aeneas

Hector, commander-in-chief of the Trojan armies,

Paris or Alexander, abductor of Helen

Astyanax,

N.B. Some commentators believe that Erechtheus was another name
for Erichthonius who was not only king of Troy, but also of Athens
(Cherbourg). See the genealogy of the House of Athens in Appendix
Note 25, page 361.

Regiment C

And they that dwelt in Zeleia beneath the nethermost foot of Ida, men
of wealth, that drink the dark water of Aesepus, even the Troes, these
again were led by the glorious son of Lycaon, Pandarus, to whom
Appollo himself gave the bow. (*Il.* II, 824-27)

This regiment was also from the region of Troy, where we find mount Ida
and the river Aesepus, the present Ise (see Part II, Chapter 1). Pandarus'
men thus came from Cambridgeshire and the east of Leicestershire (see
Map 2, Part II, Chapter 1). The Zeleians, like the Pelasgians (Regiment G),
must have come originally from the Continent, in particular from the
present Belgium, where the town of Zele, between Antwerp and Gent
reminds us of Homer's Zeleia.

Regiments D and E

And they that held Adrasteia and the land of Apaesus, and that held
Pityeia and the steep mount of Tereia, these were led by Adrastus and
Amphius, with corslet of linen, the two sons of Merops of Percote,
that was above all men skilled in prophesying, and would not suffer
his sons to go into war, the bane of men. But the twain would in no
wise hearken, for the fates of black death were leading them on.
(*Il.* II, 828-34)

Forty kilometers southwest of Glasgow, Scotland, we find Adrasteia, the
present town of Ardrossan, on the sea, while Apaesus is the western part
of Glasgow, now known as Paisley. These warriors were thus from the
present region of Strathclyde.

To the north of Glasgow we find Pitlochry (loch = lake) which
corresponds to Pityeia and the valley of Stathyre (probably a contraction
of Strath Thyre) which seems to correspond to Tereia (see Map 19 at the
end of this section on page 337).

Regiment F

And they that dwelt about Percote and Practius, and that held Sestus
and Abydus and goodly Arisbe, these again were led by Hyrtacus' son

Asius, a leader of men – Asius, son of Hyrtacus, who brought his big, high-mettled horses from Arisbe, from the river Selleïs. (*Il.* II, 835-39)

The warriors were from the east of Scotland, where the names of Percote, Practius, Arisbe and Abydos are preserved, respectively, in Perth (via *Perk[o]te), Pratis (village north of Methyl), Arbroath and Abbots Deuglie. The river Tay is probably [Prac]ti[us]. Sestus is not identified. The Selleis could be the Saline Fife, a small river in the region (see Map 19, page 337).

Regiment G

And Hippothous led the tribes of the Pelasgians, that rage with the spear, even them that dwelt in deep-soiled Larisa; these were led by Hippothous and Pylaeus, scion of Ares, sons twain of Pelasgian Lethus, son of Teutamus.　　　　　　　　　　　(*Il.* II, 840-43)

We know that in the Roman era, a thousand years after Homer, the tribes of the Belgii were living on both sides of the North Sea – on the Continent in the north of France and the present Belgium, and on the other side of the Channel in southeast England. According to Homer's works these same tribes, then known as the Pelasgians, were already established in these same regions.

'Deep-soiled Larisa' is northeast of Cambridge, the fertile region of the present river Lark in Suffolk, East Anglia (see Map 2 in Part II, page 72).

Regiments H and I

But the Thracians Acamas led and Peirous, the warrior, even all them that the strong stream of the Hellespont encloses.　　　(*Il.* II, 844-45)

And Euphemus was captain of the Ciconian spearmen, the son of Ceas' son Troezenus, nurtured of Zeus.　　　　　　(*Il.* II, 846-47)

The Thracians and the Ciconians were the only allies of the Trojans who came from continental Europe. Odysseus punishes the Cicones severely for this allegiance after the war was over (see Part III, Chapter 4). On his way home from Troy, he sacks their town of Ismarus, identified with the legendary town of Ys, now submerged in the bay of Douarnenez in the extreme west of Brittany. The Thracians and Ciconians lived in Thrace, west Brittany, which is indeed an area 'that the strong stream of the Hellespont encloses' (see Map 5). The waters off Brest in western Brittany are still called Chenal de la Helle today, and currents there are very fast indeed: up to 9 knots (18 km per hour).

It might be noted in passing that the province of Thrace in the north of Greece borders not on the Hellespont but on the Aegean Sea. Moreover, it is certainly not enclosed by the sea. (For the identification of three other places in Thrace, see Map 15, page 320–21, nos 74, 75 and 76).

The Trojans' overseas allies obviously could not sail toTroy through the Channel and the North Sea, dominated by the Achaeans, so instead they sailed from Brittany to the Bristol Channel and up the river Severn that separates England from South Wales. Homer says that the Thracian Iphidamas left his twelve ships at Percote and went by land to Ilios (Troy) (*Il.* XI, 229). This is not the Percote in Scotland mentioned in Regiment F, but is on the upper reaches of the Severn, where there is a name that is also related to Percote: Pershore (via *Perct–shore).

Regiment J

> But Pyraechmes led the Paeonians, with curved bows, from afar, out of Amydon from the wide-flowing Axius – Axius whose waters flow the fairest over the face of the earth. (*Il.* II, 848-50)

The river Axius is very easy to identify as the Exe in Devonshire, in the southwest of England. The Exe is indeed 'wide flowing' between Exeter and the sea, and it is far from Troy. Amydon may have been the ancient name of Exeter (see Map 19, page 337).

Regiment K

> And the Paphlagonians did Pylaemenes of the shaggy heart led from the land of the Eneti, whence is the race of wild she-mules. These were they that held Cytorus and dwelt about Sesamon, and had their famed dwellings around the river Parthenius and Cromna and Aegialus and lofty Erythini. (*Il.* II, 851-55)

The 'land of the Eneti' is the region of the present town of Inverness, where we find the names of Cytorus in the town of Keith, Cromna in the river Cromarty and Aegialus in the mountain [Carn] Eige. To the west of Inverness the name of 'lofty Erythini' is preserved in the lake and river Ericht and the mountains of Aird, whereas the name of the tribe of the Eneti is preserved by the Enrick river near Inverness. Paphlagonia might be the region around Papigoe near Wick, the River Parthenius having changed its name to be called Wick today. Sesamon is more uncertain, as the name also seems to have disappeared. It could possibly designate the archeological site of cairns and hut circles found near Ambusmore Lodge, north of Dornock.

Regiment L

> But of the Halizones Odius and Epistrophus were captains from afar, from Alybe, where is the birth-place of silver. *(Il. II, 856-57)*

This regiment was from the western tip of Cornwall, where we find the village of Halezy as a reminder of the Halizones, while Alybe (Greek *Halube*) was the village of Halabezack. It is indeed probable that silver was extracted from the copper ores of Devon and Cornwall in pre-Roman times, according to R.F. Tylecote in his *Metallurgy in Archeology* (1962): 'Silver is easily converted to its chloride ($AgCl$) by surface waters containing chlorine, a process accelerated by small amounts of nitrates as found in dew. It forms a whiteish-grey mass probably overlooked by early excavators.' (See Map 19, page 337).

Regiment M

> And of the Mysians the captains were Chromis and Ennomus the augur; howbeit with his auguries he warded not off black fate, but was slain beneath the hands of the son of Aeacus, swift of foot, in the river, where Achilles was making havoc of the Trojans and the others as well. *(Il. II, 858-61)*

In the absence of any geographic names one cannot be certain about the place of origin of the Mysians. Roots phonetically close to Mys – are found in the Measach falls in Scotland, and in Measham in the Midlands. I have opted in favour of the latter, simply because we have already found five regiments from different parts of Scotland. It is thus quite possible that the Mysians were from the area of Measham, in the west of Leicestershire (see Map 19, page 337).

Regiment N

> And Phorcys and godlike Ascanius led the Phrygians from afar, from Ascania, and were eager to fight in the press of battle. *(Il. II, 862-63)*

Phrygia II has already been identified as the Scottish highlands (see Part II, Chapter 4), which are indeed far from Troy. The name of their leader, Phorcys has been preserved in the Scottish family names, Forsyth and Forsyte, made famous through the *Forsyte Saga*. (In

Homer's time, Phorcys was also the name of a god of the sea and of the port of Ithaca.) For Homerian names preserved to our time *see also* Appendix Note 24, Proper names in Homer.

Elsewhere, Homer calls Ascania 'deep-soiled', and Scotland does have fertile land along the east coast, where Esk is a reminder of Asc(ania): the North and South Esk rivers lie between Arbroath and Aberdeen and there is another North and South Esk near Edinburgh, which also has a suburb called Eskbank (see Map 19, page 337).

Regiment P

> And the Maeonians had captains twain, Mesthles and Antiphus, the two sons of Talaemenes, whose mother was the nymph of the Gygaean lake; and they led the Maeonians, whose birth was beneath Tmolus. (*Il*. II, 864-66)

Elsewhere, Homer mentions other places in the territory of the Maeonians, in particular 'fertile Tarne' (*Il*. V, 44) and four more in the following passage:

> But Achilles leapt at the Trojans, his heart clothed in strength, crying a terrible cry, and first he killed Ephition, the valiant son of Otrynteus, the leader of a large contingent, whom Naïad nymph had borne to Otrynteus, sacker of cities, beneath snowy Tmolus in the rich land of Hyde. Goodly Achilles, as this man rushed upon him, threw his spear and struck him on the head, splitting his skull in two. And he fell with a thud, and goodly Achilles mocked him: "You have fallen low, son of Otrynteus, most redoubtable of men. Here is your death, though your birth was by the Gygaean lake, where lie the lands of your fathers, by Hyllus that teems with fish, and eddying Hermus." (*Il*. XX, 381-92)

The Maeonians took their name from the river Meon, which flows through Hampshire to reach the Channel between Southampton and Portsmouth. Their region of origin was the Meon valley, where we find today the towns of East and West Meon and Meonstoke. The Maeonians lived in 'the rich land of Hyde', Hyde being a name found in several places in England today, but here the context indicates Hyden Hill and Hyden Woods north of Portsmouth. As to Hermus and Hyllus, Homer does not specify that these names refer to rivers, as most translators have it. He says only that Hermus 'swirls' or 'eddies' and Hyllus 'teems with' or 'is rich in' fish. In the absence of other rivers in the region, Hermus and Hyllus could be bays on the coast. A similar problem arises with the Gygaean Lake: there is no lake in the region, and the Greek *limné* does not only mean 'lake' but also 'bay'. It so happens that there are three large bays on the south coast of England between Chichester and Southampton. The easternmost, now called Chichester Harbour, could have been Hermus, as a town on its shores, Hermitage, seems to suggest. Nearby, we find the broad peninsula of Thorney Island, which would then be Homer's 'fertile Tarne'. The second bay, Langstone Harbour, would correspond to Homer's Hyllus, situated between Hilsey and Hayling, both reminders of the ancient name. The third bay, Portsmouth Harbour, which is close to the mouth of the River Meon, would then, by deduction, have been the 'Gygaean Bay', although the name seems to have disappeared. There still remains the problem of the 'snowy' height of Tmolus, as there are obviously no snow-covered mountains in this region (or any other fertile region for that matter). Although the Greek adjective *niphoeis* normally means 'snow-covered', it might also in very ancient times have meant simply 'wet' as it is cognate with the older Sanskrit *snihyati* 'it becomes wet' (and the same Sanskrit root *sni* is found in the English 'snow', which is in any case simply a particular form of precipitation). The word used by Homer may thus simply have been used to describe the generally damp climate of southern England. This being said, the name Tmolus has disappeared, unless it has changed via *Tolus to become Dole (Woods), north of Southampton (see Map 19, page 337).

Regiment Q

> And Nastes again led the Carians, uncouth of speech, who held Miletus and the mountain of Phthires, dense with its leafage, and the streams of Maeander, and the steep crests of Mycale. These were led by captains twain, Amphimachus and Nastes – Nastes and Amphimachus, the glorious children of Nomion. And he came to the war all decked with gold, like a girl, fool that he was; but his gold in no wise availed to ward off woeful destruction; nay, he was slain in the river beneath the hands of the son of Aeacus, swift of foot; and Achilles, wise of heart, bare off the gold. (*Il.* II, 867-75)

The Carians were from Wales where we find very many names beginning with Car-: Cardigan, Cardiff, Carmarthen, Caren, etc. These were one of the peoples who spoke a language radically different from that of the Trojans themselves.

Miletus would be Milton End, not far from Homer's mount Phtires, now called Tir Phil, west of Pontypool. The river Meander ('man of the Me', the river god) is likely to have been the river Seven, which meanders through the countryside where we find May Hill, west of Gloucester. The heights of Mycale would have been in the northern

Cotswolds, where the village of Mickleton, south of Stratford–upon–Avon, is a reminder of the ancient name (see Map 19, page 337).

Regiment R

> And Sarpedon and peerless Glaucus were captains of the Lycians
> from afar out of Lycia, from the eddying Xanthus. (*Il.* II, 876-77)

It is difficult to determine where the Lycians came from. The river Xanthus can scarcely be the same one as the Scamander, that has been identified as the Cam (see Part II, Chapter 1), for in that case Homer could hardly say that they came 'from afar'. It is just possible that the Lycians came from the area of the present village of Leasgill in Westmorland on the river Kent (Xanthus), whose name is derived from the Celtic *kanto*, 'white', cognate with the Greek *xanthos*, 'fair'. (See Map 19 page 337).

Regiment S

> '. . . but what warrior was that son of Telephus whom he slew with
> the sword, the prince Eurypylus! Aye, and many of his comrades,
> the Ceteians, were slain about him, because of gifts a woman
> craved.'
>
> (*Od.* XI, 519-21)

Among the peoples of the Troad, certain translators number the Hittites, the famous people who inhabited Turkey in the Bronze Age, but certainly not England. However, Homer does not speak of Hittites, but of Ceteians (Greek *Kéteioi*), whom certain Hellenists have taken for the inhabitants of the region of Kede or Kheta in Turkey, and who were Hittites in Homer's time. In England, it is likely that the Ceteians lived in a broad region northwest of Cambridge, where the towns of Ketton (Leicestershire), Kettering (Northamptonshire) and Ketsby (Lincolnshire) are reminders of their presence (see Map 19, page 337).

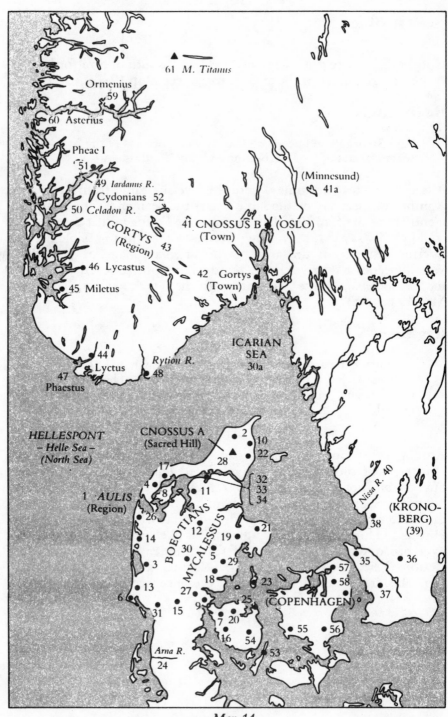

Map 14
Crete in Scandinavia. (Bronze Age.) Modern names are in brackets.

Key to Map 14

In the broader sense, 'Crete' designates the 'spacious country with 90 towns', which is Scandinavia as a whole, while in the narrower sense it covers south Norway, the territory of Regiment 17.

The main post-Homerian suffixes to place-names are as follows:

-*sted* and -*by* = town;
-*ö* and -*ø* = island;
-*skov* = forest;
-*kaer* = rock;
-*hoved* = hilltop;
-*vad* = ford;
-*torp, -strup* and -*rup* village

Regiment 1 (Peneleos)
Boeotia – Jutland, Denmark

1	Aulis	Ålborg province, rendez-vous of the Achaean fleet
2	Hyria	Hjørring
3	Schoenus	Skjern
4	Scolus	Skoldborg
5	Eteonus	Them
6	Graea	Grærup
7	Harma	Harnorup
8	Eilesium	Elsö
9	Erythrae	Erritsø
10	Eleon	Elling (also mentioned in *Il.* X, 266)
11	Hyle	Hyllebjerg (on lake Cephisus, V, 708, now part of the Limfjord)
12	Peteon	Peterstrup
13	Ocalea	region of Oksby and Oksböl
14	Medeon	Madum
15	Copae	Københoved
16	Eutresis	('good' Tresis) Dreslette
17	Thisbe	Thisted
18	Coroneia	Korning
19	Haliartus	Halling
20	Plateia	Bladstrup
21	Glisas	Glesborg
22	Thebe (lower)	Dybvad
23	Onchestus	Onsbjerg
24	Arna	River Arnå and region
25	Mideia	Midskov
26	Nysa	Nissum
27	Anthedon	Andkær

Other names in the same region

28	Cnossus (A)	Knösen (hill)
29	Scandeia	Skanderborg (*Il.* X, 268)
30	(Ikast) >	Ikarsted, 'town of Icarus'

30a	Icarian Sea	Skagerrak
31	Pramnus	Bramminge (*Od.* X, 235)
32	Niobe	Nibe ⎫
33	Achelous	Aggersund ⎬ the Niobe story
34	Sipylus	Sebbesund ⎭

Regiment 2 (Ascalaphus)
Orchomenus I – southwest Sweden

35	Aspledon	Åstorp region
36	Orchomenus I	Region of Örkelljunga and Örkened
37	(Ascalaphus)	Ask
38	(Ialmenus)	Halland
39	(Mountain of Kronos/Cronus)	Kronoberg province
40	Nysa, R.	River Nissa(n)

Regiment 17 (Idomeneus and Meriones)
Crete (in the restricted sense) – southwest Norway

41	Cnossus (B)	Town in the Oslo region
41a	(Minnesund)	Sound of the people of Minos, king of Cnossus
42	Gortus or Gortyn (town)	Horten
43	Gortus or Gortyn (region)	Hordland
44	Lyctus	Liknes in the Lista region
45	Miletus	Meling (?)
46	Lycastus	Lysefjord region
47	Phaestus	Vestbygd (site of Menelaus' shipwreck; see Part II, Chapter 6)
48	Rhytium	Ryen near Kristiansand or Ryfylke ('county of Ry') near Stavanger

Other names in the region

49	Iardanus R.	Hardanger Fjord (*Il.* VII, 135 and *Od.* III, 292)
50	Celadon R.	Sildefjord (*Il.* VII, 133)
51	Pheae I	Visnes (?) (*Il.* VII, 135) (Phaea II, Map 16, note 33)
52	Cydonians	People livingin the Iardanus region

Regiment 25 (Podaleirius and Machaon)
Danish islands

53	Tricce	Tryggelev
54	Ithome	Tommerup
55	Oechalia	Skælskör on Sjælland island

Maps

Other names in the region

56	(Corinth)	Korinth in Sjælland
57	Amnisos	('difficult port') Anisse (*Od.* XIX, 188)
58	Illithye	Illeröd (place of worship of the birth goddess Illythye, *Il.* XIX, 103)

Regiment 26 (Eurypylus)
Sognefjord region, west Norway

59	Ormenius	Hermansverk (?)
60	Asterium	Austrheim
61	Titanus M.	Tind mountain

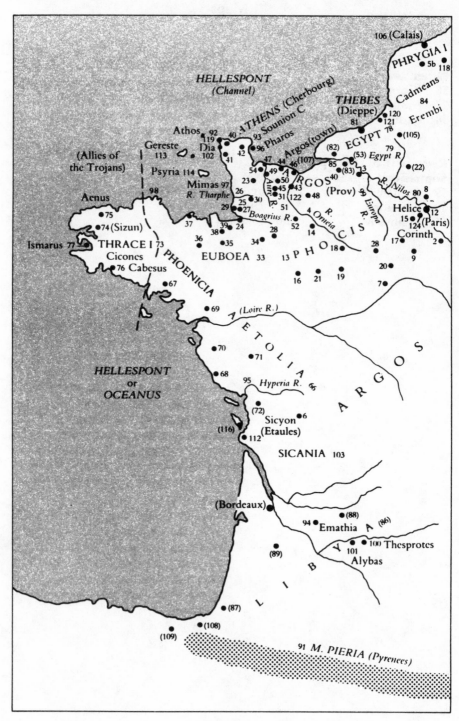

106 (Calais)

PHRYGIA I
5b
118

HELLESPONT
(Channel)

ATHENS (Cherbourg)
Sounion C

THEBES
(Dieppe)

Cadmeans

Erembi

84

Athos 92
119
Gereste
113 Dia
102

40
93
96 Pharos
Pharos

81
120
121
78 (105)

(Allies of
the Trojans)

Psyria 114

41
42

Argos(town)
47
44
46 (107)

(82) EGYPT
(53) Egypt R
79

R. Nilos 80 8

Aenus

Mimas 97
R. Tharphe

54
23
49
45
31
122
43
48

85
40
(83) 3

Helice 12
124 (Paris)
Corinth 2

75

26
29 27
25 30
51

A
50

ARGOS
(Prov)

R. Orneia
R. Europa R.

15
17
9

74 (Sizun)

37
38 39 24
36 35 34

Boagrius R.
52
14
28

28

20
7

Ismarus 77

THRACE I 73
Cicones
76 Cabesus

EUBEA 33
13 PHOCIS 18

16
21
19

PHOENICIA

67

HELLESPONT
or
OCEANUS

69
(Loire R.)

70
71

68

95 Hyperia R.

(72) Sicyon 6
(Etaules)

(116)
112

SICANIA 103

(Bordeaux)

94 Emathia
(88)
(86)

101 100 Thesprotes
Alybas

(89)

(87)

(108)
(109)

91 M. PIERIA (Pyrenees)

Map 15

320

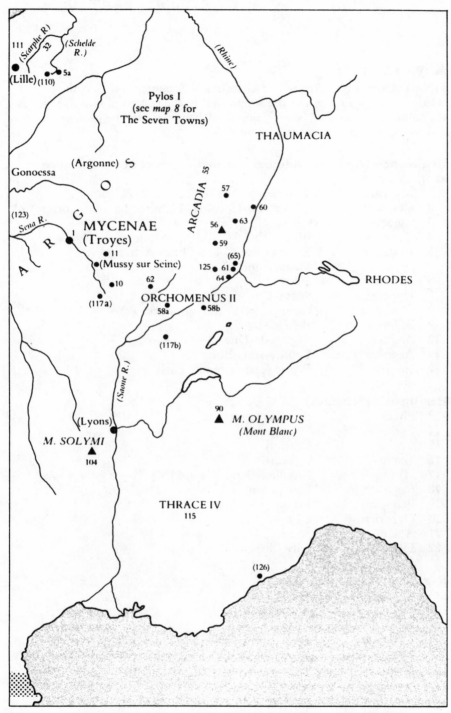

Argos in France. (Bronze Age.) Modern names are in brackets.

321

Key to Map 15

In the broader sense, Argos, the kingdom of Agamemnon, was the northern half of France and the Rhineland. In the restricted sense, Argos is the name of a town and province on the Channel coast, the present Calvados, the territory of Regiment 8.

Regiment 9 (Agamemnon, commander-in-chief of the Achaean armies)

1	Mycenae	Troyes (see Part II, Chapter 11)
2	Corinth	Courances (Corintia in Church Latin > Corrençon)
3	Cleonae	Cléon
4	Orneia R.	River Orne
5	Araethyrea	Ardres (near Calais, 5b) or Artres (near Valenciennes, 5a)
6	Sicyon	Siecq
7	Hyperesia	Suèvres
8	Gonoessa	Gonesse, plain and hill, north Paris
9	Pellene	Bellême
10	Aegium	Aignay-le-Duc
11	Aegialus II	Eguilly-sous–Bois
12	Helice	Elysée (plain); central Paris

Regiment 3 (Schedius)

13	Phocis	Beauce region
14	Pytho	Putanges
15	Crissa	Cressely
16	Daulis	Dollon
17	Hyampolis	Janville (Hiemivilla in 1130) (Greek *polis* = ville)
18	Cephisus R.	Sées (town)
19	Panopeus	Panon
20	Cyparissus	Civry
21	Anemoreia	Amné
22	Lilaea	Lilly (displaced)

Regiment 4 (Aias of Oileus)

23	Locris	St Lô
24	Opus	Pontaubault
25	Augeiae I	Angey
26	Tarphe R.	River Thar
27	Boagrius R.	River Oir
28	Cynus	Cigné
29	Callíarus	Carolles
30	Bessa	Beslon
31	Thronium	Trugny
32	Scarphe R.	Scarpe River (name displaced)

Maps

Regiment 5 (Elephenor)
33	Euboea	Town and region of St Malo (Le Grand Bé)
34	Eretria	Ernée
35	Histieia	Hédé
36	Chalcis I	Caulnes
37	Cerinthus	'hard by the sea' Cap Guérin
38	Dion	'steep citadel' Dinan
39	Carystus	Carnet

Regiment 6 (Menestheus)
40	Athens	Octeville near Cherbourg (Okke = Athene)
41	Marathon	Martinville (*Od.* VII, 80)
42	Athos	(cape near the sea, *Il.* XIV, 229) – Austhot, east of Cherbourg

Regiment 8 (Diomedes)
43	Argos	(province) Calvados
44	Argos	(town) Arromanches ('Argos on the Channel')
45	Tiryns	Thury-Harcourt (< Tirins)
46	Hermione	Hermanville-sur-Mer
47	Asine	Asnières-en-Bessin (Towns 46 and 47 'enfold the deep gulf', Seine Bay)
48	Troesen	Troarn (?)
49	Epidaurus	'on the Aure river', Bayeux
50	Mazes	Maizet
51	Aurus R.	River Aure
52	Messeis R.	Messei (village) (*Il.* VI, 457)
53	Eionae	Yainville (displaced)
54	Aegina	Aignerville

Regiment 12 (Agapenor)
55	Arcadia	'far from the sea' Vosges region
56	Cyllene	'steep mountain' Sélestat (nearby town)
57	Pheneus	Fénétrange
58	Orchomenus II	'rich in flocks' region of Orchamps (58a) and Orchamps-Vennes (58b) on the river Doubs
59	Rhipe	Ribeauville
60	Stratia	Strasbourg (Strateburgo in the sixth century)
61	Enispe	'windswept' Ensisheim
62	Mantineia	Region of Mantoche (near Gray) on the Upper Saône
63	Parrhasia	Barr
64	Tegea	Tagsdorf
65	Stymphalos	Staffelfelden (?)

Regiment 16 (Thoas)

66	Aetolia	Western France (name preserved by the village of Etaules)
67	Pleuron	Ploëren
68	Olenus	Olonnes
69	Pylene	Blain
70	Chalsis II	Challans
71	Calydon	la Caillère
72	Curetes	(tribe) name preserved by Courçon, east of La Rochelle

Trojan Regiments H and I

73	Thrace I	'Enclosed by the strong stream of Hellespont', western Brittany
74	Cicones	Thracian tribe, (village of Sizun near Brest)
75	Aenus	Henvic (near Roscoff) (*Iliad* IV, 520)
76	Cabesus	Le Cabellou (near Concarneau) (*Iliad* XIII, 363)
77	Ismarus	Engulfed town of Ys (see Part III, Chapter 4)
78	EGYPT	(See Part II, Chapter 5 and 12) Department of Seine Maritime
79	Egypt R.	River Epte
80	Nile R.	Name preserved in dozens of place-names in
(Not in Homer)		Northern France in -nil, e.g. Mesnil, Miromesnil)
81	Thebes	Dieppe
82	Bolbitinon	Bolbec ⎫
83	Phatnus	Vatteville ⎬ (not found in Homer)
84	Cadmeans	(tribe) name preserved in Cadzand and Ca(d)bourg
85	Asopus	Name of the Seine for the tribes on the left bank near the Channel (see Part II, Chapter 5), preserved in Aizier and Ste-Croix-sur-Aizier.
86	LIBYA	(See Part II, Chapter 16). The name is of Celtic origin as it figures in the genealogy of the House of Thebes (Dieppe) (see Appendix Note 25)
87	Makai	(Libyan tribe name) Macaye (village)
88	Nasamones	(Libyan tribe name) Naussannes (village)
89	Machlues	(Libyan tribe name) (Maillas < Maglacum) (village)
		(Above three tribe names not in Homer)

Other names

90	Olympus	Mont Blanc (see Part II, Chapter 18)
91	Pieria	Pyrénées (see Part II, Chapter 18)
92	Chios	(cape) Cap de la Hague (*Od.* III, 170)
93	Sounion	(cape) name preserved by the Basses du Sen (*Od.* III, 278)

94	Emathia	'lovely' Eymeth (village in Dordogne region)
95	Hyperia R.	River Sèvres (*Il.* VI, 457)
96	Pharus	(island) Tatihou island near St Vaast (see Part II, Chapter 6)
97	Mimas	'Lashed by the winds' west coast of Cotentin (Part II, Chapter 10)
98	Malea I	Cape on the Bay of St Malo (Part II, Chapter 6)
99	Europe R.	Eure river (not in Homer, but Europe was the daughter of the god of the Nile, the Seine river).
100	Thesprotes	Pirates, most probably from the region of Trespoux, near Cahors on the river Lot.
101	Alybas	Albas, near Luzech, on the river Lot (*Od.* XXIV, 304)
102	Dia (or Dié)	Diélette, formerly an island, now part of the mainland. (*Od.* XI, 325)
103	Sicania	Region of the Sicanes, where we find many place-names starting with Sic- or Seg-: Charente region
104	Solymi M.	Mountain of St Jean-Soleymieux near Retournac. (Poseidon stopped here on his return from Ethiopia [Africa].) (*Od.* V, 283)
105	Erembi	(*Od.* IV, 84), tribe of nothern France in the region of Eramecourt, called Eremburticurtis in 1118, situated near Poix-de-Picardie, southwest of Amiens
106	(Calais)	Calais was a son of Boreas, god of the north wind; Calais was related to Athens (Cherbourg) (see genealogy of the House of Athens, Appendix Note 25)
107	(Dives)	Town on the Seine Bay, ancient place of worship of Hades – Dives – Dis (see Appendix Note 21)
108	(Ermua)	Reminders of Hermes' stopover on his trip from
109	(Hernani)	Olympus to Ogygia (Mont Blanc to Azores)
110	Trito	Trit in 1170, now Trith-Saint-Léger, a Valenciennes suburb on the Schelde river. Trito was a surname of Athene (*Il.* IV, 515). North of Valenciennes we find Ath, a possible reminder of the goddess Athene 'Lady of Trito'
111	Phrygia I	Region of Flanders (Part II, Chapter 11)
112	(Etaules)	Town; reminder of the ancient region of Aetolia
113	Gereste	Island of Guernsey (Part II, Chapter 10)
114	Psyria	Island of Jersey (Part II, Chapter 10)
115	Thrace IV	(*Il.* XIV, 227) Region of Draguignan and the river Drac
116	(St Trojan)	Reminder of the victory over Troy
117	Alésia	There were many places of this name in Gaul; it is unlikely to be Alise-Sainte-Reine (117a) as it does not correspond to Ceasar's descriptions. More probable is a site near Fort-St-André (near Besançon) in the Jura, according to Guichet and Markale

118 Bouret-sur-   (In the Middle Ages: Borrais or Borrec), village;
     Canches   eponym of Boreas, god of the North Wind. For his
                      sons, Calais (*see* 106), Haemus (Map 12) and Zetes
                      (Map 17)

The Io–Isis cult (see Part II, Chapter 13)

119 Jobourg   'Io-town', west of Cherbourg
120 Incheville   'Town of Inachus', father of Io
121 Melleville   'Town of Melia', mother of Io (120 and 121 close to Le
                      Tréport on the Channel)
122 Thaon   the 'Gadfly' (*taon* in modern French); village near Caen
123 Paris   'Barque d'Isis' > Parisis, the boat of Isis is preserved
                      on the coats of arms of France's capital
124 Issy-les-   Paris suburb; Issiaco in the Middle Ages
     Moulineaux
125 Issenheim   'Home of Isis'; village near Mulhouse, Alsace
126 Eze   Village on the Riviera which had an Isis Mystery cult

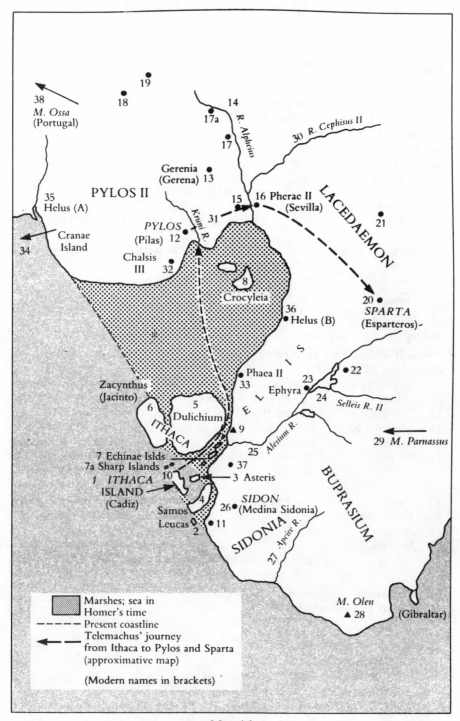

Map 16
Ithaca – Cadiz, southern Spain. (Bronze Age.) Modern names are in brackets.

Key to Map 16 (*See also* Part II, Chapter 7)

Ithaca – kingdom of Odysseus
Regiments 14 (Meges) and 15 (Odysseus)

1	Ithaca Isle	Cadiz peninsula, Odysseus' home
2	Leucas	Isla Sancti Petri (*Od.* XXIV, 11)
3	Asteris	Matagorda
4	Samus Isle	San Fernando, now part of the mainland
5	Dulichium Isle	Present region of Jerez on the mainland
6	Zacynthus Isle	Jacinto (on the mainland)
7	Echinae	'the Holy Isles', 'between Dulichium and Elis', (*Il.* II, 625)
7a	'Sharp Islands'	Cluster of rocks in the sea north of Cadiz, (*Od.* XV, 299)
8	Crocyleia	(Nuevo) Rocio
9	Aegilips M.	Gibalbin mountain
10	Phorcys	Western port of Ithaca ⎱ For details see map,
11	Rheithron	Eastern port of Ithaca ⎰ Part II, Chapter 7

Pylos II – kingdom of Nestor
Regiment 11 (Nestor)
(The older Pylos was in northern Europe: see Part II, Chapter 12 and Map 8)

12	Pylos	Pilas (Nestor's capital)
13	Gerenia	Gerena (Nestor was 'lord of Gerenia')
14	Alpheius R.	River Huelva
15	Arena	Mairena
16	Pherae	'beautiful town on the Alpheius' (*Il.* V, 544, *Od.* III, 488 and XV, 186) Sevilla (see also Note 8, *Etymology*).
17	Thryum	'ford of Alpheius' ⎱ Both names disappeared;
17a	Thryoessa	(*Il.* XI, 711-12) ⎰ probable locations shown
18	Pteleon	San Telmo
19	Mynios R.	(*Il.* XI, 722) river Molinos (?), name preserved by lake Minilla, further north

Lacedaemon – kingdom of Menelaus
Regiment 10 (Menelaus)

20	Sparta	Esparteros, name of a mountain, the nearby city having been renamed Moron by the Moors
21	Pharis	Paradas
22	Augeiae II	Algar
23	Ephyra	'of the fruitful soil' (*Il.* II, 659 and *Od.* I, 259) region of Arcos de la Frontera.
24	Selleis R. II	(*Il*, II, 659) Rio Majaceite (Selleis I was in Scotland, see Map 19).

Maps

Regiment 13 (Amphimachus, Thalpius, Diores and Polyxeinus)

25	Alesium R.	Rio Guadalete ('River of Alese' > Alete)
26	Sidon	Medina Sidonia ('Town of Sidon')
27	Apeire R.	(*Od.* VII, 11) Rio Alberite (and Rio Barbate)
28	Olen M.	Sierra de Ojén

Other names in the region

29	Parnassus M.	Sierra Bermeja
30	Cephisus R. II	River Guadalquivir. For Cephisus I, see Map 15, 18
31	Kruni R.	River Alcarayón (*Od.* XV, 295)
32	Chalsis III	La Calera (*Od.* XV, 295). For Chalsis I and II, see Map 15, 36 and 70
33	Pheae II	Not identified: probable location shown (*Od.* XV, 297). For Pheae I, see Map 14, 51.
34	Cranae Isle	Isla Canela (*Il.* III, 445) near the Portuguese border.
35	Helus (A)	Huelva
36	Helus (B)	Name disappeared; approximate site
37	(Bolaños)	Reminder of a place dedicated to Bolenos (Apollo)
38	Ossa M.	Ossa mountains east of Lisbon, Portugal

In northwest Spain we find:

– Salamis	Salamanca (Regiment 7)
– Ortygia	Ortigueira (sometimes wrongly translated as Delos, see *Od.* V, 123 and XV, 404)
– Cyprus	San Ciprián (*Od.* IV, 83, amongst others)
– Paphos	Foz (*Od.* VIII, 363)

Peoples:

Cephallenians,	subjects of Odysseus
Pylians,	subjects of Nestor
Lacedaemonians,	subjects of Menelaus
Sidonians,	subjects of Phaedimus; *Od.* XV, 118
Epeians	people from Elis and Buprasium.

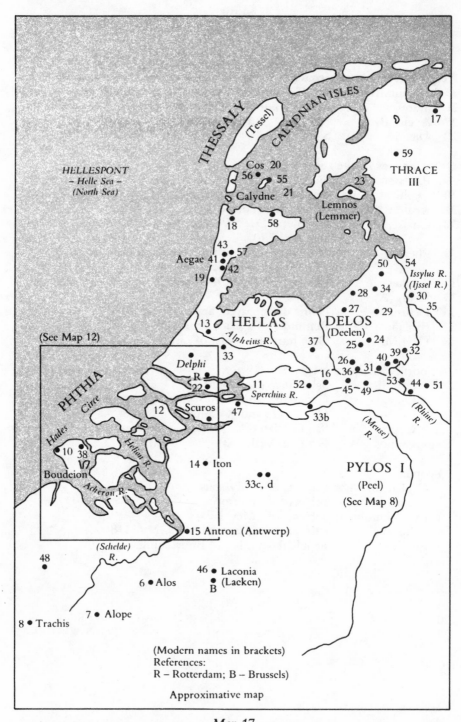

Map 17
Achaean Argos in the Netherlands and Pelasgian Argos in Belgium. (Bronze Age.)
Modern names are in brackets.

Key to Map 17   (*See also* Part II, Chapter 7)

Regions
1	Phthia	Zeeland province, very fertile region, 'mother of men' and the sacred delta of the Celts (see Part III, Chapter 10–12 and Map 12)
2	Hellas	Holland province ('Land near Helle Sea' > Helleland). (The explanation for another Holland, a region on the east coast of England, is identical)
3	Thessaly	Tessel island is a reminder of the ancient island kingdom in the north of the Netherlands
4	Delos	Region of the village of Deelen, the Veluwe, formerly a centre of the Apollo cult (see Part III, Chapter 18)
5	Pylos I	Peel region and Rhineland Palatinate (see Part II, Chapter 12). (Pylos II was in Spain, see Map 16)

Regiment 21 (Achilles)
6	Alos	Alost (in French) or Aalst (in Dutch)
7	Alope	Halluin (Alpheim in the Middle Ages)
8	Trachis	Treizennes (Trachina in the Middle Ages)
9	Scuros	Schuring, a hamlet (Achilles' home, *Il.* XIX, 326 and *Od.* XI, 509). There was another Scuros in England (*Il.* IX, 668).
10	Boudeion	Boudinkerke on old maps, hamlet now called Boudewijnskerke, 'well situated' (*Il.* XVI, 572)

Regiment 22 (Protesilaus, killed on landing and replaced by Podarces)
12	Phylace	(Greek *Phulake*), island of Flakkee (or Overflakkee)
13	Pyrasus	'Flowery' region round Brasem lake; sanctuary of Demeter, goddess of corn and harvests
14	Iton	Etten, 'mother of flocks' (region of Breda)
15	Antron	Antwerp ('Antron wharf'), 'hard by the sea'
16	Pteleus	'couched in grass' Tiel on the Waal river

Regiment 20 (Pheidippus and Antiphus)
17	Nisyrus	Niezijl
18	Crapathus	Krabbendam
19	Casus	Castricum
20	Cos	Kooy, near Helder, strategically 'well situated'
21	Calydne	Callandsoog – Calydnian islands: Wadden islands

Regiment 19 (Nireus)
22	Syme	(Greek *Sumetha*) – Smitshoek

Other names in the region
23	Lemnos	Lemmer, home of the Sintians 'of the unintelligible talk' (*Il.* I, 593; *Od.* VIII, 294, etc.)

Names related to a passage in the Odyssey (see Part III, Chapter 18)

24	Delos	Region of Deelen village
25	(Delian lake)	Delense Was
26	(Nol in 't Bos)	('sacred circle in the woods') Site near the village of Bennekom ('valley of Bennou', the Phoenix)
27	Pytho	(Greek *Puthon*) – Putten, name of the oracle of Apollo. (We found another Putten in Zeeland, Map 12)
28	(Ermelo)	('Hermes' lo') Site of Hermes worship
29	(Apeldoorn)	Town; named after Apollo of the Dorians. (< Apoldorion)
30	(Okkebroek)	('Brook of Okke') Site of worship of Pallas Okke, the alternative name for Pallas Athene.

Names that migrated to south Spain (see Appendix Note 15 The Pylians, Part IV, Regiment 11 and Map 16)

30a	Pteleos	Tiel (Regiment 22)
31	Arene	Arnhem (< Arene-hem)
32	Thryum	Dieren (< Tyron)
33	Alpheius R.	River, now called Old Rhine; town, Alphen on the Old Rhine (there are three other places of the same name, 33b, 33c and 33d
34	Aepy	Epe
35	Cyparisseïs	Schip-beek, small river
36	Helus	Heelsum on the Rhine (the noun *helus* means 'marshland')
37	Dorium	(Greek *Dorion*) – Doorn
38	Pherae	Veere (Part III, Chapter 11) (not in Homer)

Other names

39	Helicon	Ellecom; Poseidon was 'Lord of Helicon' (in some translations confused with Helice, see *Il*. XX, 404)
40	(Posbank)	(bank = hill), site of Pos(eidon) cult near the village of Ellecom (39). The height overlooks the region where the Rhine splits up into three major branches (the symbol of Poseidon's Trident)
41	Aegae	(Cognate with *aiges*, 'waves'), Poseidon's home (*Il*. XIII, 21; *Od*. V, 381 etc.) – Egmont Binnen (Egmond = mouth or bay of Eg[e])
42	(Limmen)	Aegae was situated on a deep lagoon (*limne* in Greek, preserved in the place-name Limmen), village close to both Egmond and Heiloo ('Place near Hellesea')
43	(Alkmaar)	Probably named after Alcmaeon (Greek *Alkmaion*, 'the Defender') who participated in a victorious expedition against Thebes (Dieppe, Map 15, 81)
44	(Lobith)	Village named after the 'warlike' tribe of the Lapithes (*Il*. XII, 128)

45	(Dodewaard)	Village, possibly a second Dodona (c.f. Map 18, 24), as it is a more likely place for Odysseus to have consulted the oak of Zeus
46	Laconia	(Greek *Lakonia*) – Laeken near Brussels. The name, which is the alternative for Lacedaemon, migrated to south Spain (Map 16) and south France (Lacaunes)
47	Babylonienbroek	Hamlet; 'Brook of Babylonia', (oracle, see Map 12, 57)
48	Izegem	Village; place of Isis worship and birth (gem < genesis)
49	Zetten	Village; eponym of Zetes, son of Boreas
50	Heerde	Village; eponym of the ox-eyed Here (oxhead in coats of arms)
51	s'Heerenberg	Hill; 'Mountain of Here'
52	Est	Village; eponym of Hestia
53	Pannerden	Village; reminder of the god Pan
54	Ijssel and Issel	Rivers; Homer mentions only a song, the 'Paean of Issylus'

The Amazons

The Amazons were mounted female warriors whose existence was in doubt as their region of origin was never found. A-mazon means 'without breast' these women having removed, according to legend, one breast to be unencumbered when shooting with bow and arrow or handling a spear. The following place-names might well be an indication of their region of origin:

55	(Hippolytushoef)	Village bearing the name of Hippolyta, a queen of the Amazons, or her son Hippolytus
56	(Marsdiep)	Deep of Mars or Ares, the god of war, who was the father of Hippolyta. Marsdiep is the name of a nearby strait.
57	(Oterleek)	Village that seems to be named after Otrera, the mother of Hyppolyta (in other accounts the mother was Harmony)
58	(Medemblik)	'Maiden's look', small town. The very moment Achilles killed the Amazon Pentesileia, he was struck by the expression in her eyes, fell in love with her and lamented over her dead body (legend not in Homer)

Thrace III

59	(Drachten)	Town whose name is a possible reminder of Thrace III (see Part II, Chapter 18)

Peoples

Myrmidons, Hellenes, Achaeans, Sintians, Dorians, Dolopes and Lapithes

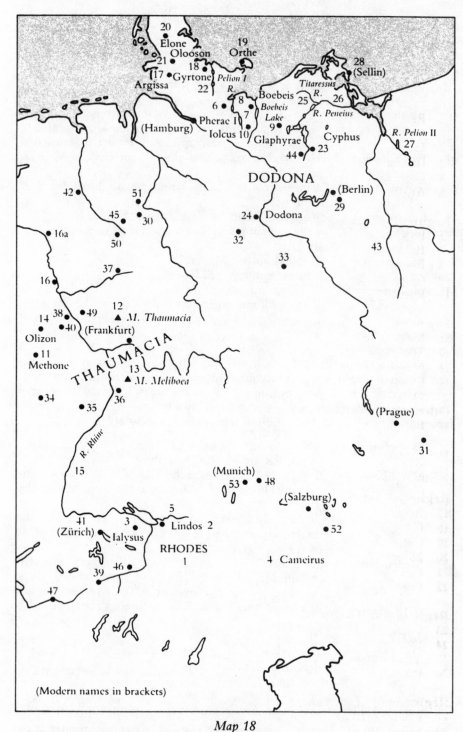

20
Elone
Olooson   19
            Orthe
21
18
17 Gyrtone
Argissa   22 *Pelion I*
                 R.   *Titaressus*
             6   8   Boebeis   R.   26
                  7   *Boebeis* 25
        Pherae I   *Lake*   R. *Peneius*
        Iolcus 10   9   R. *Pelion* II
                  Glaphyrae   Cyphus   27
(Hamburg)   44   23

DODONA

42   51   (Berlin)
    45   24 Dodona   29
16a   50 30
                32
    37   33   43

16
        12
14 38 49   ▲ M. *Thaumacia*
    40 (Frankfurt)
Olizon
11   THAUMACIA
Methone   13
            ▲ M. *Meliboea*
34   35   36
                                        (Prague)
        R. *Rhine*
                                            31
15
                    (Munich)
                    53 48
                        (Salzburg)
        5
41 3   52
(Zürich) Ialysus Lindos 2
        RHODES
        39 46   1
47   4 Cameirus

(Modern names in brackets)

Map 18
Dodona, Thaumacia and Rhodes in East and West Germany, Switzerland and Austria. (Bronze Age). Modern names are in brackets.

Key to Map 18

Regiment 18 (Tlepolemus)

1	Rhodes	(region) Rhoden (Swiss canton) and western Austria
2	Lindos	Lindau (Germany)
3	Ialysus	(St) Gallen (Switzerland)
4	Cameirus	(region) Salzkammergut, Austria
5	Argen R.	Celtic name, cognate with Argos

Regiment 23 (Eumelus)

6	Pherae	Behlendorf (?)
7	Boebeïs L.	Lake Schwerin
8	Boebe	Bobitz
9	Glaphyrae	Glave
10	Iolcus	Holthusen (?)

Regiment 24   (Philoctetes, suffering from snake bite, replaced by Medon)

11	Methone	Mettendorf (*dorf* = village)
12	Thaumacia M.	(region) Taunus, mountain
13	Meliboea M.	(region) Melibocus, mountain
14	Olizon	'rugged' Olzheim (*-heim* = -ham)

Other names in the area

15	Rhene R.	and river goddess (?) River Rhine (name cognate with Celtic *rene* = rebirth)
16	Colone	(Greek for 'hill'), Köln (Cologne)
16a	Xanthus	Xanthen (Greek *xanthos* = 'blond')

Regiment 27 (Polypoetes)

17	Argissa	Arkebek
18	Gyrtone	Kiel
19	Orthe	Orth
20	Elone	Ellund
21	Olooson	Olderup
22	Pelion R. I	Plöne, river, lake and town

Regiment 28 (Gouneus)

23	Cyphus	Kieve
24	Dodona	Dodendorf
25	Titaressus R.	River Teterow
26	Peneius R.	River Peene (also mentioned in Regiment 29)

Regiment 29 (Prothous)

27	Pelion R. II	River Plöne (or Plona)
28	Sellin	Town on the island of Rügen, reminder of the Selli, priests of Zeus in Homer's time

The following place-names do not figure in Homer but are mentioned here in support of archeological evidence that central Europe was once inhabited by the Celts, as those names are clearly of pre-Christian origin:

29	Zeuthen	Town near Berlin, name cognate with Zeus
30	Herford	Place-names cognate with Here, consort of Zeus
31	Heralec (near Prague)	
32	Athenstedt	'Town of Athene'
33	Apolda	Town named after Apollo
34	Hermeskeil	Town named after Hermes
35	Herxheim	Town named after Heracles
36	Heppenheim	Town named after Hephaestus
37	Laasphe	Laas (this name disappeared in southern Spain, see Part IV, Regiment 10)
38	Andernach	Towns named after Andarte, the alternative
39	Andermatt	name of Nike (Victory) (see Appendix Note 25)
40	Mayen	Town named after Maya, mother of Hermes
41	Aargau	(French *Argovie*) Canton; name cognate with Argos
42	Lathem	Town probably named after Leto (Latone), mother of Apollo and Artemis
43	Neisse	(Polish *Nysa*) River name identical to Homer's Nisa
44	Maronstein	'Stone of Maron', priest of Apollo.
45	Dissen	Ancient place of worship of Dis or Hades
46	Laax	Town name cognate with Laas in Lacedaemon (Laconia); returned to central Europe with the tribe of Tlepolemus (see Regiment 18)
47	Sion	Cognate with Sidon. (There are other Sions in western Europe); origin as under 46.
48	Isen	Former places of Isis worship
49	Isenburg	
50	Isendorf	
51	Isenstedt	
52	Hallstatt	Town and lake (name cognate with Helle) known for major archeological finds dating from the Iron Age Celtic culture, now known as the 'Hallstatt culture'
53	München	Town whose older name is Munich, eponym of Munichus, hero of an Illyrian legend

N.B. The origin of the Celts is discussed under Regiment 28, page 304 and Appendix Note 25, page 357.

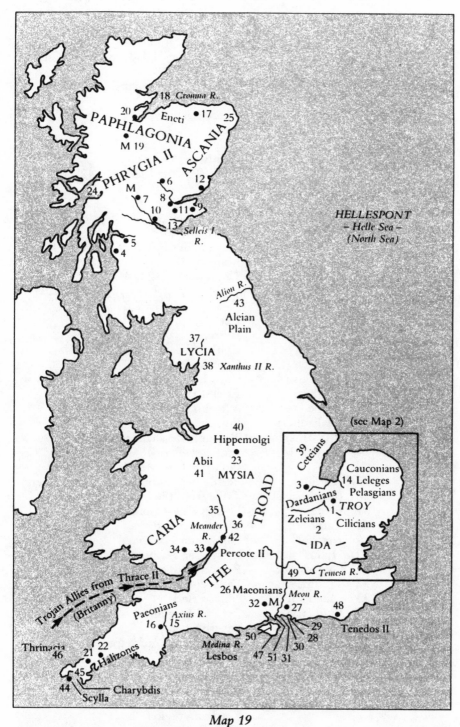

Map 19
The Troad, Phrygia II and Caria in England, Scotland and Wales. (Bronze Age.)
Modern names are in brackets.

Within the map:

PAPHLAGONIA

18 *Cromna R.*

20 · Eneti

· 17 25

M 19

PHRYGIA II ASCANIA

· 6 12

M · 7 8

10 · 11 · 9

13 · *Selleis I R.*

· 5

· 4

24

HELLESPONT
– Helle Sea –
(North Sea)

Alion R.

43
Aleian
Plain

37
LYCIA

38 *Xanthus II R.*

(see Map 2)

40
Hippemolgi

Abii 23

41 MYSIA

39 Ceteians

Cauconians
14 Leleges
Pelasgians

3 ·

Dardanians
TROY
1 ·

Zeleians
2

Cilicians

IDA

35

CARIA *Meander R.*

34 · 33 · 36 · 42 THE TROAD

Percote II

49 *Temesa R.*

Trojan Allies from Thrace II (Britanny)

26 Maconians

32 · M · 27 *Meon R.*

· 48

Paeonians
16 · 15 *Axius R.*

29
28

Tenedos II

Thrinacia
46

21 22

Halizones

Medina R.
Lesbos

50

47 51 31

30

45

44 Charybdis
Scylla

Key to Map 19

Regiment				
A	1	Troy	Gog Magog Hills (See Part II, Chapter 2 and Map 2)	
B	2	Ida Mounts	Ditton Woods (Map 2 [38])	
C	3	Zeleia	Shelton (Map 2 [32])	
D	4	Adrasteia	Ardrossan	
	5	Apaesus	Paisley	
E	6	Pityeia	Pitlochry	
	7	Tereia M.	Strathyre mountains	
F	8	Percote I	Perth (Percote II: see no. 42)	
	9	Practius	Pratis	
	10	Sestus	Stirling (?)	
	11	Abydus	Abbots Deuglie	
	12	Arisbe	Arbroath	
	13	Selleis R. I	River Saline Fife (For Selleis R. II, see Map 16, 24)	
G	14	Larisa	Lark (see Map 2 [8])	
H		(Thracians)	Allies from France (Map 15, 73–77)	
I		(Ciconians)		
J	15	Axius R	Exe river	
	16	Amydon	Exeter	
K	17	Cytorus	Keith	
	18	Cromna R.	Cromarty river	
	19	Aegialus M.	Carn Eige mountains	
	20	Erythini	Ericht, river, lake and region	
L	21	Alybe	(Greek *Halube*) Halabezack	
	22	(Halizones)	Inhabitants of Halezy	
M	23	(Mysians)	Tribe of Measham region	
N	24	Phrygia II	Scotland (Part II, Chapter 4) (For Phrygia I, see Map 15, 111)	
	25	Ascania	'fertile' region of Scotland (Esk rivers)	
P	26	(Maeonians)	Tribe from the Meon valley region	
	27	Hyde	Hyden Hill region, near East Meon	
	28	Tarne	Thorney Island	
	29	Hermus	Chichester Harbour	
	30	Hyllus	Langstone Harbour	
	31	Gygaean Bay	Porthmouth Harbour	
	32	Tmolus M.	Dole Woods (?)	
Q	33	Miletus II	Milton End	
	34	Phtires M.	Tir Phil heights	
	35	Meander R.	Severn river	
	36	Mycale M.	Mounts near Mickleton	
R	37	Lycia	Leasgill region	
	38	Xanthus R. II	Kent river (Xanthus R I is the Scamander)	
S	39	(Ceteians)	(Greek *Keteioi*)Tribe of Ketton and Kettering region	

Other names in the Iliad

40	Hippemolgi (XIII, 5)	The lordly people from the region of Hipley Hill, Derby, 'who drink milk'
41	Abii (XIII, 6)	'the most law-abiding folk' from the region of Abney Low, Derby
42	Percote II (XI, 229)	Pershore (< Perct-shore), landing site of Trojan Allies on the Severn/Avon
43	Aleian Plain (VI, 201)	Region near the river Allen and Allendale town, Northumberland

Names in the Odyssey (XIII, 363)

44	Scylla	St Michael's Mount
45	Charybdis	Carbis Bay
46	Thrinacia	Land's End
47	Lesbos	Isle of Wight
48	Tenedos II (III, 159)	Denton (near Newhaven) (For Tenedos I, see Map 2, 28)
49	Temese R.	River Thames

Related names not in Homer

50	(Methymna R)	Medina river
51	(Solen)	Solent

Albion

Although this ancient poetic name for England is not mentioned by Homer, it is of mythological origin. It was thus far often believed that Albion was cognate with Latin *albus* (white), a reference to the chalk cliffs on the Channel, but it now appears to be an eponym of Alebion (stress on the first syllable) who, very appropriately, was a son of Poseidon, the god of the Ocean. As a cross-reference, we read in classical mythology that Heracles passed through the 'land of Alebion', after he had stolen the cattle of Geryon (*see* Map 2, nos 47 and 48, on page 72).

Appendix Notes
Nos 1–25

Note 1   The Iliad in Greece (Part I, Chapters 1 and 4)

The map on the opposite page appears in the translation of Homer by
R. Flacelière and V. Bérard and is intended to help readers to locate the
Homeric names in Greece. It is in fact incomplete, because it is still possible
to find other names borrowed from the *Iliad* in modern Greece, but a
majority of Homeric names have never appeared in that country and for
those that did, it was in haphazard fashion. Some of the most glaring
anomalies, in addition to those mentioned in the text, are:

1 The river Axios in the extreme north of Greece should be in Trojan
   territory;
2 The river Xanthe, in the north of Greece, should be in Turkey;
3 The river Achelous is in Greece, whereas Mount Sipyle, near this river
   according to legend, was believed to be in Turkey;
4 Various Greek islands, such as Euboea, Delos and Rhodes, are not islands
   in Homer;
5 Larissa is a town in Greece, instead of a river in Turkey;
6 The difficulties encountered in trying to locate the names of the Troad in
   Turkey have been discussed, with a map, in Part I, Chapter 3 and in Part
   II, Chapter 1.
7 Description of places (e.g. 'fertile', 'sandy', 'surrounded by the sea')
   seldom fit the Greek setting.

I shall stop there, before confusing the reader altogether. The reason why
more detailed maps have never been published in translations of the *Iliad* is
simple: it would be useless. It has never been possible to draw a map
showing the origins of all the Achaean and Trojan regiments in Greece and
Turkey, despite various efforts by specialists in the field.

Note 2   Trinities (Part I, Chapter 2)

The real reason why Zeus does not want to choose the winner of the
Golden Apple among Here, Athene and Aphrodite is not that he is afraid of
hurting the losers, but because he knows that they really form a Trinity,
three aspects of the same divinity, he himself being part of the Trinity Zeus/
Poseidon/Hades.

In this context it is interesting to recall the biblical story in which the
Lord appears before Abraham in the form of three identical men (Genesis
18). Although the text is not explicit on this subject, the generally accepted
interpretation is that of the Trinity.

Greece and the Aegean.

The Christian Trinity, the Father, the Son and the Holy Ghost is, of course, well-known, but the concept is found in other religions, even though it has different significance and scope. Examples are:

The Egyptians:	Osiris/Isis/Horus
The Babylonians:	Anau/Enhil/Ea
The Rig-Veda:	Varuna/Indra/Mitra
The Hindus:	Brahma/Shiva/Vishnu
The Norsemen:	Odin/Thor/Baldr
The Gauls:	Lug/Ogmios/Cernunnos

Note 3   Women in the Bronze Age (Part I, Chapter 2)

Female readers of Homer may wonder whether Bronze Age society was as
sexist as ours has been until very recently. But they can be reassured on this
point. For a start, it appears that women had access to the Mysteries, which
meant access to education. This is borne out by classical mythology which
tells us, for instance, that a certain Melissa was torn to pieces by the women
of her village when she refused to reveal the secrets of her initiation. This
legend also puts an end to the debate on the question whether women could
attain the rank of Druid. There were not only High Priestesses, but what is
even more significant, the symbolic head of religion and science (which
were inseparable at the time) was a woman: Circe. Religion was not male
dominated either, most gods having spouses with their proper functions,
including the highest, Zeus, whose consort Here had her own assignment as
we have seen in the story of Io (Part II, Chapter 13). It may not even be
surprising that the chief god had a consort, as religious beliefs were inspired
by the observation of nature, where all manifestation of life has a male and
female aspect. Besides, people believed in the transmigration of the soul, so
that reincarnation could take place at random in a male or female body. The
human body was considered to be the 'envelope' of the soul which was as
temporary and perishable as the 'leaves of the mighty forest' as Homer put
it.

Women also had access to the warrior class, as evidenced by the
redoubtable Amazons, although this must have been the exception rather
than the rule, as warfare was undoubtedly a predominantly male
occupation, judging by the *Iliad*. Only in times of war and defeat were
women in a bad position as the victors used to kill the men while keeping
the women, cattle and other riches for themselves. Although captivity has
never been pleasant, it was at least preferable to death, in particular when a
warrior fell in love with his captive, as was the case with Achilles who was
so deeply attached to 'his' Briseïs that he lost interest in the Trojan War!

Note 4   The Translation of Homer (Part I, Chapter 2)

Throughout this book, Homer has been cited in the authoritative translation
by A.T. Murray without any modification. Although Murray's language
seems old-fashioned, as it dates from the first quarter of this century, it has
the merit of rendering the original very closely, which is of great
importance for the interpretation of various details. Those who prefer to
read Homer in modern English will enjoy the excellent translation by
E.V. Rieu, keeping in mind that some detail may be lost. For instance,
where Homer calls Circe 'the terrible goddess with the human voice', an
expression which needed explanation, Rieu and some other translators call
her Circe, 'the Witch', an epithet which turns out to be incorrect.

What all translations have in common is that they are made in a certain
context, which for the *Iliad* and the *Odyssey* was always assumed to be the
Mediterranean. This of course very much determines the choice of

synonyms or even the rendering of the names of peoples, the 'Achaioi' often becoming the 'Greeks' or the 'Keteioi' the 'Hittites', to fit the scene.

I did not attempt to present my own translation (with only one, argumented, exception) to avoid any suspicion of adapting Homer's text to the requirements of my thesis.

Note 5   The Ogamic Script (Part I, Chapter 5)

Several hundred Ogamic inscriptions have been found on stones in England and Ireland, most of them in the southwest of the latter country. It has been possible to decipher them thanks to Irish manuscripts of the Middle Ages, such as the Book of Leinster and the Book of Ballymoore, which contains the 'Ogam tract', an exposé of about seventy varieties of Ogamic writing. The name itself is derived, according to some, from the Greek 'ogmos' (furrow), while according to others it comes from Heracles' alternative Celtic name, Ogmios.

Ogamic writing has also been found on stones in Spain and North America but it is difficult to date the stones.

Here is the complete alphabet, though it should be noted that the vowels do not appear in all versions:

B	L	V	S	N
H	D	T	C	Q
M	G	Ng	Z	R
A	O	U	E	I

Note 6   Indo-European Languages (Part I, Chapter 5)

Here is an amusing example to illustrate how the languages of Europe resembled each other much more 2,000 years ago than they do today, not only from East to West, but also from North to South, as shown by comparing two main branches of Indo-European, Germanic and Romance.

Gothic, known above all through the Bible translation by Wulfila (about 311–383 AD) is an ancestor of the Germanic languages, just as Latin is the predecessor of the Romance languages, but at that time the two had many features in common. For example, 'we had' was *habaidedumes* in Gothic, *habebamus* in Latin. Both words contain the same components, literally 'have-did-we', and the same root *hab* and the same suffix *mes/mus* (we) can be recognized. The grammatical form was subsequently simplified and the Germanic languages became more analytic, i.e. prefixes and suffixes tended to split off into separate words:

Gothic	Habai-ded-umes	approx 300 AD
Old High German {	habaiddum	approx 600 AD
	habadum	approx 1200 AD
Modern Dutch	wij hadden	
Modern German	wir hatten	contemporary
Modern English {	we had	
	'if we'd known!'	

This 'erosion' of the Germanic languages has ended up by making their verb systems very different from those of the Romance languages.

Note 7 Metrics (Part I, Chapter 5)

Homer's poems are written in dactylic hexameters, lines of six feet, five of three syllables, with the first syllable stressed and the other two atonic, while the sixth foot is a spondee of two long syllables, with the first one stressed:

$$|\acute{\angle}\ \cup\ \cup\ |\acute{\angle}\ \cup\ \cup\ |\acute{\angle}\ \cup\ \cup\ |\acute{\angle}\ \cup\ \cup\ |\acute{\angle}\ \cup\ \cup\ |\acute{\angle}\ \breve{\angle}\ |$$

Meter has the advantage of making the oral composition of a poem and the memorization of a text easier, and helps prevent accidental changes being made. But why should Homer have preferred the dactylic hexameter to other meters? The rhythm of this type of verse is in fact poorly suited to the Greek language so that it is doubtful that the original language was Greek, as R. Flacelière notes in the introduction of his French translation of the *Iliad*: 'the dactylic hexameter seems to be a borrowing, an imitation of a foreign model rather than an invention of the Greeks themselves, since the lines contain an abnormally high proportion of short syllables for their language, and thus require a particular effort on the part of the poet'. This tends to confirm my hypothesis that the *Iliad* and the *Odyssey* were initially composed in a language other than Greek and subsequently translated into Ionian Greek, while retaining the original meter. According to Watkins and Kurlowicz early metrical forms of verse seen in archaic Irish and Vedic Sanskrit, as well as in Homeric Greek, appear to be related.

Here are the famous first two lines of the *Odyssey*, where the poet invokes the Muse and asks her to relate the adventures of Odysseus:

Appendix Notes

$$\overset{\prime\prime}{A}\nu\delta\rho\alpha\ \mu\text{oι'}\text{έννεπε},\ \mu\text{οῦσα},\ \pi\text{ολύτροπον},\ \text{'ὸς}\ \mu\text{άλα}\ \pi\text{ολλὰ}$$
$$\pi\lambda\acute{\alpha}\gamma\chi\theta\eta,\ \acute{\epsilon}\pi\epsilon\grave{\imath}\ T\rho\text{οίης}\ \text{'ιερὸν}\ \pi\tau\text{ολίεθρον}\ \text{'έπερσέ}$$

Disregarding the accents of the Greek text, which do not indicate stress but music, the scanned version reads as follows:

Andra moi	ennepe	Mousa po	lutropon	hos mala	polla
Planchthé e	peî Troï	és hië	ron ptoli	ëthron é	perse

A very close translation is:

> Tell me, Muse, of the resourceful man who wandered so much after he had sacked the holy city of Troy.

Translation by A. T. Murray:

> Tell me, O Muse, of the man of many devices, who wandered full many ways after he had sacked the sacred citadel of Troy.

Translation by E. V. Rieu:

> The hero of the tale which I beg the Muse to help me tell is that resourceful man who roamed the wide world after he had sacked the holy citadel of Troy.

Translation by Robert Fitzgerald:

> Sing in me, Muse, and through me tell the story ot that man skilled in all ways of contending, the wanderer, harried for years on end, after he plundered the stronghold of the proud height of Troy.

Note 8   Etymology (Part 1, Chapter 6)

In seeking to identify the geographic names found in Homer with the current place-names of western Europe, my first guide was the well-established rules of etymology.

There were additional difficulties, however, because we know very little about the evolution of place-names during the first millenium BC or about the influence of successive migrations of peoples of different tongues in Europe. For example, England was invaded by the Romans, the Scandinavians, the Angles and the Saxons, but the last invasion, by the Normans of William the Conqueror in 1066, brought about a radical change in the language. Old English was a highly inflected Germanic language, very closely related to Old Norse and Icelandic; Modern English is a highly analytic language, still with a large proportion of Germanic words, but with in addition a very large proportion of Latin-based words. Spain was occupied for a long time by the Moors, who spoke Arabic. Geographic names have suffered the consequences, sometimes changing so much as to become unrecognizable, sometimes being totally replaced by a new name. However, the fact that Homer sometimes mentions several names in the same region has greatly facilitated the task, for in those cases there is only one region in Europe where it is possible to find the roots of a number of place-names that correspond with those of the text. I have always been guided by phonetics rather than by the orthography, for it makes no difference to the sound whether the spelling is, for example, 'f' or 'ph', and in any case for the Homeric names we have to transliterate from the Greek. The way in which sounds change over the course of time depends very much on whether the syllable concerned is stressed or unstressed. It so happens that the majority of Homer's names have the stress on the first syllable. For example, 'Pelasgians' can become 'Belgians' only if the first syllable is stressed and the others not: *Pélasges* > Pelges > Belges; similarly for *Egypte* > Epte and *Chary*bdis > Carbis.

When consonants change, they generally become voiced: f > v, k > g, p > b, s > z, t > d, though there are cases where the reverse occurs, and there can even be changes in both directions in the same word: Thebes > Dieppe. The 'l' and 'r' are readily interchangeable, as is demonstrated today by many Japanese when speaking European languages – they have no 'r' sound in their own language and have the greatest difficulty in making the distinction between it and 'l'.

If the first of two vowels is aspirated, it may mutate to 'h' or 'g': Iardanos > Hardanger; Ialus > Gallen.

Unstressed vowels tend to disappear, in particular the short 'o' (omicron): Gonoesse > Gonesse, but even the long 'o' (omega) can disappear if it is unstressed: Kolône > Colne (in England), > Köln (in Germany), but > Coulogne (in northern France).

It appears that the Greek letter eta was a 'long' e (epsilon) and pronounced é as in French 'pré' rather than è as in French 'père'.

The 'u' (upsilon) has become 'y' or 'i' in our orthography: Mukéné > Mycenae, Pulos > Pilas. The pronounciation of the Greek k (kappa) seems to have been similar to the c in modern European languages in that it sounded like 's' when followed by the vowels e and i.

Certain names have changed very little, if at all, since Homer's day: Maeon > Meon; Gérenia > Gerena, while others have become totally unrecognizable though still following the normal rules of sound change: Phéras > Vélas > Véla > Vila > Sevilla ('se' being an indicative pronoun).

Since the rules of etymology often leave a fairly broad margin for interpretation, I have always tried to reduce this margin by taking account of other factors. First, a resemblance of sound by no means proves that there is an etymological link. I have also taken account of the cultural and geographic context. When there were several places in Europe with the same name in which I was interested, it was necessary to select the one in the same region as related Homeric names. This task is greatly facilitated by the list of armies in Book II of the *Iliad*. This list is of inestimable value, for here Homer groups together towns and rivers of the region of origin of each regiment. It is much more difficult to identify isolated geographic names.

Appendix Notes

Note 9   Gog and Magog in the Guildhall (Part II, Chapter 1)

In addition to the biblical references to Gog and Magog, there is, according to the *Encyclopedia Britannica*, 'an independent legend of Gog Magog (which) surrounds the two colossal wooden effigies in the Guildhall in London. They are thought to represent survivors of a race of giants destroyed by Brutus the Trojan, legendary founder of London (Troianova, or New Troy) who brought these to act as porters at the gate of the royal palace. Effigies of Gog and Magog are known to have existed in London from the time of Henry V. The earlier figures were destroyed in the Great Fire (1666) and were replaced in 1708. The second pair was destroyed in an air raid in 1940 and replaced in 1953'.

Note 10   Geographical Names in Homer (Part II, Chapter 1)

One of the problems in Homer is that the same name can designate several things, for example, a river, the god of that river, a town or hill on its banks, or the region around it. The same name may also be that of a warrior or a horse.

What is more, there may be more than one town or river of the same name: there are two rivers called Selleïs, two towns called Scuros, two regions called Pylos, three Chalsís and four Thraces. However, once this fact is known there is usually no difficulty in seeing from the context which of the alternatives is being referred to.

Note 11   Temese – The Thames (Part II, Chapter 1)

There is also a village called Temse south of Antwerp in Belgium, called Tamise by the Walloons, a name clearly of the same origin as Temese, which would tend to confirm that the Pelasgians (Belgians) lived on both sides of the Straits of Dover in Homer's time, as we know was the case in the Roman era. Since Athene was going to Temese for bronze, she must have been going to England, not Belgium. There is also a village called Tamisa in Italy, but the Celts did not arrive there until after the Bronze Age, as was the case with Yugoslavia, where there is a river Tamis between Beograd and the Roumanian border.

Temese has never been found in the Mediterranean, and all attempts to identify Homeric Temese and Taphos (where the iron came from) as mining regions in the Mediterranean have failed.

Note 12   Europe (Part II, Chapter 5)

In mythology, we find several Europes or Europas, the best known being the daughter of Agenor, king of Sidon (Medina Sidonia in Spain). She was kidnapped by Zeus, who had taken the form of a white bull for the occasion. He abducted her on his back, taking her all the way to Gortyn in

347

Crete (southern Norway), where he fathered several sons on her, Minos (founder of the Minoans), Rhadamanthus and Sarpedon. On her death, Europa was given divine honours, while the bull, Zeus' temporary disguise, became the zodiacal constellation of Taurus. Homer does not mention Europa by name, but refers to her as the daughter of Phoenix (*Il.* XIV, 322). Neither does he call the 'old continent' Europe as in his time it was called Argos, in its broadest sense.

Another Europe was the daughter of the Nile river god. Since we have identified the Nile as the Bronze Age name for the Seine, it is not so surprising to find a reminder of Europe close by, in the southern confluent of the Seine now called Eure. This name is a contraction of Europe in the same way as the northern confluent of the Seine, the Epte, is a contraction of Egypt, the stress in each case having been on the first syllable of the word and the second syllable being lost.

Note 13   The Sea Level (Part II, Chapter 7)

As Cailleux already noted last century, the sea level does not remain constant due to climate change over periods of several centuries. It has been calculated that the sea level could rise by as much as 100 metres if all polar ice melts. It will never come to that but we are again in a period of rising sea level which is all the more worrying as it is accelerated by global warming due to air pollution. The chart opposite, published by Dr H. Wind in a Dutch newspaper, shows all areas in Europe which might be flooded if the sea level rises only a few metres. These regions include those mentioned in this book as having had a different geographical aspect in the Bronze Age when sea levels were also relatively high: in particular East Anglia, Cadiz province, western France and the province of Zeeland. However, the islands in the latter region appear to have been spared in Homer's time, not only because they were already protected by dykes but also because the level of the land was higher at the time than it is today. It has indeed been established that the soil of the Netherlands is slowly but constantly sinking over time. Only during the fifth to ninth centuries were most of the islands in Zeeland believed to be engulfed. But place-names were retained by sailors to designate sandbanks and other obstacles to be reinstated when the population had returned to reclaim the land.

Note 14   Iphigenia (Part II, Chapter 11)

The sacrifice of Iphigenia by her father on the advice of the seer Calchas before the Achaean fleet sailed to Troy is not related by Homer, but by Aeschylus (525–456 BC) in his drama *Agamemnon*, an episode of which is reproduced below. It is particularly interesting for us to read about 'surging tides' at Aulis, now identified in northern Denmark (see Map inside Front Cover). The name of the river god Strymon, whose son was said to have been killed at Troy, has been preserved as an adjective in the Dutch language, where a 'lashing wind' is called *striemende wind*, which refers

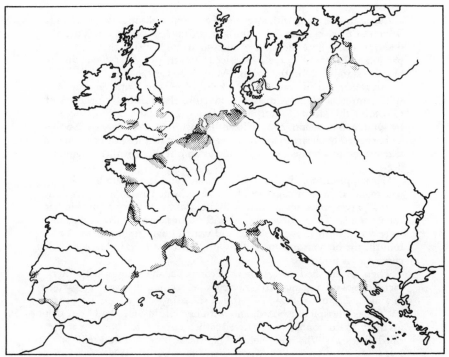

Low-lying areas in Europe.

mainly to the prevailing southwesterlies which indeed can blow over the North Sea for many weeks on end. This explains perfectly why the Achaean fleet was so long prevented from sailing in a southwesterly direction to Troy in England. Although Aeschylus situated the scene of the sacrifice of Iphigenia in Aulis, it is more likely to have taken place in Agamemnon's capital, Mycenae, now Troyes in France, for reasons set out in Part II, Chapter 11. The great dramatist was clearly inspired by a theme that originated far from him in space and time:

> . . . the Achaean folk, on the shore over against Chalcis in the region where Aulis' tides surge to and fro, were sore distressed by opposing winds and failing stores; and the breezes that blew from the Strymon, bringing them grievous leisure, hunger, and tribulation of spirit in a cruel port, driving the men distraught, and sparing nor ship nor cable, by doubling the season of their stay, began to wither by wasting the flower of Argos; and when the seer, urging Artemis as cause, proclaimed to the chieftains another remedy, more grievous even than the bitter storm, so that the sons of Atreus smote the ground with their staves and stifled not their tears –
>
> Then the elder king spake and said: "Hard is my fate to refuse obedience, and hard, if I must slay my child, the glory of my home, and

at the altar-side stain with streams of a virgin's blood a father's hand. Which of these courses is not fraught with ill? How can I become a deserter to my fleet and fail my allies in arms? For that they should with passionate eagerness crave a sacrifice to lull the winds – even a virgin's blood – stands within their right. May all be for the best."

But when he had donned the yoke of Necessity, with veering of spirit, impious, unholy, unsanctified, from that hour his purpose shifted to resolve that deed of uttermost audacity. For mankind is emboldened by wretched delusion, counsellor of ill, primal source of woe. So then he hardened his heart to sacrifice his daughter that he might prosper a war waged to avenge a woman, and as an offering for the voyaging of a fleet!

Her supplications, her cries of "Father," and her virgin life, the commanders in their eagerness for war reckoned as naught. Her father, after a prayer, bade his ministers lay hold of her as, enwrapped in her robes, she lay fallen forward, and with stout heart to raise her, as it were a kid, high above the altar; and with a guard upon her lovely mouth, the bit's strong and stifling might, to stay a cry that had been a curse on his house.

Then, as she shed to earth her saffron robe, she smote each of her sacrificers with a glance from her eyes beseeching pity, and showing as in a picture, fain to speak; for oft had she sung where men were met at her father's hospitable board, and with her virgin voice had been wont lovingly to do honour to her loved father's prayer for blessing at the third libation – What next befell, I beheld not, neither do I tell.

(Aeschylus, *Agamemnon*, 186–247; translation: H. Weir Smyth, Loeb Classical Library)

Note 15   The Pylians (Part II, Chapter 12)

In the *Iliad*, Homer mentions two military expeditions led by Pylians. In the first case (*Il*. VII, 134), they appear to be the people living in 'sandy' Pylos (on the shores of the lower Rhine), who are associated with the Arcadians (living on the shores of the upper Rhine, in particular Alsace), attacking the area of the river Iardanos (Hardangerfjord, Norway).

In the second case (*Il*. XI, 706), they are the inhabitants of the city of Pylos governed by Neleus (Nestor's father), hence Pilas in southern Spain.

Since Homer also tells us that Nestor's grandparents were the first to settle in Pylos (Spain), it can be assumed that they were Celts from the lower Rhine (sandy Pylos), and there are in fact a number of place-names in southern Spain that closely resemble those of Holland: Arene – Arnhem (via ★Arene-hem, 'hem' being 'house' in Old Saxon), Alpheíus – Alphen (there are several places of this name in the Netherlands), Thryum – Dieren, Dorion - Doorn, Elos – Elst and Aepy – Epe (see Map 17 in Part IV). Other Celts from the north must have followed this emigration movement, which would explain how two brothers, Menelaus of Sparta (Esparteros in Spain) and Agamemnon of Mycenae (Troyes in France), had their kingdoms so far apart.

Note 16   Celts and Germans (Part II, Chapter 12)

The country we call France today, was, as we have seen, called Argos by
the Celts in Homer's time and subsequently Gallia by the Celtic Gauls in
Roman times. To the Romans, 'Gallia' sounded like 'Land of the Roosters',
as *gallus* is Latin for rooster (and, of course, the cock has become the
emblem of France). The present name of the country stems from the
Franks, a Teutonic tribe who invaded the territory around 500 AD. As to the
people of central Europe, they never called themselves Germans nor their
country Germany, which is probably not a German word at all. According
to the Italo-American linguist Mario Pei, it comes from a Celtic root
meaning 'neighbouring', seemingly akin to the Latin *germanicus* meaning
'having the same parents' (whence the English 'germane'). The Germans
themselves call their country Deutschland, meaning 'Land of the people'
from the Gothic root *deudisko*, meaning 'people'. The French name for that
country, Allemagne, is a reminder of the Alemani, a tribe living in the
Black Forest in Roman times. Germany was often equated with Prussia,
which is a contraction of Borussia, the Russians themselves being of
Swedish Viking descent. They were called Rus for the first time by an Arab
diplomat, Ibn Fadlan, who arrived in Russia in 922 AD.

Note 17   Oedipus (Part II, Chapter 13)

It might be asked why all the texts dealing with the murder of Laïus by his
son Oedipus insist on the fact that the event took place at the intersection of
three roads. The two vehicles could just as well have disputed the right of
way at a crossroads or simply on a narrow road. Since the story is one of
incest, the intersection of three roads could be interpreted as a female
symbol by placing the scene of the crime between 'brackets':

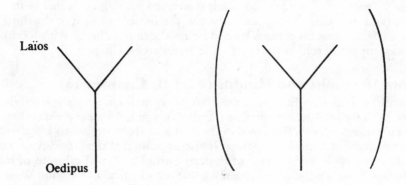

The son is obliged to kill his father if he is to possess his mother, for the
father obviously cannot let him beyond the crucial point.

Note 18   Creation (Part II, Chapter 13)

It is puzzling for readers of classical mythology that the principal god of the ancients, Zeus, was not the Creator of the Universe. Not even his father Cronus, but his grandfather Ouranus was believed to be the origin of everything. Apparently, the ancients realized that Creation had been a very lengthy and complex process taking place in various stages, which R. Emmanuel has categorized, very briefly resumed, as follows:

In the *first* stage, only lifeless matter was created in a timeless universe. This was ascribed to Aea (or Gaea), the Earth-Mother, and Ouranus (the Heavens). They had several children, the youngest of which, Cronus, castrated his father with a sickle. That was obviously the end of Ouranus' creative role and the first stage of Creation.

In the *second* stage, Cronus (also spelled Kronos or Chronus, meaning: Time) added the time element in creation with the introduction of the cycles of sun, moon, the year, the seasons, the tides and so on, with the help of his wife Rhea, an appropriate name, as it means 'she who streams' or 'moves'. The cycles were symbolized by their children, which were swallowed by Cronus at their birth. There was thus still no continuity in Nature as each cycle was cut off with Cronus's sickle. (Think of the Old Year still often represented on cartoons as a bearded old man with a sickle and a timer.) Only the youngest son, Zeus, escaped this fate, thanks to the intervention of his mother who gave Cronus a stone to eat, wrapped in cloth, instead of the young-born.

Once grown up, Zeus started the *third* phase: he threw his father in the Tartarus and liberated his brothers and sisters, the cycles, which he needed for the final phase of Creation, life, which needs the cycles in eternal succession, so that, for instance, plants produce the seeds for their next generation. Zeus was cut to pieces by the Titans and dispersed in the Universe. He was thus crucified into the matter, meaning that he is present in every particle of Nature. But Zeus continued his reign together with Here (and the other Olympians) who put the finishing touch to the third phase of the Creation process by endowing the human being with Reason, as was implicitly told in the myth of Io (see Part II, Chapter 13).

Note 19   Celts and Hindus (Part II, Chapter 13)

Countless studies on European pre-history, ancient languages and religions have brought to light a surprising number of similarities between cultures of the various peoples that lived in the vast area from Ireland to India and from Scandinavia to North Africa. It also appears that the Druids had much in common with the Shamans of Eastern Europe and the Brahmins of India.

In this book we found many names that are identical in East and West. Cultural exchange over such great distances must have taken place both via the Mediterranean and over land via the Russian plains. The first route was taken by the 'Sea Peoples' who must have been Celts from the Atlantic coastal areas, who arrived in the countries around the Eastern

Mediterranean around 1,500 BC. Conversely, peoples from the Levant sailed west to venture out in the Atlantic in search for tin and amber.

The Celts gave new names to existing places in the East including a name for the newly discovered continent: Asia, after a daughter of Oceanus, while Persia was named after Perseus and India after Indus. Other Europeans were in contact with India and Persia via the land routes from the north as evidenced by the origin of the Hindu religion, as described in the *Encyclopedia Britannica*, India was invaded around 1,500 BC by European peoples living in Siberia and Russia who called themselves Aryans. They brought with them their language, Vedic Sanskrit (which is much older than classical Sanskrit), the horse and the Vedic religion. Hinduism then developed slowly from the synthesis of the sacrificial cults of the invaders with the religions of the various indigenous peoples.

According to the same source, Iran had known even earlier contacts with the northern invaders, as evidenced by a near-kinship between Sanskrit and the earliest Iranian language. In Europe, Sanskrit grammar and word roots were also very similar to those of the 'younger' classical languages, such as Greek, Latin, Gothic and Celtic. Linguists therefore classify virtually all the languages which were spoken between Ireland and India as 'Indo-European' languages, which include the Semitic languages but exclude those whose structure, verb conjugations and word roots are of entirely different origin, such as Basque, Finnish, Hungarian and Turkish. The modern language which is closest to Sanskrit is, according to Mario Pei (*The Story of Language*), Lithuanian, spoken on the Baltic coast. Cultural exchanges between West and East could have taken place here as in Homer's time the influence of the Druids extended as far east as Poland (see Part IV, Regiment 28). West Europeans still use many Sanskrit words today, such as Zodiac, Paradise, Karma, Shakra or Mandala, while many are familiar with 'oriental' notions such as reincarnation and karma which may well be of European origin.

Note 20   The *Odyssey* in the Mediterranean (Part III, Chapter 1)

To give the reader some idea of the extent to which commentators have been forced to betray the text when trying to fit the *Odyssey* into the Mediterranean, here are a few remarks on Victor Bérard's maps at the end of this note (English-speaking readers may be more familiar with the more recent book by Ernle Bradford, *Ulysses Found*, which describes an itinerary close to that of Bérard):

1. It can be seen immediately that Calypso here does not live on 'a sea-girt isle, where is the navel of the sea' (*Od.* I, 50), for Bérard locates her on the island of Peregil, in the Strait of Gibraltar.
2. From Cape Malea, Odysseus was driven for nine days by a northerly storm, according to the text, whereas on the map the course from Greece to Tunisia (Bérard's Land of the Lotus-eaters), is almost due west. What is more, the distance covered is less than half what would be expected (over 2,000 km) in these circumstances.

3. The Isle of the Phaeacians is just off the west coast of Greece, even though Nausicaa says to Odysseus: 'far off we dwell in the surging sea, the furthermost of men, and no other mortals have dealings with us' (*Od.* VI, 204-5).
4. Circe is situated on Monte Circeo in Italy, which is not a 'low' island, but a hill 541 metres high. In citing Homer's text, Bérard conveniently leaves out the phrase saying that the island is flat.
5. When Hermes leaves Mount Olympus to take Zeus' message to Calypso, he steps first on Pieria, then flies a long way over the sea (*Od.* V, 50-4). As Mount Pieria in Greece is just to the northwest of Olympus, Hermes' journey cannot be shown on this map because it is impossible to reconcile with the text.
6. The land of the Cicones, Thrace, does not fit Homer's description of a place 'that the strong stream of the Hellespont encloses' (*Il.* II, 845).
7. Already in the last century, scholars had strong reservations about the identification of Odysseus' Ithaca with the Greek island of Ithaki or Thiaki, as evidenced by the works of Völcker (1830), Herscher (1866), Draheim (1894), Dörpfeld (1900) and Rothe (1905).

The list of inconsistencies can be extended at will. It is perhaps fair to say that most commentaries to date have remained too much on the surface of the stories and not really concerned themselves with trying to establish whether there was an underlying cohesion and purpose in the *Odyssey*, such as the compilation of an oral maritime chart for trading, or possibly military, purposes, while the profound symbolism of the texts has been treated in too piecemeal a fashion. The serious shortcomings in most attempts to explain Homer show that the mentality of the ancients is little understood and that their ability to describe places and events

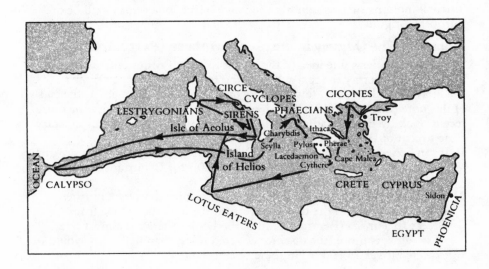

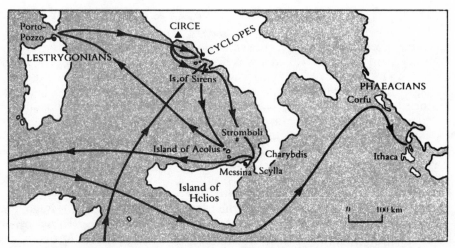

The wanderings of Ulysses in the Mediterranean, after Victor Bérard.

with great accuracy and memorize them for oral transmission over the centuries has been very sadly underestimated as such an exploit would indeed be impossible in modern society.

Note 21 Cicero on the Nature of the Gods (Part III, Chapter 11)

The god of the underworld, whether called Hades, Dis, Dives or Pluto was extremely important for the ancients, for reasons explained by Cicero:

> The earth in all its power and plenty is sacred to Father Dis, a name which is the same as Dives, 'The Wealthy One', as is the Greek [version of] Pluto [Hades]. This is because everything is born of the earth and returns to it again. Dis it was who is said to have married Proserpina, a name of Greek origin in the form 'Persephone'. Proserpina is identified with the seed of the corn and hence comes the legend of her mother's search for her when she had vanished below the earth. Her mother was named Ceres, from *gero* [to bear] because she is the bearer of the corn. The same accidental change of the first letter is also seen in the Greek name Demeter, from Ge Meter (Mother Earth).
> (*The Nature of the Gods*, Book II, translation C. P. McGregor, Penguin Classics.)

Hades' alternative name, Dives, is preserved by the French coastal town of Dives on Seine Bay. For clarification, I added square brackets to the text cited above which seems to be somewhat hastily written. We know that Cicero was not only a busy lawyer, but also a prolific author who dictated his books to his secretary Tiro, who took them down in shorthand.

Note 22   Whirlpools and Waves (Part III, Chapter 15)

In the Inner Hebrides off the west coast of Scotland, there is probably one of the world's most dangerous whirlpools, the Corryvreckan between Scarba and Jura islands, and it was here that Gérard Pillot thought he had found Homer's Scylla and Charybdis.

In the summer of 1975, I went to Scotland to see if it was possbile to visit the site by motorboat. This turned out to be a thoroughly irresponsible enterprise, for it nearly ended badly for the skipper (who had been extremely reluctant to try the trip), myself and a dozen tourists, to whom I owe my humble apologies. Weather conditions were excellent, blue sky and no wind, and we had very detailed charts so that we could take the least dangerous possible route and pass beside the whirlpool precisely at the time of slack water. Being unfamiliar with the area I had gravely underestimated the danger, for half way between the islands we were met by the huge, long swell of the Gulf Stream. It was here that I realized just what Homer meant when he spoke of 'waves as high as mountains'. Neither the North Sea, which can be very dangerous, nor the Mediterranean ever have waves so high as that. And when I crossed the Aegean between Athens and Rhodes in a storm so violent that all the passengers and nearly all the crew were seasick, I was nowhere near so impressed.

Although this Scottish whirlpool and the site correspond in themselves quite well to Homer's description of Scylla and Charybdis, it had to be rejected for other reasons.

Note 23   Viticulture (Part III, Chapter 21)

It is generally believed that viticulture came to France during the Roman occupation, but nothing could be further from the truth. From archeological evidence we know that vineyards existed as far north as Sweden in the Bronze Age, long before Rome was even founded. Today, the northern limit of viticulture is much further south, from East Anglia through Luxembourg and the Moselle region to Franconia. In the Middle Ages viticulture still existed in the Netherlands, judging by the old street name 'Wijngaard' (Vineyard) in Middelburg on the island of Walcheren (Hades). In Homer's day, wine was the most important drink for everyone, the first drops always being offered to the gods. Grape harvesting time was a joyful period, just as it still is today, as is evident from Homer's description of the scene on the shield forged by Hephaistus for Achilles:

> Therein he set also a vineyard heavily laden with clusters, a vineyard fair.
> . . . And maidens and youths in childish glee were bearing the honey-sweet fruit in wicker baskets. And in their midst a boy made pleasant music with a clear-toned lyre, and thereto sang sweetly the Linos-song with his delicate voice; and his fellows beating the earth in unison therewith followed on with bounding feet mid dance and shoutings.
>
> (*Il.* XVIII, 561-570)

Note 24   Proper Names in Homer (Part IV, Regiment N)

On rereading the *Iliad* and *Odyssey* and situating the action in western
Europe, one may still have difficulty in believing that the proper names are
of western European origin because 'they look so Greek' and because they
are no longer given to people in this part of the world. The first problem is
in many cases simply a question of spelling, while the latter is due to the
fact that names generally do not remain popular for ever. Few people these
days have medieval first names, although the Middle Ages are as yesterday
compared to the Bronze Age. However, on closer scrutiny, it appears that
many Homeric first names (surnames were not yet in use) have survived,
with relatively little sound change, though the spelling looks quite different.
I have already mentioned the example of Phorcys, chief of Regiment N
from Phrygia (Scotland), whose name is perpetuated in the Scottish family
name Forsyth(e). In England, the Trojan name Phorbas became the
surname Forbes, while in the Netherlands Altes survived unchanged to
become a surname. In the United Kingdom, Marpessa is still occasionally
given as a first name; Peleus became Pélé in Iberia and Pelle in Scandinavia;
Neleus and Chloris became Nelis and Kloris in the Netherlands, surviving
as somewhat old-fashioned first names in the countryside; Alastor is now
Alistair in England; Rhene is now Renée in France and many other
countries, while Theseus and Calais became place-names in France: Thésée
and Calais. The reader will discover still other examples for himself on
rereading Homer.

It is curious that Homer calls the girls Briseis and Chryseis after their
fathers, Brises and Chryses. According to other ancient sources, their real
names were Hippodamia and Astynome respectively. The former was said
to be tall and dark, and the latter small and fair.

Note 25 The Principal Gods

The following list gives, in the first column, the Homeric (Celtic/Greek)
names of the gods, with the Latin equivalent in brackets. The second
column gives any alternative Celtic names and the third column the specific
functions. It should be noted, however, that the equivalence is often only
approximate. For example, Zeus was of a different nature from the Roman
Jupiter, while the Celtologists are not certain of the attribution of some of
the alternative Celtic names. There is indeed a definite confusion in the
functions and origins of some of the gods that will never be resolved.

Homeric name (Latin in brackets)	Alternative Celtic name	Functions
Zeus (Jupiter)	Taranis (the Thunderer) (Irish: Dagda), Lug	Chief god
Poseidon (Neptune) 'The Earthshaker'	Nechtan, Manannan, Llyr	God of the ocean and the subconscious; guardian of the Grail
Hades (Pluto)	Dis(-Pater), Dives, (Irish: Dagda)	God of the Underworld, but also life (rebirth)

Here (Juno)	An[n]a, Dana, Don	Chief goddess
(Pallas) Athene (Minerva)	(Pallas) Okke, Onka (Irish: Brigit)	Goddess of arts, wisdom and crafts
(Phoebus) Apollo 'The Archer God'	Bolenos, Beltaine (new fire) Maponios, Grannus, Borvon	God of light, arts and divination
Ares (Mars)	Teutates (god of the tribe)	God of war
Artemis (Diane)	Artio	Goddess of hunting and forests
Aphrodite (Venus)	Morgane (born of the sea) Branwen	Goddess of love
Hermes (Mercury) (or Argeîphontes = 'Slayer of Argus', a monster)	Lug (white, brilliant) Fionn	Guide of the initiates, messenger of the gods, god of eloquence, trade, travellers and thieves
Hephaestus (Vulcan)	Goibniu (Irish: Lochan)	God of fire and metal working
Persephone (Proserpine)	Etaine	Wife of Hades
Heracles (Hercules)	Ogmios, Malios, Melkarth	Demi-god, son of Zeus, renowned for his twelve labours
Kirke (Circe)	Nehalennia	Initiatrice into knowledge (the Mysteries) Head of the Gnostic religion
Nike (Victoria)	Andarta, Andrasta	Goddess of victory
Iris	(Irish: Leborcham)	Messenger of the gods (the rainbow was her scarf)
Demeter (Ceres)	An(n)a, Anu or Dana, Dön	Goddess of agriculture and fertility
Dionysus (Bacchus)	Cernunnos	God of the vine and wine, and of abundance
Helios (Sol)	Mabon	Sun god

Zeus was worshipped under this name in Gaul and gave his name to *jeudi* (Thursday), while his alternative Celtic name, Lug, has survived in the names of certain towns, such as Lyon, Laon and Leyden, which are all derived from Lugdunum, as is well attested.

Athene's alternative name Okke was used by both the Celts and the Greeks, but the name Athene was itself definitely pre–Greek according to explanatory Greek dictionaries. Athene had no mother, as she emerged from the forehead of Zeus: the goddess of wisdom symbolized the 'third eye'.

The identification of Borvon with Apollo is confirmed by the Latin inscription on a votive altar dating from the Gallo-Roman era:

Deo Apollini Borvoni et Damonea C Daminius Ferox, civis Lingonis, ex voto.

The name is preserved in many place-names in France, such as Bourbon-l'Archembault, Bourbon-Lancy, La Bourboule, and by the Bourbon dynasty.

Hermes gave his name to *mercredi* (Wednesday) through his Latin equivalent, Mercury.

Aphrodite gave her name to *vendredi* (Friday) through her Latin equivalent Venus (*Veneris dies* = day of Venus).

The names of the Nordic gods live on in the names of the days of the week in the Germanic languages, for example in English:

Tuesday	Tyr's day
Wednesday	Woden's day or Odinn
Thursday	Thorr's day or Donar (German Donnerstag)
Friday	Frigg's day or Freyja (wife of Odinn)
Sunday	Sun day
Monday	Moon day

The Indo-European origin of these gods, like those of the Celts, is well-established. For example Tyr corresponds to the Vedic god Diauh and to Zeus and his latinized version Jupiter (= Zeus-pater, ['Zeus the father'], via Zejup > Jup).

The Genealogy of the Gods and the Celts

N.B. The kinship between Achilles and the Celts is based on the theogony of Hesiod (presumably eighth century BC) and P. Grimal's *Dictionary of Classical Mythology* citing additional sources such as Apollodorus and Parthenius.

Gaia or Aia was the Earth Mother; Pontus was the male personification of the sea.

Nereus, the 'Old Man of the Sea' had fifty daughters (the Nereids, who symbolized the waves and various other aspects of the sea) of which only three are mentioned here. His wife Doris was a 'rich haired' daughter of Oceanus. (For more names of Nereids see key to Map 12 Part III, Chapter 10, pages 197–8, Notes 51 and 52.)

Amphitrite had a son (Triton) with Poseidon, originally the river god of the Rhine (Map 17, 40).

Galatea is called 'very famous' by Homer as she is the legendary mother of the Celtic peoples.

Thetis was married to Peleus, a mortal, father of Achilles and king of Phthia (the present province of Zeeland and adjacent regions in the Netherlands and Belgium (Maps 8 and 12).

The seagod Triton is always represented with a fish tail and a trident (Plate 8 b).

Achilles was the legendary hero of Homer's Iliad.

The Celts, Gauls and Illyrians settled throughout Europe (see Map 10) including western Greece, where Homer's orally transmitted epics would be put in writing.

The Principal Gods

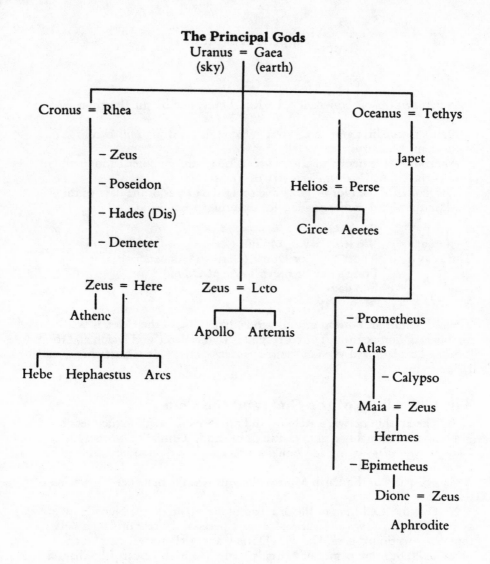

Uranus = Gaea
(sky)   (earth)

Cronus = Rhea

– Zeus

– Poseidon

– Hades (Dis)

– Demeter

Oceanus = Tethys

Japet

Helios = Perse

Circe   Aeetes

Zeus = Here

Athene

Zeus = Leto

Apollo   Artemis

Hebe   Hephaestus   Ares

– Prometheus

– Atlas

– Calypso

Maia = Zeus

Hermes

– Epimetheus

Dione = Zeus

Aphrodite

The origin of the Celtic peoples

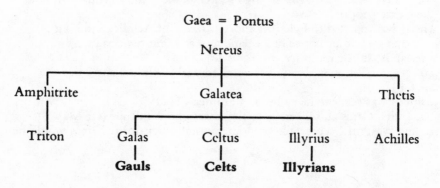

Gaea = Pontus

Nereus

Amphitrite   Galatea   Thetis

Triton   Galas   Celtus   Illyrius   Achilles

Gauls   **Celts**   **Illyrians**

House of Thebes
(Dieppe)

House of Mycenae
(Troyes)

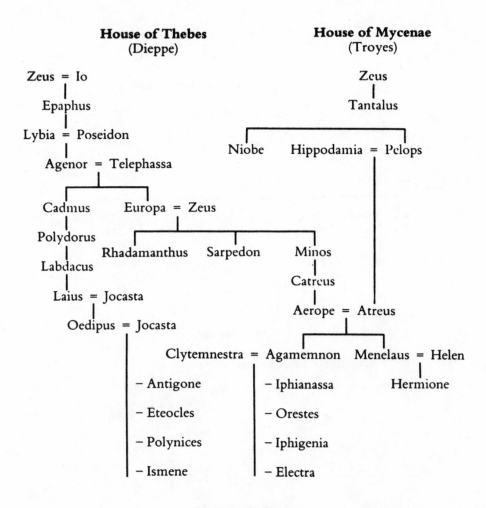

House of Athens
(Cherbourg)

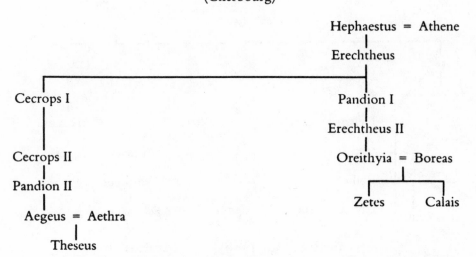

Principal Descendants of Prometheus

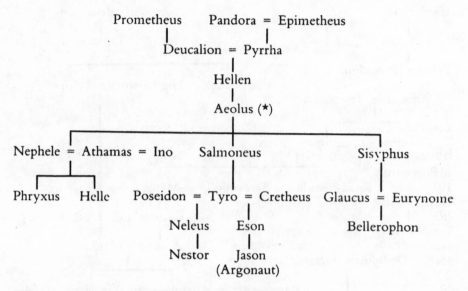

(*) For other descendants of Aeolus, see below:

Genealogy of Helen

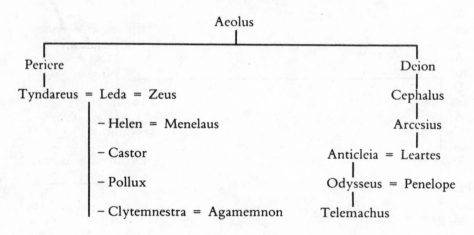

Bibliography

Homer
The Iliad and *The Odyssey*, translation by E. V. Rieu, Guild Publishing,
  London and Penguin Classics, Harmondsworth, 1969 and 1970.

The Celts
Ambelain, R., *Les traditions celtiques, doctrine initiatique de l'Occident*, Danglès,
  1977.
Chadwick, N., *The Celts*, Penguin, 1985.
Dillon, M. and Chadwick, N., *The Celtic Realms*, Weidenfeld & Nicolson,
  London, 1967.
Duval, P-M., *Les Celtes*, Gallimard, Paris, 1977.
Hubert, H., *The Greatness and Decline of the Celts*, Constable, London, 1987,
  2 Vols.
Le Roux, F. and Guyonvarc'h, C-J., *Les Druides*, Ouest-France, 1986.
Markale, J. *Les Celtes*, Payot, Paris, 1973.
  Chartres et L'énigme des Druides, Pygmalion, Paris, 1988.
Muir, P., *Reading the Celtic Landscapes*, Michael Joseph, London, 1985.
Newark, T., *Celtic Warriors*, Guild Publishing, London, 1986.
Powell, T. G. E., *The Celts*, Thames & Hudson, London, 1985.
Ross, A., *The Pagan Celts*, Batsford, London, 1986.
Rutherford, W., *The Druids, Magicians of the West*, Aquarian Press,
  Wellingborough, 1983.
Savoret, A., Visage de Druidism, Dervy-Livres, Paris, 1986.

Archaelogy and History
Bord, J. and C., *Ancient Mysteries of Britain*, Paladin, Grafton Books, 1987.
  Mysterious Britain, Garnstone Press, London.
Bosch-Guimpera, *Les Indo-Européens*, Payot, Paris, 1989.
Hondius-Crone, A., *The Temple of Nehalennia at Domburg*, Meulenhoff,
  Amsterdam, 1955.
Kruta, V. and Forman, W., *The Celts in the West*, Orbis Publishing,
  London, 1985.
Renfrew, C., *Before Civilization*.
  Archaeology and Language: The Puzzle of Indo-European Origins, Jonathan
  Cape, London, 1987.
Sandars, N. K., *The Sea Peoples, 1250-1150 BC*, Thames and Hudson,
  London, 1978.

Religion and Mythology
Bailey, A. A., *The Labours of Hercules*, Lucis Trust, 1981.
Bies, J., *Art, Gnose et Alchimie,* Le Courrier du Livre, Paris, 1987.

363

Boyer, R. and Lot-Falck, E., *Les religions de l'Europe du Nord*, Fayard-Denoël, Paris, 1974.
Brunton, P., *The Secret Path*, Rider, London, 1983.
Campbell, J., *The Masks of God*, 4 vols, Penguin Books, 1985.
Coquet, M., *Les çakras et l'initiation*, Dervy-Livres, Paris, 1985.
Dumézil, G., *Les dieux souverains des Indo-Européens*, Bibliothèque des Sciences Humaines, Paris, 1977.
   L'oubli de l'homme et l'honneur des dieux; esquisses de mythologie, Gallimard, Paris, 1985.
Eliade, M., *Birth and Rebirth*, 1958.
   Histoire des croyances et des idées religieuses, Payot, Paris, 1987.
Gennep, A. van, *Rites of Passage*.
Green, M., *The Gods of the Celts*, Allan Sutton, Gloucester, 1986.
Hamilton, E., *La mythologie*, Marabout Université, (translated from English), Paris, 1978.
Le Cour, P., *L'évangile ésotérique de Saint Jean*, Dervy-Livres, Paris, 1987.
MacCana, *Celtic Mythology*, Newnes Books, 1987.
Mallinger, J., *Des initiations antiques aux initiations modernes*, Planquart, Lille, 1980.
Rutherford, W., *Celtic Mythology*, Aquarian Press, Wellingborough, 1987.
Naddair, K., *Keltic Folk and Faerie Tales*, Century, London, 1987.
Sorval, G. de, *Initiation chevaleresque et initiation royale*, Dervy-Livres, Paris, 1985.
Vries, H. de., *La religion des Celtes*, Payot, Paris, 1984.

Symbolism, Esoterism and Numerology

Ares, J. d', *L'éveil initiatique*, Collection Atlantis, Vincennes, 1982.
Berteaux, R., *La voie symbolique*, Edimaf, Paris, 1986.
Boucher, J., *La symbolique maçonnique*, Dervy-Livres, Paris, 1948.
Creusot, C., *La face cachée des nombres,*, Dervy-Livres, Paris, 1982.
Dahlke, R., *Mandalas der Welt,* Heinrich Hugendubel Verlag, Munich, 1985.
Emmanuel, R., *Pleins feux sur la Grèce antique, La mythologie vue par ses Ecoles des Mystères*, Dervy-Livres, Paris, 1982.
Franz, M. L. von, *Individuation in Fairy Tales*, Spring Publications, Zurich, 1977.
   Zahl und Zeit, Ernst Klett, Stuttgart, 1970.
Gerardin, L., *Les mystères des nombres*, Dangles, 1985.
Jung, C. G., *Psychologie et alchimie*, Buchet Castel, Paris, 1970.
Levi, E., *The Mysteries of the Qabalah*, Aquarian Press, 1984.
   La Clef des grands mystères, Diffusion Scientifique, Paris, 1987.
Markale, J., *Le Graal*, Retz, Paris, 1982.
Ouellette, D., *Rebirthing According to Spirit*, 1982.
Portal, F., *Des couleurs symboliques*, Trédaniel, Paris, 1984.
Prieur, J., *Les symboles universels*, Fernand Lanore, Paris, 1982.
Rousseau, R-L., *Le language des couleurs*, Dangles, 1980.

Bibliography

Souzenelle, A. de, *Le symbolisme du corps humain*, Dangles, 1984.
Wirth, O., *La Franc-Maçonnerie*, Dervy-Livres, Paris, 1986.

Reference Works

Bauer, W., Dümotz, I. and Golowin, S., *Lexikon der Symbole*, Fourier Verlag, Wiesbaden, 1985.

Chevalier, J. and Gheerbrant, A., *Dictionnaire des symboles*, Laffont/Jupiter, Paris, 1982.

Gittenberger, F. and Weiss, H., *Zeeland in Oude Kaarten*, Lannoo, Bussum and Mappamundi, London, 1983.

Grimal, P., *The Dictionary of Classical Mythology*, Blackwell Reference, Oxford, 1986.

Pei, M., *The Story of Language*, New American Library/Meridian, Harper and Row, New York, 1984.

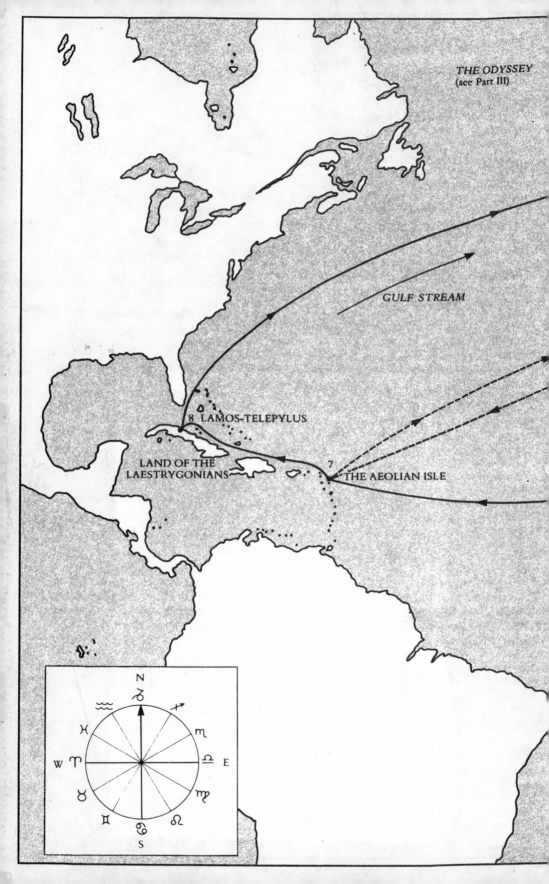

THE ODYSSEY
(see Part III)

GULF STREAM

8 LAMOS-TELEPYLUS

LAND OF THE
LAESTRYGONIANS

7

THE AEOLIAN ISLE